Please remember that this is a library book,
and that it belongs only temporarily to each
person who uses it. Be considerate. Do
not write in this, or any, library book.

Pagan Religion

ꝺoveɦouse stuꝺies in literature

Volume 5

ꝿeꝺieval & renaissance texts & stuꝺies

Volume 152

Edward Lord Herbert of Cherbury.

Edward Herbert

Pagan Religion

A Translation of
De religione gentilium

Edited

by

John Anthony Butler

Dovehouse Editions
Ottawa
Canada

Medieval & Renaissance
Texts & Studies
Binghamton, New York

1996

Acknowledgements

This book has been published with the help of a grant from the Humanities and Social Sciences Federation of Canada, using funds provided by the Social Sciences and Humanities Research Council of Canada.

Pegasus Limited for the Advancement of Neo-Latin Studies has generously provided a grant to assist in meeting the publication costs of this volume.

Canadian Cataloguing in Publication Data

Main entry under title:

Herbert of Cherbury, Edward Herbert, Baron, 1583–1648
    Pagan religion : a translation of De religione gentilium

(Medieval & Renaissance texts & studies ; 152)
Translation of: De religione gentilium.
Includes bibliographical references.

ISBN 1-895537-21-5 (bound); 0-86698-193-4 (bound)

1. Religion–Philosophy.   2. Religions.   I. Butler, John Anthony, 1950–
II. Title.   III. Series.

B1201.H33D4713 1995   291'.01   C95-900454-8

Copyright © Dovehouse Editions Inc., 1996
Typeset in Canada by Carleton Production Centre, Nepean.

Printed in Canada

For distribution write to:

Dovehouse Editions   Medieval & Renaissance Texts & Studies
1890 Fairmeadow Cres.   State University of New York
Ottawa, Canada K1H 7B9   Binghamton, N.Y. 13902-6000

ISBN 1-895537-21-5 (bound)   ISBN 0-86698-193-4 (bound)

Frontispiece: Edward Lord Herbert of Chirbury from *The Life* (4th ed.) London: J. Dodsley in Pall Mall, 1792. Engraving by A. Walker from the painting by J. Oliver.

This book is for my colleague
Donald Beecher

"Mitto tibi sanam non pleno ventre salutem,
Que tu distento forte carere potes."

(Milton)

Contents

Acknowledgments

I would first like to thank my two funding organisations, the Social Sciences and Humanities Research Council of Canada and the Canadian Federation of the Humanities. A Private Scholar Grant from the first enabled me to travel to Wales to study Herbert's manuscripts in the National Library at Aberystwyth. The second not only contributed significantly to the production costs of the book, but allowed me to use suggestions made by various readers; I think that these helped make this a better book, and I am grateful to these anonymous and hard-working people. My first personal debt is to Professor Don Beecher of Carleton University, Ottawa, Canada, editor-in-chief of Dovehouse Editions, without whose encouragement the book would, quite simply, never have been finished. He knows my predicament, which need not be discussed here, and if I emerge successfully from it, much credit will go to him. Secondly, I would like, as usual, to thank Professor John Teunissen of the University of Manitoba, who has offered moral support over the years and who kindly read over and commented upon the Introduction. Other colleagues from the University of Manitoba have also helped me with some scientific and philosophical difficulties; they include Professors Carl Matheson and Michel Feld of the Department of Philosophy, Professor Terence Day of the Department of Religious Studies, and Professor Jim Keller of the Department of English. I am also, of course, indebted to Professor Mario Di Cesare and the staff of MRTS for accepting this work for publication. A special thanks to Professor Judith Flynn, Head of the Department of English, for finding me employment at the last minute, and to Lucia Flynn for producing the final copy of the text. Lastly, I would like to thank Sylvia, who was always there and always patient with Lord Herbert, who has been the other man in her life for eight years, not to mention with me, an often unemployed and unwillingly peripatetic scholar.

Ottawa, Ontario/Winnipeg, Manitoba
1990–1995

Introduction

1. The Nature and Scope of *De religione gentilium*

Lord Herbert of Chirbury wrote this work in 1645 as an expansion of his earlier philosophical treatise *De veritate prout distinguitur a revelatione, a verisimili, a possibili et a falso* (1624), in which he had suggested the existence of a common foundation to all religions as a possible starting-point for a search for religious peace and the settlement of sectarian strife. In the present work Herbert cites further evidence for the claims made in his previous book, and at the same time he makes an attempt to clarify his intentions. The earlier work was the product of a young man of scholarly inclinations heavily influenced by the work of his illustrious contemporaries, particularly his friends Hugo Grotius and Daniel Tilenus, both of whom read the work before Herbert published it, and whose approval he had eagerly sought. *De veritate* received wide publicity, thanks in part to Herbert's own efforts, and was read by, amongst others, Descartes, Campanella, Mersenne and Gassendi. Descartes and Gassendi wrote extensive comments on it. By 1645 Herbert was an established philosophical voice, and while he did not live to see some of the reaction to his new book, it too provoked comment, and Herbert's name would be established as one of the "fathers" of the English deist movement which would come to fruition early in the following century with the work of John Toland, the Earl of Shaftesbury, and others.

Herbert's primary purpose in *De religione gentilium* was to establish, using evidence from ancient religions (mostly, but not completely, Graeco-Roman religion) the existence of his five Religious Common Notions as the basis for all religions. These are as follows: 1. There is a Supreme Deity; 2. The Supreme Deity ought to be worshipped; 3. Virtue and Piety are essential components of every religious system; 4. Vice must be expiated through some form of repentance; 5. There are rewards and punishments after death. The Religious Common Notions are innate; they existed in man before the formal establishment of religious systems, and indeed were the cause for the systematisation of belief into religions. They are present in all human beings, having been imprinted on the mind by God, and were therefore present in pagans at all stages of history. As John Hopkins stated some centuries later, "the higher reaches of religion, as of philosophy, are the same; the supreme believers worship the same Supreme God everywhere" (89). Herbert believed that if he could prove, through evidence from ancient religions, that this were true, then all virtuous human beings at every stage of human history would be eligible for salvation, and sectarian claims of privilege or election would be invalidated.

Herbert believed that when humanity realised that the Common Notions were universally present and always had been, religious strife would end. To justify this idea that Common Notions were in fact "common" to all, Herbert decided to examine the very foundations of religion as they had been before the advent of modern religious "systems" such as Christianity, Islam or Buddhism. In his search backwards Herbert was not being radically original; his methodology was an established convention and as such would have been acceptable to its scholarly theological and philosophical readers. As Frances Yates remarked, however, "the great forward movements of the Renaissance all derive their vigour, their emotional impulse, from looking backwards" (1), and Herbert's work was no exception. He went back beyond the early Christian fathers, beyond the Gospels, beyond the Old Testament to find his ultimate spirituality. Herbert, Basil Willey states, "goes beyond Christianity itself, and tries to formulate a belief which shall command the universal assent of all men" (85). That Herbert wished to get "assent" implied that his system would be rational rather than belief-based, and it is the rational basis of Herbert's system which would have its far-reaching influence in the eighteenth century. Herbert went back to the great notion of Being itself, to concern with man's place in the cosmos and his relationship to nature, and he found that the ancients, particularly the Stoics and Neo-Platonists, had laid the ground for him. In his own time, Herbert found intellectual allies in the work of men like Comenius, who wished to draw all knowledge together into one coherent system, and he may even have shown interest in the mysterious doctrines of the Rosicrucians, who had surfaced in 1614 with a manifesto of their own proposing a synthesis of all that was known.

Herbert intended to demonstrate that religion had once been a unified system which had, through the passage of time, become fragmented and alienated from its purer origins. He believed that it was possible to promote a system which rested entirely upon the Religious Common Notions, which were the implicitly-shared foundation of all religious systems, and which constituted "a primal religion of perfect purity and simplicity" (E. Hill 40). The examination of ancient religions could, he thought, demonstrate the truth of the Common Notions, although it might reveal on the other hand that Christianity, far from being the superior system, was merely one of the fragmentary systems which had developed out of the old religion, and that it, too, could not provide the religious certainty that seventeenth-century humanity craved. As W.K. Jordan pointed out:

> In *De religione gentilium* [Herbert] advanced the radical opinion that all institutional religions were only relatively true and, he added, relatively false. No religion is entirely devoid of truth. . . . and it is the task of the critic to examine religious systems dispassionately and comparatively. (Wiley 98)

To suggest this, even in veiled form, was theologically radical, and is one of the reasons for considering Lord Herbert as a seminal eirenic thinker. If Jordan is correct, and I believe he is, then Herbert is suggesting that religious belief, like any other belief, is open to intellectual and rational examination and that it does not, by special virtue of its being religious belief, carry any privilege as knowledge. As Herbert states about pagan religion early in the work, religions do indeed contain some truth, but no one religion contains all the truth, and consequently no one religion has any inherent right to claim that it does. In *De veritate* Herbert had argued against philosophers who claimed to know the whole truth, and in the present work he extends his scepticism to theology.

For Herbert to think eirenically was not in itself particularly radical. During his lifetime Europe was racked by the devastating Thirty Years' War (1618–48), and England suffered a Civil War (1640–48). There had been terrible religious wars in France, Spain and the Netherlands during the last years of the previous century. Herbert had seen action in the Thirty Years' War as a volunteer, and he participated reluctantly in the Civil War; it can hardly be argued that Herbert derived his eirenicism purely from his military experiences, but he was an observant man, and the world he inhabited was at war during most of his lifetime. Since seventeenth-century wars were concerned almost equally with religion and politics, it is not an unwarranted assumption to make a connexion between his experiences and his beliefs. The young Herbert who had cheerfully volunteered to fight in the Spanish Netherlands matured into the older man who saw through the veneer of religion and came to understand the futility of war. It was this man, further disillusioned by the English Civil War, who wrote *De religione gentilium.* For Herbert, what human beings needed was an easily-understood, rational, and fundamental set of religious beliefs to which they could adhere because they were non-denominational and transcended the formal existence of entities like "church" and "organised religion." They had their being in the very depths of the human soul, where they had been implanted by God according to his divine plan. This set of religious beliefs was what Herbert called "the ancient religion of the gentiles," or pagan religion at its oldest and purest stage.

Herbert's assertions about the Religious Common Notions had their origins in *De veritate*, where he organised them into a *religio rotunda*, explaining as follows:

> For what is sufficient is due to God; excess is due to us. Why, then, as I have said elsewhere following the law of common reason, can we not apply the same rule of the perfect sphere of the religion of God that we apply to any circle? If anything is added to it, or taken away from it, its shape is destroyed, its perfection ruined. . . . I would, indeed, firmly maintain that it is impossible to remove any feature from religion. But whether anything can justifiably be added to the orb of religion, as is possible within a circle, I am not so certain, though the shape of a visible circle is continuous, so that no part of it is hidden.   (121)

D.P. Walker correctly indicates that this idea might have posed certain problems for Herbert's readers because it is now "much more difficult to take [the Religious Common Notions] as the basis for a Christian superstructure" (168). Quite so; but why must readers assume that Herbert intends such a basis? And why is it so crucial for later scholars and commentators to turn Herbert into an apologist for Christianity? Indeed, as Jordan suggested and Walker implied, perhaps Herbert's eirenicism was not meant to privilege Christianity at all. Eugene Hill recognises this possibility, suggesting that Herbert was "neither a Protestant nor even a Christian" (9), but most readers do not go that far. There is certainly a veil or veneer of orthodoxy in much of what Herbert says, but it is likely there because Herbert was a public figure, an aspiring politician, and his true views, if clearly-expressed, would not exactly have won him friends in influential places. By 1645, however, Herbert knew that his political career was over; he was sixty-three years old, he had held no political post since 1624, and he was living more or less in scholarly obscurity. If there is anything "orthodox" about *De religione gentilium* it is an orthodoxy of discourse; certain things had to be said in certain ways, and they had to be expressed in terms which readers could understand. Walker's contention that even the earlier *De veritate* was "a truncated, eirenic Christian apologia" (167) is inaccurate; his own description of the book does not bear out this claim, and it is certainly inappropriate as a description of the present work. Hill, for example, points to Herbert's description of the infant Zeus as "the first god that the ancients ever adored bawling in a cradle," a not-so-subtle double-edged piece of sarcasm, an ironic slam at Christianity with that little word "first" saying it all, and the words "adored" and "cradle" the clinchers (Hill 45).

Whatever Herbert's reasons might have been for the comparative mildness of his discourse (and it is, as we have demonstrated, by no means all so mild), many readers were upset by what he had written, and with good reason. The independent divine Richard Baxter, an admirer of George Herbert's poetry, complained in *More Reasons for the Christian Religion* (1672) that there seemed to be no place for Christ in Edward Herbert's system of philosophy. For Baxter, of course, Christ was essential, "not to make repentance needless, but to procure it" (558), notwithstanding Herbert's assertion in *De veritate* that sin was "an almost necessary compulsion" (180) which God would almost automatically forgive. To suggest that repentance was possible directly through God rather negated the whole point of the Incarnation, at least as far as Baxter could see, and this was, for him, blasphemous. Herbert appeared to suggest that any religious system, that is, any non-Christian system, could offer repentance, and that God would accept it. But things got even worse; Herbert, after reluctantly allowing the probability that the Decalogue was a genuine revelation, subjects it to rigorous analysis and concludes by explaining that "revelation adds nothing to what is already known by the light of nature [i.e. reason]" (Walker 169). Baxter, however, had put his finger firmly on the central controversy of Herbert's work; where was Christ, and what role did He play? The answer was, according to Herbert, nowhere and none.

If modern scholars have seen fit to remark on Herbert's circumspection, his contemporaries hardly noticed it. We have already seen that Richard Baxter found fault with Herbert's demotion of Christ, and scholars on the Continent were even more vehement in their condemnation of Herbert. They certainly knew what he was about, and they ringingly denounced, in somewhat rabid tones, what they believed to be Herbert's heresy and blasphemy. Herbert's eirenicism cut the heart out of their beliefs by suggesting that cherished Christian tenets needed to be abandoned if religious peace were to be attained. In his *Dissertationes duae contra Herbert de Cherbury Baro Angliae* (1675), Johann Musaeus, Professor of Theology at the University of Jena, accused Herbert of proposing the replacement of Christianity with what Musaeus called "Cherburianism," a natural theology based on rational principles rather than upon revelation and divine law. Musaeus noted that Herbert's Religious Common Notions tell us nothing about the truths of Christianity, and he flailed away at Herbert's scandalous demotion of Christ.

Christian Kortholt in his *De tribus impostoribus magnis* (1692) created an unholy Trinity consisting of Hobbes, Spinoza and Herbert, thus confirming what Rosalie Colie later called "the official view of English deism's heretical (and English) descent from Lord Herbert . . . through Hobbes and Spinoza" (26).

Kortholt made a connexion between Herbert's "reason" and Spinoza's notion of *scientia intuitiva*, and he went on to surmise that Herbert's obsession with reason rather than revelation would lead mankind back to the state of nature which was described so well by Hobbes. There is little doubt that Musaeus and Kortholt, together with Baxter and several others, fully understood where Herbert's thinking was leading. They were not mistaken about the tone, either; as Eugene Hill observes, "numerous passages beg to be read as malign side-swipes at Christianity" (288–90). The implications of Herbert's thought for the deist movement will be discussed later in this introduction.

The weakest part of Herbert's argument is his stress on the argument of *consensus gentium*, believing as he did that it transcended religious, political, philosophical and ethnic considerations. Universal consent cannot be assumed or proved, but Herbert's insistence on its validity is not a careless philosophical assertion or an amateurish blunder. Human beings are capable of reason, wherever they are; Herbert saw his system as reasonable, indeed one that had been implanted upon human reason by God, and therefore reasonable human beings would consent to it. For him, all humans except madmen and children were reasonable. His belief in reason transcended all considerations; from early days, when Herbert tells us in his *Autobiography* that he learned several languages "to make my selfe a Citizen of the world as farr as possible" (17), to his death, he sought common humanity. Citizens of the world must perforce take the world as they find it, accepting differences between human beings as they accept linguistic differences, at the same time never losing sight of that common humanity shared by all with whom they come into contact. To bother about learning others' languages is analogous to learning their customs and religions, and just as some words may be commonly recognisable, so may some religious beliefs. Language may divide, but it may also unite; commonly-held religious beliefs can only help to show us that we are commonly human. Herbert argues that if people only understood each other's beliefs to be based on his Religious Common Notions, then their human bonds would be strengthened. Under current systems of belief the opposite was true, but just as it was never God's intention to consign all pagans to Hell because they did not know Christ, neither could it be His intention to consign all those to Hell who did not follow a particular creed or denomination. The further back in history Herbert investigated, and the more religions he examined, the more he found they had in common.

The result was a system that could not have been called specifically Christian, because its Christian elements were virtually unrecognisable amidst the Platonic, Neo-Platonic, Stoic and Hermetic elements, not to mention the "gnostic, astrally-centered pantheism" which D.P. Walker noticed that Herbert "superadded" (188).

In *De veritate* Herbert had set about supplying humanity with the appropriate epistemological principles for the holding of certain common beliefs, amongst which he identified religious principles. For Herbert, both religion and philosophy were epistemic systems requiring the same methodology, a point alluded to by one of Herbert's nineteenth-century admirers, Baron Charles de Rémusat, who wrote in 1824 that "in his search for religious truth, [Herbert] found his philosophy" (I, 175), a judgment which is still sound. Thus it was logical that Herbert should attempt to supply a religious system which would replace all the others by including their basic tenets within itself, and by doing so would obviate the need for religious conflict. Herbert was assuming, of course, that people would, in the long run, somehow prefer to act rationally and logically rather than letting themselves be governed by their passions. His system would not depend upon divine revelation, because even if God did reveal himself directly (which Herbert doubted), whatever he had revealed would have been quickly taken over by the priests in order to secure their spiritual power over the common people.

The Religious Common Notions, then, are the root and foundation of every religion. As the Cambridge Platonist Henry More put it in his *Antidote against Atheism* (1653), they are "whatever is *noematically* true, that is to say, at first to all men in their wits, upon a clear perception of the terms" (Sorley 80). To demonstrate this, Herbert isolates some of the formal elements of reason to show how all religions contain, to some degree at least, the same amount of "truth" (Bedford 184). One may determine what is true against what, for example, is claimed by priests as true, by the judicious application of what was known in the seventeenth century as "right reason," a term frequently employed in the 1650s by the Cambridge Platonists and by orthodox theologians. Right reason is God-given (Nathaniel Culverwell called it "the candle of the Lord"), and indeed was designed by God so that human beings could use it to sift out truth in the midst of falsehood. As Benjamin Whichcote remarked a few years later, "The first operation in religion is mental and intellectual" (Sorley 76). The remarks of More and Whichcote, both eminent Cambridge Platonists, could have just as well been made by Herbert, whose philosophy influenced them both. "Here is contained," Margaret Wiley explains, "the use of the sceptic *isosothenia*, the use of reason to prepare the ground for faith . . . and the sceptic tendency to judge a statement of belief by its intention" (99). The agenda or "intention" of priests was not to help people understand their relationship with God, but to ensure that the priests themselves, by discouraging the use of right reason, would remain in control of the spiritual lives of the people. Their truth was to become religious truth. For Herbert, right reason consisted not in the subordination of one's powers of reasoning to priests, but a conscious exertion of what every person has. Thus anyone can apprehend the Religious Common Notions and attain salvation. "Canst thou by reason more of Godhead know/ Than Plutarch, Seneca or Cicero?" Dryden asked in a poem whose title was borrowed from Herbert's *Religion laici*. For Herbert, the answer would have been "No," for those pagans possessed exactly what we possess, reason and the Religious Common Notions. In the present work Herbert suggests, furthermore, that not only can we not know "Godhead" more than the pagans, we also cannot claim revelation as anything more than a confirmation of what we already know by right reason.

As we have seen, Herbert expends considerable energy in attacks on the priesthood, and we may suppose that he did not mean merely the long-dead priesthood of antiquity. At the same time, he has to deal with the more disagreeable aspects of ancient religions such as human sacrifice, mutilation, sacred prostitution and superstition. He also has to explain some of the more salacious exploits of the gods. The latter, which the pagans themselves questioned, Herbert suggests might have been invented by the priests of one god to discredit the reputation of a rival deity! As for the other matters, these were plainly and simply instituted by the priestly castes. Less harmful aspects of pagan religion, such as hero-worship, he simply explains as the equivalent of the adoration of saints. Herbert's main target is the priests themselves, who have contrived a "priestly" religion in the place of the older, "pure" religion. He claims, for example, that monotheism was the rule until the priests, for reasons best known to themselves, proclaimed polytheism, which effectively placed all the power, spiritual and temporal, in their hands. This, of course, had serious ramifications for the common people.

Modern scholarship, unfortunately, does not entirely bear Herbert's theory out. There is no certainty, for example, that even the most ancient forms of religion were ever monotheistic. Even Judaism, that most monotheistic-appearing religion, is open to question; Larry Hurtado points out, for example, that "a number of Jewish groups worked with the idea of God having . . . a chief agent who was second only to God in rank" (18). Herbert was correct in his idea that all religions did at least have a "supreme" god; as the priest in Chapter XV admits, "Nothing is more certain and beyond a doubt that there is a Supreme God and that he is the First Cause." However, Herbert's suggestion that the spread of cults might have weakened the worship of the Supreme God has some truth in it, and it would seem to follow that because of this proliferation people did lose touch with the older beliefs. One need only glance at the mind-numbing list of gods in the Egyptian pantheon, or remember that the Greeks had a god or goddess for every river and stream, or consider that the Romans had tiny gods who presided over functions of the human body.

Lord Herbert was well aware of differing traditions within Christianity itself, as can be seen from his allusions to gnosticism and by his claim that polytheism and syncretism somehow fragmented and ultimately destroyed the foundations of the old religion. But how legitimate was Herbert's claim that this state of affairs had always been the case? R.L. Fox argues, for example, that syncretism, the merging or combining of cults, might actually have strengthened some cults (34); if you combine Ra, Jupiter and Zeus into one god, and convince worshippers that this is a legitimate action, you have a "new" cult with three times as many adherents. The Roman emperor Alexander Severus (222–35) seemed to have this in mind when he collected together his famous Pantheon. Of course, as Fox tells us, syncretism would be seen negatively "by those who see the history of paganism as a gradual corruption by Oriental influences; [it] merged the gods of the East with traditional cults and undermined their stability" (35). But syncretism was one way of getting from paganism to Christianity, a fact not lost on the emperors Valerian and Gallienus (as we shall see later) or on Julian "the Apostate," who did not fail to see its potential when he tried to make the Sun the Supreme God. The great persecutions of Christianity under such emperors as Decius, Trebonianus Gallus and Diocletian strengthened Christianity rather than destroyed it; they became preludes to the ultimate triumph of Julian's "pale Galilean." In Chapter XV Herbert's priest looks back beyond the syncretism of his own times and wistfully remembers the attractive old astral religion, its Stoic ethics and Neo-Platonic spiritualism.

For all the holes which modern scholarship in its wisdom can poke in his ideas, Herbert's eirenicism has not been lost in the darker reaches of history. It has found echoes, however faint, in our own times. The contemporary theologian René Guénon, for example, suggests that there was a "primordial tradition" behind every religious system, which he defines as "a body of the highest universal truths" (Needleman 11). Those "universal truths" are, to all intents and purposes, Herbert's Common Notions writ new. In *The Transcendent Unity of Religions* (1984), Frithjof Schuon argues that religions "converge" in God, in "absolute, categorical, undifferentiated Unity," as Huston Smith notes in his Introduction (xiii). Elsewhere Schuon himself writes:

every initiative taken with a view to harmony between the difference of cultures and for the defence of spiritual values is good, if it has as its basis a recognition of the great principal truths and consequently also a recognition of tradition or the traditions. (Needleman 39)

Lord Herbert courageously advocated the need for going back to "primordial tradition," because therein lay the heart and soul of all religion. When tradition became shrouded in the mists of polytheism and syncretism, or when religion was used by the priesthood for political gain, people lost sight of it and lost their anchor to the world above the sublunary. Man's reasoning powers, worked upon by fear, would lose their force, belief would become mere lip-service and religion reduced to empty rites and ceremonies. Herbert's insistence that the old religion be recovered and possibly revived was, for him, the only way to combat the inherited sectarian strife handed down to his contemporaries by the vicissitudes of historical inevitability. The collapse of the old religion became the paradigm for his own troubled times. It also afforded him a glimpse of a Golden Age which could still, he hoped, be grasped by those prepared to risk the attempt.

Finally, in any discussion of Herbert as a philosopher of religion, the question of whether Herbert was a "deist" usually comes up. We have seen that he believed in a Supreme God, but what kind of a being was it? What was the relationship between this God and human beings? Did Herbert believe that this God had created the earth and its contents? How close was Herbert's conception of a Supreme God to any kind of "orthodox" Christianity? Deism is usually thought of as an eighteenth-century phenomenon, with John Toland and the Earl of Shaftesbury as its prominent spokesmen. But deism originated long before their time; Pierre Viret, in his *Instruction chréstienne* (1563), described deists as people who, while they do not actually deny the existence of God, "yet with regard to Jesus Christ and all that to which the doctrine of the Evangelists and the Apostles testify, they take all that to be fables and dreams" (Craig 73). In Viret's terms, then, Herbert would most certainly be a deist, because he was sceptical about miracles and was reluctant to grant Christ much of a role in his system. Early deism was, perforce, virtually an underground movement, but some of its doctrines found expression outside France; Herbert's library contains, for example, Lucilio Vanini's *De admirandis naturae reginae deaeque mortalium arcanis* (1616), a work which led to its author's prosecution and death at the stake.

Any attempt to define deism must recognise that there are several versions of it. Perhaps the commonest is the one which assumes belief in a God who, after he had created the universe, took no further interest in his creation. In the words of Van A. Harvey, this deism "regards God as the intelligent creator of an independent and law-abiding world, but denies that he providentially guides it or intervenes in any way with its course or destiny" (66). Here we see a difference with Herbert, who cites "Universal Divine Providence" on the very first page of the present work. R.L. Emerson defines deism as "the belief that by rational method alone man can know all the true propositions of theology which it is possible, desirable, or necessary to know" (390). Emerson goes on to list a number of metaphysical and epistemological propositions to which this deist might assent, and the list includes all of Herbert's Religious Common Notions. A further qualification to this particular definition is that deism can be either positive or negative in nature; John Orr, for example, states that positive deism "presented the content of . . . the religion of nature," and "often . . . claimed that it was the original and universal religion." This should sound familiar, but, perhaps more significantly, Orr points out that positive deists hold that the original religion had been "more or less concealed and corrupted by the various religions of priestly invention" (14). However, when Orr defines negative deism he also touches upon some of Herbert's assertions, for negative deists deny "special revelation, miracles, supernatural prophecy, providence and the incarnation of Christ" (15). Herbert expressed great scepticism about miracles, revelation and prophecy, but, as we have seen, he did accept the idea of Divine Providence. On the incarnation of Christ he was, it seems, indifferent; for Herbert, Christ has little relevance at all, incarnate or otherwise, for it is not Herbert's purpose to privilege Christianity.

On the other hand, if Herbert is to be judged by the application of the above criteria, he is certainly a deist. The difficulty is that his deism is eclectic; it is very difficult to securely pin him down in a category. Emerson's definition seems to fit best, but it is not specific enough. On the other hand, whilst Herbert answers to all of Orr's points for positive deism, he also shows signs of negative deism. Thus it seems appropriate to widen our criteria for deism such as Herbert's so that it will include the following characteristics: 1. A disbelief in, or at least a strong scepticism about miracles; 2. An impersonal conception of God, but not a denial of his existence altogether; 3. Providence, rather than God directly, controls the workings of the universe; 4. Reason is given by God to man, and therefore a scepticism about revelation is a logical consequence of that gift. It must be noted, however, that some deists, such as Herbert's self-proclaimed disciple Charles Blount, went a good deal further than some of these points suggest. In his *Anima mundi* (1679), Blount declared that Christ was merely a fantastic miracle-worker in the tradition of Apollonius of Tyana; he uses the word "juggler"! It would therefore appear that Thomas Halyburton was right to describe Herbert in 1714 as "the Father of English deism," and that other writers against deism, notably Leslie (1698) and Leland (1745) were of the same opinion. Whatever the truth of these assertions, the deist label certainly stuck to Herbert, and it probably originated with Blount, eager as he was to associate himself with a man whom he termed "the great Oracle and Commander of his Time for Wit, Learning and Courage" (*Religio laici* [1682], 49).

From what has been said above, it is obvious that *De religione gentilium* is not a work easily pigeonholed. It is certainly not another Christian apology, but a real polemic, a call for religious rethinking if not for complete re-organisation. It stresses rationality over belief and philosophy over theology. It is not meant to be an attack on the shortcomings of paganism, which was Herbert's friend and mentor Vossius's agenda in his book. It was not purely historical or archaeological either, as his other friend John Selden's *De diis Syris* (1617) had been. On the contrary, Herbert often claims that pagan religion had been maligned by those who studied it in subsequent eras, that its good points had been seriously misinterpreted, overlooked or glossed over by Christian commentators. Indeed for Herbert, pagan religion had the power to highlight the religions which had superseded it, for it had given them of its best. Herbert's work is in the humanist tradition, mankind-centred, concentrating on what can be said about our response to the divine as the unifying aspect of our own humanity, not on its divisive aspects. It expresses the hope, formulated towards the end of a murderous civil war, that human beings can, using their God-given rational faculties, make the world a better place.

The actual arrangement of the work is quite straightforward. Herbert restates the Religious Common Notions and then argues that salvation, rather than being selective, is universally-ordained by God. Judgment, Herbert argues, should be based on general evidence of guilt or innocence, not its particularisation in Christianity. He leaves no room for notions such as Calvinism's predestination of the elect. Then Herbert begins his analysis of religion in general, showing how it originated and developed, and how the Common Notions may be shown working within pagan religions from their very inception. Ancient religion began, he tells us, with the worship of heavenly bodies, which were seen as evidence of permanence as opposed to the transitory lives of human beings. In Chapters III through XII Herbert details the origin of the worship of stars, planets, gods and heroes. Much of the evidence he presents is drawn from Greece and Rome, but there are also allusions to ancient Egypt, the ancient Near East, India, and even South or Central America. In Chapters XIII and XIV Herbert shows how ancient man developed faith in a Supreme God who had created the cosmos, and how a priesthood arose which institutionalised religion in order to perpetuate its own power. Polytheism was introduced, together with oracles and other meaningless rituals through which the priests were able to keep the common people in ignorance, fear, and subservience to their wishes. The priests were fully responsible for sectarianism, religious wars, schisms and persecutions. Ordinary people, who possessed the Common Notions as well as the priests, became afraid to exercise what they intuitively knew. In Chapter XV Herbert demonstrates how pagans, like Christians, had a system of rewards and punishments after death, and that they encouraged piety, virtue and repentance in life. In Chapter XVI Herbert returns to his attack on the priests, asserting that as they destroyed the old religion by adding to it, so might Christianity find itself undermined in his own times. "The Five Articles . . . ought to provide the best means for attaining a better life," Herbert ringingly concludes; "I condemn all those who oppose the implementation of Universal Peace and Divine Providence" (366).

2. The Life of Lord Herbert of Chirbury[1]

Edward Herbert was born at Eyton, Shropshire, probably on March 3, 1582. His father Richard Herbert (c. 1555–96) was an M.P. and local official, and his mother Magdalen Newport (c. 1563–1627) was the patron of John Donne and a great lover of learning. At the early death of her husband she married Sir John Danvers (c. 1576–1655), the future regicide and an early authority

---

[1]The spelling "Chirbury" has caused some consternation amongst readers of my biography of Lord Herbert, and calls for some explanation here. This spelling was used by Rossi in his three-volume study of Herbert, and when I first saw it I believed it to be an Italian approximation of the name, if not a misspelling. I then came across two articles by Mr. George Herbert (now Earl of Powis), "A Note on Lord Herbert of Chirbury and his son Richard" [*Huntington Library Quarterly* (1942): 317–32], and "A further Note on Lord Herbert of Chirbury and his son Richard" [*Huntington Library Quarterly* 46, 4 (1980)], both of which point out that the "ir" spelling was used in Herbert's time. Mr. Herbert has subsequently supplied further information; the patent of nobility for Herbert used the "ir" spelling, and the village from which the title is taken still uses it. Nowhere does the "er" spelling occur; the Saxon name of the village was Cyriebyrig, and the 1638 Parish Register (which I have seen), has "Churbury." Mr. Herbert also stated:

> The ER in Herbert was undoubtedly pronounced as if it was AR. See the present pronunciation of DERBY, HERTFORD etc. Some of the wills include HERBERT and HARBERT in the same document. So, if ER was pronounced AR and if CHIRBURY was pronounced as it now is, why did anyone write it ER?

I am indebted to the Earl of Powis for clearing up this matter. I only hope that it will satisfy those readers who thought me pedantic, eccentric, or both.

on ornamental gardening. Edward Herbert had numerous siblings, amongst whom may be mentioned the eminent poet George Herbert (1593–1633) and Sir Henry Herbert (1591–1672), who held the post of Master of the Revels for nearly half a century. Edward was privately educated, but at the age of sixteen he went up to New College, Oxford; as was normal practice for young men of his class, he did not take a degree, although (by his own account) he took his studies very seriously indeed.

In 1598 Herbert married his cousin Mary Herbert of St. Julian's, by whom he had several children but with whom he seems not to have been very happy. In 1603 James I conferred the Order of the Bath on young Edward Herbert, and a few years later we find him travelling in Europe, where he saw service, together with at least two of his brothers, as a volunteer first with the English army in the Low Countries and then with Prince Maurice of Nassau. In 1619, through the good offices of Sir George Villiers, later the Duke of Buckingham, Herbert obtained the post of Ambassador to France, where he remained until 1624. During his stay in France Herbert completed *De veritate*, his first philosophical treatise; at the same time, he was actively engaged in writing poetry, the nature of which was chiefly lyrical and "metaphysical." His experiments with the latter form of poetry no doubt owed something to Herbert's close friendship with Donne, although he also counted Ben Jonson as a friend and was well-acquainted with second-rank poets as well; Aurelian Townshend had accompanied Herbert on his first journey to Europe (1608), and in 1619 he took Thomas Carew along as his secretary. During the course of his sojourns in Europe Herbert cultivated the acquaintance of such intellectual luminaries as Grotius, Tilenus, Isaac Casaubon and many others. In addition to his scholarly and literary interests, Herbert was also a musician; he played the lute, collected Italian music, and himself composed a few pavans and galliards.[2]

Herbert's ambassadorship in France was less politically successful than his stay was intellectually rewarding. Proud and choleric by nature, Herbert first quarrelled with and then nearly came to blows with Louis XIII's favourite, the duc de Luynes, and then found himself on the wrong side as he expressed disapproval of James I's proposed Spanish match for the Prince of Wales. He also overstepped the mark by outwardly proclaiming his sympathy for the deposed Bohemian king, Frederick V of the Palatinate (another personal friend), and by his outspoken support of the French Protestant cause. The frankness of Herbert's letters to his superiors and to the King

---

[2]Paul O'Dette has recorded selections from Lord Herbert's lute-book for Harmonia Mundi. It includes a "Pavane compos'd by mee," a beautiful but melancholy piece which amply expresses Herbert's depressed state of mind in his later years.

and his unwillingness or inability to play the appropriate diplomatic games led to Herbert's recall, and never again did he hold public office. James I rewarded Herbert's services with the Irish barony of Castle Island, but he did not pay the debts which Herbert had incurred as ambassador, a state of affairs which led to a lifetime of anxiety for Herbert. He also felt slighted by the Irish peerage, but this was remedied in 1629, when Charles I conferred on him the barony of Chirbury in the English peerage.

Thus the Herbert who returned to England in 1624 was a disillusioned, bitter man, whose ambitions had been severely curtailed. He now turned his attentions full-time to scholarship and poetry, which pursuits occupied him for the rest of his life. Lord Herbert was no mere aristocratic amateur; he spent twenty-four years of his life almost exclusively on serious writing projects, many of which were variations on the same philosophical and theological themes. If Herbert was an amateur, it was in the old-fashioned sense of that word; he was a serious thinker and his books attracted attention from other serious thinkers. Herbert's readers included Descartes, Campanella, Mersenne, Hobbes, Gassendi and Grotius; several of these readers, notably Descartes and Gassendi, commented at length on Herbert's philosophy in writing. Descartes, who confessed to having difficulties with the Latin text of *De veritate*, read the French translation (probably by Mersenne or Herbert himself) in 1637, and the next year made his judgment after completing his own *Discours de la méthode* (1638). He stated that while Herbert "has several maxims which seem to me so pious and so much in accord with common sense that I wish they may be approved by orthodox theology," he "cannot be in complete agreement with this author's opinions." Nevertheless, Descartes concluded on a note of high praise. "I consider," he wrote, "that he is much above ordinary minds" (Walker 170). Gassendi, who prefaced his remarks with the opinion that Herbert was "a second Verulam" (Jones 117), attacked Herbert from the point of view of a destructive sceptic, concluding that "truth, in my judgment, is hidden from man's eyes" (Gassendi 110). In spite of Gassendi's criticisms, he was the last philosopher the ailing Herbert visited on his trip to France in 1647.

Herbert's endeavours in other fields should not go unmentioned. Besides his poetry in English and Latin and his two major philosophical works, Herbert also produced a political biography of Henry VIII (1639), an account of the Duke of Buckingham's ill-fated invasion of France, the *Expedition to the Isle of Rhé* (1630), *Religio laici* (1645), *De causis errorum* (1645) and his autobiography, which first saw print in 1764, a product of Horace Walpole's Strawberry Hill press. Herbert was probably also the author of *A Dialogue between a Tutor and his Pupil*, which was finally published in 1768.[3] His brother Sir Henry Herbert issued the *Poems on Several Occasions* in 1665.

When the Civil War broke out, Lord Herbert found himself rather unwillingly a royalist (his cousin the Earl of Pembroke was a Parliamentarian); unpublished papers about the nature of kingship indicate that he had grave doubts about Charles I which went beyond mere irritation that his salary arrears were still owing. In 1644 Herbert and his daughter Beatrice, besieged in Montgomery Castle, surrendered to the Parliamentary commander Sir Thomas Middleton, and Herbert compounded with Parliament in order to save his London house and library. For these actions he was censured in his own time and roundly castigated by his Victorian biographer, Sir Sidney Lee. However, throughout these later years Herbert's health, never strong, had been failing steadily, although he did go to France for a final visit in 1647 to attend an intellectually-stimulating dinner at the exiled court of Queen Henrietta Maria, whose guests included Descartes, Hobbes and the Duke of Newcastle, erstwhile tutor to the Prince of Wales, poet, playwright and rather poor general. Herbert died in 1648 and lies buried in the parish church at Montgomery. He was sixty-six years old.

Lord Herbert of Chirbury was a colourful and enigmatic figure. As a young man (so he tells us) he was renowned for his good looks, sweet-smelling sweat and amorous proclivities, although in regard to the latter he takes pains to tell us that he remained faithful to his wife for the first ten years of their marriage. He fought duels on flimsy pretexts, needlessly exposed himself to enemy bullets in battle, challenged people to single combat and was on the whole rather arrogant, aggressive, and quarrelsome. Something happened, however, which made Herbert's brain take over from his body, and in an age of gifted contemporaries he became known for his wit, erudition and powerful intellect. He spoke French, Italian, and Spanish fluently, and was acquainted with German and Portuguese. As a teenager he had been made to learn Welsh so that he could converse with the Herbert tenants in their own language, and he was fluent in Latin. Herbert's Greek was somewhat shaky, but passable, and he knew some Arabic and Hebrew. His library amply demonstrates his wide range of interests; it includes works

---

[3]This work is probably Herbert's, and modern scholars, with the exception of Mario Rossi (III, 531–33) agree that it is. Gawlick provides a lengthy introduction to his facsimile edition, and H.R. Hutcheson and Robert I. Aaron are also convinced (Butler 522–23). R.D. Bedford says that the book is full of views that are, at least, "Herbertian" (189), and Eugene Hill, the most recent author of a book on Herbert, has no doubts (46). For further details, see my Lord Herbert of Chirbury, Appendix III, 506–10.

on geography, history, mathematics, medicine (he liked to try out remedies on unsuspecting friends and tenants), travel, military strategy, politics and music. Jonson described him as "all-virtuous Herbert," who was "so many men" that he could not be encompassed. William Lewis, the first translator of *De religione gentilium*, called Herbert "this Glory of his Country, and Ornament of Learning," and even the cynical Horace Walpole, after laughing himself "sick" over Herbert's *Autobiography*, had to admit in his preface to that work that Herbert had "supported the dignity of his Country, even when his Prince disgraced it." Walpole's summary of Herbert's achievement is as apt as anyone's:

> Valour and military activity in youth, business of state in middle age; contemplation and labours for the information of posterity in the calmer scenes of closing life: This was Lord Herbert. (A2)

Finally, since Lord Herbert wrote an autobiography, it may be legitimately asked how he viewed himself. Herbert's account, unfinished as it stands, is still a curious footnote to his career. He seems to have begun it quite late in life (we do not know when) and he gets only as far as the end of his ambassadorship. What made Walpole laugh was Herbert's self-advertising, his bragging about love-affairs, his military prowess and duelling skills, all of which make interesting, indeed racy reading. He says very little about his intellectual activities, although there is an extended passage on the "vision" he had before deciding to publish *De veritate*.

The answer is that Herbert did not intend to tell "us" about himself; the autobiography was intended for his own immediate posterity, not as an exercise in self-analysis, although Margaret Bottrall sees in it "Herbert's brave attempt to disguise a sense of failure from himself and his posterity" (81), a judgment which perhaps has more than a grain of truth in it. Douglas Bush calls it "a naive appeal to the traditional code of chivalry" (241), which makes Herbert sound like an English Don Quixote, but again, there is some truth in that, too. The world into which he was born was still the Elizabethan age, and by 1648 all which that had represented was in ashes. Delaney flatly states that the book is "flamboyant self-dramatization" (122), a judgment which seems to cast pejorative assertions on the man because he was not terribly modest. And of course, as all autobiographies are, Herbert's places himself at centre-stage. What would be the point of writing an autobiography in which one purposefully set out to marginalise oneself? In the end, objective readers must suspend judgment because Herbert never finished the book. Perhaps he simply felt that his books could speak for themselves, but that the author needed to ensure that he was remembered for who he was, not for what he wrote. Men like Herbert need "for short

Time an endlesse Moniment," as Spenser put it, and to build one the words needed to be set down.

3. Paganism and Pagan Religion

It is perhaps not so well-known that the word "pagan" is a Christian coinage which appeared in texts no earlier than the fourth century C.E. The word does not appear in the Bible (the translators preferred "heathen" with its pejorative overtones), and in its everyday sense *pagani* simply meant "civilians," that is, people "who had not enlisted through baptism as soldiers of Christ against the powers of Satan" (Fox 30–31). Herbert uses the word *gentiles*, but "gentiles" to a twentieth-century reader usually carries the meaning of "those who are not Jews." In the present work Herbert discusses the Greeks, Romans, Egyptians, Arabs and Indians (of various kinds), and it seemed more accurate to translate Herbert's *gentiles* as "pagans." Herbert's friend and contemporary Hugo Grotius used the word in his *Against Paganism, Judaism and Mahumentanism*, a work whose English translation appeared in 1676. Thus the word "pagan" is understood here to mean simply "non-Christian," in as neutral a way as that term could have been used by a seventeenth-century writer.

The phrase "pagan religion" also needs some clarification, and this task is rather complex. A.D. Nock, for example, states that it may be defined as "essentially a matter of cult-acts" (Fox 31), and indeed most writers on the subject, including Herbert, emphasised the importance of cult-acts in pagan religion. After all, pagans did not possess either revelation or "faith" in the Christian sense, and neither did they see God as personal, except perhaps for some megalomaniacal Roman emperors who declared themselves actually to *be* gods, which is, I suppose, about as personal as one gets. As E.R. Dodds points out, however, "to anyone brought up on classical Greek philosophy, faith was the lowest grade of cognition, the state of mind of the uneducated" (Fox 31). Herbert takes issue with this in Chapter XV, but it would seem that only Cicero (one of Herbert's favourite sources) in Book III of *On the Nature of the Gods* came anywhere near to admitting that faith might have some useful function, and the person who voices the opinion happens to be a Pontifex Maximus. At the same time, writers on religion have recognised with William James that the pagan, while a "mere natural man without a sense of sin," also had "his own peculiar religious consciousness" (85), which James identifies as "full to the brim of the sad mortality of this sunlit world" (86). We may perhaps also note that St. Paul, too, grudgingly admitted that he had learned something from the pagans (whom he calls Gentiles), who although they "have not the law," nevertheless "do by nature the things contained in the law . . . which shew the work of the law written in their hearts" (Romans 2:14–15). These observations, and those which Cicero attributes to Cotta, indicate that for some pagans, at least, religion was more than mere "cult-acts."

Now if pagan religion was more than cult-acts, could it be defined? From the above quotations, we may deduce that pagans had no sense of sin (James) and that they may have followed Christian practices without knowing that their value-systems overlapped (St. Paul). Let us look at the Latin word *religio*. In 257 C.E. the reigning emperors of Rome, Valerian and Gallienus, wrote on the vexatious subject of Christianity to one of their provincial governors. The emperors had no trouble defining the Christians as people who did not "follow the Roman religion [*religio*]," and they ordered that Christians should be "forced to observe Roman religious ceremonies" (Fox 31). Fox contends, quite rightly I believe, that Valerian and Gallienus were concerned with much more than mere sacrificial or ceremonial lip-service to Jupiter, Mars or Hestia. It is true that they were not thinking of "faith" as a Christian would see it, but they seemed to have wanted their subjects to embrace a particular "attitude" towards the sacred. They saw religion as a force in peoples' lives, and they considered that the Roman religion was under threat. Fox's contention is made stronger, I believe, by the fact that we are not dealing, in the case of Valerian and Gallienus, with lunatics or tyrants. Valerian, before his elevation to the purple in 253, had been a distinguished soldier and senator; his son Gallienus was a highly-cultured man who had been trained in philosophy and who himself wrote poetry. Their combined reigns (253–68) covered an extremely turbulent time in Roman history, and both men deserved, one can say with hindsight, to have lived in better times. Valerian, defeated and captured by the Persians, lived out the remainder of his days in captivity; his skin was stuffed with straw after his death so that the Persian people could have a permanent reminder of their triumph over Rome. Gallienus, rushing from one part of his empire to another to crush hydra-like usurpers, had little time for poetry or philosophy. And paganism, in part because of the disintegration of the empire, had less than a century to go before it was abolished forever by Constantine the Great as the official religion of the Roman Empire. Paganism enjoyed a brief resurgence under Julian "the Apostate" (361–63), but the Persians also put his life to an end, thus leaving the path clear for his Christian successor, Jovian, to issue the Edict of Universal Toleration (364), which ended "official" paganism for ever.

This being said, what accounts for the significant revival of an interest in paganism during the Renaissance? Paganism itself, to be sure, had survived, more or less run underground, since the dawn of Christian supremacy, but it really came into its own again during the sixteenth century. Jean Seznec believes that the main impetus for its survival came from the discovery of the *Sacred History* of Euhemerus, a third century B.C.E. writer who advanced the claim that the gods had once been mortals. Euhemerus's work found its way into Latin literature first through a translation by the Roman poet Ennius (Seznec 12–13), and subsequently through the works of the Christian writer Lactantius. Other writers, including Diodorus Siculus, Eustathius, and Eusebius, all of whom are cited by Herbert, took up Euhemerus's ideas. Diodorus, for example, quoted Euhemerus as stating that the god Uranus "was a gentle and benevolent man, familiar with the movements of the stars; he was the first to honour the heavenly gods with sacrifices, and that is why he is called Uranus, or Heaven" (Grant 75). Herbert cites several Christian Euhemerist writers in the present work, including Tertullian, Arnobius and Minucius Felix. Further development took place at the hands of humanist historians and mythographers, and paganism began to take on a new lease of life, finding its expression in the poetry, art, and sculpture of the Italian Renaissance. Euhemerus's ideas appealed to intellectuals, who had found it difficult to take the myths of the gods and the heroic legends, which had been presented in the works of Homer and Hesiod, either literally or seriously. At the same time, Euhemerism allowed for the emergent Roman civilisation to claim that its ancient rulers should be worshipped as gods.

Euhemerus and his followers, many of whom were also Homeric commentators, promoted their thesis through historic as well as through epic and heroic examples; the cult of Alexander the Great, the deified Seleucid kings and Roman god-emperors were all part of the propaganda of Euhemerism. There was, of course, opposition to Euhemerism, because it could not offer the same emotional and spiritual power as myth and epic; indeed, what could Euhemerus's demystification of the heroic accomplish in the lists against Homer or even Hesiod? Euhemerism did appeal to the Christian fathers who found themselves at the forefront of establishing the new religion, for it gave them a weapon with which to belabour their pagan opponents. We find Ignatius of Antioch, for example, exhorting the church at Magnesia-on-the-Maeander to dismiss paganism as "the teachings and time-worn fables of other people," explaining further that "nothing of any use may be got from them" (Staniforth 89). Augustine, an oft-quoted source of Herbert's, frequently mocks pagan religion in his *City of God*; he presents, for example, an amusing discussion of "bearded Fortune" in Book IV (Augustine 150). It may have struck some educated pagans as somewhat surprising that the very people who rejoiced in their own "god-made-man" Christ should suddenly take exception to the rather more plausible "man-made-god" of the ancient religions. The Christians, it seemed, wished to bring their God down to the level of a man, while claiming that there was something reprehensible about a good man being raised up by the immortals to join their number.

From being a weapon in the war against the pagans, Euhemerism evolved into what Seznec terms "am auxiliary to historical research" (13). If the gods had been people, historians could find out where they had lived and what they had done. Eusebius does something of the kind in his work on church history, and a massive compilation by Isidore of Seville, the *Etymologiae*, sought to apply Euhemerus's ideas directly to history, going as far as to construct "dynasties" from mythical god-kings and attempting to date them (Seznec 14). By the Middle Ages it had become quite common for scholars to make parallels between Christian wisdom and pagan lore, and special positions were granted to such figures as Zoroaster, credited with the invention of magic and treated as a legitimate authority by Herbert. Indeed, Herbert himself demonstrated latter-day Euhemeristic tendencies, claiming, for example, that some of the more salacious female deities of the Near East must have at one time been famous prostitutes, and that Saturn was a great Latin king. The latter idea Herbert found mentioned in Boccaccio's *Genealogy of the Gods*, itself a Euhemeristic work.

What, then, is this "ancient religion of the gentiles" as it was seen by Herbert? Does his conception differ much from the Euhemeristic offerings of his predecessors? Or is it what D.P. Walker termed "the ancient theology," which he defined as "a certain tradition of Christian apologetic theory which rests on misdated texts?" (2). The "misdated texts" to which Walker alludes are, of course, the so-called Orphic Hymns, various Hermetic *libelli*, and certain Platonic, Neo-Platonic and gnostic material. What are we to make of Herbert's allusions to the Seven Sages, to Pythagoras and other mystical magi, or to trace elements of even older religious systems? Walker goes on to mention still other strange ideas which he finds in Herbert, such as "good natural magic and astrology, numerology, powerful music, patriotic national history [so that, for the English and French, the Druids became Ancient Theologians]" (175). Put all this together with myth, fable, allegory, and Biblical typology; we now have a potent mixture of ancient theology, and Herbert does devote large parts of his treatise to an exegesis of ancient rites, lustrations, ceremonies and myths, all the while interspersing the discourse with Biblical citations and allusions.

Herbert's use of this material confirms that he took pagan religion seriously as a religion, and was not prepared to dismiss it as Christian theologians had. And it was not, for him, a series of "cult-acts." Present-day religion was linked to pagan religion by the fact of the Religious Common Notions; it was alienated from it proportionate to the amount of priestly innovations, dogmatism and obscure doctrinal hair-splitting that the centuries had produced. Pagan religion had its failings, but it nonetheless took us back to the primordial collective soul of humanity; it was the foundation of modern religions, and it had been misunderstood for generations of theological speculation. Herbert was also attracted to the "ancient theology" because it was so all-encompassing and therefore universal in a sense that Christianity could never be.

One main link between Herbert's system and the old religion is, according to Walker, that both are astrally-centered, because the stars and heavens, observed by man through innumerable ages, were forever providing observers with evidence of order and stability in the universe. Cicero had noticed, for example, that "the very aspect of the heavens declared that they were not the work of chance . . . there is someone in command whose orders are obeyed" (*NG* 129). From this observation it is easy to see how the pagans began to venerate the stars themselves as divine, naming them with names that were already well-known. "*Nomen, numen*—the name was enough to lend divine personality to each luminous body moving in the heavens" (Seznec 37); the naming-process must have gone back at least as far as Homer and Hesiod, first with whole constellations and then individual stars and planets. Herbert himself noted that the ancients, desperately looking for something that was not "transitory and passing," looked upon the stars alone as possessing "a certain eternal and therefore happy state," and worshipping them not as gods themselves, but as "visible ministers" of the Supreme God (6). Herbert's notion of stars as "visible ministers" implies that they possess some kind of intelligence, an idea which may also be found in Aquinas. While God himself may remain invisible and ineffable, human beings may have knowledge of God's creation.

In *De l'infinito, universo e mondi* (1584), a book which Herbert owned, Giordano Bruno stated that God is "wholly in the whole world," and that the universe, "because it has no margin, limit or surface" is also infinite. However, the worlds within it are finite, and Nature is "an organic whole which stands in the centre of the world-substance" (Copleston 3, II, 70). The stars and planets make up the universe; they are the eternal objects of God, whose splendour (which we can see) links the human and the divine. We invoke them as divine, and they demonstrate to us that God's eternal objects are apprehendable, at least insofar as we can know that they are immutable. It is this limited understanding of the divine which allows us to partake of the divine nature.

The limited perception and understanding which can be gained of the heavenly bodies led mankind to speculate about the order and purpose of the universe itself. Throughout the present work Herbert insists, as Walker points out, "that the pagan cult of natural objects [stars, planets] and of men [heroes] was of a symbolic nature" (177). Herbert borrowed Vossius's distinction between direct worship (*cultus proprius*) and symbolic worship (*cultus symbolicus*). He amasses evidence to show that ancient writers believed that the heavenly bodies were somehow "alive," citing Plato, the Stoics and Aquinas to prove his point. He enlisted an eirenicist Jesuit theologian, Adam Tanner, to show that if Aquinas was correct, then the ancients were justified in considering the stars worthy of worship. As Herbert puts it, "those things that are higher seem to deserve greater worship than those that are lower," and that height betokens immutability; "sempiternal felicity," he declares, " is enjoyed in the heavens and stars" (10). At the same time, the stars did not themselves become gods, he insists, until the priests and "false prophets" made them so and told the people to worship them directly.

In ancient times the stars, planets and heavens were regarded by many as the dispensers of universal fate (*heimarmene*) to the natural world. The sky itself, as Hans Jonas states, became "the purest embodiment of reason in the cosmic hierarchy, the paradigm of intelligibility and therefore of the divine aspect of the sensible realm" (121). The emperor Julian wrote of the Sun, for example, that he "had an extraordinary longing for the rays of the god . . . [which] penetrated deep into my soul" (I, 359). Small wonder, then, that Herbert's own "vision," which he described in his autobiography, came from "the serenest Skye that ever I saw being without Cloud," and that he addressed a prayer not to the Christian God or Christ but to something more ancient than either, "thou Eternal God Author of that Light which now shines upon me, and Giver of all inward Illuminations" (*Autobiography* 121). The outer light mirrors the inner light, the intellectual spirit not of Christianity but of gnosticism, "the deification of the heavens or of the chief heavenly bodies" (Jonas 259), which is, of course, the theme of Chapter III of the present work. This deification, Jonas further states, "*is for the most natural and universally operative reasons* [italics mine] an element in all ancient religions [except the Jewish one]" (259). Herbert himself described the fixed stars as "God's eternal Law," and the planets as "His prophetic book," asking "why should the Supreme God . . . not inscribe certain immutable principles of His laws in the stars . . . Why should God not show certain reasons both of present and future things in the planets?"

In view of the above, as well as Walker's observation that Herbert demonstrates gnostic elements in his theodicy, it might be useful here to look very briefly at gnosticism. It is also germane to the discussion to note that in Chapter XIII Herbert mentions two gnostic writers by name, Marcus Cerdon and Apelles, both of whom were disciples of the better-known gnostic thinker Marcion. Furthermore, the hierarchy of gods which the pagan priest outlines in Chapter XIV and which Herbert found "not uncomely" has definite gnostic overtones, and may be at least tentatively linked to the theodicy of the gnostic Valentinus (fl. 138–58 C.E.). When Pope Clement I (c. 90–100) issued a decretal against the gnostics, he asserted that priests, and in particular the Bishop of Rome, held their authority directly from God, who in turn had delegated it "to certain rulers and leaders on earth" (Pagels 40). This is an early example of a priest of an "established" church attempting to monopolise spiritual if not temporal power as well, excluding others from interpreting God's word by asserting that he alone has "authority," which presumably came from revelation. Clement also mentions the gnostics in his decretal, and threatens death to anyone who disobeys him.

In Valentinian gnosticism, the God whom Clement I had worshipped and from whom he claimed to derive his authority was a savage, sadistic demiurge with a very unreliable demeanour, whom the Christians had mistaken for the Supreme God. Only through *gnosis*, which may be defined as a form of "secret knowledge," could the spirit be delivered from the prison of the body and thus attain salvation. Valentinus, using the Gospels as his authority, claimed that Christ himself had imparted this knowledge to his disciples, who had taught it "only in private, to certain persons who had proven themselves to be spiritually mature" (Pagels 17). Valentinus posited a hierarchy of "Aeons," which corresponds strikingly to the system expounded by Herbert's priest. The Supreme God, Bythos, is "the unbegotten Monad and perfect Aeon;" his consort, Sige, is also Bythos's thought (*ennoia*). They are the powers above the next group, the "supercelestial" demiurges. From these all other Aeons emanate in a downward hierarchy, until man appears, formed by a Creator whom Valentinus identified with the Old Testament God. The Creator, who had the outward image of Bythos, was known by the Valentinians as The Demiurge (Kelly 23–24). Gnosis, of course, is the direct worship of Bythos, although the latter does not concern himself with human affairs. This system, then, is close to that posited by Herbert's priest, and it is not surprising that his readers looked in vain for orthodox Christianity in it. From early times gnosticism was under fire; Irenaeus's *Adversus haereses* appeared in about 180, followed by Hippolytus's *Elenchos against all the Heresies* (c. 225), Epiphanius of Salamis's *Panarion* (c. 375) through to Philastrius and Theodoret in the fifth century C.E. Heresiology, of course, was a going concern of the Catholic and Protestant churches down to (and including) the present time.

The Renaissance revival of interest in paganism might never have come into being had it not been for medieval mythographers, theologians and philosophers, who took the interpretations of their predecessors a little further at a time and brought the old ideas to life. As Leonard Barkan remarks of the mythographer Natalis Comes (c. 1520–82), he "is at least as reductive and moralistic as the earlier commentators, and his Platonism seems to be an innovation only until one had read Arnulf and John of Garland" (171). It is as if the centuries have been compressed; "the spirit of paganism and metamorphosis," Barkan continues, "is resurrected from the dead and at the same time alive as though there had been no interval of dormancy" (172). The same can be said of the raw materials of pagan religion, which were seized upon by Herbert as evidence for the Religious Common Notions and as proof that mankind had always held certain beliefs no matter what God he happened to worship.

4. Herbert's Mythography

When Lord Herbert decided to turn mythographer, he had a radically different reason for doing so than any of his predecessors, however much he mined their material. To understand how different Herbert's purpose was, it is useful to consider what some of his mythographical predecessors (and sources) were doing while they accumulated, studied, and interpreted stories about the Greek and Roman gods. Let us consider as examples only some of those whom Herbert cites. To the eminent Roman scholar M. Terentius Varro, myths were often a means to an historico-political end; as Michael Grant points out, Varro's *De lingua Latina*, far from being merely a treatise on the Latin language, was also part of "the official version, or legend, of the Augustan régime" (*RM* 29). The later Latin mythographer Fulgentius took the ancient myths and legends, imposing upon them "an allegorical interpretation, mostly in terms of ethics and turning on etymologies of the names of principal characters" (Fulgentius 17). We have already seen how Augustine ridiculed pagan religion in his *City of God*; when he refers to it he usually wishes to demonstrate the superiority of Christian beliefs, that is, of his own set of myths and rituals. As for Herbert's more modern authorities, their treatment of myth was informed by the Renaissance interest in paganism as a source for the works of artists and poets, a purpose clearly explained by writers such as Du Choul and Cartari in their prefaces. Vossius, who is Herbert's chief source, wants readers to see how superior Christianity is to "idolatry," which places him closer to Augustine than to his own times. Selden's interest, on the other hand, is purely historical. In his treatment of pagan religion, Herbert differed from all of the above; he accumulated evidence not so much to show how far away paganism was from Christianity, but how close the pagans had come to supporting his contentions about the foundations of religious belief.

Herbert certainly did not condone all aspects of pagan religion. "When I understood how ridiculous some of their religious rites and ceremonies were," he wrote, "I was at first inclined to concur with the accepted view," the latter, one assumes, being Augustinian in nature. He details his surprise at the "fallible and finite attributes" (1) bestowed by the pagans upon their gods. In spite of this, he wishes that "modern theologians would be more tolerant" (3) about pagan beliefs and myths. Even if the pagans "mixed superstition with truth . . . [and] polluted their souls with such crimes as could not be expiated with any amount of repentance," they still "know about the most rational and intelligible parts of divine worship" (6).

One of the problems that Herbert encountered as he attempted to put a "positive" face on pagan religion and emphasise its ethical aspects was the so-called "immorality" of the gods, an easy and constant target for Christian writers, not to mention some Greeks and Romans as well. Herbert appears to be moving in the direction taken by a modern scholar on this subject:

> the gods' lusts, though in themselves something which would get them life imprisonment in a modern society, were not trivially exercised but exist in order to beget significant offspring who have a god at the head of their genealogy. It is doubtful whether this mythology is best viewed as implementing irresponsible male fantasy.   (Dowden 163)

Herbert needed to address this question simply because it would be raised by his Christian critics. In Chapter XIV Herbert blames the introduction of polytheism by the priests for any immorality in pagan religion, suggesting that it was levelled as a charge by one cult against another. Walter Burkert notes that polytheism has difficulties when it comes to legitimating a world-order of ethics, because each deity protects his or her own "turf" and, as any readers of ancient epics know, each deity also has a favourite mortal, sometimes because he or she is the parent of that mortal. The sexual mores of the gods are inextricably bound up in the way they behave towards mortals, and mortals, for their part, have to learn to live with what the gods do, that "dialectic of amoral gods and religious morality," as Burkert puts it (247). "Greek gods," we are told, "do not give laws" (Burkert 248), and there was no equivalent of divine revelation, where gods come down to earth and deliver instructions.

At the same time, Herbert would have understood that the Greeks and Romans nevertheless had a sense that they owed certain duties to the gods and that they should avoid offending them; after all, one of the Religious Common Notions states that "virtue and piety are the principal points of the divine cult," and another one points out that "divine judgment, reward, and punishment exist both in this life and the next" (3). Thus the pagan gods, whatever they might do sexually amongst themselves and amongst mortals nevertheless, as Homer tells us, "love justice and good deeds" (*Odyssey*

14.83) in mankind, and will act accordingly. "I cannot but think," Herbert added, "that after leading good lives, [the pagans] partook fully of Divine Grace" (6).

As we have mentioned, the Greeks themselves recognised the need to resolve the contradiction between what the gods did while at the same time encouraging "justice and good deeds" amongst mortals, and punishing them if they did not live up to standard. The Pre-Socratic philosopher Xenophanes, for example, complained that "Homer and Hesiod have attributed to the gods all things which are shameful and a reproach among mankind: theft, adultery, and mutual deception" (Freeman 22). Xenophanes, however, is blaming not the gods themselves, but two poets who "attributed" these vices to them. This allowed the Greeks to distinguish between a "theology of poets" and what might be called "state theology," which, according to Burkert, was "very much a civic duty" (246). A fine distinction, this, and one which allowed Plato to banish "lying" poets from his polis. It also gave Herbert a precedent, or at least an analogy, for blaming the priests, who had tampered with an older and purer form of religion, likely monotheistic in nature and certainly more ethically "correct" than would have appeared from ancient evidence.

When Herbert cites mythographers, he usually prefers classical authorities to moderns, most particularly Varro, Cicero, Dionysius of Halicarnassus, and Servius. Of Greek authorities, the historian Herodotus is the most frequently-cited, together with Pausanias. It is sometimes difficult to tell whether Herbert cited his Greek authorities directly or from Latin sources; his Latin was superior to his Greek, but there are some passages from Aristotle, Homer, and Plato which appear in Greek. Of the moderns, Cartari is Herbert's chief mythographic authority, but he cites Du Choul and Selden as well. Fulgentius, whom one might expect to find more often, is cited once or twice, and some others, such as Natalis Comes, are not mentioned at all. Herbert's main church authorities are Augustine and Jerome, and for comparative mythography (which usually means Central or South America), he relies on José de Acosta. Philosophical interpolations from Aristotle and Plato occur fairly often amongst the mythographical detail, and there are five references to the emperor Julian, who for Herbert seems to have represented the philosopher-king. Julian is discussed at some length (with quotations from Ammianus Marcellinus) on two of these occasions.

Of the modern mythographers cited in this work, Herbert's largest debt is to the erudite, prolific, and sometimes prolix Dutch scholar Gerard Jan Vossius (1577–1649), whose name is invariably prefaced with the honorific "learned." Vossius's great work of comparative mythography, *De theologia gentilium sive de origine ac progressu idololatriae* (1642) is a massive compilation of religious, theological, philosophical, mythographical and linguistic material, systematically marshalled to show how pagan "idolatry" developed and to demonstrate how it was, ultimately, irreconcilable with Christianity. Vossius made connexions between Graeco-Roman and Old Testament mythology, some of which Herbert accepted, others which he rejected. Vossius argued that Christianity had conquered paganism not simply because God had ordained its triumph, but because it was, inherently, the better religious system. Paganism, Vossius asserted, had borrowed and then debased, with the help of Satan, the original truth of the Judaeo-Christian tradition. Since the pagans had already been corrupted by Satan, and since their reason (like all reason) was subject to deception (as Descartes had suggested with his "evil genius" hypothesis), the pagans had absolutely no chance of salvation. Herbert completely disagreed with Vossius on this major point. Salvation, for Herbert, came through the Religious Common Notions, which, he had demonstrated, were present in all humans, known intuitively, and not subject to the errors of reason. Corruption, Herbert argued, was not due to the machinations of Satan (who, like Christ, merits scarcely a mention) or to faulty reason, but to the power-lust of the priests. Furthermore, Vossius's evidence pointed to the exact opposite of what he claimed. Lastly, as D.C. Allen perceptively remarked:

> Herbert's. . . . book marked the beginning of the end for the whole theory that
> etymological investigations and comparative biographies would show the Old
> Testament behind all other religious theory and history.   (78)

The Old Testament was not the ultimate source of religion, according to Herbert; in fact, evidence taken from it showed that Judaism had adopted rites, ceremonies and beliefs from more ancient cultures, and this implied that Christianity, based upon Judaism, did not have the authority of that which was more ancient than itself. Herbert, in a word, used Vossius's evidence to show that Vossius had been wrong.

Herbert did, however, find much in Vossius that was useful. We have seen above that he used Vossius's distinction between direct and symbolic worship, and he agreed with the Dutch scholar that Sun-worship was the oldest and most central part of pagan religion. Vossius's great erudition and the vast amount of source-material he used provided Herbert with a veritable gold-mine of useful information, backed up with the authority of modern scholarship. It appears sometimes that Herbert needed to see whether Vossius had included an authority before he himself would use it; Vossius's book became an encyclopaedia, and it supplemented, in one convenient place, Herbert's own considerable reference-library.

Lest anyone assume from the foregoing that Herbert was in any way an epigone, let it be noted that he differs from Vossius not only in the intentions of his work, but on many details of scholarship also. For example, Vossius stated that in pagan times both the sun and the stars were a *cultus proprius*, and that the pagans were therefore wrong to worship them. Vossius used the word "symbol" in reference to heroes such as Hercules, who ascended into heaven as a demigod and to whom the pagans raised altars and temples. Vossius argued that the pagans, who had no revelations, could only seek God in one way, through the worship of idols such as Hercules. This meant that they were not worshipping God himself, but Hercules, falsely attributing divinity to a mere mortal who had been a part of God's creation. Herbert argued that the devotees of Hercules were not worshipping Hercules, but God *through* Hercules, and thus the cult of Hercules was a *cultus symbolicus*. Similarly, the stars and planets, in Herbert's system, blazon forth in their own immutability that of their Creator, who is beyond comprehension; worship of these heavenly bodies would be, for Herbert, symbolic, even though they themselves were immutable. God does, after all, have the power to create that which is immutable. Vossius does not seem to have allowed this. In fact, Herbert's theology is symbolic throughout, because that is the only way it can be true both to his conception of ancient religions and his eirenic intentions. If it were not, the foundations of his Religious Common Notions in primordial antiquity would be weakened, and any evidence gathered from non-Christian sources open to question. Herbert emphasised that he would "completely reject the opinion of the pagans" if they paid *direct* worship to heavenly phenomena, but if "the worship was originally symbolic of the Supreme God in the stars, sometimes of the stars in heroes," he would accept it.

Herbert drew on two other continental sources for his mythography, *Le imagini colla sposizione degli dei degli antichi* (1556) by Vincenzo Cartari (c. 1520–75) and, to a lesser extent, the *Discours de la réligion des anciens Romains* of Guillaume du Choul, published in the same year. Cartari's book was designed as one of those ubiquitous Renaissance handbooks for artists; his publisher, Marcolini, said that it would be useful "to all who take an interest in antiquity," but especially to artists, who could use its copious illustrations to help them come up with "a thousand inventions with which to adorn their statues and painted panels" (Seznec 251). Herbert often refers to Cartari for the physical descriptions of deities under discussion; he probably found it very useful that Cartari did not confine himself to Classical antiquity and included illustrations of Syrian, Egyptian, Persian and Scythian deities as well. Cartari had another desire, too, for the use of his book; he wished, he said, "to promote a better understanding of the ancient literatures" (Seznec

251), a sentiment with which Herbert concurred. Of Du Choul we know very little, but his "beautiful book, magnificently illustrated," as Seznec describes it (247), is cited several times by Herbert and evidently had a wide readership.

A brief mention should be made of some of the works that Herbert did not use, notably two English works on mythography, Stephen Batman's *Golden Booke of the Leaden Gods* (1577) and Abraham Fraunce's *Third Part of the Countesse of Pembroke's Yvychurche* (1592). Batman, like Vossius, condemned paganism in a polemical introduction, which is perhaps why Herbert did not bother with his book, and the scholarship is decidedly inferior to that of Vossius. Herbert may have known a third English work, Richard Lynche's *Fountaine of Ancient Fiction* (1599), which was a paraphrase of Cartari, but Herbert's command of Italian was more than adequate, and we may suppose that he preferred Cartari himself to Lynche. Another rather curious omission was Jean Boem's *Customs, Laws and Rites of all Peoples* (1520), which Mircea Eliade praises as "the first general history of religions" (277), and which contains useful information on Asia and Africa. These works are deserving of mention because they were available for Herbert to consult, and Boem's book in particular (which is not listed as being in Herbert's library) is a particularly interesting omission.

As a mythographer Herbert employed several identifiable methodologies, all of which are now old-fashioned, but whose use by Herbert shows that he was abreast of his own times in his research. Following the divisions and definitions proposed by Ken Dowden, we can determine that Herbert principally employed three methods: historicism, allegory, and comparative mythology, also known as "natural allegory" (Dowden 23–27). Historicism may be defined simply as the belief that myth is actually history which has been distorted by the passage of time. Herbert's assertion that Saturn was an ancient king, or the theories of Euhemerus, are examples of this method. Dowden defines allegorical mythography as the belief that myths are "disguised theology or philosophy" which somehow conceal their "real" meanings and secrets "from those who do not understand allegory" (24). This method leads mythographers to make philosophical and theological connexions which are often bizarre and usually unsubstantiated. Herbert does this when he speaks with certainty of "symbolic" meanings, or when he discusses ideas such as whether the stars have "intelligences" or are "alive."

The third method, comparative mythology or natural allegory, is perhaps the most interesting one because it was new, and Herbert was the first English mythographer to employ it. It is based on the assumption that primitive man, feeling awe before natural phenomena, personified their abstract qualities and came to worship them. Herbert discusses this in Chapter II; the ancients, he wrote, "finding that everything in the sublunary world had a beginning . . . began to observe the heavens and the stars." From observation they proceeded to outright worship, as he tells us. This method was developed by the great nineteenth-century German mythographer F. Max Müller, but it is essentially being employed in the present work by Herbert, who attempts to use linguistic analysis to find connexions between the names of deities and reconstruct original meanings through comparative philology. This theory maintains that as language changed, the original myths "ceased to be understood and their sense could only be recovered by identifying the meanings of the myths and the names of the participants in the myths" (Dowden 27). The discussion of the Arabic words for God and the comparison with other names in Chapter III is a good example of Herbert's employment of this method.

5. Philosophical Trends in Herbert

With a writer like Herbert, especially when the topic is to a great extent theological, it is sometimes difficult to make a distinction between theology and philosophy. In fact, one ought probably to classify what Herbert is doing in both his major treatises as "philosophy of religion," but that phrase would have made no sense in 1645. In this section I will attempt to trace some of the major "purely" philosophical influences in the present work, on the understanding that readers realise that the categorisation is purely a matter of convenience.

Douglas Bush has noticed a "Platonic strain" in Herbert which he considered explained the latter's "conception of the universe as a harmonious organism and . . . the correspondences between it and man" (Wiley 98). Mario Rossi, whose three-volume study of Herbert is the starting-point for all modern scholarship on the subject, felt that the main influence on Herbert was not Plato but Aristotle. Rossi argued that while some Platonic elements were indeed discernible in Herbert, they are more accurately Neo-Platonic, "and further removed from Plato than Aquinas was from Aristotle" (I, 293). R.D. Bedford, who has examined Herbert's philosophy very thoroughly, agrees in part with both Bush and Rossi, stating that Herbert was bound up with "the Platonic heritage" (84), which could be traced back through the Hermetic tradition to Plotinus and from thence back to Plato himself. However, Bedford considers that all this was filtered through the Renaissance interpreters of Plato, notably Telesio and Patrizi. Herbert cites Patrizi quite frequently in the present work, and there are also quotations from other Renaissance Neo-Platonists such as Pico della Mirandola and Marsilio Ficino. In fact, Bedford's assertion that Herbert provides a synthesis of Plotinian,

Hermetic and Neo-Platonic doctrines in a comprehensive theory of nature is a sound one, based on the idea of harmony which Bush had already noticed. The entire doctrine, Bedford states, "rests upon the assumption that truth is a certain harmony between the world and the mind" (85). Finally, W. von Leyden has commented upon Herbert's "Platonic approach to ethics, with its emphasis on morality and its implied critique of ethical naturalism" (119).

The presence of Neo-Platonic elements in Herbert necessitates a short discussion of Renaissancē English Neo-Platonism, particularly as there is agreement amongst Herbert scholars that Neo-Platonism is important to Herbert. Renaissance Neo-Platonism developed from an earlier synthesis of Platonism with Christian doctrine and pagan Hermeticism. Plotinus, the father of Neo-Platonism, believed in "a hierarchical universe that descends through several levels from the transcendent God or One to the corporeal world," together with "an inner, spiritual experience that enables the self to re-ascend through the intelligible world to that supreme One" (Kristeller I, 52). Plotinus's work was continued by his disciple Porphyry, and from there, through Proclus (whom Herbert cites in the present work) to Michael Psellus, who introduced into Neo-Platonism various Hermetic and Zoroastrian doctrines. Perhaps the most famous of the early Renaissance Neo-Platonists was Georgios Gemistos Plethon (c. 1356–1450). This eminent Greek philosopher was also a mythographer; he attempted an allegorical explanation of ancient Greek myths which drew fire upon him from churchmen as being too "pagan." Plethon's name is curiously absent from Herbert's book, although he is cited more than once by Vossius. In addition to incursions by Christianity, Zoroastrianism and Hermeticism, Neo-Platonism also absorbed some of the Augustinian tradition along with Christianity.

It is not surprising that Herbert cites the name of Marsilio Ficino (1433–99) on several occasions; Ficino was the translator of both Plato and Plotinus, not to mention of the Hermetic *libelli*, into Latin. Ficino set out his own philosophical system in his *Theologica Platonica* (1474), in which he attempted to synthesise Neo-Platonism and Christianity by placing man at the centre of the cosmic hierarchy and developing the theory of "Platonic love." In the latter doctrine, Ficino suggested that there were two Venuses, surnamed Urania (celestial or divine love), and Pandemos or Terrestris (earthly love), a doctrine adopted by Herbert in *De religione gentilium*. Ficino also pointed out, as Charles Trinkaus states, that "man's freedom is not restricted to divine foreknowledge and that man's actions are not determinate as are the movements of nature" (Eisenbichler 143). What this implied, in effect, was that man had a rational soul which could be employed freely in the contemplation of all kinds of knowledge, human, cosmic, or divine. All man cannot do is become God himself. Thus it was both logical and legitimate for man to speculate about the nature of the divine because he was in fact already part of it. Ficino's placing of man at the centre of the cosmos had implications for the theories which Herbert advanced about the after-life and salvation, for he declared that all men, regardless of their origin or background, possessed souls. The soul, Ficino said, "is the greatest of all miracles in nature . . . the soul is all things together" (Kristeller I, 129). The pagans, then, had possessed souls, which meant that they were redeemable, although Ficino himself did not go quite that far. For Ficino, love and attraction, centred in the soul, are the unifying force in the world, and man proves this whenever he acts humanely, otherwise "he removes himself from the community of mankind and forfeits his human dignity." If Ficino was not expressly clear about salvation, his system, at least as far as Kristeller is concerned, allowed "that a reasonable proportion of mankind will attain eternal happiness" (I, 133).

Herbert clearly wished to go beyond Ficino. He asks on the first page of *De religione gentilium* "whether . . . eternal, universal salvation of the entire human race might be intended" (1). His positive answer contradicts Vossius; Herbert finds, he says, that even some scholastics might grant this point, in that "saving grace" might be possible to "anyone who does all he can to obtain it" (5), and that, together with more modern authorities, convinced Herbert that "some means should be available for everyone to come to God." He felt, moreover, that "the best of the pagans" would have been eligible for salvation, too. "I intend to demonstrate," Herbert wrote, "that Universal Providence is extended to all mankind" (5).

Closely connected with the Italian humanists was a revival of the ancient philosophy of Stoicism, whose influence on Herbert is unmistakeable. Seneca is cited early in Chapter III, and there are frequent references to him and other Stoics throughout *De religione gentilium*. Rossi has argued convincingly and at length that Stoicism was important to Herbert (I, 280ff), and it is possible that Herbert knew Sir Richard Barckley's *Discourse of the Felicitie of Man* (1598), a work of so-called "radical Stoicism," which is defined by Sidney Warhaft as a system in which "virtue may flourish without any external aid," and in which "the wise man . . . gains his eminence through conscious exertion of will and natural reason" (83). Herbert always stresses the role of right reason over compulsion, and of nature as the teacher of morality. Stoicism appealed to Christians because of its aversion to worldly pleasures and its emphasis on inner peace and reconciliation with a world over which the individual had little control. Joseph Hall, in *Heaven upon Earth* (1606), for example, "attempted to identify Stoic tranquillity with Christian peace" (Rivers 49), and to make it dependent upon divine Grace. John Smith, one of the Cambridge Platonists, remarked that "It were not worth while to live in a world . . . devoid of God and Providence, as it was well-observ'd by the Stoic [Marcus Aurelius]" (Patrides 190). Herbert was clearly attracted by the Stoic idea that man could be virtuous without reference to anything outside himself, a notion which again reinforced his contention that the pagans could have been endowed with a capacity to lead virtuous lives as a result of something within their own nature, something which they shared with all humanity through the ages.

Herbert's insistence that man had within him the means to be saved even without Christianity obviously led to a great deal of controversy. If Herbert was right in his Stoic ethical stance, then there was certainly no necessity for Christ in his system, for the doctrine of original sin did not apply to the pagans. A good example of the opposing view is that held by Milton, who put Stoic tenets in the mouths of the fallen angels in the first two books of *Paradise Lost*, and in *Paradise Regained* turned Christ into an anti-Stoic philosopher railing against those who "stand alone" (IV, 531–62), that is, arrogantly and without the aid of divine Grace. Other objections to Herbert's doctrines were, as we have seen, raised by Richard Baxter in England and several Lutheran divines on the Continent, all within a few years of Herbert's death.

The last philosophical influence I shall discuss here is that of Tommaso Campanella (1568–1639). Herbert corresponded with Campanella shortly before the latter's death, and had sent him a copy of *De veritate*. It is singularly unfortunate that Campanella, old and weakened by torture and ill-treatment at the hands of his own church authorities, died before he could write his comments. However, Charles Diodati (also a friend of Milton's), who acted as Herbert's "agent" in Europe, reported that Campanella had expressed his verbal approval of the book. Unlike Herbert, Campanella saw a need to furnish a proof for God's existence (for Herbert, it was, of course, a Religious Common Notion known intuitively), and in his *Philosophia universalis seu metaphysica* (1639) he posited a hierarchy of "states of perfection" in which he ranged all finite things and placed God at the top, being the highest state of perfection. Finite things, for Campanella, are made up of two opposing elements, being and not-being. To properly understand being we must first know ourselves, as Socrates taught us, and to that extent all knowledge is self-knowledge. Herbert had promoted that idea in *De veritate*; for both Herbert and Campanella man was a microcosm of what was happening in and to Being itself. God is therefore reflected in his creatures, and it follows from this that "knowledge of the best being known to us is the key to knowledge of being in general" (Walker 188–89). In *Atheismus triumphatus* (1631), Campanella had proposed a kind of universal religion in the form of what he called "natural Catholicism," which would "introduce the Millennium, the City of the Sun" (Yates 388). Herbert's system might well be termed "natural Protestantism," but in essence it is similar to Campanella's. The discussion of the heavenly hierarchy in Chapter XV of the present work may owe something to Campanella, and in Herbert's universal religion the Millennium would rest upon the Religious Common Notions.

6. The Translation

The work presented here is a translation made from the first printing (Amsterdam, 1663) of *De religione gentilium*, reissued in facsimile under the editorship of Günter Gawlick as the second volume of a three-volume set of Herbert's philosophical writings (Stuttgart: Friedrich Frommann Verlag, 1967). There is one MS copy of the work extant, written in an unknown hand, which Gawlick believes dates from about 1645, the year in which scholars agree that the work was written. Herbert had been in touch with Vossius, who was to print it, and was promised that it would be issued in 1646. However, there were various delays; Herbert's death in 1648, and finally Vossius's death in 1649 put paid to the printing of the work for several years, until Vossius's son Isaac issued it in 1663 (Gawlick xv). In 1705 it was translated into English by William Lewis, an Anglican minister, as *The Antient Religion of the Gentiles, and Cause of their Errors Consider'd* (London: printed for John Nutt). No subsequent English translation has appeared until the present one.

All Herbert's major philosophical works were written in Latin, and his style as a Latinist has come in for a fair amount of discussion. When the eminent antiquarian Sir William Dugdale tried to read *De veritate* in 1625 he gave up, noting that "it much passeth my understanding, being wholly philosophical" (Levy 397). We have already seen that Descartes, too, had trouble with the same book, and waited until he could read it in French. Nathaniel Culverwell, who admired Herbert's work, remarked in his *Elegant and Learned Discourse of the Light of Nature* (1651) that Herbert's language required paraphrasing because it was, as he put it politely, "somewhat cloudy," and Thomas Halyburton, attacking deism early in the next century, complained about "his Lordship's singularity of notion" (45). Sir Sidney Lee, hardly a master of the plain style himself, suffered from Herbert's Latin diction, which he found "obscure, where precision is least dispensable" (xii).

Some of the blame for this scholarly whining can be placed upon the shoulders of Dr. Thomas Master (1603–43). Master was a voluminous author, scholar, and Latin poet (he wrote a long Latin poem on the enthralling subject of Herbert's "shovel-board" game [Moore Smith 93–94]). Master acted as a kind of research assistant (Anthony Wood called him a "drudge") and also, as Wood remarked, "had a hand in Latinizing . . . *De veritate*" (III, 84). In fact, the Latin in the present work is not as difficult, and perhaps Herbert's skills as Latinist had improved after his "drudge's" death. There are, to be sure, many repetitive words and phrases, most of which I have quietly expunged (a practice one wishes Lewis had indulged in more than he did), and Herbert has a habit of over-explaining himself and citing a plethora of examples, some of which do not seem to have much to do with whatever point he is making. Herbert, like many Renaissance scholars, argues through *"accumulatio ad verecundiam"* (my Latin), the piling-up of Classical authorities, and putting up with this is a necessary adjunct to reading him. However, he sometimes appears to get tired of his own learning, and will show a rather aristocratic (should one say cavalier?) impatience, breaking off with a remark to the effect of "if you want more on this, go and look it up yourself." On the other hand, far from demonstrating the author's lordly arrogance, it may show that he believes his readers to be intelligent enough to do what he suggests.

William Lewis, it must be said here, was a fine, if somewhat literal-minded translator. Because he works so closely to Herbert's text, he provides an excellent basis for the modern translator to refer to from time to time, and he often shows an ability to turn a "Herbertian" phrase authentically. However, Lewis had his own agenda in presenting Herbert's book to the world in English, and the modern translator needs to be aware of this fact. Lewis wanted Christianity to be privileged; he wanted Herbert's book to show that it had triumphed over paganism and other religions, and he seems to have thought that Herbert, who does after all speak of "errors" in pagan religion, ultimately wanted the same end. Further evidence that Lewis did have something of the sort in mind can be gleaned from the omissions in his translation; if he feels that a passage might inflict moral or spiritual damage upon an unwary reader he simply removes it. All such passages have been restored, including Prudentius's poem about the Vestal Virgins and their salacious practices with gladiators. When it comes to verse passages, Lewis tends to translate badly; he thinks that anything in Greek or Latin can be beaten into English hexameters, and he bashes away manfully and mercilessly at those stubborn words to make them fit that metre and the rhyming couplets in which it is employed. In short, when it comes to translating verse, Lewis is no Dryden or Pope, but rather a second-rate Laurence Eusden. Unfortunately the present translator cannot reach even those exalted heights in verse, and has attempted either to find good modern translations or to render the passages in literal prose.

No particular attempt has been made to somehow imitate Herbert's Latin style in English, although I have taken care not to use words with which Herbert would not have been familiar. Herbert's sentences are long, which the attention-spans of the general reader often are not, so they have been broken up, for the translator cherishes the hope that Herbert's work will be read by students of the period and by others interested in the intellectual history of the seventeenth century. This translation is an attempt to render Herbert's work in readable English while retaining some flavour of the original. To the latter end, for example, I have retained some of the honorifics with which Herbert often prefixes scholars' names, and I have not turned the Latin names of the more familiar ones back into their native forms; thus Grotius is not modernised to "de Groot" or Lipsius into "Lips." On the other hand, Drusius, who is not well-known, is rendered as "van der Driessche" because that is the name under which he was listed after an almost fruitless search for a biographical sketch. I have retained Herbert's occasional asides and the odd piece of scholarly invective, because these at least point to a personality behind the book, and a "plain" translation, such as this purports to be, is all too prone to losing the individual behind his work; I hope that this has not happened. The model for a translator of Herbert is Meyrick H. Carré's *De veritate* (1935), with its plain, straightforward, and accurate English, without being flat and impersonal; even the sesquipedalian effusions of the learned Dr. Master are put by Carré into something like lucidity.

The major addition to this translation is, of course, the notes. In the seventeenth century, few scholars would have needed explanations or biographical details of Herbert's sources, of which he cites a formidable number. Many of them are people whose names and accomplishments mean little even to the most learned modern specialist, and no apologies are made for the use of biographical data drawn from many sources, ancient and modern. The notes also attempt to explain what Herbert might have found useful in these authors, and wherever possible supply information on modern translations. I have also indicated whether the work in question was a part of Herbert's library, donated to Jesus College, Oxford, and listed by Fordyce and Knox in their article. Herbert himself supplied a number of marginal references, which in this translation have been converted into footnotes and contextually explained when necessary. If the exact location was not supplied by Herbert, I have attempted to find it, cite it and translate it. Some of the references were so vague that this was not always possible.

The present translation is offered, then, as an attempt to further accessibility of an important and influential seventeenth-century thinker, whose importance has declined in a Latinless age. If Herbert is not seen as significant beside Descartes, Hobbes, and Grotius, it is perhaps because he has not been read as widely in Latin as they have been in the vernacular. Yet this man, whose writings were considered crucial by the Cambridge Platonists and the eighteenth-century deists, whose books felt the anger of Continental theologians and were banned by the Pope, deserves re-establishment as an important philosopher in his own right, the first English writer to tackle comparative religion and to promote eirenicism at a time when peace was under constant threat. Herbert is the bridge between Bacon and Hobbes, and his rationalist outlook looks forward to Berkeley and Butler as well as to Shaftesbury and Toland. In many ways Herbert was the last of the Elizabethans, but in others he was the first English rationalist. For these reasons he deserves to be heard and read again, and in this present work, "a bold and provocative piece of writing" (E. Hill 42), his voice rings out clearly and distinctly.

Pagan Religion

I

The General Purpose of the Work

After pondering for a long time over many matters, such as whether in some manner eternal, universal salvation of the entire human race might be intended, and that consequently the certainty of a universal Divine Providence might be necessarily inferred, a great number of doubts began to occur to me. I found that several Fathers of the Church not only held the ancient public religion of the pagans up to ridicule, but absolutely condemned it, and that theologians in the centuries following were no more lenient about anything which occurred outside their own agenda,[1] so much so that for a long time the greater part of humanity seemed doomed to a sentence of eternal punishment.

As this dogma seemed to me too harsh, and as it actually contravened the attributes of the Supreme God, I began to investigate the books of the pagans themselves. However, I perceived from their own histories that their gods were often not only mere mortals, but sometimes people of the vilest kind, and when I understood how ridiculous some of their religious worship, rites, and ceremonies were, I was at first inclined to concur with the accepted view. On further consideration, however, it seemed that this was altogether incompatible with the dignity of a Universal Divine Providence, and I began to make careful enquiry as to whether the god of those attributes was indeed the same one who presides over us. To us, for example, God is perfect, almighty, eternal; the pagans, however, sometimes ascribed to God imperfect, fallible and finite attributes, which they did to such an extent that not only the Heavens, planets, stars, etherial and aerial spirits, but even humans, such as were deserving of their country, or rulers (some of whom were very wicked), when they were still alive, were by popular acclaim translated to immortality. Pallor, Trembling and Fear themselves were designated gods, and anything considered a little above human strength by the feelings of the rabble was immediately taken by the pagans for a god.

---

[1] Agenda. It may be necessary to apologise for the use of this somewhat over-used "buzzword." Herbert's phrase translates literally as "erected boundaries," which is awkward and archaic. The word "agenda" suggests that the theologians had their own reasons for their attitude, which is, I believe, what Herbert is saying.

Yet it is evident that where either Highest, or Best and Greatest[2] was an added attribute, that our universal God and Father is indicated by these titles. This homonymity is obvious, and with it we may clear the doubts that may appear by a comparison of our God with theirs. However, as far as the holy things and the rites of the pagans were concerned, it was plain to me that the common people and populace probably hated them. Ceremonies and rites were simply an invention of the priests, and for that reason not the common people, who just listened to what they were told, but the priests themselves must shoulder the blame. The priests, in fact, may be criticised as having themselves introduced superstition and idolatry, and I perceived, without a shadow of a doubt, that they sowed strife and contention everywhere amongst the pagans. I therefore thought that I should not, as some theologians have done, make hasty generalisations about the future state of the laity, because of their total devotion and subjection to the priests' authority. Their great defection from pure worship of a Supreme God could be justly blamed upon their Colleges of Priests, and I was led from there to enquire whether amongst such heaps of superstition some trace of truth might be discovered by which they might be extricated from the labyrinth of error in which they now found themselves. These five principles occurred, which are not so much mine, but are held as indubitably true by all, a universal world meeting-point. They are as follows: [1] there is a Supreme God, [2] he is owed worship, [3] Virtue and Piety are the principal points of the divine cult, [4] we should be repentant of our sins, [5] Divine judgment, reward and punishment will be given in the next life as well as in this life.[3]

I will explain in more detail at the end of my book the place of these principles in the religion of the pagans after I have dealt with the following

---

[2] Herbert always uses the term "[Deus] Optimus Maximus" to denote the Supreme God; this was the term often employed by the Romans to describe Jupiter. Unless the context requires the full title, I will use "God" to indicate the Supreme God whom Herbert believes is behind all the surface polytheism of the ancients. Herbert himself employs the abbreviation "O.M."

[3] Here Herbert refers to the five Religious Common Notions which he presented in *De veritate*. These universally-held innate ideas (*notitiae communes*) are apprehended through Natural Instinct, and because they are innate, they are true in any philosophical system which is based upon reason. As Herbert put it in *De veritate*, "Religion is a common notion, [and] no period is without religion. He explains that the task of the philosopher of religion is "to search for what is by universal consent acknowledged in religion and compare these universal principles with one another." The results of such a comparison would, he holds, be that "what is universally acclaimed as religious truth must be recognised as Common Notions" (121).

parts of their religion and shown where a thread may be found so that we may see how the most enlightened pagans got out of the labyrinth. The reader, by the way, should not think that I am using the word "labyrinth" lightly here; once there were four labyrinths constructed with marvellous skill, that is, the Cretan, the Egyptian, the Lemnian and the Italian[4] from which the superstitions of all religions chiefly spread to the outside world.

I sincerely wish, then, that modern theologians would be more tolerant in what they lay down concerning the souls of the pagans. The most rigid of them, who are unrefined in human learning, explain things rather like this: "After the Fall of Adam all mankind was formed out of a degenerate mass; some, through God's pleasure and the intervention of the death of Christ, were elected to eternal glory, but the larger part, even those who had never heard of Christ,[5] were condemned and doomed to eternal perdition. The most innocent and virtuous lives that pagans could lead would be of no use to them; their works were merely moral, and therefore insignificant." I saw at once that these writers grounded the causes of eternal salvation upon God's pleasure and the death of Christ; their opinion was not based upon reason, but only on dogma, the origin of which nobody seemed to know. I could not believe that these theologians were so intimate with God's secret counsels that they could establish anything with certainty. I therefore ignored them because they were entertaining base and unworthy thoughts about the the most gracious and good God, not to mention about the generality of mankind as well. How could I believe that a just God could take pleasure in the eternal punishment of those to whom he had never

---

[4]The familiar labyrinth, the home of the Minotaur, is the one built by King Minos of Crete, probably at Knossos. We may identify the Egyptian one as the funeral temple of Amonemhat III (see Herodotus 2, 148). The one at Lemnos may have been constructed by the first Pelasgian settlers of that island, and the Italian one may be a reference to a labyrinth supposedly built during the time of Septimius Severus (193–211).

[5]There was considerable controversy over Herbert's mentioning (or rather not mentioning) Christ in both *De veritate* and the present work. Only in this redaction of what he calls "the most rigid" of the Church Fathers does Herbert allude to the salvific quality of Jesus. The lack of importance which Christ evidently had in Herbert's system attracted reactions ranging from the regretful (Richard Baxter) to the vituperative (Lutheran divines who attacked the present work after Herbert's death). As he downplays the nature of sin in general, and denies original sin in particular, it is not suprising that Herbert saw no need for a "saviour" of any kind. Furthermore, as he argues here, the implication is that Christ could hardly "save" people who had lived in a pre-Christian era. For further discussion of Christ's place in Herbert's system, see Butler, *Lord Herbert of Chirbury*, Chapter IX, 398–436.

afforded a method of salvation, and whom he necessarily foresaw as being damned absolutely, with no possibility of escape? I could not understand that people could call that God Greatest and Best who had created men only to condemn them without their knowledge and against their will.

I then encountered other theologians, who claimed that Christ was revealed at the moment of their death to those pagans who had lived honest and pious lives, and that they therefore could enter Paradise. But this appeared to me very improbable, as it was an opinion founded neither on historical evidence, tradition, nor rational conjecture. However, I must admit that these theologians showed much more compassion towards humanity than the others, although they had no solid evidence for their assertions.

Lastly, I consulted those known as the Scholastics, to see whether their feelings about the pagans were any more just and intelligible. They skipped around from faith to reason and then immediately back to faith with amazing agility, and while I found that they were very clever at hair-splitting, I received no satisfaction from them whatsoever. However, together with other axioms which I found established amongst them was this one: "Saving grace will not be denied to anyone who does all he can to obtain it."

I then turned to other writers, especially Crell,[6] a very learned man who has written about the souls of the pagans; he cites several excellent passages from the church fathers about this subject, and I found that they thought that the best of the pagans, through God's infinite mercy, might be eligible for eternal salvation. I soon adopted this opinion, because I was unable to see how the problem of Universal Divine Providence could otherwise be solved in order that some means should be available to everyone to come to God. Understanding, as I did, that Nature or Common Providence supplied us in this world with all that was necessary for food and clothing, I could not conceive that the same God either could or would leave anyone deprived, either by Nature or by Grace, of the way to obtaining a happier state. If the

---

[6]Jan [Johann] Crell (1590–1633) was a Socinian divine from the College of Rakow, Poland. The work which Herbert read was probably *De Deo et eius attributis* (1630). He may also have known a further work (in Latin) by Crell which appeared in English rather too late for him to have used in the present work, *A Learned and Exceeding well-compiled Vindication of the Liberty of Religion* (1646). Socinianism appealed to Herbert because it was rational and ethical; it rejected original sin, the doctrine of the Trinity, and other orthodox positions which it considered had no Biblical basis. The Socinians held that God was absolute, and could therefore forgive anyone He wanted, when He wanted to. "Socinian books," Czeslaw Milosz notes, "were the strangest Polish contribution to European thought," and he goes on to call them "the most daring reinterpretation of Christian faith in its encounter with rationalism" (115).

pagans did not make as good use of these things as they might have done, the Best and Greatest God was hardly to blame for their mistake.

I am aware of the commonly-held opinion that Common Providence is not sufficient without the concurrence of Grace and Particular Providence. I intend, however, to demonstrate that Universal Providence is extended to all mankind. The Holy Scriptures testify, and learned theologians agree, that the pagans worshipped the same God as we do, had the same abhorrence of sin, and believed in rewards and punishments after this life. I cannot but think, then, that after leading good lives, they partook fully of Divine Grace, especially because they knew about the most rational and intelligible parts of true divine worship. On the other hand, I am not going to defend the greater part of pagan religion, which I have always considered foolish, incongruous and absurd, but will present only those truths which shine out from a profound darkness. When the pagans mixed superstition and fiction with truth, or when they polluted their souls with such crimes that could not be expiated with any amount of repentance they justly condemned themselves, but let glory be to the great God for ever. Whether these means for attaining a better state are sufficiently effective for eternal happiness is something that will be treated of in later chapters.

II

The Beginning of
Religious Cults amongst the Pagans,
what they meant by God,
and what they chiefly worshipped

In all ages, once human knowledge exceeds its present limits, humanity tries to find a happier state than the one it presently enjoys and indeed, the poor and miserable condition of humanity, as well as religious worship and sound philosophy calls for it. There has been hardly anyone alive who has found so much delight, satisfaction and enjoyment in this life as to persuade himself that he was designed for it alone, or who, after a judicious searching of his conscience, had no hope of, nor from a strong impulse of mind did not earnestly wish that there might be something better. The mind is so noble in its own nature that it directly desires eternal objects and ultimately may only be satisfied with them.[1] Our fragile and precarious state declines even at the height of our enjoyment of sensual pleasures, and the ancients therefore believed that they should not be satisfied with this state of affairs. Because they were world-weary and satiated, they looked for something beyond themselves, even though they did not know what it might be, which is how the notion of an "Unknown Deity" first arose. By inspiring humanity with the desire for something eternal and happier, God was tacitly revealing himself as life eternal and perfect happiness.

Now, we cannot worship the dignity of God as we should because even the deepest intelligence cannot penetrate it; and so God reveals himself in the most wonderful fabric of the world. As the ancients contemplated and viewed the parts of that world, they were troubled by that first anxious enquiry, namely, whether there could be anything here, or somewhere else, that was eternal, knowing very well that transitory and passing things cannot produce anything except that which is transitory and passing. Finding that

---

[1] In *De veritate*, the highest form of truth is *veritas intellectus*, through which the mind comes to apprehend the truth of the intellect by making judgments about the value of subjective constructions.

everything in the sublunary[2] world had a beginning, and was therefore subject to mutability, they began to observe the heavens and the stars, discovering that only they possessed a certain eternal and therefore happy state. Scrutinising them more closely, the ancients deduced that Motion, Heat, Light and Influence[3] were at least the secondary causes of all things that could be seen here on earth. The most learned of the ancients deduced the rule and reason of those things which stayed the same from the Fixed Stars,[4] of those things that changed from the Planets, and of those things that are subject to variation from both. The convenience of this opinion led them to pay much homage and worship, not so much to God himself but to his visible ministers. Therefore the name "*god*" was given to a star, but not quite in the same way we take it, because the name *god* was not simply then given to stars, but to all things which were beneficial to mankind, and even to some things that were harmful, as scholars know very well.

Amongst the stars, those that were of the first importance and of the greatest splendour and virtue were the Sun and Moon; these, together with the rest of the planets, were deified before the Fixed Stars. Amongst the planets, after the two great lights, the star called Phosphorus or Venus[5] was the most celebrated, which, as the others were later, was worshipped everywhere under various names. The next was Mercury, as, like Venus, it was the servant or companion of the Sun and moved round it, sometimes

---

[2]In Renaissance cosmology, the sublunary world is that part of the cosmos located below the sphere of the Moon. In metaphysical poetry such as that of Donne, or of Herbert himself, it is the world of the senses, or phenomenal world.

[3]Motion and Influence were often denoted the same concept, that is, a movement or exertion in the macrocosm which had influence on the microcosm; as Herbert wrote, "The little World the Great shall blaze" ("A Description," Smith 3).

[4]The sphere of the Fixed Stars is the first circle above that of the Planets. Christopher Goodman, in *The Fall of Man* (1616), notes that "the stars in general intend the earth's fruitfulness; each one in particular hath his several office and duty" (Tillyard 54). The ancients believed that the stars rather capriciously acted either for good or evil, and that humans could do little about it.

[5]Herbert correctly claims that Venus was the most "celebrated" star. Initially, the Greeks only had one planet, Hesperus (Venus), and they made no distinction between the Fixed Stars, which made up constellations, and the Errant or Wandering Stars. According to the astronomer Eratosthenes (284–204 B.C.), there were five of the latter, each corresponding to a deity. Planets were not named *for* gods; rather, the divine name denoted the possession of the planet by the god (Seznec 39). As time passed, the owners of the planets changed, which caused a great deal of confusion; Hera, for example, "took over" Venus, and Hercules got Mars from Ares. Phosphorus was a general term for Venus as the morning-star.

above it and sometimes below it. The ancients could not have observed as much about Mars, Jupiter or Saturn, although the erratic planets, with the exception of those discovered by Galileo's telescope, were very well-known a long time ago, as they were distinguished by their colours. Venus was always white, Mercury blue, Jupiter red and yellow, Mars the colour of blood (almost purple or black), Saturn lead-coloured and pale. It was also seen that the planets did not sparkle like the Fixed Stars do, although Mars sometimes flashes his rays in a threatening manner.

In the ages following, some distinguished philosophers attributed imagination or Internal Sense to the planets, and others thought they had feeling, sight and hearing, senses with which Hippocrates[6] credits fire. Still others believed that they were alive, intelligent, and rational, not wishing that such noble bodies should lack noble spirits.[7] It is not, then, very remarkable that mankind was prone to paying them adoration and worship, even though it was an inferior kind of worship, because Nature has implanted in man a duty to venerate anything from which he has received benefits. What is more, everyone prefers those things which move by themselves to those that are motionless, that which is shining and splendid to the obscure and dark, the good to the bad, and the eternal to the transitory. Because of this, the pagans believed that the Stars, especially the Sun and Moon, deserved greater worship and reverence than any person at all, notwithstanding that person's being at the apex of honour and glory. According to José de Acosta[8] and others, the Indians are of the same opinion to this day; they worship everything whose influence they see as being most prevalent in day-to-day life.

As religion advanced in complexity, the pagans began to ask whether there might be any God or Deity which presided over the Stars themselves, and when they observed not only different, but contradictory effects in the Stars,

---

[6]Hippocrates of Cos (c. 460–375 B.C.) was the great physician of the ancient world. Unfortunately the so-called *Corpus Hippocraticum*, a collection of writings ascribed to him, is of a later date. G.E.R. Lloyd has edited *The Hippocratic Writings* (Harmondsworth: Penguin Books, 1978).

[7]Spirits. Herbert's Latin suggests "forms," but it was pointed out to me, correctly I believe, that the word "form" could mislead modern readers. In Aristotle (and in Aquinas) what we term "soul" or "spirit" is the "form" of the material body, and the usage of the word "form" in these philosophers is not the same as Plato's employment of the term.

[8] José de Acosta (1539–c. 1600), a Jesuit, was Professor of Philosophy at the University of Ocaña. In 1571 he went to South America as Principal of Peru, and upon his return to Spain became Superior of Valladolid. Herbert refers to his *Historia naturas y moras de las Indias* (1591), which was translated by Edward Grimston as *Of the ancient superstitions of the Mexicans and Indians of America* (1604).

they were soon convinced, and acknowledged one Supreme Power who governed all things and to whom they believed the profoundest adoration was due. However, the pagans still retained a certain veneration for the stars, because it was by their eternal nature that men were first led to the knowledge of a Supreme Power.

The worship of a Supreme Power is engraved upon the heart, and is therefore more ancient in itself, but also because our ancestors received their first indications of its existence from those splendid eternal bodies, the Sun and Moon, and the most universal, if not the most ancient worship was paid to the stars, as many scholars can testify. At last, by degrees, our ancestors came to adore the Supreme Power; the strength, wisdom and goodness of God was shining through his works, and he was thus made intelligible; in fact they could not know him any other way. In earlier times people hoped that divine worship and love would effect a better life; this drew them to the Stars, the most illustrious of the Supreme Power's works, and thus they worshipped God himself through his handiwork. At that time there was no other religion.

Here another question arises, as to whether any worship of God other than a blameless mind and holy life could be instituted. The pagans initially had nothing to direct them but the Common Notions imprinted on their minds. After a time, a group sprang up who persuaded them to invent rites and ceremonies; this is proved by religion's formerly being called *deisidaimonia*[9] or the same word YWH, which the Jews use to signify both God and Demons, as Vossius observes. This group asked if anything of grandeur deserved external worship, and if even earthly majesty is chiefly supported by rites and ceremonies, should not the greatest adoration be given to that God from whom all things originate? And should not His chief ministers also be reverenced, because the Supreme Power cannot be worshipped the way he should be if those who come before him in order, if not in dignity, are neglected? Sacred rites should be performed to the Stars and will thus, through them, centre on God himself: this is the only way there is to approach the Supreme Power. These, and other specious reasons, prevailed with the rabble, who remained ignorant of the adoration, rites, and ceremonies that should be given to the Supreme Power.

---

[9]*Deisidaimonia* usually means, in Classical Greek, "fear of the gods" or "religious feeling." The verb form *deisidaimoneo* means "to have superstitious fear." In New Testament Greek, the same meanings apply, but there is a third one, indicating "religion in general." The word *daimon*, of course, does mean "demon," and refers to both good and evil versions of the same.

In due time, as the Rabbis[10] tell us, false prophets arose and told the people that they had been commanded by God to worship this or that star, and finally all the stars; that they must make sacrifices and oblations to them, build temples, and set up idols to be worshipped by women, children and the rest of the ignorant. To this end, they showed them things of their own invention, which they said were the image of the Star as revealed to them by prophecy. Then people began to raise up images not just in temples, but under trees and on top of mountains or hills. Afterwards, they got together and worshipped these things publicly, saying that good and evil came from them and that they should therefore be worshipped and adored. Their priests promised that their worship would bring prosperity and great increase of everything, and thus were able to tell them what to do and what not to do.

The same Rabbis, and others too, show that there arose impostors who pretended that Stars, Spheres or Angels themselves spoke to them, delivered instructions about how they should be worshipped and told them what rites to perform and what to avoid. So it was all over the world that images came to be worshipped, chiefly by sacrifice and adoration, as the Rabbi says. The impostors publicly declared, moreover, how they came to have the information from the god (for so they called the Star); they said that they had been all night in the temple and the commands had been delivered or revealed in a dream. At that time, there was no better evidence for the truth of the oracles.

This custom originated with the Egyptians; they were the first to have knowledge of the gods or stars, and they built temples and ordered solemn assemblies to meet in groves. The custom passed to the Syrians and their neighbours, and then to the Greeks and Romans; almost all superstition and religion came from the East, and it was not extirpated until the reign of Constantine the Great, who, understanding what went on in the temples under the pretext of religion, abolished the old customs. By this means, then, many harmful superstitions and abuses were imposed upon the ignorant and credulous common people, who believed it impious to question them, even though they were supported by no better authority than that of a dream.

The priests could not have done this so easily if they had not introduced prophecies of things to come, delivered invariably in ambiguous and doubtful

---

[10]Herbert refers to a number of Jewish scholars in his book. The chief ones seem to be Simeon ha-Darshan and Abraham ben Ezra, but there are marginal notes mentioning others (see Chapter IV). Herbert's authorities here would have been Vossius and Selden, and Maimonides's famous work on idolatry is translated by Vossius as the first part of *De theologia gentili*.

terms, which if they happened to be only marginally true, gained vast credit and authority. If, on the contrary, they were wrong, the priests still got what they wanted, for if anything bad or unfortunate happened, they simply said that it was caused by the sins of the people, which had made God deviate from his usual kindness. The priests made them offer up sacrifices (a great part of which fell to their own share), persuading them that it was the only way to appease the angry god. But if something good happened instead of the evil which they had foretold, the priests said that their prayers or other devotional acts had enabled them to ward off the impending evil. They never, therefore, ran any risks about the outcome of their prophecies, for however things fell out, the priests were always right, and never lost their reputation or esteem with the common people.

The priests also made observations on the course of the stars, their rising, setting and various conjunctions; this was especially the case in Egypt, where, the weather being temperate, the priests could lie in the open air all night. They made many promises through the prediction of the fertility of the seasons and other similar things, which caught on with the common people, but as this could not be carried out without charge, the priests were able to cause stipends to be settled on themselves. By this means the lowest persons soon grew very rich, and at last gained such repute and esteem that the most important people of their country were elected to their College. Nothing could have been more conducive to keeping the people in absolute subjection than making them believe that only the priests knew the mind and will of God and could deliver oracles. At last the very Caesars themselves were elevated to the priesthood, and even Cicero served as an augur.

Later, divine honour was paid to the seven planets, especially to the Sun, Moon and Phosphorus (also called Lucifer, Hesperus, Vesper, Venus etc.) and then to Mercury, who is called Marcolis, Margamah, Hermes and Splegon, and then to the rest. Next come the stars, particularly the Great Dog, who is known as Sirius. Next Pisces, who were called Syrian deities, and who were equivalent to Cupid and Venus, were worshipped, first by Eastern peoples and then by others.[11] Observing that storms arose from

---

[11] [Herbert's marginal note]: German. in Arat. The quotation is from Germanicus Caesar's redaction of Aratus:

> Hanc Pisces abdunt orti tortumque Biformem
> cum geminis Pisces Aquilonis provocat aura,
> ille etiam surgit, qui tristos respicit austros;
> Piscibus ille simul surgit, sed liberat ora,
> cum pernix Aries in caelum cornuo tollit.
> Pisces educunt Cepheida; laetior illa
> Nereidas pontumque fugit caeloque refertur. (l. 695–701)

Orion, winds from the Goat and Kids, rain from the Hyades and Pleiades, heat from the Caniculi and the fore-parts of the Lion,[12] the ancients also particularly honoured them with divine worship.

They then went on to ask whether Heaven itself ought not to be worshipped, as well as the Stars, as it alone seemed so immense and so infinite. The most famous philosophers, as well as the priests, agreed that it should, and not only Aristotle, but his master also was of this opinion, for he gives the following reason:

> Everything which has a function exists for that function, but the activity of a god is immortality, that is, perpetual life. Therefore perpetual motion is necessary in a god. Therefore, since heaven is of this nature (i.e. is a divine body) it has a spherical body which naturally rotates.[13]

So the priests and philosophers not only made the stars into gods, and acknowledged that there was a Supreme Power that governed them, but also deified Heaven itself. The seven planets had seven governing intelligences, grouped in order whereby it was believed that the intelligence of the lunar orb was less than that of the solar, and those of the seven planets less than that of the *Primum Mobile*.[14] These intelligences, or movers of the planets, were constituted with deference to the Supreme Mover. Then it was asked, whether this heaven we see is a body or not, and if it had right, left, top, bottom, thick parts or thin parts? Was it moved by an appetite, for the ancients believed that motion could not exist in any living thing without appetite. Many such things were discussed by learned men, but they had no effect on the more stupid common people, who needed only to know that the heaven, which contained the stars, should be worshipped as a god.

This plurality of gods led to variety of worship. The natural consequence of diversity, which the crafty priests manipulated to their own advantage, was the invention of rites and forms of religion; the priests declared what worship must be paid and what sacrifices had to be made to please, appease or propitiate each god. Many extravagant cults arose, and spread all over the world, the priests everywhere imposing their imaginary dreams on the people. What seems worse is that while people ought to expect true piety to

---

[12]The former are the "lesser dogs," as distinguished from Sirius, "the great dog." Seznec notes (38) that the Lion (Leo) represents the Nemean Lion which was killed by Hercules. The mythological significance was given to the constellation by Eratosthenes.

[13]Aristotle, *On the Heavens* II, iii, 1. 8–13.

[14]In the Ptolemaic cosmogony, the Primum Mobile's sphere was next to the Empyrean. Its movement sets the movement of the other spheres in motion.

lead to peace of mind, or that sincere repentance will make up for deviation from it, the priests reduced everything to the rites and ceremonies which they themselves performed. It was as if their gods would listen to no-one but them, and that they were the only mediators between gods and men.

Once the worship of the heavenly bodies was established in the world, people then asked whether the Earth itself ought to be worshipped, and the following reasons were given. When people saw that, after the Sun and Stars, the Earth assisted the most in providing life, nutrition and animal life, our ancestors venerated it greatly, and the most eminent philosophers gave it first place amongst the elements, calling it the oldest god. According to them, Nature first created the Earth, and then everything else for its use. The priests also referred to the Earth as *Antiqua Mater*[15] (the Old Mother), whom, they claimed, had married *Caelum* (Heaven); thus they made Heaven male and Earth female, which is why the Greeks and Romans called them the Nuptial Gods (*Dii gamelioi*). There were many reasons for the worship of the Earth; if we respect our parents, said the priests, then we ought to reverence the Earth so much more, because not simply our parents, but everything else as well originated there, and it is into the Earth's bosom that we are received after we leave this life. Also, while the Heavens are far superior to all other entities, they are so remote from us that they are only the objects of sight; the Earth, on the other hand, allows us to live on her. Within her sphere all our rights and all our authority is defined, indeed exists only by her courtesy, and this, too, is a reason for our veneration of her. Credulous and ignorant people were soon persuaded by this to worship the Earth; according to Varro,[16] Caelum and Terra were made the principal

---

[15] Herbert uses the Latin name for Gaia (Ge), the daughter of Chaos and mother of Uranus (Caelum). She mated with her son to produce a great number of offspring, notably the Titans, Kronos (Saturn), and Rhea, who, at Gaia's instigation, dethroned Uranus. Kronos was deposed in turn by his son, Zeus. She had produced Uranus alone, "without Love the desirable" (ML 32). She was usually identified with Cybele. The fullest account may be read in Hesiod, *Theogony* 117ff; 820ff.

[16] Marcus Terentius Varro (116–27 B.C.), Roman soldier and politician, was also a great philologist. He wrote the *Antiquitatum rerum hominum et divinarum*, which contains a great deal of information about religious customs as well as detailed descriptions of the gods and their temples. Varro was also the author of the celebrated treatise *De lingua Latina*, which, unfortunately, is not extant in its complete state, Book IV being mostly missing. Augustine commended Varro for his monotheism and his disgust at idol-worship.

[Herbert's marginal note]: Varro l. 4 de L.L. The source here is either Lactantius (see below) or possibly Augustine, who supplies several fragmentary quotes from this part of Varro's book.

gods, being called Serapis and Isis in Egypt, Daantes and Astarte by the Phoenicians, and Saturn and Ops in some other regions.

The next question was whether Fire, as well as Earth, deserved to be worshipped. Now, because earthly things act by heat, Fire resembles spirit rather than matter, and, like the Stars, it emits its rays beyond the extent of its heat. Also, again like the Stars, it is not subject to decay, and never ceases to exist as long as fuel is provided for it. For these reasons, it was accounted a place amongst the number of the gods. Its worship was very ancient, as I shall show later, but I refer you to the theologians to show how it related to the glory of the Supreme God — it was called by the Jews "a consuming Fire." The priests, not yet overwhelmed by these many forms of worship, next proceeded to adore Water. Heat, they claimed, cannot undertake the act of creation, but by itself would destroy everything, and the coolness of water kept the violent heat of the fire at bay. Its moisture softens the dryness and hardness of the earth, and it reduces things to an equable temperature. It is also found above the earth, and supplies mankind with its necessary and convenient nourishment; people can live longer without food than without drink. All things come from water, as this example proposed by a very ingenious philosopher long ago shows. Suppose, he says, that there is a great container capable of holding several acres of earth. When it is accurately weighed, sow corn or herbs there, which will be watered only by the rain. Weigh the first crop, and for several years afterwards weigh all the produce. Then plant oak, beech, fir, elm or some other trees there, and let them grow to their fullest extent. Cut them all down and weigh everything together, and the weight will equal that of the earth put in the container at the beginning, yet the weight of the container will remain the same. This experiment proves that all new matter came from Water which fell upon the Earth. It was for this reason that divine worship was paid to Water. The Persians believed that water was so sacred that it was impious to wash their hands in it, to spit or blow their noses into running streams, or to throw anything dirty into them at all.

Air was the only element left to which worship was not yet paid. But its vast extension seemed to advance its claim, as its three regions, reaching from the Earth to the Moon, must be nearly a hundred thousand times larger than our globe of earth and water. Also, without air man would be blind, deaf, and dumb; there is no other element that the lungs breathe, and though a person in good health may live four days without food or drink (and I am not speaking of people with asthma, of whom we have some strange stories), yet he cannot live one moment without air. Some philosophers have tried to prove that air is divine, notably Anaximenes,[17] Diogenes Apollionates,[18] and also Ennius[19] amongst poets. Varro says that Jupiter was called Air by the Greeks, and is the wind and clouds, as well as the rain; from rain comes cold and the wind becomes air again.[20] This is confirmed by the common Latin expressions *sub dio vel sub Divo*, and *sub Iove*, in the open air; Jupiter was sometimes taken figuratively by the ancients for the Air, of which more later. Thus anima, the soul, is derived from *aiein*, to blow or breathe. Lactantius quotes Varro as saying that "the soul is air received by the mouth, made tepid in the lungs, heated in the heart, and thus diffused in the body."[21] The ancients did not confine their worship to the noblest and most excellent parts of the world, but thought also that they should praise

---

[17]Anaximenes of Miletus (fl. 546 B.C.) held that all things arise from air. When rarefied, air turns into fire, and when it condenses, wind, clouds, water, earth and stones are produced. He believed that the cosmos was governed by natural or physical, rather than moral laws. For translation of his fragments, see Freeman 19-20, Robinson 41–50 (with a discussion).

[18]Diogenes Apollionates (fl. 440/30 B.C.) held that air is the principle of the soul and of intelligence. He also postulated that the earth was flat and round, surrounded by heavenly bodies made of fire-filled pumice (see Freeeman 87–90).

[19]Quintus Ennius (240–169 B.C.), an early Roman lyric poet, also wrote many tragedies, comedies, fables and satires. He also introduced the Romans to epic poetry with the *Annalium libri xviii*, a poetical history of Rome of which 550 lines only survive (Grant, *Myths* 34). The work to which Herbert alludes here is the *Sacra historia*, a poetic rationalisation of Greek mythology. It was epitomised by Lactantius in prose, which is the likely source for Herbert, as Ennius's works survive only in fragments.

[20]Curiously enough, Augustine usually sees Juno, not Jupiter, as being the air. Jupiter, "the soul of this material universe," he says (paraphrasing Vergil), "from above" embraces Juno, "the air spread out below him" (*City of God* IV, 11 [148]).

[21]Caecilius Firmianus Lactantius (250–317) was appointed a professor of rhetoric by Diocletian, and later served as tutor to Prince Crispus, the ill-fated son of Constantine I. Amongst his many works we find *De opificio dei*, a discussion of the body/soul dichotomy, and the *Divinae institutiones*, a comprehensive survey of religious beliefs. The latter work included the argument that all the gods of the ancient world were ordinary people whom idolatry had raised to immortality.

The origins of this theory may be found in the writings of Euhemerus (c. 300 B.C.), whose fragments, together with those of Ennius, were collected by Lactantius. Ennius's work on the old gods was, in fact, a Latin translation or paraphrase of Euhemerus. Christian scholars were very interested in Euhemerus, for his works provided them with ammunition for their attacks on pagan religion (Seznec 12–13). Some of these Christian writers, such as Clement of Alexandria, Arnobius, Minucius Felix, Julius Firmicus Maternus and St. Augustine, are all quoted by Herbert in the

the Universe itself as the most beautiful image of God. Of this I shall have more to say later.

Their adoration grew so extensive that they eventually began to worship Man himself. Consisting of the four elements, to which divine worship was already paid, and deriving the noblest part of his origin from heaven, Man also excelled the elements themselves, because he contained many things within him that the qualities of the elements, however they were mixed, could not produce. Not only did man excel all other animals, but one man could be more excellent than another, and so the ancients worshipped those whose great achievments or whose noble and brave acts advanced them above others. Thus they came to worship Virtue herself as being worthy of the highest veneration.

All that remains now is to note how some worship was paid to certain animals, but as this was limited to a few nations only, particularly those of the Egyptians, I shall leave them out. A general superstition may be termed a sort of religion, but that which is limited geographically may not. I have called nothing *religion* except that which has been generally accepted in most parts of the world. I have also presented the oldest and most universal sorts of worship, which I have collected from the most eminent authorities extant. With the exception of Judaism — because, according to sacred scripture, the Jews were the most ancient people, and thought to worship a particular god unknown to other nations — there was no other universal religion. Neither is there any to be found at present in the West Indies, except where Christianity has taken root, or in the East Indies, where Islam has spread itself. I do not deny that some particular rites were intermingled with this general worship, but the Indians, to this very day, except for the adoration of Man, agree about them, as we find in the testament of many reputable scholars. It is therefore clear that the ancients worshipped first the Supreme God and Moderator of all things, then the Sun and Moon, Phosphorus and Mercury, and afterwards the rest of the planets and fixed Stars, especially Canis and Pisces, Arion, Arcturus and Corona, the Goat and Kids, Hyades and Pleiades, Caniculi and the fore-part of the Lion, and finally the four elements. In short, all the important parts of the world, and finally the Universe itself, as God's

---

present work. Franz Cumont commented that many of these attacks were aimed at "an idolatry long since extinct, and at gods whose existence had been reduced to a mere literary convention" (Seznec 13), and errors perpetrated by "Euhemerists" were being quoted until well into the Middle Ages.

The quotation comes from *De opificio Dei*: "Varro thus defines it: 'The soul is air conceived in the mouth, warmed in the lungs, heated in the heart, diffused into the body.'" (Lactantius 50). As noted previously, Book IV of Varro's treatise is missing, and Lactantius is another source for fragments from it.

most perfect image, were worshipped, each in a different way, as can be seen from their rites and ceremonies. As we have noted, that which had an extraordinary influence on inferior beings, and especially upon humans, was taken for a god. Everything was the object of ethnic adoration in its several degrees, but in respect to those things which had most to do with virtue or piety, the ancients had recourse not only to religion, but to philosophy: the laws and internal principles were engraved upon their hearts.

These, then, were the deities and gods whom the ancients worshipped, and they also thought that adoration was due to those who had deserved well of their country or of mankind in general. It now remains to prove and corroborate those things, or at least the most important of them, through the testimonies of ancient authors, so that it will be clear exactly what the religion of the pagans was.

III

Why there were
so many Names given to God,
and what they were

The names by which the ancients called their gods were numerous; everyone styled them according to country, language and inclination, and different epithets were also added to the number of names. Seneca says that God may have as many names as the benefits he dispenses, so that if, as Oenomaeus[1] and Hesiod[2] demonstrate, there were thirty thousand names for God, then his benefits must supposedly equal them.[3] Indeed, because the blessings of the Greatest and Best God are numberless, it does not seem strange that he was worshipped under innumerable names. The attributes of the Highest God are infinite, and his virtues are beyond our comprehension and expression; however, it is my opinion that he cannot be represented to us in any better terms than those used by the Indians, namely Greatest and Best. He cannot be termed "Best" without the infinite power and will to do good, nor "Greatest" unless he distributes his goodness universally. And at this point we must embark on a very difficult task, groping in the dark mists of time with the spirits of our ancestors.

I shall begin with Judaism, although Joseph Scaliger[4] raises an objection here, seeming to agree with the opinion of the dynasties mentioned by

---

[1]Oenomaeus of Gadara (fl. 120 A.D.) was a Cynic philosopher, a few of whose fragments are extant. He wrote a book attacking the truth of oracles, and appears to have suggested that human free will is stronger than divine destiny.

[2]Hesiod (8th century B.C.) wrote the *Theogony*, a work on the origins of the gods, and the *Works and Days*, a poem about farming, cosmology, and ethics which was translated into English (as *The Georgics*) by the poet and dramatist George Chapman (1618). A fine modern verse-translation of both works has been made by Richmond Lattimore (Ann Arbor: University of Michigan Press, 1978).

[3][Herbert's marginal note]: Sen[eca]. l. 5 *De Ben[eficiis]*. c. 17.

[4]Joseph [Justus] Scaliger (1540–1609), son of the great Renaissance polymath Julius Caesar Scaliger, edited Manilius's work on geography, and was himself the author of *De emendatione temporum*, in which he claimed that the historical works of the ancient Persians, Jews, and other civilisations could teach us as much as those of the Greeks and Romans.

Manetho,[5] namely that there were ages long before Adam. And although Diodorus Siculus[6] and the Chinese chronology[7] mention things done many thousands of years before the Creation of the World according to Moses, our first authority is derived from ancient Jewish books, and I shall describe the origin of names given to God by them. It does not much matter for our purposes that according to ancient writers the Jews took many of their religious rites from the Egyptians, for the ancient Egyptian language died out with their religion, leaving only a few fragmentary traces in some authors and some hieroglyphics, which are preserved in Rome and some other places. At the same time, however, it must be mentioned that after Deucalion's flood[8] and other disasters, the Egyptian monuments, because of the constant purity of the air, remained intact for a long time. Nothing is now left that is important.

We will begin by noting the opinion of Sanchuniathon[9] that EL[10] signified

---

[5]Manetho (fl. 280 B.C.) was an Egyptian, appointed High Priest of Heliopolis by Ptolemy I. He composed a history of Egypt which he claimed was based on ancient documents to which he had access. His book traced the history of Egypt from the earliest times down to 323 B.C. (the death of Alexander the Great). Manetho established the dates of the Egyptian dynasties from the old king-lists.

[6]Diodorus Siculus of Agyrium (d. c. 21 B.C.) wrote, in 30 years, a history of the world. Modern scholars, however, have repayed his diligence by considering his chronology confused and misleading. Johann Herold made a translation of his works (Basel, 1554).

[Herbert's marginal note]: Diod[orus] Sic[ulus], l. I. The reference is to Diodorus on the date of the creation of the world.

[7]Herbert is probably referring here to a compilation made by the Chinese historian Ssu-ma Ch'ien (1st century B.C.). I am indebted to Mr. Jiang Jong Zhu, M.A., for this information. Lord Herbert owned an anonymously-edited *Regni Chinensis descriptio ex variis authoribus* (Leyden, 1639) from which he may have obtained this information.

[8]Deucalion was the son of Prometheus, who advised him, together with his wife Pyrrha, to build an ark, because Zeus was going to flood the world. After the flood went down, the similarities with the Noah myth become rather tenuous. Hermes advised Deucalion to throw his mother's bones over his shoulder, and as he did so, a new race sprang up (see Ovid, *Metamorphoses* I, 318ff).

[9]Sanchuniathon (?14th/13th century B.C.) is thought to have been a Phoenician historian who wrote a treatise on the myths of his country. His authority and indeed existence have been questioned by scholars for centuries, but ancient Ugaritic texts bear out Philo of Byblos's claim for Sanchuniathon's historicity (see *OCD* 949; du Mesnil du Buisson 35–36).

[10]El was also the Supreme God of the Canaanites (Teixidor 46), and his name

God amongst the Hebrews, being admittedly a Phoenician word (although the Phoenicians and Jews were great enemies, their languages were but dialects of one another). We may also add the authority of Porphyry[11] as quoted by Eusebius[12] and that of Vossius.[13] Saturn, then, called Israel[14] by the Phoenicians and after whom, posthumously, an altar was named, had, while he reigned, a single child by a nymph called Anobret. The child's name was Jeoud, which meant "an only-child" in Phoenician, and when his country became embroiled in a most dangerous and bloody war, the King, dressed in royal robes, sacrificed his son on a specially-built altar.

Three things may be understood here. First, Israel, that ancient Phoenician king, was identical to Saturn. Secondly, he had a son, whom the Phoenicians called Jeoud. Thirdly, Jeoud was sacrificed by his father. Now, how can it be shown that this originated from a confusion between Israel the grandson and Abraham the grandfather, who was commanded to sacrifice his son? In Genesis 22:1 it states "Take thine only Son," but in Hebrew the word is *Jebid*, which comes very close to the Phoenician Jeoud. Also, in the Orphaics or Onomacritus[15] Abraham is called *monogenes*, only-begotten;

---

is associated with Poseidon, who in some Phoenician settlements was known as the Creator of the Earth (Teixidor 42).

[11]Porphyry (c. 232–305) is known chiefly as a disciple of Plotinus and the editor of the latter's works. He also wrote a treatise on theurgic practices which survives in fragments, and his works were edited by Marsilio Ficino.

[12]Eusebius, Bishop of Caesarea (c. 260–340) was the author of *The History of the Church*, which traced the history of Christianity down to the time of Constantine I. He also wrote a brief chronicle of universal history, in which he claimed that the Bible was superior to all pagan philosophy and theology. His main objective was to prove that Judaeo-Christian religion actually preceded pagan mythology in time, and like many of his contemporaries, Eusebius exhibited Euhemerist tendencies, even making the claim at onepoint that the Babylonian god Baal was the first king of Assyria, "and that he lived at the time of the war between the Giants and Titans" (Seznec 14).

[13]Vossius I, iv, 322–23. References to Vossius are to his *De theologia gentili* (1641), reissued in 3 volumes by Garland Press (1976).

[14]The name, in Hebrew, means "God strives."

[15]Onomacritus of Athens (fl. 520–485 B.C.) was a poet who may also have been a priest of Dionysus; the latter reason is cited for his possible authorship of those poems which are ascribed to mythical or semi-mythical figures such as Orpheus, Musaeus, and Linus, and Aristotle says that Onomacritus was a compiler of Orphic hymns. Herbert has certainly been doing his homework, as he refers to "Orpheus or Onomacritus." He may have got the information from Damascius's *De principiis* (see Grant 106), a work which he often quotes. An "Orphic" poem, the *Rhapsodic*

here, Abraham and Isaac are confused, as Abraham and Jacob had been previously.

It is easy to see that objections might be raised here, particularly that it is hardly believable that the Phoenicians would take Israel for their Supreme God, who, as Moloch or Saturn, was founder of a neighbouring nation for which, as sacred histories show, they had a mortal hatred.[16] It seems that the citation from Eusebius must have been faulty, and that for *Israel* we ought to read *Il*, for people who use abbreviations often write *Il* with a small line drawn over it for *Israel*. But this cannot be correct, because IL in Phoenician is the same as EL in Hebrew, one of the ten names of God.[17] Sanchonianthon, quoted in the same book by Eusebius,[18] tells us that they called the god Saturn, not Israel:

> When Uranus took over his father's kingdom, he married Gaia and had the following children by her: Saturn, Betylus and Dagon,[19] who are also called Sito and Atlanta.

Theogony, was a source for Neo-Platonists, and is quoted by Vossius as being by Orpheus (I, xviii, 143)

[16]Herbert is correct. The chief god of the Phoenicians was Baal-Shamin, for whom see Teixidor 27ff.

[17]Names of God. Herbert's etymologies are largely correct (they are based on Vossius and Selden), but perhaps modern scholarship can clarify the point for those who are interested. The basic name EL means "God," but it can be applied to any god, true or false (see Genesis 35:2, for an example). J.C. Connell (*IBD* I, 570) notes that Deuteronomy 5:10 well illustrates the confusion that the names of God might cause: "I the Lord (Yahweh) your God (elohim) am a jealous god (el)." The Canaanites, as we have already seen, add to the confusion by calling their chief God "El." The three names in Deteronomy are explained thus by Connell:

Yahweh (anglicised to Jehovah) is the most familiar. It is the vocalised Tetragrammaton (YHWH) which was so sacred that it could not be spoken. The Jews avoided it by using *Adonai*, "my Lord," instead. Scholem notes that YHWH is the source from which the entire Torah derives (43).

Elohim is either singular or plural. The former means "the One Supreme Deity," and denotes all that appertains to being that Deity.

Interchanging these names also takes place in the Old Testament. For example, in Genesis 27:30 we find Abraham worshipping the Supreme God (El) under the name Yahweh.

[18][Herbert's marginal note]: Eus[ebius] *Ora[tio] in Consta[ntino] laudem.*

[19]The principal God of the Phoenicians. The origins of the name, according to K.A. Kitchen, are "lost in antiquity" (*IBD* I, 353). The notion that Dagon was a fish-deity came from a confusion of his name with Hebrew *dag*, "a fish." He is linked with, although probably not identical to, Atergatis. See also Vossius I, xviii, 143.

Sanchoniathon makes this clearer later: "The companions of This, who is the same as Cronos,[20] are called *Elohim*, that is, Saturnians." *Eloein* there is nothing else but the Hebrew *Elohim*. Any schoolboy can tell how Angels, Judges, false gods and even the Supreme God came to be called in the beginning of the books of Moses, and everywhere else in scripture. I remember a conversation I had with the incomparable Hugo Grotius, now ambassador from the most illustrious King of Sweden to his Most Christian Majesty [of France], in which he hinted this much, and Vossius agrees.[21] It is most likely that the pagans, particularly the Phoenicians, formerly sacrificed only sons, as ancient authors tell us. Sanchoniathon writes that "the Phoenicians sacrificed their most precious only sons to Saturn," and this is confirmed by Porphyry, and by Vossius. Damascius[22] also states, "Saturn was called *El*, *Bel*,[23] and *Bolathen* by the Phoenicians and Syrians."[24] Servius[25] tells us that HL was the Sun; in those parts, he says,

---

[20]Cronos was worshipped in Hellenistic times, appearing on the coins of Antiochus IV Epiphanes (175–164 B.C.). Philo says that he is the same as El (Teixidor 46), the head of the Ugaritic pantheon. See Genesis 14, and a 9th century B.C. inscription at Karatape which calls El "the Creator of the Earth."

[21]Hugo de Groot [Grotius] (1583–1645), the eminent Dutch jurist, statesman and theologian, was a personal friend of Herbert's, whom he probably met when Grotius was ambassador to the Court of St. James in 1613. In 1619 Grotius was imprisoned in The Hague, but he escaped in a book-crate to Paris, where Queen Christina of Sweden made him her ambassador. As Herbert was then English ambassador to the French court, the two men renewed their friendship, and Herbert sought Grotius's advice about publishing *De veritate* (1624). While Grotius is best-known for his *De jure belli ac pacis* (1625), he wrote a number of theological works, including *De veritate religionis Christiani*. Herbert owned a number of works by Grotius (*FK* 98–99). The conversation Herbert claims he had with Grotius is also recorded by Vossius (I, xviii, 143), which is rather strange, but it is possible that all three of them were present.

[22]Damascius the Syrian (4th century A.D.), rhetorician and philosopher, was the last head of the Athenian School, closed down by Justinian I in 529. Damascius moved to Persia, then returned to Greece and wrote *Doubts and Solutions of the First Principles*, a Neo-Platonic work showing a marked debt to Proclus.

[23]Bel was the principal god of Babylon. His name was a title of Marduk; the word is Sumerian, but there are obvious links with the Hebrew *ba'al*, "lord."

[24][Herbert's marginal notes]: Damas[cius] in Isidor, *Apud Photium*. Servius, *De belo Phoenice*.

[25]Marius [Maurus] Severus Honoratus (4th century A.D.), the Roman grammarian, was the scourge of generations of luckless schoolboys, including Herbert. His *Commentarii in Bucolica, Georgica et Aeneidem Virgilii* was first printed in Venice

they all worship the Sun, which in their language is called *Hel*, from which derives Helios, but more of this later, when we come to discuss Sun-worship. This is enough about the name EL, whose plural is *Elim*, which also means Angels (Exodus 15:13) and *Elohim*, whose singular is *Eloah*. I shall add only that *Elohim*, the name by which God, who created Heaven and Earth, is known, has many ramifications, and you may see their interpretations set out by Gordon.[26]

Turning now to the other name, *Jehovah* or *Jah*, I shall cite further evidence from Vossius. *Iacchus* comes from *Jah*, one of the names of God, from which we get *Hallelu-jah*, that is, "praise the Lord." While they were dancing, the pagans used to shout the name *Jah* or *Jach* very loudly. It seems also that they employed the Tetragrammaton, a word of four letters, which they might have pronounced *Jave* or *Jehave* like the Samaritans, from which I may deduce that *Iache* in Epiphanius[27] means the same. But whether it ought to be pronounced *Jeheve*, as le Mercier[28] and van der Driessche[29]

(1471), and contains much valuable information on rhetoric and style. A modern edition, *Servianorum in Vergilii carmina commentariorum*, was prepared by E.K. Rand and others (Lancaster, Pennsylvania: Harvard University Press, 1946), but there is no modern translation.

[26] James Gordon of Lesmore [Gordonius Scotus] (1553–1641), Scottish Jesuit scholar, was made confessor to Louis XIII, which makes it possible that Herbert knew him in 1619–24. Gordon wrote *Opus chronologicum* (1613–14) and *Opuscula chronologicum, historicum, geographicum* (1636). Herbert owned a copy of his *Controversium epitomes* (1620) [*FK* 98].

[27] Epiphanius of Samos (c. 310–402) was the author of the *Panarion*, a work whose avowed intent was "to describe and refute the eighty heresies facing the one truth like the eighty concubines of the Song of Songs 6:8–9 who surround and celebrate the unique bride, but have no part with her" (Vallée 65). He was very knowledgeable about pagan rites and symbols, linking them with heresies, and he is particularly hard on the Gnostics, a group with whom Herbert probably had some sympathy. Herbert owned his *De prophetarum vita et interitu commentarius Graecus* (1529), edited with notes by Albino Torino (*FK* 98).

[28] Jean le Mercier [Mercerus] (c. 1502–70), a distinguished French scholar of Hebrew, Chaldean and Aramaic, was Professor of Hebrew at the College Royal de France from 1546. He wrote many works on ancient languages, the ones which Herbert would have found most helpful here being the *Tabulae in grammaticum linguae Chaldaeae* (1560), *Alphabeticum hebraicum* (1566), and *Decalogum commentarius Rabbi Abraham, cognomento Ben Ezra* (1568). See also Vossius I, iv, 326.

[29] Jan van der Driessche [Drusius] (1550–1616), was a Belgian linguist. A Protestant, he fled to England with his father in 1567, and subsequently became Professor of Oriental Languages at Oxford (1571). He returned home and occupied a similar

think, or *Jehovah*, as it states in the Puncta masoritica[30] I am not going to
decide here; allow me to note that there seems to be no great absurdity in
the opinion of those who derived the Greek word *Bacche* from pronouncing
the word aloud. With respect to this, it is very well-known that *Vau* is
often interchangable with B, so *Varro* in Greek would become *Barron*, and
Virgilius would be *Birgilios*. If you will not allow *Bacchus*, *Iao*[31] certainly
derives from either the Tetragrammaton,[32] or *Jah*, which can be found in
Exodus 28 and, often, in the Psalms. I wish that Labeo's book[33] from which
Macrobius[34] cites the following passage, was extant:

----

post at the University of Leyden (1577), where he produced his Chaldean grammar
(1602) and commentaries on the Pentateuch, Ruth, and Origen. Herbert would have
known his *Tetragrammaton vel De nomine dei proprio* (1604), and he owned a copy
of *De sectis Judaeicis* (1619) [*FK* 97].

[30]Herbert is referring to an Old Testament word *masoreth* which means, loosely,
"tradition." It became the term of reference for the body of that text relating to the
Hebrew Bible, compiled in the 10th century by a group of Jewish scholars. The
word as applied to this text first appeared in Samuel Purchas's *Pilgrimage* (1613),
and the term "Masoretes" came to denote the group of scholars themselves.

[31]Carus calls Iao "the god with the adorable name (i.e. Abraxas)," and links
him with Aesculapius because he bears a cock's head. There is a drawing of a
gem showing Iao with a cock's head and legs made from snakes. The serpent is
"the emblem of mystery, of eternity, of wisdom, the prophet of the gnosis" (Carus
226–27).

[32]The literal translation of the Greek is "a four-letter word." It refers to the
Hebrew word YWHW, the unspoken name of God. The Tetragrammaton itself
became a mystical symbol, and its pronunciation was kept secret by the priests, in
case blasphemers should use it. For further details, see Scholem 42–44.

[33]The "Labeo" to whom Herbert refers is probably M. Antistius Labeo (d. 10
A.D.), a celebrated Roman jurist and mythologist who may have written *De oraculo
Apollinis*. However, Macrobius (see n. 31) refers to a Cornelius Labeo, whose name
is found nowhere else, and to whom Herbert, like other subsequent scholars, ascribed
the above-mentioned book. Macrobius's mistake caused this non-existent Labeo to
be credited with other works as well.

[34]Aurelius Ambrosius Theodosius Macrobius (fl. 400 A.D.), a Roman grammar-
ian, wrote a commentary on the *Somnium Scipionis*, a lost work of Cicero. This
work in turn seems to have been based on the incident in Plato's *Republic* where
Er, son of Arminius, returns from the dead. Macrobius was much in vogue in the
Middle Ages, being cited by, amongst others, Chaucer, in *The Parliament of Fowles*.
Macrobius's work was printed in Florence (1515).

Apollo Clarus, being consulted about which of the gods was called *Jao*, stated that 'Jao is the supreme god above all, Jupiter at the beginning of Spring, and the Sun in Summer, but Jao is soft and delicate in Autumn!'[35]

Macrobius then subjoins the power of this oracle's god and the interpretation of the name; *Liber Pater*[36] and the Sun are designated by *Iao* from Cornelius Labeo in his book *De oraculo Apollonis Clarii*. This can all be found in Vossius.[37] Later it will be explained how the expurgation of crimes by certain rites, especially the vannus,[38] which is mentioned in the scriptures, was attributed by the pagans to *Iao*.

It may be understood from many sources how the God of *Sabaoth*,[39] that is, of Hosts (one of the names of God in scripture), was the *Liber* or *Bacchus* of the pagans, but particularly from Aristophanes, who always calls Bacchus or Liber by the name *Sabbasion*, Lucian[40] in *Deorum consiliones*

---

[35]There was an oracle of Apollo at Clarus (Klaros), north-west of Ephesus (see Pausanias I, 233). Ceyx, the lover of Alcyone, was drowned on his way to consult it.

[36]Originally, Liber and his female equivalent Libera were Italian gods connected with wine-making and viticulture (Rose 166), and only later came to be identified with Dionysus (Bacchus) and Persephone (Proserpina). Rose adds that "an absurd Latin etymology" was concocted for the name Proserpina.

[37]Vossius II, xiv, 374–80.

[38]The *vannus* is a winnowing-fan.

[39]The word *Sabaoth* derives from the Hebrew *saba*, "host," and Yahweh *sabaot* is thus the military or apocalyptic Lord of Hosts. The reference Herbert gives (I Samuel: 5) does not seem to be correct, but there is a reference to the Lord of Hosts in I Samuel 1:3).

The word *Sabbath* comes from the Hebrew *sabat*, "to stop or desist." The connotations should be obvious. Later on in the chapter, Herbert gets the meanings the wrong way around.

[40]Lucian of Samosata (c. 114–200), Greek barrister and satirist. His modern translator, Paul Turner, quotes a 10th century encyclopaedist referring to him as "Lucian the Blasphemer, the Slanderer, or . . . the Atheist." Lucian's habit of making uproarious fun of everything utterly scandalised the anonymous Christian writer, who went on to rail at the "filthy brute" who "attacks Christianity and blasphemes Christ Himself" (7), and cites with great relish a rumour that Lucian was torn to pieces by dogs. Lucian wrote many stories and satirical sketches, and was in great vogue amongst late mediaeval and Renaissance cultural critics; his admirers included Erasmus, Sir Thomas More (who made some Latin versions), Ariosto, and Ben Jonson, to name a few. Lucian also wrote *De dea Syria*, a work on the Syrian goddess Astarte. Paul Taylor's brilliant translation of *The Satirical Sketches* (Harmondsworth: Penguin Books, 1961) is now sadly out of print.

Harpocratione on the word *Sabos*, and Eustathius[41] in the *Oxiengnosis* of Dionysius.[42] It may also be confirmed by an ancient inscription, "Q. Nunnius Alexander dono dedit Jovi Sabazio" (Quintus Nunnius Alexander dedicated it to Jupiter Sabazius),[43] and in the ancient parchment manuscripts of Apuleius[44] he is called Sabadius. In the rites of Sabazius,[45] a snake was put on the chests of initiates, and Arnobius[46] writes:

> The sacred ceremonies and rites of initiation of Saebadius may serve as a trial of truth; a yellow snake is placed on the chests of those who are consecrated, and taken out again from their lower parts.[47]

Vossius believes that Saebadius and Sabazius are the same,[48] as does Julius Firmicus Maternus, who notes that "those who worship Jupiter Serpens, when they are initiated, draw a snake through their bo-

---

[41] Herbert has Eustachius, but this seems to be a misprint. The reference is probably to Eustathius (d. 1194), Metropolitan of Thessalonica, whose commentary on the *Iliad* and *Odyssey* contains a great deal of information on geography, language, mythology and history. Rabelais makes some rude remarks about him in the Preface to *Gargantua and Pantagruel*.

[42] Dionysius of Alexandria (d. 265), philsosopher and bishop, headed the theological school at Alexandria. During the persecutions ordered by the emperors Decius (250) and Valerian (257) he suffered very hard times, which he recorded in an amusing manner. When Gallienus ascended the throne (258), he returned home and wrote his treatise *On Nature*, which contains much information about pagan ceremonies.

[43] Quoted from Vossius II, xiv, 376. Modern scholars equate Sabazius with Dionysus (Burkert 420, n. 32) and Vaillant, quoted by Burkert, says the name means "Liberator," cf. Slavic *svoboda*, "liberty" (420).

[44] Lucius Apuleius (114–after 170) of Madaura in Africa, apart from being the author of *Metamorphoses seu de asino aureo* [*The Golden Ass*], also wrote *De daemone Socratis*, a work dealing with spirits, which Apuleius saw as an intermediary life-form between gods and mortals.

[45] Sabazius was a Phrygian import, whom the Greeks believed (as Herbert states) to be the same as Dionysus. He was worshipped in Athens during the latter part of the 5th century B.C., and the snake was his cult-symbol.

[46] Arnobius of Sicca (fl. 305 A.D.) was a Numidian theologian who wrote the *Adversus nationes,* an early attack on paganism. He is quite a learned writer, and draws on the work of Varro and Lucretius. Because of the nature of his work, Arnobius is assumed to have been a Christian writer, but nothing is known about him.

[47] Arnobius, Book V [Herbert's textual note].

[48] Vossius II, xiv, 376.

soms."[49] That snake, to some, symbolised the Deity, to others the World, and to still others Youth or Regeneration when it discarded its skin. When it drew up its tail and tucked it under its throat it signified Time, and, according to Pierino,[50] it was placed in the hand of Saturn and so came to mean the Earth moving around the Sun. The Greeks and Romans were unaware of the name Sabazius, which others had taken from the Egyptians or Syrians. Cicero says "they are new gods and must be worshipped by watching throughout the night."[51] And Aristophanes, that most witty of ancient comic poets, is worried that Sabazius and some other gods, being taken for strangers, might be turned out of the city! Sabazius comes from the Hebrew word *tsava* which means "warfare" or "army." Thus in I Samuel:5, Psalm 24:10[52] and elsewhere, the God of Sabbath (Hosts or Armies) is quite different from the Jewish Sabaoth, which means "rest," and is contrary to the opinion of Plutarch, who derives *Sabbaton* or *Sabbathum* from Sabazius.

There is another celebrated name of God used in scripture, *Adonai* (Psalm 24, Isaiah 19:4).[53] This is derived from *adon*, Lord or Master, in which sense it may be found in Plautus,[54] where by *donni* or *adoni* he means my lord, or

---

[49]Julius Firmicus Maternus (fl. 334 A.D.) wrote the *Mathesis*, a treatise on astrology. He believed that the soul was divine, and as such was superior to the stars. Firmicus also wrote a Euhemerist work, *De errore profanorum religionum*, in which he urged the emperors Constans I and Constantius II to stamp out paganism. Herbert owned a copy of the latter work (*FK* 83).

[Herbert's marginal note]: Iul[ius] Firm[icus], *De error[re] prof[anorum] rel[igionum]*.

[50]Pierino or Pierio Valeriano [Pierinus] (1477–1558) was an Italian scholar whose main work was the *Hieroglyphica* (Basel, 1556), which is quoted here by Herbert. It is a mine of information on ancient learning, and Herbert may have read about Pythagoras's supposed journey to Egypt in it. The author makes the claim that hieroglyphs "mean nothing less than the revealing of the nature of things, divine and human" (Seznec 100, n. 75). Valeriano was one of the first scholars to draw serious attention to the antiquities of Egypt, and he demonstrated conclusively that Egyptian civilisation had been very influential on that of Greece.

[Herbert's marginal note]: Pierius in *Hierog[lyphica]*.

[51][Herbert's marginal note]: Cic[ero] 2 *De leg[ibus]*.

[52]The reference in I Samuel:5 is to "the God of Israel" who "smote [the men of Ashdod] with emerods." Psalm 24:10 refers to "the Lord of hosts, he is the King of glory."

[53]In Psalm 24 (see also above) God is called "the Lord strong and mighty," "the Lord mighty in battle," "the Lord of hosts" and "the King of glory." Isaiah 19:4 also has "the Lord of hosts."

[54]Titus Maccius Plautus (c. 254–184 B.C.) was the great Roman comic dramatist,

master.[55] Macrobius says that by Adonis the pagans meant the Sun, and if you look at Assyrian religion, where Venus Architidis (actually Atergatis) and Adonis were highly revered, you will find that Adonis was the Sun.[56] This is what the Phoenicians now believe, according to Macrobius:

> Naturalists worshipped the upper hemisphere of the earth, which we inhabit, under the name of Venus, and called the lower part *Proserpina*. The Assyrians and Phoenicians understand her as a mournful goddess, because the Sun's annual motion is through the twelve signs of the zodiac, six upper and six lower, and when the Sun is in the lower the days are short, and they imagine the goddess mourning, having left him to Proserpina. As we said before, she is the goddess of the lower hemisphere and the Antipodes; they call it 'the return of Adonis' when the Sun passes the six lower signs and begins to adorn the hemisphere with more light and longer days. They also tell how Adonis was killed by a wild boar, which they see as the emblem of Winter, as it is rough and hairy, liking dirty places which are covered with hoar frost. Winter becomes, as it were, a wound on the Sun, and its heat and light is lessened, causing the death of animals over a large area.

Adonis was called *Gingras*[57] in Phoenician; this was the name of a flute, and his worshippers sang mournful songs, of which mention is made in Isaiah 28 and Jeremiah 8:7[58] where the Hebrew word, while it does not mean flute, does mean crane or goose, the pipe being made of a goose pipe, and *gingrire* being the proper expression for the noise of a goose. Aldrete[59] derives the word *gingras* from the Syriac root *ghenaq*, which means "to hunt," but this seems far-fetched to me.

---

author of plays such as *The Rope* and *Miles gloriosus*. He adapted the Greek "New Comedy" to the Roman stage.

[55][Herbert's marginal note]: Plau[tus] in *Poenul*.

[56]Macrobius states: "In the story which they tell of Adonis being killed by a boar the animal is intended to represent winter . . . and so winter, as it were, inflicts a wound on the sun, for in winter we find the sun's rays ebbing" (*Saturnalia* I, 21, 140). Herbert gives the reference also in the margin.

[57]The etymology here is quite correct. The Latin word *gingrina* means "a small flute," and *gingritus* denotes the noise that geese make, together with the verb *gingrire*, "to cackle like a goose."

[58]There is no mention of "mournful songs" or anything similar in Isaiah 28; Jeremiah 9:7 does indeed mention "the turtle and the crane and the swallow."

[59]Bernardo Alderete [Hispanus Aldrete] (1558–c. 1632) was an eminent Spanish scholar who specialised in oriental languages and history. He wrote *Varias antiquedades de España, Africa, y otras provincias* (1614).

In the sacred rites of Adonis, people had to whip themselves very severely, as if they were celebrating Adonis's funeral; they also shaved their heads as the Egyptians did for the dead Apis. But if any women wished to keep their hair, they had to prostitute themselves to strangers for one day, and if anything proceeded from this action it was dedicated to Venus. After the day of mourning was over, they made a bed for Venus and Adonis, and the next day celebrated Adonis's restoration to life. These holy rites were called the Adonia, and they are probably referred to in Ezekiel 8:

> And he led me to the door of the Gate of
> the House of the Lord, which is to the
> north, and there sat women lamenting for
> Thamur.

St. Jerome understands Thamur as Adonis,[60] as does Procopius,[61] who says that Mars changes himself into Adonis, but Plutarch says that Adonis was Bacchus.[62]

Now, because stars were worshipped under men's names, and men under the names of stars, the authorities are very confusing, so much so that it is difficult to determine what belonged to the stars and what to men. This is an important observation in reference to the legends of the old gods, and also in elucidating obscure scriptural passages, for history sometimes changes from the gods and their rites to men of the same name, and vice versa.

---

[60]This was actually known to Christian writers since the time of Origen (see Teixidor 154–55 n. 38).

[61]Procopius of Caesarea (c. 490–565), Byzantine politician and historian, was the author of the notorious *Secret Histories*, which chronicled the reign of Justinian I and Theodora. More importantly for Herbert, Procopius also wrote a *Military History* in eight books and the *Edifices*, a work dealing with the architecture of Justinian's reign, which was published in 562.

[62]*Thamur* is another name for the Phoenician god *Tammuz*, the lover of Ishtar. Frazer mentions a Babylonian hymn to Tammuz called "The Lament of the flutes for Tammuz" (429), which makes the *gingras* connexion less tenuous. Frazer (428) and the *OCD* (7) agree that Adonis and Tammuz are related, and that the name Adonis is simply the Semitic title *adon*, "Lord." Rose (32) comments that the identification of Tammuz and Adonis is not certain, but they are at least "of the same type," namely vegetation-gods and consorts of a mother-goddess. As for the parallels between Aphrodite/Adonis and Ishtar/Tammuz, Morford and Lenardon (121) consider that the Cybele/Attis combination is closer. Teixidor (154) favours the identification of Tammuz with Adonis.

There is also the question whether Adonis means not only the Sun but "grain," and evidence for this may be gathered from Ammianus Marcellinus:[63]

> The women, according to the custom of their country, used to lament in a very doleful way when their expectation was frustrated in the first fruits, as did the worshippers of Venus in the sacred rites of Adonis, which symbolically represent ripe fruit.

There were gardens sacred to Adonis, about which the scholiast on the 15th *Idyll* of Theocritus[64] says, "they used to sow bread, corn and barley in some gardens near the city, and called them the gardens of Adonis." We could introduce other instances of these gardens, but this is enough about the name Adonai and its acceptance by the Phoenicians, who worshipped the Sun under this name. There are other names of God mentioned in the scriptures, and recorded by Jerome as *Schaddas*[65] and so forth, concerning which you may consult the commentators.

The above were the most solemn names used by the Hebrews for the Supreme God, all of which the pagans applied to the Sun, except Sabazius, as has been pointed out. Thus, although the Hebrews worshipped a deity superior to the Sun under the same name, the pagans did not mean the Sun or any other deity (unless they esteemed it as the clearest representation of the Supreme God, and, as Plato says, his most sensible image) but only worshipped the Supreme God himself. I am more inclined, therefore, to believe that almost all ancient religion was symbolic, and that they do not worship one thing in another, but one thing out of another. The priests, always

---

[63] Ammianus Marcellinus (c. 330–400), a soldier, was the last great pagan historian of Rome, being a fervent admirer of the emperor Julian, whom he accompanied on his campaigns. His *Later Roman Empire A.D. 354–378* has been edited and translated by Walter Hamilton (Harmondsworth: Penguin Books, 1986).

Herbert has accurately cited the Latin, which reads: "Feminae vero, miserabile planctu, in primaevo flore succisam spem gentis solitis fletibus conclamabant, ut lacrimare cultrices Veneris saepe spectantur in sollemnibus Adonidis sacris, quod simulacrum aliquod esse frugum adultarum religiones mysticae docent" (XIX, ii; Vol. 2, 123).

[64] Theocritus (c. 308–240 B.C.), author of the *Idylls*, is credited with the invention of pastoral poetry. An anonymous translation into English first appeared in 1588. Robert Wells has produced a good modern translation (Harmondsworth: Penguin Books, 1989). Idyll 15, "The Festival of Adonis," is a miniature dramatic sketch about two women who are going off to join in the festivities (Wells 100–06).

[65] The proper form of the name is *Shaddai*, which means (in Hebrew) "the mighty one."

so careful and industrious at keeping the people dutiful, were exquisitely ingenious both in loading them with superstitious forms and rites, and in enriching themselves.

Some people assert that the Hebrews took the above-mentioned names of god from the pagans, which seems very unlikely to me, as almost all the religion of the Greeks and Romans came from the East. I do not deny, however, that some particular rites were invented by their priests, but in any case, it is very obvious that the sacred rites of Hebrews and gentiles differed very little in most ways, and will be very clear from what follows.

This is all concerning the names of the Supreme God as *El*, *Elohim*, *Jah*, *Jehovah*, *Sabaoth* and *Adonai*. I will now examine the different names used by the pagans for the Sun.

IV

The Worship of the Sun
and his Several Names

The adoration of the Sun, so not only scripture, but Homer, Hesiod and the ancient historians tell us, was both ancient and universal. It was generally thought that the Supreme God had made heaven his home (as immortal things are suitable to immortality), and the pagans could not think of anything more conspicuous or worthy of worship and adoration. They therefore lifted their eyes and hands devoutly up to heaven, not only in great adversity or difficulty, but also in prosperity did they direct their prayers there, because they did not know from where else anything good could come.

Then they began to think it strange that God, who required worship from everyone, should hide himself from them, and for this reason the pagans venerated the Sun as a god, not himself supreme, but the next noblest and most excellent representative. Other people, however, thought that the world itself, being full of God, was [itself] his most exact image. Those who worshipped the Sun instead of the Supreme God himself were like people who, when they come to a great potentate's court, take for the king the first richly-dressed person they see, and pay to him the respect which should be reserved only for majesty itself. The Inca of Peru was more correct when asked whether he acknowledged any god superior to the Sun, and answered, "I do not take the Sun as the Supreme God, but only as his minister, who, as he goes around the Earth, performs his will and pleasure."[1] That was a very astute answer; how could anything be thought of as supreme which could reduce all sublunary life to ashes if it were allowed to act unrestrained? The Sun, then, was the sensible representation of the Supreme God, and as such was worshipped by the wisest of the pagans, who knew very well that God himself could not be reduced to one thing, and that even universal Nature was insufficient to represent him according to his true dignity.

---

[1] Herbert's source for this story, given in the margin, is Garcilaso de la Vega's *Historia de las Incas*. Garcilaso (1503–36) was an eminent Spanish poet and soldier, who was in the vanguard of a poetic revival in the early sixteenth century, and who wrote sonnets, odes and eclogues. He was praised highly by Cervantes in *Don Quixote* (II, lviii) and died fighting in the service of Charles V.

No-one knows what shape the Sun is, whether it is four-sided, polygonal, or, as common opinion has it, round. If it were angular, the angles might not be visible because of our weak sight, or its very remoteness, as happens with square towers, might make it seem round. But if, as Anaximander[2] thought, the Sun is a hollow fiery furnace, it would still seem to be, as optics demonstrates plainly, protruberant. We must pass over the shape as being uncertain. It may be proved, however, by mathematical demonstration, that the Sun is one hundred and sixty-six times, or, as some say, one hundred and forty times, larger than the Earth, and of such incredible swiftness that it moves at one million miles per hour, exceeded only by the velocity of the Firmament. In twenty-four hours, its diurnal motion, it goes 42,308,437 paces, which, so says Patrizi,[3] if a bird could do the same, it would have to fly 1884 times around the world in an hour, that is, 31.66 times per minute.

Lastly, the Sun emits so bright and splendid a light when it brings the day that all the other stars and sublunary fires, if combined in one body, could not compare with it for light and heat. For these reasons the pagans called it divine, and also because spring, summer, autumn and winter, which in turn caused the beginning and end of all animals and plants, followed one another by its motion. The Egyptians, in whose system [the Sun] is called the Sole God of Heaven, paid the greatest worship to it, although they still honoured the stars with divine reverence; they called it Osiris, but Plutarch notes that the name "Osiris" stands for many other pagan deities besides the Sun. Yet really, it should refer [only] to him. Diodorus Siculus, commenting on Macrobius (Book I, 21) states that Helios [Osiris] first ruled over the Egyptians by that name as a star in the heavens, and Statius writes "Whether with the Anthemonians we call/ You rosy Titan, or the fruitful/ All-producing

---

[2]Anaximander of Miletus (c. 610–530 B.C.) was "the . . . greatest of the three Milesians who presided in succession over the first school of Greek philosophy" (Cornford 7). In his one surviving fragment he wrote that "things perish into those things out of which they have their birth according to that which is ordained" (Freeman 19; see discussion in Robinson 23–31). He may have been the first philosopher to construct a systematic theory of the origin of the universe.

[3]Francesco Patrizi [Patricius] (1529–97) was Professor of Philosophy at the University of Ferrara. He is best-known as the author of *Nova de universis philosophia* (1593), a work in which he advocated that all religions be brought together in a moderated form of Catholicism. Patrizi also believed that Platonism might be made into a kind of proto-Trinitarian doctrine and that Christianity might therefore be brought into conformity with it (Walker 116). Patrizi was also the editor of the *Oracula Chaldaica*, thought to be the works of Zoroaster, and he also wrote on history, rhetoric and the theory of poetry. His eirenic tendencies, though somewhat weaker than Herbert's, were obviously attractive.

Osiris."[4] In the Egyptian language "Osiris" means "many eyes," thus Osiris illuminates the world with many rays, as Diodorus Siculus tells us.[5] The Egyptians also called the Sun Horus, and worshipped at Heliopolis the form of a bull, called Mnevis, consecrated to him. They also gave games in his honour here and carried sacred images of the gods in horse-drawn carriages; Servius says that these images, or *xasna*, were small figures carried in litters which were inspired with prophetic power. Perhaps it is to this practice that Amos alludes in "Ye have borne the the tabernacle of your Moloch" (5:26). Tabernacles or chariots, serving as temples, were drawn by oxen, horses, or donkeys, and sometimes even by men. The ancient ceremony of sun-worship was to extend the thumb upright and lay it upon the mouth (this was done for other gods, too), then turn the body round about. The Romans turned to the right, the Gauls to the left, or so the scholars tell us. The pagans traditionally prayed towards the rising sun, but the Israelites, on the contrary, turned towards the west when they prayed. The Christians have revived the former custom, turning towards the east. The Egyptians also called the sun Typhon, of whom more later.

The Phoenicians also worshipped the Sun, and we note that Phoenicia was a part of Syria, situated on the coast and known as Canaan in the Scriptures.[6] Canaan, St. Jerome says, produced Sidon, from whom the city took its name, and it was also the border of Canaan. I must admit, however, as Arias Montanus[7] tells us, that there were twelve other nations with that name [Canaan], whose people, according to Herodotus, crossed

---

[4]Publius Papinius Statius (c. 45–96), the Roman epic poet whose career was involuntarily cut short by order of the Emperor Domitian. Statius was the author of the *Silvae* and two epics, the *Thebaid* and the *Achilleis*. The Anthemonians are the inhabitants of Anthemos, a city in Mesopotamia, north-west of Edessa in the Osroene district.

The quotation is taken from the *Silvae*: "Seu te roseum Titana vocari/ Gentis Anthemoniae ritu, seu praestat Osirim/ frugiferum" (cited in text).

[5]Osiris has a name "the Eye of Ra" (Budge I, 236) and, as Ra is the Sun-god, Osiris assumes the power of his rays. Unfortunately Osiris has many other names, more than 200 of which are listed by Budge, without translation (II, Chapter X). Herbert probably got his information from Herodotus or Plutarch. Budge reprints the latter's version of the Osiris myth in full (II, Chapter XI).

[Herbert's marginal note]: Diod[orus] Sic[ulus] I; Macr[obius] I, *Sat*[*ires*] c. 2.

[6][Herbert's marginal note]: Gen. 10.15. "And Canaan begat Sidon his firstborn, and Heth."

[7]Arias Montanus (1527–98), a Spanish humanist, was the editor of the so-called *Polyglot Bible (1572)*. He attended the Council of Trent with the Bishop of Segovia, and afterwards became chaplain to Philip II of Spain, a post he retained after refusing

the Red Sea and lived on the Syrian coast. However, as Pliny later described it, the Phoenicians spread all over Syria, which I find even more curious, because it is very likely that religious worship, after Egyptian times, came from Phoenicia into the West. The Phoenicians were also credited with the invention of writing[8] and of distance navigation; Critias,[9] according to Athenaeus, said "the Phoenicians invented letters", and Dionysius of Alexandria states:

> The Syrians live inland,
> And next to the shore, the Phoenicians.
> Descended from Erythian stock,
> They first built ships and sailed the stormy seas,
> Instituted trade over the ocean,
> And taught the observation of the stars.
> They colonised Joppa and Gaza, the Elian towers,
> Ancient Tyre and pleasant Berytis,
> The shores of Byblos, then Sidon's fertile soil,
> Famous for its rivers, they occupied,
> And rich Tripolis, Orthosia and Marathus.

And Festus Avienus,[10] following this, writes:

---

the king's offer of a bishopric. His nine-volume work on Jewish antiquities (1593) was well-respected and translated into several languages.

[8]The Phoenicians certainly seem to have been the originators of the alphabet, although of course writing existed before alphabets. Ancient writing-systems (cuneiform, hieroglyphics) transcribed either words or syllables, while alphabets transcribe sounds, and are therefore simpler. It is impossible to say whether Herbert considered this distinction or not. The Phoenician writing system reached Greece around 700 B.C. (Jean 52). The origin of the claim for the Phoenicians' invention of writing may be found in Herodotus (5.57–58).

[9] Critias (c. 450–404 B.C.), Athenian poet, philosopher and politician, was one of the "Thirty Tyrants" imposed on Athens by the Spartan general Lysander. He had been a pupil of Socrates (see Plato, *Timaeus*) and had made original contributions to the philosophy of religion, maintaining that there were no gods and that the moral trappings of religion were only useful for political ends. Critias is quoted with respect by Sextus Empiricus, Philostratus and Clement of Alexandria, one of whom must have been Herbert's source because he left no extant works. Critias was killed in battle.

[10]Rufus Festus Avienus (fl. 360–90) was a poet of history and geography, amongst whose works were the *Descriptio orbis terrae* and *Ora maritima*, which were paraphrases of Dionysius of Alexandria. If not very original, Festus has been credited with "considerable energy and liveliness of style" (Smith I, 432).

By the salt-flowing sea
Is the country of Phoenicia.
Here from the Red Sea
People moved, the first to improve shipping
And learn navigation, the first
To open trade with the world, the first
To discover the Pole-star.

What Strabo[11] tells us about their sailors in particular worshipping the stars will not seem very strange to us, as they carried their religion to far and distant places, trading all over the Mediterranean until they almost colonised the Carthaginians and Iberians. Strabo says that the Phoenicians held most of Spain and Africa before Homer's time, retaining it until it was destroyed by the Roman Empire. They used to place *pataici* (deities) on the stern of their ships, but even Hesychius[12] cannot say in what form they were carved or painted. However, Cartari[13] says that the Phoenicians represented their gods in neither human nor animal form. The Phoenicians also worshipped the Sun under the name of Baal, or Bal, called Bel by the Assyrians.[14] Servius states:

---

[11] Strabo of Amasia (c. 63 B.C.–19 A.D.) wrote a geography of the Roman Empire in 17 books, most of which still survive. It is less well-known that he also compiled a continuation of the historical work of Polybius.

[12] Hesychius of Alexandria (5th century A.D.) was a grammarian who compiled a dictionary of rare words. There is a 15th century MS surviving, albeit in poor condition, which shows that Hesychius was generally accurate about the words he defines. For Herbert not to find a word in Hesychius meant that it was truly obscure.

[13] Vincenzo Cartari [Cartarius] (c. 1520–75) was an Italian mythographer and author of *Le imagini colla sposizione degli dei degli antichi* (1556). This work was translated into French by du Verdier (1581) and into English by R. Linche under the title *The Fountaine of Ancient Fiction* (1591). Cartari's book was widely-read as the pre-eminent authority on the appearance of ancient deities. "No-one had ever spoken of [the gods'] statues and representations before," claimed his publisher, Marcolini (Seznec 251). Cartari intended his work to be used as a reference book for artists and poets who wished to accurately represent ancient gods.

[14] Herbert's derivations are correct. Baal was originally a northern Semitic fertility-god whose name came simply to mean "Lord." The Bel mentioned in the Old Testament is actually the Assyrian god Marduk, upon whom the title Bel, "Lord," was conferred by King Tiglath-Pileser I of Assyria in about 1200 B.C. This god was synonymous with the Hebrew god Yahweh (Sykes 26) and was also worshipped in Egypt.

[Herbert's marginal note]: Serv[ius] I *Aeneid*.

It is evident that the Assyrians worshipped Saturn (i.e. the Sun) and Juno. These deities were afterwards worshipped by the Africans. In their language, God is called Bal, and Bel by the Assyrians. These are Saturn and the Sun.

The Sun, as we have seen, was also worshipped by the Phoenicians and Arabians, who called it Adon, Adonis, Adoneus or Gingras.

The cult of the Sun existed in Judah, too, long before the reign of Josiah,[15] who destroyed the horses that the kings of Judah had dedicated, and who burnt the chariot of the Sun.

We now come to Mediterranean Syria, where, besides Judaea, is Commagene, consisting of Seleucia, Antioch, Apamea and Laodicea (where Commagene is known as Tetrapolis), Caelo-Syria and Cava Syria. Here the Ammonites worshipped the cult of the Sun under the name Moloch or Milcom, which means "Lord of the Universe." This is the god of the Ammonites mentioned in I Chronicles 2:5 and 7, Leviticus and II Chronicles, where it appears that parents made their children pass through fire in Moloch's honour — not burned alive, but, as some say, purged and purified.[16] They were carried or led by priests, or even, on priestly orders, by their parents, between two great fires where ben Ezra thinks that they were burned, grounding this on II Kings 17:31, "those of the Sepharvaim burned their children in the fire to Adramalech and Anamelech."[17] It is not important that some people think Moloch is Priapus, for the latter stands for the generative power of

---

[15]Josiah was king of Judah 640/39–609 B.C. His reign is noted for the king's thorough purging of idolatry. Josiah demolished sacred groves, burned idols and restored the old religion of Abraham and Moses in the kingdom of Judah.

[16][Herbert's marginal notes]: R[abbi] Solomon Jac[ob], R[abbi] Marmen[ides], R[abbi] Ioseph Karo.

Moses ben Maimon, or Maimonides (1135–1204) was the great judge, codifier and Biblical exegete, author of the *Moreh Nebuchim* [*Guide for the Perplexed*]. In the latter, Maimonides showed that Judaism was in harmony with philosophy, but was also capable of offering insights beyond the merely rational. Grotius was much influenced by this work in his writings on Christianity.

Rabbi Joseph Karo (1488–1575) was a Spanish scholar who wrote the *Shulcham Arukh* (Venice, 1564), the standardisation of the Jewish Code, containing information on rituals, festivals, the law and the duties of Jews.

There were several rabbis named "Solomon Jacob," but I have been unable to determine which one Herbert means.

[17]Abraham ben Ezra (c. 1092–1167), the eminent Spanish Biblical exegete and Jewish scholar, well-known to readers of Browning as "Rabbi ben Ezra." His commentaries on the Decalogue were translated into Latin by Jean le Mercier [Mercerus]. The Sepharvaim are the people of Sepharvais, a city captured by the Assyrians, possibly located near Damascus.

the Sun, or that others would make him equivalent to Mercury, for *melech*, not *molech* means "messenger," thus denoting the function of Mercury.[18] Moloch's image was divided into seven compartments. In the first, a small ape was offered up; in the next, a tortoise; in the third, a sheep; the fourth, a ram; the fifth, a calf; the sixth, an ox; the seventh, a male child. According to Rabbi Simeon's *Yalkut*[19] and Buchheim's[20] notes on the Chaldaen paraphrase of Leviticus, men were sacrificed in honour of the Sun, although lesser victims were used for other gods. The cruel and bloody priests believe that the Supreme God expected such noble sacrifices, and to this end they persuaded parents to destroy their own children, thus imitating Saturn or Time, which destroys everything that comes into the world. Minucius Felix[21] states that this custom also prevailed in some parts of Africa.

In Syria, Apamea and Emesa the Sun was worshipped together with Mercury and Mars, as may be understood by Julian's "Hymn to the Sun."[22] The name there was Elagabalus or Alagabalus, which word came to the

---

Adramalech (modern Adrammelech) was a god brought by the Sepharvaim to Samaria, and children were indeed sacrificed to him (see II Kings 17:31). Some scholars derive the name from *'ddr mlk*, i.e. "the king [Moloch] is powerful." Anamalech (modern Annamelech) came with the other god to Samaria. Scholars link his name with *'An*, the male version of *'Anqat*.

[18]The etymology is as follows. The Hebrew *melek*, "king," and *boset*, "shame," were combined to make the derogatory word *molek*, hence the *OT* appellation of "abomination" to Moloch. The Punic word *mlk*, moreover, denotes "sacrifice" or "offering."

[19]Simeon ha-Darshan (13th century) was a Jewish scholar from Amsterdam, author of the *Yalkut Shimoni*, a compilation of rabbinical wisdom. There is a MS of this work dating from c. 1308, and a printed version appeared in Salonika (1521). Herbert may have known M. Prinz's Latin translation of the latter (Venice, 1566). Information courtesy of Dr. Moshe Stern, Department of Religion, University of Manitoba.

[20]Paul Buchheim [Paulus Fagius] (1504–49) was professor of Hebrew at Strassburg (1544) and Cambridge (1549). He translated Elijah Levy's Chaldaen dictionary (1541) and wrote books on Biblical interpretation and Hebrew linguistics. Mary I had him exhumed and burnt as a heretic (1551) but he was rehabilitated ten years later by Elizabeth I.

[21]Minucius Felix (fl. 200–40), a Roman lawyer, was the author of a dialogue betweeen a pagan and a Christian. The former employs Fronto's defence of paganism against the Christian, who bases his arguments on Cicero, Seneca and the Stoics.

[22]Flavius Claudius Julianus (331–63), philosopher, poet and Roman emperor (361–63), known as "the Apostate." He dedicated himself to eradicating Christianity from the Empire. Julian did not persecute, but set up a cult of the Sun, which he placed in the centre of a pantheon of gods. Julian wrote extensively on religion,

Romans as Heliogabalus;[23] the latter part of the word deriving from the old Arabic *gabal*, "inventor," or *gebel*, which means "mountain." As an ancient inscription "Sacerdos Solis Dei Elagabali" shows, priests were consecrated to him, of whom Festus Avienus writes:

> To the fire-bearing breast of the Sun
> They dedicate their lives.
> High Libanus swells to the summit,
> But yet they fill his temple with cedars.

In Syria-Palmyrena, named for Palmyra (which the Hebrews call Thamur), they also worship the Sun. The city was built by King Solomon, and Vopiscus, in his life of Aurelian, mentions that there was a temple of the Sun there.[24]

Vossius, having passed through Judaea, Caelo-Syria, Commagene and Seleucia, then goes to Mesopotamia, Babylonia and Syria, where he observes that the ancients took "Syria" in such an extensive sense that it included all these lands. Thus Pomponius Mela says: "Syria is called Coele, Mesopotamia, Damascene, Adiabene, Babylonia, Judaea and Sophene,"[25] and Pliny states that Syria

> was formerly a great tract of land called Palestine, where it joins to Arabia, Judaea and Coele; then it was called Phoenicia, and, more inland, Damascene. In our time it is rather South Babylonia, and between the Tigris and Euphrates, Mesopotamia; where it passes Taurus Sophene [it is called] on this side Commagene, and beyond Armenia Adiabene it was formerly called Assyria.

---

his works including four *Orations* and *De diis et mundo*, a treatise on mythology. Harold Mattingly remarked that he was "intolerant of any nonsense that was not his own" (*OCD* 470).

[23]The reference is to M. Aurelius Antoninus (c. 201–22), the deranged emperor Elagabalus or Heliogabalus, who reigned 218–22. He imported the cult of the Sun to Rome, and himself pretended to divine status, which did not, however, prevent his murder.

[24]Flavius Vopiscus wrote biographical sketches of the emperors Aurelian (270–75) and Carinus (283–85) which are part of the *Historia Augustae*, a work on the emperors from Septimius Severus (193–211) to the end of the 3rd century. Aurelian, the self-styled (with some justification) "Restitutor Orbis," conquered Palmyra and captured its queen, Zenobia.

[25]Pomponius Mela (fl. 37–50) was a geographer and an epigone of Strabo. In his *De chorographia* he divides the world into zones and continents, commenting extensively on the customs of each area. His first modern editor was Schott (1579), himself quoted by Herbert in Chapter XV.
[Herbert's marginal note]: Mela l. I, c. 11.

From Herodotus, Trogus[26] and others it is very obvious which part of Syria used to be called Assyria. Cicero says there were Chaldaeans in Judaea.[27] The Sun was called Belus by the Assyrians, Syrians or Chaldaeans and Babylonians, not historically, for Nimrod was known as Belus, but properly accepted under that name as Universal Nature, the celestial nature of the Sun. There is a gemstone, which, as it shines like the Sun, was called "the eye of Belus"; Pliny says that it is white and has a black "pupil" or "apple" in the middle which shines like gold.[28] This stone was most sacred to the god of the Assyrians, who called the sun Adad and the earth Atergatis.[29] Macrobius writes:

> The Assyrians call the supreme god they worship Adad, which means One. They revere him as the most powerful, but they also have a goddess whom they call Atergatis, and to these two, as the Sun and the Earth, they ascribe all power. There is a most impressive image of Adad darting down rays, by which it may be seen that the celestial influence is contained in sunbeams sent to earth. There is also a very splendid image of Atergatis, emitting rays upwards from every part; anything that the earth produces is made by the power of those rays.

Whether this Adad is the god mentioned in the Book of Joshua is a matter for discussion amongst learned scholars, and may be read about in Vossius.

In Arabia, so Strabo tells us, they set up an altar on the roof of a house and burned frankincense to the Sun every day. In the same country, according to Theophrastus,[30] the Sabaeans take myrrh and frankincense to the Sun's

---

[26]Pompeius Trogus (1st century A.D.), a zoologist and botanist, wrote the *Historiae Philippicae*, a compendium of universal history. Its length (44 books) rather belies its intent, and the author's style, leaden and ornamental, is made worse by a propensity for moralising. Trogus's many digressions, however, are a source of interesting vignettes of the customs, religions and belief-systems in places such as Parthia and the ancient orient.

[27][Herbert's marginal note]: Tull. [Cicero] I *De div*[*ino*].

[28][Herbert's marginal note]: Plin[y], l[iber] 37, c. 12.

[29]Adad was the Assyrian storm-god, ruler of the gods and the equivalent of the Babylonian god Marduk.

Atergatis [Atargatis] was a goddess chiefly worshipped in Heliopolis, and, as Herbert notes, she was also known as Derceto. Lucian mentions a temple of hers which was still considered holy in his time, although it had been long ago destroyed by Antiochus IV Epiphanes. Atergatis was half-fish, half-woman; as a fertility goddess she was sometimes identified with Aphrodite (*OCD* 112) and later became fused with the constellation Virgo. In Greece and Rome she was known as "the Syrian goddess." Her consort was Hadad (Adad).

[30]Theophrastus (c. 372–287 B.C.) succeeded Aristotle as head of the Peripatetic

shrine, which was considered the most sacred of all, and was guarded by
armed Arabians. Also in Arabia was the cult of Baal-peor, who is mentioned
in the Scriptures,[31] and whom St. Jerome equates with Priapus. If this were
true, Priapus must have been mystically substituted for the Sun, as Orpheus
states, "Carrying/ A light shining on Earth, I call you Phaneta/ And King
Priapus." Phaneta, according to Macrobius, was the Sun, and if Priapus was
the Egyptian Horus, then he was indeed the Sun. Suidas tells us:

> The image of Priapus, known as Horus to the Egyptians, is human in shape,
> with a sceptre in his right hand denoting all that is dry (the Earth). Also, he
> holds his penis in his left hand because he makes hidden seeds appear in the
> open. His wings show that he moves quickly and the roundness of his dish
> shows his circular form, in which he is worshipped as the Sun.

At Lampsacus there was another Priapus, from whose distorted history some
incredible tales have developed, but I have thought it best to omit them here;
it is enough for my purpose to prove that Priapus anciently and mystically
stood for either the Sun or the Universal Generative Power of Nature, into
whose embraces women who were about to be married were placed in order
to free them from unnecessary modesty, as we can see from Lactantius (I, i,
20) and Arnobius (Bk. IV).[32]

Some of these ancient priestly inventions were not simply impious and
stupid, but lewd, obscene and sordid also. For example, the worshippers
of the idol Belphegor[33] amongst the Moabites were a very nasty lot in
appearance as they piled up great heaps of mud and offered excrement
instead of frankincense. But the Moabites and Midianites had some rites
that were even worse; their Belphegor, like Priapus, had an erect penis, and
they used the same ceremonies as in the sacred mysteries of Venus, openly
allowing all sorts of lust and licentiousness. Thus Numbers 25:12–13 tells
how the Israelites, invited to the sacrifices of Belphegor, were initiated into
his rites and copulated with the daughters of Moab. From II Kings 25:2 and
II Chronicles 15:16 we may see that Maacha, King Asa's mother, presided
over these rites. St. Jerome, in his commentary on Hosea 4, shows that

---

School of Athens. His *Characters*, much imitated in the seventeenth century by
Overbury, Hall and others, was translated by Herbert's mentor Isaac Casaubon
(1591).

[31]Baal-peor was an Arabian deity whom the Israelites liked so much that they set
up a temple to him (Numbers 25:3), an act for which they were brutally punished by
their "jealous" God (Numbers 31:16).

[32]These notes are given as they appear in Herbert's text.

[33]See Baal-peor. An additional feature of this Moabite deity was his erect penis.

women seemed prone to this worship. It is not surprising that in the first book of Athenaeus,[34] Priapus is often called Bacchus, for it is evident that Bacchus, or Liber, was an incarnation of the Sun. As for Chamos,[35] which Jerome says was another name for Belphegor, we need not bother with him at all, for his rites were very sordid and little relevant here. Yet we cannot omit noting that in Baisampsa, an Arabian city, the Sun was universally worshipped; as Estienne[36] notes, its name, which means "House of the Sun," intimates this.

The Persians also worshipped the Sun under the name of Mithras. This is plain from Hesychius who, in addition to others, says that "amongst the Persians Mithras signifies the Sun." Suidas confirms this, and gives an ancient inscription "DEO SOLI INVICTO MITHRAE, & OMINPOTENTI DEO MITHRAE" [To the Only Invincible and Omnipotent God Mithras]. Herodotus has a story of the Persians' method of worship, how "amongst all the gods they worship the Sun alone, and sacrifice horses,"[37] and Trogus states that "the Persians believed the Sun to be the only god, and horses were sacred to him." Ovid, in the *Fasti*, writes: "The Persians placate radiant Hyperion with a horse;/ A slow victim will not please the swift god."[38] What is said here of the "only" god should be taken to mean the Supreme God, for, as Hesychius indicates, while Mithras was the "primary deity amongst the Persians" they also worshipped the Moon, Venus and the Elements, as we will show later on. Now, as the Sun was thought the best representative of the power and majesty of the Supreme God, almost all the pagans therefore worshipped it.

---

[34] Athenaeus of Naucratis (fl. 200 A.D.) was the author of a witty dialogue called *Deipnosophistai* (*The Learned Feast*). It has been described as "a work illustrative of ancient manners, a collection of curious facts. . . . As a body of amusing antiquarian research it would be difficult to praise it too highly" (Smith I, 401).

[35] This Moabite god (see Numbers 21:39) demanded the sacrifice of children. Solomon built him a temple (II Kings 23:17) which was destroyed by Josiah. Milton describes him as "Chemos, th'obscene dread of Moab's sons" (*Paradise Lost* I, 406).

[36] Herbert probably refers to Robert Estienne (1503–59), but the name Stephanus was used for all three members of this illustrious French family of scholar-printers. Robert is the likeliest candidate here; he edited a critical version of the New Testament (1523) and wrote the *Thesaurus linguae Latinae* (1532), described by Sir Paul Harvey as "the best Latin dictionary of the time" (280). However, his son Henri (1531–98) wrote a *Thesaurus Graecae linguae* (1572).

[37] Herodotus 1. 131.

[38] Ovid, *Fasti* I, 385 [28].

The Persians were of the opinion that there were two principles: Oro-mazes [Ahura-mazda], the fountain of good, and Arimanes [Ahriman], the source of evil: one harmed, whilst the other helped. You may say that one was like Jupiter, the other like Vejupiter, between which the Sun acted as arbitrator. This is noted by Plutarch. Zoraster, the most ancient of philosophers, called one of them Oromases, or Oromasdes, the other Ari-manius, between whom was Mithras; the Persians also refer to Mithras as the mediator. He is also known as a threefold entity such as power, wisdom and kindness, or heat, light and influence, coming together as reason. The Persians kept a perpetual sacred fire going in honour of Mithras as did the Vestal Virgins amongst the Romans. Just as the Sun was the image of God, so fire was the image of the Sun, and there were priests known as *Pyrathoi* who hourly sang a choral song before the fire, holding verbena-branches in their hands. They covered their lips with veils hanging from their turbans and tied to their jaws with ribbons, which Strabo said appear in the shrines of Anaitidos, where later the fire, which was previously the symbol of the Moon, becomes the symbol of the Sun. The Persians sacrifice a pedigree white horse, which was also done amongst the Massagetae, as Herodotus relates (Bk. I). Xenophon, in his *Anabasis*, says that human beings were burnt and sacrificed to the Sun, but he is less than certain about it. There was also a gemstone known as Mithrax, rivalling the Sun in colour, which is found in Persia. As well, there are the Manichaean patriarchs,[39] whom Augustine says worship the Sun as an intermediary between the principles of good and evil: "You praise the Sun as it completes its orbit,"[40] and "It is acceptable to your vanity to attribute the virtue of your child to the Sun and wisdom to its light,"[41] words which illustrate the superiority allocated to the Sun. Whether this would have been a symbolic cult or a divine one is uncertain. Indeed, I am inclined to agree with the most learned Vossius that the Manichaeans, like [other] pagans, transformed this symbolic cult into worship of the Supreme God. It could hardly be granted that so eminently important a part of Nature, the sum of everything in the system, could be set up as a cult, and worshipped as supreme, in ignorance that its framer was a demiurge. The Sun was, therefore, excellent as an emblem of the Supreme God, but they paid a superior form of worship to the unknown divinity as

---

[39]They were the followers of Manes (c. 215–75), a Persian mystic who taught that there were two ultimate realities, Good and Evil, or Light and Darkness. The teachings of Manes were frequently attacked by Augustine.

[40]Augustine, *Contra Faustum*, Bk. XX, Ch. 5 [Herbert's note].

[41][Herbert's marginal note]: Aug[ustine], *L[iber] adversus Manich[aos]*.

being much greater. How widespread this cult of the principles of good and evil was we will discuss later.

And truly Adam, by his fall, became the fountain of all evil, indeed, I may say, the bubbling spring of it. In another place we will examine the Serpent, who is the symbol of the Devil. Certainly, all Christian theologians unanimously ask for the guidance of the Saviour of mankind on the question, and they take those matters into which we are enquiring for the truth, as evil. It is not said in vain that evil may be concealed from what is right, but will be brought to light by God's justice and the guilty criminal will suffer [divine] vengeance; human judgment, tending as it does towards sin, I say plainly, may do evil, but the worst actions result not from original sin in itself, but in many instances come from a misunderstanding of God's Providence.[42]

Amongst the Ethiopians the cult of the Sun is known as that of Assabinus, who in Ethiopian is the Jupiter of the Greeks and Romans. Neither is it a problem, as Vossius thinks, whether in the East and in some parts of Africa, neither Jupiter nor Uranus are exactly the same as Caelius, but the Sun is. Here also cinnamon is sacred in the ancestral rites, about which arts, the false customs and fraudulent inventions of the priests, you may read in Theophrastus (IX, 5), Pliny (XII, 19) and Solinus (Ch. 31).[43]

In Cyrene,[44] particularly in Marmarica, which is called "the sacred land of God" by Diodorus Siculus (Bk. XVII)[45] and in the land of the Ammonites, there was a temple of Amon, who is worshipped as Jupiter amongst the pagans of Libya, and who is known to them as the Western sun-god (Macrobius I, 21).[46] The Libyans think that Amon is the Western sun-god. There is

---

[42] This rather obscure passage does not appear in Lewis, and it is quite easy to see why. It is one of the few times that Herbert mentions Christ, and he does not assign to Christ any particular divine assets. Furthermore, Herbert suggests that original sin is not at the heart of the evil that mankind experiences, an idea which is in direct contradiction to Augustinian theology. Man, Herbert suggests here, often errs when he judges his fellows, because he does not have a sufficient understanding of God's intentions. It may be assumed that this is a result not of Adam's transgression, which Herbert almost mockingly characterises as the "fountain" (fons) and the "bubbling stream" (scaturigo) of sin, but of priestly distortion of God's revelations, if indeed they were revelations at all. The passage seems to be rather digressive in nature; Herbert rather suddenly pulls back and gets into his comparative studies again.

[43] These citations are Herbert's own notes.

[44] A port to the north of Great Syrtis, founded by Thereans and Cretans in about 630 B.C. (*OED* 249).

[45] Herbert's note.

[46] Herbert's note.

another temple to Amon in Meroe, on an island in the Nile, but it is inferior to the other one. This god is depicted as having the horns of a ram, by reason of which, so Macrobius tells us, that animal is as powerful as the Sun's rays. Others wish to turn the twisting and bending of the ram's horns into a sign, a doubtful and involved communication from Amon, which, in order that they might understand its obscurity, they credited in antiquity as being the truth. Amongst the Ethiopians there was the table of the Sun, for which see Herodotus on Thalia. Also in what manner the Ethiopians performed the sacred rites of the Sun and of Memnon, whose statue spoke just when the Sun's light covered its eyes, you may read about in Philostratus's *Life of Apollonius* (Ch. 3).[47] The Carthaginians, too, who arose from a colony of the Phoenicians, worshipped the Sun, and, as Servius establishes from a reference in Ennius, "It was the custom to sacrifice young girls to their gods." And Piscennius Festus repeats that the Carthaginians habitually sacrificed their male enemies to Saturn.[48] When they were defeated by Agathocles, king of Sicily, they thought that their god was angry, and therefore, as a serious method of expiation, they sacrificed two hundred of their noblest male children.[49] I have now shown that Saturn was superior to the Sun. Other authors also confirm this, from whom it is clear that this truly impious and barbarous custom, which Tiberius permitted in Gaul and in Africa, spread to a large area of the world.[50]

That will be enough about the names and the cults of the Sun amongst oriental peoples. However, I do not deny that some amongst them may make sense in another way, if Mela may be believed, who says that the Atlantes, an African people, cursed the Sun, the plague of their fields, both as it rose and as it set. But what could the priests not do, whether by superstition or by cunning? It is certain that the Sun, entering Aries, raises up poisonous

---

[47] Herbert's textual note.

Memnon was a mythical Ethiopian king who went to Troy to assist Priam, his uncle. He was killed by Achilles, but Zeus made him immortal. The statue to which Herbert refers is the so-called "colossus of Memnon," which is actually a huge statue of Amenhotep III, and it stood in front of a temple to Isis. When it was restored, it ceased to sing.

[48] [Herbert's marginal note]: Lac[tantius], Bk. I, Ch. 31. Source of citation from Piscennius Festus.

[49] Agathocles (361–289 B.C.) reigned as tyrant of Syracuse from 317–289, and proclaimed himself king of the eastern part of Sicily in 304. He was engaged in a war with Carthage for a good part of his reign; his near-capture of the city occurred in 310.

[50] [Herbert's marginal note]: Tertul[lian] in *Apolog[ia]*.

vapours in Africa, but it consumes these when it proceeds to Leo, so much so that afterwards the deadly plague lingering amongst the Africans, by which thousands of people have perished, leaves off altogether, and after a time the infection is extinguished.

The Greeks and Romans worshipped the Sun under a number of names, but especially as Apollo, of whom more later. Macrobius is quite right when he says that "the names of the gods signify their several virtues," for there are a great number of names in the various nations, as this author demonstrates. Plato tells us in his *Cratylus* that the first is Phoebus, which signifies splendour, and then the name Apollo itself, which is the Sun. Thus Cicero: "The name of Apollo too is Greek, and he is identified with the Sun, just as Diana is identified with the Moon."[51] See also [the Emperor] Julian's *Hymn to the Sun*. The Emperor Heliogabalus, himself known in Syria as the Priest of the Sun, built a temple on the Palatine Hill in Rome, to which he ordered carried the image of the Great Mother, the Vestal Fire, the Palladium, the Ancile[52] and all the sacred objects of Rome, as well as those of the Jewish and Samaritan religions. He undertook to convert to Christianity so that all secret cults could be controlled by the priesthood of Heliogabalus. Antoninus Varius built a temple to the Sun in Rome, called the Apollinaria, and one to the Moon called the Delia, for whose rites you may refer to Proclus in his *Chrestomathia apud Photium*, in the following place:

> They crowned the wood with laurels, and ornamented it with various flowers, on top of which copper spheres were placed, from which smaller ones hung. In the middle of the wood they arranged a purple crown, and smaller crowns also, which from the top were placed as a final touch. All around were clothed in saffron robes. The higher one stood for the sphere of the Sun, which they called Apollo; the lower was the sphere of the Moon, and the small globes the stars.

There were solemn games instituted in Apollo's honour, known as the Apollinares,[53] which Cicero mentions in his *Philippics*. There is a great deal more which could be said about the mystic cult of the Sun, but it will be explained at a more opportune time where Apollo is discussed in relation to the Sun. It will be collected from the most ancient authorities as well as from the most universal, and you will also find information about modern-day Indians.

---

[51]Cicero, *NG* II, 68 [151].

[52]The Ancile (Herbert has *ancilia*) was a shield which was supposed to have fallen from heaven during the reign of Numa Pompilius, and its preservation was linked to that of Rome.

[53]The games took place on July 5, and were more accurately known as the *ludi Apollinaris*.

As to the books of Apollo preserved in the Capitol, which were consulted by the priests in times of emergency, or at least were seen to be consulted, and prophecies and predictions of the future taken from them, or revealed, they are not part of the present discussion, and it will be more proper to discuss the sacred books of antiquity in another place.

V

The Names of the Planets
and their Relation to the Sun

Knowledge of the Planets amongst the pagans was not very ancient, and we have already indicated that some of their names were subsumed by the Sun. The first was Saturn, whose name, as we showed with evidence from Servius, Damascius and others, agrees with the Sun; the slow movement of this planet was unknown at that time. Macrobius, citing Homer, and Cornificius[1] prove that Jupiter is the Sun, as does Philo Byblius[2] citing Sanchoniathon from Eusebius:

> they believed this god to be the only governor of Heaven, and they called him
> *Baalsamin*, which in Phoenician means "Lord of Heaven" and is Zeus in Greek.

However, the Sun was not worshipped as the Supreme God, only as His representative, so that it came to be worshipped symbolically under these names, and, as we have noted, the diversity of its virtues led to its being given several names at different times and in different places.

Amongst the more ancient pagan theologians Mars was one of the Sun's names, particularly Mars *Silvanus*,[3] as Cato calls him. This might derive from silva, wood or quantity, or from hyle, the material from which elements are made, such as base fire, air, earth and water. This is explained by Macrobius:

---

[1]Herbert is probably citing Lucius Cornificius (fl. 50–10 B.C.), the author of *Rhetorica ad Herennium* and the *Etyna*, a work often quoted by Macrobius. Smith states that he is "rather worse than the usual wretched authorities of the ancients" (I, 858). There was also a Quintus Cornificius (c. 82–42 B.C.), a rhetorician turned soldier who has also been credited with writing the *Rhetorica*.

[2]Philo[n] Byblius (c. 47–after 120), the grammarian, was the translator of Sanchuniathon. He is cited from Eusebius by way of Porphyry, and may be identified with the Philon Herennius Byblius mentioned by Suidas as the author of a work on cities and their famous men. He also wrote on rhetoric and Jewish history.

[3]Mars Sylvanus [more properly Silvanus]. Herbert seems to be correct. Silvanus was a Latin god of woods and groves, and there were also lesser gods called Silvani. Mars's sister was known as *silvarum dea*, the goddess of the woods, and there is no reason why Mars himself should not have had a slightly less aggressive incarnation as Lord of the Woods.

The attributes with which Pan (or Inuus as he is called) is represented enable those who are the better endowed with understanding to perceive that he is the sun. The Arcadians in their worship of him call him "the Lord of the *Hyle*," meaning to indicate, not that he is the lord of the forest but ruler of all material substance . . .[4]

The glosses of Philoxenus[5] and Papias[6] make Silvanus the same as Pan, and there is more on this in Vossius, but it seems to be more far-fetched when he equates Mars Sylvanus to Pan than when he reduces Pan to the Sun. What similarity could there be between Mars, the god of war, and [Pan], the common sustainer of all things? My opinion is that Silvanus (the epithet given Mars by Cato) refers simply to a wood full of trees, because when their god was angry, people were afraid that savage wolves, always lying in wait, would devour their flocks. Thus Horace writes "lest the martial wolves the flocks [devour]," and Cato, in the work cited above, advises people to sacrifice an ox to Mars Silvanus. Cato, who was a very pious man, believed that Mars, the war god, had command over even the wild beasts in the wood, and he advises people to offer sacrifices and prayers to Mars under this name. From all of this, we have good reason to conclude that the learned Vossius has not sufficiently proved that Mars was once a name for the Sun.

Vossius also says that Mercury, called *Stilbon* by Cicero,[7] *Cyllenius Ignis* by Vergil,[8] and *Communis Stellis* by Apuleius, was the Sun, but this does not seem correct to me, either.[9] What he alleges as proof agrees either with the

---

[4]Macrobius I, 22 (Davies 147). Dionysius calls Pan "the most ancient and the most honoured of all the gods" to the Arcadians (I, 32, 5).

[5]Philoxenus of Alexandria (dates uncertain) was an Athenian grammarian who taught in Rome and wrote a commentary on Homer. His *Glossary* was published in 1573 by Henri Estienne.

[6]Papias (d. ?163 A.D.) was an authority on ancient Christian traditions. St. Jerome said that as a young man Papias had known the apostle John. Papias also wrote *Explanationum sermonum domini*, a work dealing with the spoken words of Christ.

[7]The name Stilbon means "the shining one" or "the brilliant one." Cyllenius derives from Mount Cyllene, in North-eastern Arcadia, where Mercury was born. There does not seem to be any connexion between Mercury and the Sun, apart from the name Stilbon being applicable to both.

[8]This name, translated as "the fire of Cyllene," refers to Mt. Cyllene, the traditional site of Hermes's birth. The *Fourth Homeric Hymn to Hermes* refers to Hermes as "lord of Cyllene and Arcadia rich in flocks" (Morford & Lenardon 179).

[9]Vossius also adds that Mercury was known as Seches by the Babylonians. He derives the name from the verb *silbein*, following Hesychius (Vossius II, xxii, 470–71).

name of the star, or with some men that had the same name; I will not deny, however, that Mercury was somehow connected with the Sun by a kind of symbolic virtue. Curious seekers of nature's secrets had a great respect for the power of this star, and believed that [Mercury] listened readily to men's prayers; it was believed that he was allied not only to other stars but to people as well, especially concerning things that related to study or politics. The ancients believed that one man was wiser than another according to [Mercury's] influence.

The greatest venerator of Mercury amongst the ancient philosophers that I have read about was the Emperor Julian, for as he believed the Sun to be the supreme god, so he understood Mercury as the chief minister, companion and dispenser of benefits. As Ammianus Marcellinus writes:

> Julian always arose at night and secretly prayed to Mercury, whom theological doctrines say is the swiftest sense of the world. Afterwards he settled himself down to study, and it is incredible with what wisdom he investigated knowledge of the most important things; having acquired, as it were, more than ordinary help, he ascended to the sublime, and successfully learned the most abstruse parts of philosophy.

It was believed that Mercury was in charge of souls after this life, but because those mystical things related about the star are confused by the ancients with historical or mythical facts about other Mercuries, we cannot say anything for certain about their secret observations. The Magi[10] believed his power to be very great, that it could make things good or evil, and that it could redouble its influence. It has been amusingly observed, "what can a bad companion not do, when a malignant star can make someone wicked?" but this is beside the point. Let me only note that Saturn and Jupiter signify the Sun and Universal Nature; I do not think that Mars and Mercury did the same, unless I can find more convincing arguments than the ones which have already been presented. So much for the names and worship of the Sun amongst the ancients; what names it had in common with men who were deified I will discuss later.

---

[10]The Magi. This term is not reserved only for the Three Wise Men of Bethlehem, but applied to all Persian or Egyptian sages. Their task was to interpret dreams and to show the symbolic and allegorical meanings of sacred objects.

VI

The Worship of the Moon, and its Various Names

The Moon comes next after the Sun, as it supposedly governed the moist generative principle in the same way that the Sun does the warm one. Pliny calls the Moon "the Earth's most familiar star, designed by nature as a remedy for darkness." Its influence was considered most effective, because by reason of its proximity it seemed to exert more force upon Earth and Water than any other star. I will not say anything about the size, distance [from the Earth], or phases of this planet, as this information can be found elsewhere; I will note, however, that the most distinguished philosophers believed that as well as being a planet it was a kind of earth. Orpheus writes: "He built another infinite Earth, called Selene/ By the immortals, Meene by men / It contains many mountains, cities and houses." Thales, Pythagoras, Anaxagoras, Heracleides,[1] and Ocellus[2] follow this opinion as well.

It is very apparent that [the Moon's] surface is rough and uneven, even to those that observe it without a telescope; the great Author of Things arranged it that way so that it would dispense more light everywhere upon this inferior globe. If it were smooth and completely even, it could only reflect the Sun's rays from one point or part; Galileo has demonstrated this by hanging a mirror against a smooth wall on which the sun is shining. If it were round, such a bright light would not be cast, for flat mirrors show the sun to us much less than others. The surfaces of the Moon and Earth,

---

[1]Heracleides [Heraclides] of Pontus (c. 390–310 B.C.), a philosopher, also wrote Homeric commentaries. Homer had said some uncomplimentary things about the gods, and writers such as Heracleides felt that they should not be taken literally, but allegorically or symbolically. There were "literal" meanings and "deep" meanings, the latter being more truthful than the former. The eminent Greek scholar Leo Allatius (1586–1669) edited Heracleides's treatise, *De incredibilibus* (1641). His printer set the author's name as "Heraclitus," but Allatius's identification of Heracleides as responsible for the work is borne out by modern scholarship. Herbert prints "Heraclitus," following Allatius.

[2]Ocellus of Lucania (5th century B.C.) was the probable author of a treatise entitled *On the Whole*, in which he said that both man and the cosmos were eternal, that is, they did not "come into being" (Freeman 81).

therefore, were made rough and uneven so that they might diffuse more light and be mutually useful to one another, lighting each other reciprocally when the sun is absent. The influence of [the Moon] is very great upon the sea and all moist things, and its effects on the brain, that citadel of the soul, can be very strange, so that people who are out of their minds are called "lunatics," see Matthew 4:24. In Matthew 17:15 there is a person called "lunatic" who is described in Luke 9:39 as "demoniac," while in Mark 9:17 and 25 he is called "dumb and deaf."[3]

As the Sun was called *Baal* or *Moloch*, Lord or King,[4] in the East, from where religion originates, so the Moon is *Baaltis*,[5] or Queen of Heaven. Poets, in particular Aeschylus and Euripides, made her the daughter of Jupiter. Amongst the orientals and Africans she was called *Urania*, the Celestial, and Luna in the vernacular which the Romans derived from the Greeks. On a coin of Julia Symiamira,[6] who was the Syrian mother of [the Emperor] Heliogabalus, the phrase "Celestial Goddess" appears. At first she was worshipped under the name of Celestial Venus by the Assyrians, as Pausanias[7] tells us, and he also mentions that the Phoenicians and Greeks received that name from them. Vossius has sufficiently proved that the Moon was called Celestial Venus, and you may refer to him. The name of the Moon

---

[3]These are the Biblical references: "those which were lunatick" (Matt. 4:24); "Lord, have mercy on my son, for his is lunatick" (Matt. 17:15); the Luke 9:39 reference is not quite accurate; the son here "foameth;" Mark 9:17 "my son, which hath a dumb spirit," and "deaf and dumb spirit" (Mark 9:25).

[4]Cf. Milton, *Paradise Lost*, "First *Moloch*, horrid King besmear'd with blood/ Of human sacrifice and parents' tears" (I, 392–93). Milton was using the same source as Herbert, namely Selden's *De diis Syris*.

[5]There is a Baaltak worshipped in Palmyra, as well as Belti; the latter is identified by Teixidor with Allat (116 n. 44).

[6]Julia Symiamira [Julia Soaemias Bassiana] (d. 222) was from Emesa in Syria. She claimed that her son Elagabalus had been fathered by the emperor Caracalla (d. 217); this allowed her to prevail over the emperor Macrinus (217–18) and gain even more power during her son's reign. She was probably a priestess of the Sun, and therefore directly responsible for introducing the rites of the Sun to Rome.

[7]Pausanias (fl. 150 A.D.) was a Greek historian and travel writer. His *Guide to Greece* (Peter Levi, tr. Harmondsworth: Penguin Books, 1971; rep. 1986) was the result of nearly 20 years' travelling in Greece during and after the reign of Hadrian (117–38). His account covers the history of nearly every temple and city, providing a wealth of information on local customs, beliefs, and religions. The Greek text was printed in Venice (1516), and a Latin translation was issued in Basel (1550).

amongst the Assyrians was also *Astarte*,[8] and her image, like that of Isis, had cow's horns, symbolising the horns of the Moon. For the Jews, Astarte was *Ashtoroth*, and Solomon is said to have built a temple for Ashtoreth, the idol of the Sidonians.[9] In the Septuagint the name appears as Astarte. Her body was either all fish, or part human, part fish. If Baaltis is the Moon in Dio Cassius,[10] as she appears to be in Sanchoniathon, Baaltis, contracted to *Beltis*, must mean "Lord."[11] The prophet Jeremiah, according to Jerome's interpretation, calls her Queen of Heaven (7:18; 44:17–19, 25).[12] According to Cicero, there was a Syrian Venus called Astarte, married to Adonis,[13] and it is she, very probably, whom Aelius Lampridius[14] calls *Salambo*. The word *salazein* in Anacreon[15] means "to mourn," and this was the most important part of the sacred rite of Adonis. I cannot easily believe that this Astarte was the Moon, but rather some woman of that name, whom Cicero, in the passage just cited, calls "the fourth Venus," and here I must again beg to disagree with Vossius. The Syrian goddess, or Juno Assyria, worshipped at Hieropolis, may also be the Moon, as may Atergatis and *Derceto*, of whom

---

[8]Herbert is wrong. Astarte "was never a Moon goddess, even though late Hellenistic syncretist ideas presented her as such" (Teixidor 36). The sources which Vossius and Herbert used are Pausanias and Lucian.

[9]Cf. Milton, "On the Morning of Christ's Nativity": "And mooned *Ashtoroth/* Heav'n's Queen and Mother bothe" (199–200). Herbert cites II Kings 23:13, which reads: "And the high places that were before Jerusalem, which were on the right hand of corruption, which Solomon the king of Israel had builded for Ashtoreth, the abomination of the Zidonians . . . did the king [Josiah] defile."

[10]Cassius Dio Cocceianus (fl. 193–after 229) was a Roman politician and minister of the Emperor Alexander Severus, with whom he held the consulship in 227 and 229. He wrote a *History of Rome* from ancient times until 229.

[11]The word probably means "Lady" rather than "Lord" (Teixidor 37).

[12]Biblical references are as follows: "make cakes for the queen of heaven" (Jer. 7:18 [Herbert has 16]); "burn incense unto the queen of heaven" (Jer. 44:17–19); "burn incense . . . . and pour out drink offerings unto her" (44:25).

[13]Cicero, *NG* III, 57–59 (217).

[14]Aelius Lampridius [Spartianus] (3rd century A.D.) was another compiler of the *Historia Augustae*. His section covers the period from Hadrian (117–38) to Alexander Severus (222–35).

[15]Anacreon (b. c. 570 B.C.), the elegant and tasteful Greek lyric poet who celebrated the pleasures of life in his verse. He was also the author of hymns to various deities, such as Artemis, Dionysus and Eros. Herbert is quite correct about his usage of *salazein*.

more later when we discuss Earth-worship. The same name very often, if not always, signifies the Moon and the Earth.

Amongst the Babylonians and Assyrians there was *Mylitta*,[16] whom Herodotus, in his first book, counts as a goddess; Vossius takes her to be Venus Urania, and subsequently the Moon. That goddess, however, was not Venus Urania, but another, called, according to Herodotus, *Aphrodite*. Cicero says that there were four Venuses: this one sprang from the foam of the sea and so was named Aphrodite. She had, by Mercury, Cupid, her second son. In my opinion she was not the Moon, but some lascivious woman whom the Greeks had deified, as Flora had been amongst the Romans. The religious rites mentioned by Cicero and Valerius Maximus[17] connected with religious worship are sufficient demonstration of her lewdness. Mylitta, then, was no celestial being, but a mere animal deity, whose temple was known as *Succoth Benoth*,[18] meaning "tabernacle of the daughters," where women went to meet their lovers and which the Babylonians erected when they had driven the Israelites out of Samaria.[19] As Selden[20] tells us, Benoth is derived from Venus, or the other way around. Neither is *Nebo*[21] one of the

---

[16]Mylitta was a Babylonian goddess, as Herodotus correctly testifies, and she may have been connected with Ishtar. The story about the temple prostitution is correct, as Mylitta may have been a goddess of childbirth.

[17]Valerius Maximus (fl. 14–37 A.D.) wrote *De factis dictisque memorabilibus*, a work in 20 books, the first part of which deals with the rites and prodigies connected with oracles and religious worship.

[18]The information provided by Herbert is mostly accurate. The Succoth-Benoth was an object made by Babylonian exiles in Samaria after Shalmaneser V had captured the city (722 B.C.), and the name does mean "booths of the daughters" in the Masoritic texts (see Chapter III n. 30). The place where it was venerated *may* have been connected with ritual prostitution, but it may also simply have been a place where female images were carried. Benitu is another name for Ishtar (*IBD* III, 1490).

[19]See II Kings 17:30: "And the men of Babylon made Succoth-benoth, and the men of Cuth made Nergal, and the men of Hamath made Ashima." (Herbert's note).

[20]John Selden (1584–1654), lawyer and scholar, was a close personal friend of Herbert's and the executor of his will. His chief work in the field of religion was *De diis Syris* (1617), an extensive study of the religions of the ancient Near and Middle East. His work had considerable influence on that of Vossius (see Introduction). Selden made an important collection of Oriental MSS and also worked on rabbinical law. Other works of Selden's deserving of note are *De jure naturali* (1640) and the *Table Talk* (1689), collected by his secretary Richard Milward.

[21]Jerome is close. The Babylonian god *Nabu* (Nebo) was the son of Marduk-Bel. The name Nabu is Sumerian. There was a temple to Nabu at Hermopolis.

names of the Moon, but of the Sun, if we may rely on Jerome's authority; he thinks that Nebo is the same god as Chamos and Belphegor, whom we have already discussed. What is certain is that the Sun and Moon were the chief deities of the Babylonians and Assyrians, although they were worshipped under other names, the most important being Venus Urania. Herodotus says that she had a very ancient temple which was destroyed by the Scythians. It is not known whether *Anitis* or *Anaitidos*[22] were names for the Moon, although Plutarch seems to think so. Strabo tells us that the Armenians, as well as the Medes and Persians, had a law that virgins should prostitute themselves for some period of time to Anaitidos, and afterwards no-one refused to marry them.

This obscene invention of the priests or priestesses also existed elsewhere, as Herodotus says, for such degraded creatures would unfortunately devote themselves to this rite, and continue as good "virgins" as they were before, for two or three years. Agathias[23] has some evidence to prove that Anaitidos was not Venus Urania, but the Aphrodite who, as we and Vossius say, mystically symbolised the star Luna. Strabo,[24] amongst others, tells us that this kind of worship was very popular amongst the Persians, Babylonians, Medes, Parthians and Armenians and that in Zelitica, an Armenian province which takes its name from the city of Zela,[25] the kings did not keep court in palaces, but in the temples of the Persian gods. The kings, then, were themselves priests, and in all likelihood they handed over to men the virgins dedicated to Venus, which custom, according to Garcilasso de la Vega, is still observed amongst the Peruvians. Vossius has more information about the rites of Anaitidos and their correspondence with the Saturnalia.

The Arabians, imitating the Eastern people, also worshipped the Moon; although religious worship in the East had many names, it was essentially the same, for the Sun, Moon and Stars were everywhere venerated. I question very much whether the Arabians worshipped the Moon under the name

---

[22]These names are actually alternative names for Anthat, the goddess of love and the lover of Baal. The name is Ugaritic, but there is a better-known Zoroastrian version, Anahita, who was a river-goddess and an associate of Mithras. Anahita was the Mother-Goddess of Armenia.

[23]Agathias (c. 537–82), a Greek lawyer and rhetorician, wrote the *Myrensis historiarum*, an "honest and impartial" (Smith I, 63) account of the years 553–58, particularly concerning itself with the Persian Wars under Narses. Agathias is a detailed and learned writer, but rather vague in some of his historical generalisations.

[24]Book XII (Herbert's note).

[25]Zela is in Pontus, and it did have a large Persian temple, whose priests ruled the city until about 64 A.D.

Altitat,[26] as Vossius seems to think, because Venus Urania, which he says is the Moon, seems to me rather to be the Morning or Evening Star. This can be seen in a passage from Herodotus which Vossius himself quotes:

> They sacrifice to the Sun, Moon, Earth, Fire, Water and Wind as the first objects of adoration, and then they learned from the Assyrians and Arabians to sacrifice to Urania. The Assyrians call Venus Mylitta, the Arabians Alitta, the Persians Mithras.

Nothing is more obvious than that the word *selene* means the Moon, and that the Mylitta of the Assyrians and the Alitta of the Arabians was the same as Venus Urania. Therefore they saw Venus and the Moon as separate deities, although Vossius insists that Urania is only the Moon, in spite of being taken for both. Perhaps he thought that this star was so well-known that it would merit worship, but, by his leave, what star is brighter or more splendid than Venus in her opposition to the Sun? I am sure, therefore, that the Moon was worshipped in Arabia under this name, although not everywhere else; Urania is also Venus, and perhaps may also stand for Fortune, evidence of which may be found in Philastrius:[27] "There arose another heresy in Judaea, the worship of a Queen whom they call the Fortune of Heaven, and in Africa the Celestial." This cult I shall examine elsewhere.

What Vossius has to say about the Arabian deity *Ciun*[28] seems to me to be pertinent to Hesperus and the Moon. Amongst the Egyptians the Moon

---

[26]Altitat (Alitta) is probably one of the goddesses to whom the *Koran* refers in the so-called "Satanic Verses." Their Arabic names, according to modern notation, were Al-Lat, Al-Uzzah and Manat. N.J. Dawood notes that they represented, respectively, the Sun, Venus, and Fortune (Introduction to *The Koran* 9), which makes Herbert and Vossius both wrong, Al-Uzzah being Venus. The verse reads "Have you thought on Al-Lat, and Al-Uzzah, and, thirdly, on Manat?" (The Star 53:7). The worship of Al-Lat (Allat) was interchangeable with that of Astarte in Palmyra. The ancient Arabs worshipped Venus as a warrior-goddess, but Teixidor points out that identification of Allat and Venus is a problem, because "under Hellenistic influence, Allat became identical with Athena" (68). In Herodotus, Allat is Aphrodite Urania, or Astarte (3.8).

[27]Philastrius [Philaster] (fl. 375–90) was probably the Bishop of Brixia (modern Brescia) who wrote a work attacking various heresies. It was printed in Basel (1539) under the title of *Philaster*.

[28]More properly, Chiun. This goddess was worshipped in Egypt and was the equivalent of the Roman Venus. She is described in Amos 5:26, "But ye have borne the tabernacle of your Moloch and Chiun your images, the star of your god, which you made yourselves." Chiun stands on a lion, with two snakes in one hand, a flower in the other (Durdin-Robertson 54).

was worshipped also, and here she was known as Isis, as Diodorus Siculus tells us, and Plutarch as well; assuming this is correct, Isis sometimes stands for that moisture which is the principle of generation. Her statue had horns, representing those of the Moon, and her shoes were made from palm-fronds. In this way she is also described by the Greeks, and calves were the appropriate sacrifice for her, as sacrificing a cow would have been considered blasphemous. *Apis*, called *Epaphos* by the Greeks, was principally consecrated to her. Thus Ammianus Marcellinus writes:

> amongst those animals in former days that were sacrificed, *Mnevis* and Apis were the most noteworthy; Mnevis to the Sun, Apis to the Moon and so on. Apis is not merely an ox, but only one that has 29 particular marks on him.

It was said that he was born from lightning or from the brightness of the Moon, and that he delivered oracles; when he was dead they called him Serapis, but whether this is the same as the Hebrew Seraphim has not been established by Gesner.[29] Eusebius, quoting Dionysius, says that Isis may be rendered in Latin as Prisca, the Moon, as if she were always old, being known that way, and she is depicted with four horns. Of this Ovid remarks, "You can make a Bacchus just by adding horns." According to Diodorus Siculus, Bacchus had horns. Of his rites Apuleius has the following to say:

> As the priests of Bacchus ran up and down the streets and around town like fanatics in the celebration of his sacred mysteries, making a horrible noise with their cymbals and brass instruments, so at the Feast of Isis or the Syrian Goddess they slash their arms and rip their muscles with their teeth. They receive presents of brass and silver, those that brought them striving to outdo each other's generosity.

Pausanias tells us that the people of Mount Cithaeron[30] also worshipped Isis, and gave two fairs in her honour every year. It is likely that the Israelites worshipped the Golden Calf in an imitation of the Egyptians, for when the children of Israel begged Aaron to make them gods to go in front of them, because they did not know what had happened to Moses who had led them out of Egypt, Aaron asked them, "Which of you hath any gold?" When they

---

[29]Conrad Gesner [Gesnerus] (1516–65) was a Swiss scholar who held the Chair of Philosophy first at Basel and then at Zurich. He wrote mainly on medicine and biology, but also had an interest in theology and ancient philosophy. He wrote a commentary on Xenocrates (1559) [see Chapter 7], and relevant works include *Partitiones theologicae, pandectorum universalium liber ultimus* (1549) and *M. Antonii imperatoris Romani et philosophi De seipso* (1558).

[30]Mount Cithaeron is in Boeotia, but there is no mention of a temple to Isis being there (Pausanias I, 312).

gave him some, he threw it into a furnace and made a calf. I am not going to describe here what sort of adoration was paid to the ox in various parts of the East Indies, as it will be more logical to do this when I come to discuss their religion.

Amongst the Africans also there was a cult of the Moon. Herodotus says "the Africans in general make sacrifices to the Sun and Moon only." Amongst the Greeks there was also a cult of the Moon, her name there being Artemis, mentioned by the author of the Acts of Apostles, "Great is Artemis of the Ephesians."[31] The Romans had a cult of the Moon under the name of Diana, which may be a shortened version of *Dea* or *Diva Jana*. Vossius notes that as Janus was the Sun, so Jana was the Moon, but Janus is not always the same as the Sun, nor Diana the same as the Moon, for there was a [King] Janus who reigned in Italy before Saturn, and taught the people agriculture, for which he was later deified and paid divine honours. Diana and the Moon are not the same, as is evident from Dionysius of Halicarnassus: "Tatius[32] had tablets sacred to the Sun, Moon, Saturn, Rhea, Vesta, Vulcan, Diana, Quirinus and other deities." He placed those sacred to Juno *Quirita* in all the courts, where they remain to this very day. From this it seems certain that the Moon and Diana were separate goddesses, and so were Diana and Juno, both of whom Vossius would have as the Moon. Although each of these goddesses, through some kind of symbolic virtue, might seem to be properly joined to the Moon, I believe they were originally as distinct as those that were deified animals, afterwards made into gods or stars. I readily acknowledge that Diana and the Moon were originally worshipped as each other, but this is not the case everywhere with Juno, although Vossius has very plausible reasons for believing it. He says that *Eileithyia*[33] was the Moon, but Homer says there were many Eileithyias, who protected women in childbirth, so it is more likely that the name referred to Juno *Lucina*, who

---

[31] Herbert is taking a certain liberty here; the phrase is, of course, "Great is Diana of the Ephesians" (Acts 19:28). Herbert's self-styled disciple Charles Blount used this as a title for one of his deist works.

[32] Titus Tatius (6th century B.C.), King of the Sabines, captured the Capitol after the rape of the Sabine women by the Romans, and became, with Romulus, joint ruler of the Romans and Sabines. He was probably an historical figure; his entry in the *OCD* states that "there is evidence that he enlarged the city and established several cults" (880).

[33] The *OCD* (309) and Rose (166) identify this goddess with Juno Lucina of the Romans. The Greeks also used her name as a title for Hera as a childbirth goddess, but she had a widespread cult of her own as well. Rose notes (16) that she is sometimes said to be the sister of Ares.

took care of women who were in labour, and not to Diana. I do not deny that it may, according to various interpretations, seem to refer to Diana herself.

The names of ancient gods were very confused, being the same as those given to the Stars and the Moon, and when historians, poets or philosophers mentioned them, they all tried to make the different words of several countries fit their own senses. This is why those of their writings which have been handed down to us (some being understood literally, others mystically or symbolically, still others full of poetic license) have so complicated matters that it is very difficult for us now to make accurate versions of the truth. We may learn from Servius that *Ceres* was a name for the Moon, as he says in his commentary on [these lines from] Vergil's *Georgics* I: "You brightest lamps/ That lead the year's procession across the sky;/ Liber and nurturing Ceres. . . .[34]

The Stoics say that there is only one God, one and the same power, to which we give different names according to the diversity of its functions. They call Sol either Bacchus or Apollo, and Luna they name Ceres, Juno, or Proserpina. But Servius is alone in his opinion that Juno was a name for the Moon, except for Apuleius, who incorrectly makes Diana, Juno, Venus and Bellona the same. The ancients thought them separate genealogically and historically, and also their ornaments, age, habits, images, temples, methods of worship sufficiently prove this, so it is unnecessary to insist further on it. Now, while in some ways these two goddesses may seem the same, for it was believed they had equal powers, ancient history shows us that their religious rites and so forth were so vastly different that I cannot see any pretext at all for identifying them with the Moon. This is even more evident when we consider that the ancients mixed the attributes of most of their deities, so that Isis is sometimes the Moon, sometimes the passive nature of things; Rhea and Ops are sometimes Diana, at others the Earth. Ovid has this to say about Rhea or Ops, also called the Mother of the Gods: "Before the Mother Goddess a piper sounds a bent horn; / When he plays, who would deny a small offering? /We know that no sum comes from Diana's command, /And yet her prophet has plenty to live on."

In Pausanias we find that *Suada*[35] is a name for Diana, and Venus, on account of some symbolic attribute, is sometimes taken for the Moon, but it was impossible that she could be called Juno, because Venus (an animal deity) was believed to be protectress of prostitutes, and Juno was their sworn enemy. Thus in [King] Numa's law it says "Do not let a prostitute approach Juno's temple; if she does, she must, with her hair hanging loose, sacrifice

---

[34]Vergil, *Georgics* I, 5–7 (Wilkinson 57).

[35]I do not find the name Suada for Artemis (Diana) in either volume of Pausanias.

a female lamb."[36] Macrobius says that the word Venus was of late origin amongst the Romans, and Varro agrees, stating that even in the time of the Roman kings it was neither Greek nor Latin. Selden confirms this, deriving Venus from the Hebrew word *Benet*,[37] the story of that celebrated prostitute, together with her most obscene rites, coming from the East.

Under Romulus and Numa the ancient Romans did not believe in any of the Greek animal gods, nor in any of their myths about gods conversing with mortals, as can be seen from Dionysius of Halicarnassus. *Proserpina* or *Persephone* mystically signifies the Moon, but only when she is under our hemisphere; Orpheus, at the beginning of his hymns, invokes the goddess in this way: "Protectress of time, ancestress of light, / Most beautiful, splendid and horned," and then, "the most honourable wife of Pluto / Celebrated giver of life," which is to be interpreted either mystically or historically. Other authors say that she was Pluto's wife, but they are ambiguous, sometimes worshipping a person under the name of a star, or vice versa.

Persephone and Ceres were believed to preside over the *Manes*[38] or shades, which are souls departed from their bodies. Both Theocritus and Porphyry say that Proserpina was also known as *Meletode*. The theologians often referred to souls as melissi (bees), because of the sweet pleasure they enjoy once freed from the body. Porphyry says that the Moon is Queen of Procreation, and used to be called Apis, and bees that were produced from oxen were called *bugeni*, which name is also given to souls going forth to regeneration.[39] Not all such souls were called bees, but only those which had led just lives here, and could return again after they had done the bidding of the gods; the little bee is an insect that usually returns whence it came,

---

[36]Numa Pompilius was the second King of Rome, the traditional dates of his reign set at 715–673 B.C. Probably an historical figure, Numa is said to have established the College of Priests. For further information on Numa and the cult which was established in his name, see M. Grant, *Roman Myth* 134–41.

[37]The Hebrew word *benet* means "daughters." Selden (or Herbert) is simply following the rule that "v" can be substituted for "b."

[38]Their name derives from an old Latin adjective *manus*, meaning "good." Cicero notes that the dead used to be considered a kind of collective divinity and that they were worshipped as deities. The word *Manes* also applied to the gods of the Underworld and to deified ancestors (*OCD* 533). From the 1st century B.C. onwards, epitaphs would often begin "Dis manibus sacrum" ("sacred to the Manes of") followed by the person's name.

[39]Bees produced from oxen. Herbert is probably referring to the passage in Vergil, *Georgics* IV, 294–314, where the poet describes how bees can be produced from the carcass of a bullock:

and it is an example of justice and temperance, therefore solemn sacrifices were performed with honey.

The Moon when she illuminates those under her is called *Libera*, as the Sun is Liber; this is mentioned by Livy, Tacitus and Macrobius. Hecate is also the Moon, properly called Triodis, or Three Ways; hence Varro calls Diana Trivia, because in Greek cities she was placed where three roads met. The Scholiast on Aristophanes says "they used to worship Hecate in places where three roads, called the Moon, Diana and Hecate, met." A lavish feast was provided for her, and it was set down purposely in a place where three roads met, so that the poor could carry it away. The rites did not involve any howling, like others did, but there were hymns and songs performed by respectable women, as Servius tells us in his commentary on Book IV of the *Aeneid*. As Hecate had three faces, so her dog Cerberus had three heads; as Tibullus[40] says "[Cerberus], who has three tongues and as many heads." The head on the right is a horse's, that in the centre a fierce man's, and that on the left a dog's. Hesiod says that he has fifty heads, and Horace, in his second Ode, calls him the beast with a hundred heads.

This is enough about the various names of the Sun and Moon amongst the pagans; it is evident that a great variety of names derived partly from the great diversity of attributes found in the two great lights beyond that which could be seen in other stars, and partly from human beings who were turned into stars. Stars, at the same time, were worshipped as humans, and humans as stars, so that all those ancient heroes and heroines, either by their own merit, or the credulity of common people, had some particular heaven or star assigned to them. This is why the Sun, Moon and Stars had so many different names, but the Sun and the Moon had more. Thus Diodorus Siculus says,

> when the first people contemplated with admiring astonishment the world above them and universal nature, they believed that the gods were eternal. They especially believed it of the Sun and Moon, calling the first Osiris, the second Isis. . . .

Meanwhile the moisture in those softened bones
Warms and ferments, and little animals,
An amazing sight, first limbless, then with wings
Whirring, begin to swarm, then gradually try
The thin air. . . .   (L.P. Wilkinson, tr., 134)

[40] Albius Tibullus (c. 60–19 B.C.), Roman elegiac poet, was celebrated for his restrained, elegant and tender poems about love, peace, and the charms of country life. A modern translation by Philip Dunlop (Harmondsworth: Penguin Books, 1972) includes the *Tibullan Collection*, poems written by Tibullus's contemporaries and included with his works.

VII

The Cult of the Five Planets

Other stars and planets, not simply the Sun and Moon, were once honoured and worshipped, some being more prominent than others. From Plato's *Cratylus* we know that stars in general were worshipped, and he shows what the oldest universal religion was: "I suspect that the sun, moon, stars, and heaven, which are still the gods of many barbarians, were the only gods known to the aboriginal Hellenes."[1] Plato also states in the *Timaeus* and *The Laws* that the world is divine, and so are the Heavens, Stars, Earth and Souls.[2] Xenocrates[3] says that the Planets, Fixed Stars, Sun, and Moon are divine, and so do many distinguished philosophers, which we can see from evidence in ancient authors, especially the Stoics, who said that a star was a divine body made up of Aether, by which was to be understood Jupiter, as Ennius writes: "Behold a supreme brightness / The Jove whom all invoke." St. Augustine teaches that the stars were thought by the Stoics to be parts of Jupiter, and from them they derived not only life, but intelligence and wisdom too.[4] Philo terms them "purest minds," and "divinely beautiful images." Aristotle goes even further; he says that the stars, because they are composed of Aether, are always moving and growing, and they must therefore have souls, very quick senses, and extreme swiftness. He thought it was very absurd that the cause of animal generation should not itself have a soul, and several modern philosophers still hold this opinion.[5] Many very respectable Christian writers, whom Vossius lists, have also thought that the Stars were alive, in particular Aquinas;[6] he also notes some who were of the

---

[1] Plato, *Cratylus* 397d (Hamilton and Cairns 435).

[2] Plato, *Timaeus* 89–90 (Hamilton and Cairns 1208–10), and *Laws XII, 959b* (Hamilton and Cairns 1503).

[3] Xenocrates of Chalcedon (396–314 B.C.) was a Platonist philosopher. He succeeded Speusippus as head of the Athens academy. It is not clear from the context to which of his works Herbert is referring.

[4] Augustine, *City of God* X, 29 (416).

[5] Aristotle, *On the Heavens* II [*passim*] (McKeon 398–470).

[6] Aquinas is writing in support of Alexander of Aphrodisias against Averroes (Ibn Rushd), the Arabian philosopher. He concludes that "just as any heavenly body has from another its motion, so likewise from another does it hold existence"

opposite opinion; for example, a learned Jesuit [Adam Tanner][7] says in his dissertation on Aristotle's *On the Heavens* that if stars are alive, they may be worshipped with the same adoration as is paid to saints. Amongst people who, after this life, locate eternal happiness in Heaven and the stars, that which is above deserves greater praise than that which is below, and eternal objects more than transitory things.[8]

The old pagan philosophers and priests thought that it was very indecorous not to worship things from which they believed everyone originated, and where they believed (by divine permission), their souls would return. Thus, after the Sun and Moon, the other five Planets were worshipped and adored; the chief reason given by learned men may be found in Cicero's *On the Nature of the Gods*:

> The motion of those five stars which are falsely called erratics is very admirable; nothing which eternally progresses and returns in the same way could be called erratic. What is even more amazing about these stars is that sometimes they are hidden, and then re-appear, sometimes they precede each other and then follow; at times they move slowly, then quickly, then not at all. From their unequal motions come the great mathematical years, which occur when the Sun, Moon, and the five erratics, having gone on their courses, come back to their original places.[9]

Venus

After the Sun and Moon, the bright Morning and Evening Star had the next greatest adoration paid to it, as it was the most conspicuous of the five so-

---

(*Commentary on Physics*, VIII, lect. 21, 1154). Aquinas had noted earlier that "if we allow that a heavenly body is not composed of matter and form, it must be admitted, nevertheless, that potentiality for non-being is somehow within it" (1153). See Clark 67–69.

[7] Adam Tanner (1572–1632) was Professor of Theology at Ingolstadt and author of the *Theologica scholastica*. At what must have been considerable risk to himself, Tanner advocated liberty of conscience for "infidels" on the ground that since they were unchangeably ignorant of the true faith they could hardly be called heretics. Tanner also wrote powerfully against witch-burning, torture and indiscriminate executions, all of which beliefs must have struck a sympathetic chord with Herbert. The reference is also used by Vossius (II, xxx, 460).

[8] Compare the discussion here (and earlier) about the heavenly bodies with orthodox Catholic dogma. Cardinal Robert Bellarmine writes in *The Mind's Ascent to God* (1615) that "the sun's course shows God's greatness" (121) and that the sun "stands for God" (126), lending light to the moon. Taken all together, "the heavens through the moon and the stars provide us a step for climbing up to God" (125).

[9] Cicero, *DRG* II, 40–47 (McGregor 138–41).

called lictors to the Sun, or, as Homer says, "Hesperus is the most beautiful [star] in the aetherial orb." Amongst the Greeks it was called Phosphorus, amongst the Romans Lucifer, as is the Moon called because of the great light she gives in the night. Afterwards it was called Venus, as it was the daughter of Caelum and Dies; according to Cicero it had a temple in Elis. This celestial Venus is not Aphrodite who came from the foam of the sea and who with Mercury bore Cupid, neither was she the daughter of Jupiter and Dione who was afterwards married to Vulcan, and who with Mars gave birth to Anteros.[10] She is not Astarte, born in Syria and Tyre, who, as Macrobius tells us, had a statue on Mount Libanus, her head veiled, her face sorrowful, holding up her clothes with her left hand and looking as if she were weeping. But that she was the daughter of Caelum and Dies, and sometimes came before, sometimes after the day, was an agreeable invention. These other names of Venus have nothing that symbolically matches our Phosphorus, though it must be acknowledged that Aphrodite is often used by the ancients as a name for this star.

There was also Venus *Lubentina*, mentioned by Cicero, and Venus *Libentina* in Plutarch, who also calls her *Epitymbia*; she had a small statue at Delphos, and, if we may believe what Plutarch says, when they sacrifice to her they summon from hell the spirits of the dead. It was generally thought that as Venus presided over birth, so she did over death, but I think that Venus is the one that Pausanias places amongst the Parcae, and to whom the Athenians dedicated a statue. Venus *Coelestis* or Urania the daughter of this Venus or Parca mystically signifies, according to Plato, Divine Love. There was also Venus *Victrix*, Venus *Barbata* and Venus *Calva*, of whom you may find more amongst the ancients. Dionysius of Halicarnassus[11] and others mention temples of Venus in Thrace, Zacynthus, Paphos and Rome, as well as amongst the Leucadians and the people of Actium. He also speaks of Venus *Libitina*'s treasures, of which more when I come to Juno *Lucina*. I have already discussed that obscene rite of Venus *Mylitta*, and Firmicus has

---

[10]See Chapter XII.

[11]Dionysius of Halicarnassus (1st century B.C.) was a rhetorician and historian who worked in Rome. His *Antiquitates Romanae* in twenty books traced the history of Rome down to the time of the First Punic War, but he is generally considered by modern scholars to be rather inaccurate. Herbert, however, often cites him as an authority on religious customs.

Several editions of his work were available to Herbert; Robert Estienne (Paris, 1546), whom Herbert cites elsewhere, edited the Greek text. A good Latin translation by Gelenius (Paris, 1549) could also have been consulted by Herbert.

added others, but they are so sordid and filthy that I would be ashamed to repeat what he says.

Amongst the Hebrews, Lucifer was also sacred to Venus, as we may understand from the targums[12] on Joshua 14:12 and others, as Vossius points out. The Ishmaelites of antiquity worshipped Venus, and, as Euthymius Zigabenus[13] says, the Saracens took her from them and continued [to worship her] until the time of the Emperor Heraclius, calling the star Chabar or "the Great" in their language. The Mohammedans imitate them, calling it Venus *Cubar*, which comes from "Cabir" in Hebrew, and means "great" and "strong."[14] Vossius, quoting Cedrenus's[15] *Chronicles*, adds the Saracen prayer, "Allah, oua kubar," which he says means "God, God, greater Egg, great Kubar," or Luna and Venus.[16] But Selden, together with Vossius, says that Cedrenus is wrong about *oua* as it is merely a conjunction, and they say that it means "God, God, and that great Goddess." In my opinion, however, Euthymius has given a better interpretation than any of them: "God, God, the greater, and that great Goddess." The word "greater," omitted by them, is inferred by him, and makes more sense. Although the Saracens invoked the star Kubar by the name of "the Great," they still acknowledged a greater God, *Allah*. And St. Jerome, in his *Life of St. Hilarion*, states that the Saracens, who, like Mohammedans today, ended their week on Friday which they call

---

[12]Targums. These are Aramaic translations, interpretations or paraphrases of the Old Testament made after the Babylonian captivity.

[13]Euthymius Zigabenus (12th century A.D.) was a Byzantine monk and theologian who lived in the Convent of the Holy Virgin at Constantinople. His book on the dogma of the Greek church was translated by Paolo Zini (1555), and he also wrote a commentary on the Psalms.

[14]The Arabic word *kebir* does indeed mean "large" or "great." There is further discussion on this in Chapter XI.

[15]George Kedrenos [Cedrenus] (11th century A.D.) was a Byzantine monk and historian who wrote a history of the world from the Creation to 1059 A.D. He has been described as "a man of no imagination or talent" (*NBG* IX,243), but a Latin version of his work was published by Xylander in 1566.

The following passage, introduced by the reference to Zigabenus, refers to Astarte or the Arabian goddess Artasamain, a personfication of the planet Venus. Her name means "the Morning-Star of Heaven" (Teixidor 68–69).

[16]Both Vossius and Selden are wrong about the Arabic. Nothing here about either eggs or goddesses; the phrase (usually transliterated "allahu akbar") simply means "God is great." What some Islamic scholars of today might make of the link between Venus and Kubar perhaps does not bear thinking about, although of course the ancient Arabians worshipped a multiplicity of deities, including goddesses, until Mohammed showed them the true path.

Giume (Sunaxis), worshipped Venus or Lucifer, and also swear by Venus, whom they call the "running bright Star," and believe it will write down the actions of every soul. I will not discuss whether in Amos 5:26, "But you have borne the Tabernacle of your Moloch and Chiun, your images, the Star of your God" refers to this, although St. Jerome says that here Cochiab is Venus, Lucifer or Benoth, but whether Siccuth is the same as Succoth is the question I am not qualified to determine, and leave it to those who are more skilful in Hebrew. Acosta tells us that the worship of Lucifer extended at last to the Indians of Peru.

I could add many other facts about Venus: she waxes and wanes like the Moon, and she is fullest when she is farthest away from Earth, horned when she is waning and near the Earth. She goes through an eclipse like the Moon, although this is also the case with Mercury and Jupiter, as Mersenne[17] says he observed through his telescope. St. Augustine, quoting Varro, says, "Castor[18] wrote that there was such a prodigy in Heaven that the star Venus changed colour, size, shape and course, which has never happened before or since." These things are not really to the point, which is only to show what the most ancient universal religion was, and I will now discuss Mercury and his worship, Mercury, after Venus, being the most visible star.

As Vossius has correctly observed, Mars, Jupiter and Saturn, being above the Sun, have neither evening rising nor morning setting, and the Moon, on the contrary, has neither evening setting nor morning rising. Mercury and Venus, which move round the Sun, are for half the time above the Sun, half the time below, and so have both rising and setting.[19] People therefore began

---

[17]Marin Mersenne (1588–1648), French priest and polymath, was another of Herbert's close friends in the academic world. Apart from helping to publicise Herbert's first book, and perhaps making the French translation, Mersenne displayed a wide range of tolerance towards religious beliefs of all kinds, and his voluminous correpondence reveals his erudition and broad-mindedness. He may have been instrumental in introducing Herbert to Descartes and Gassendi. Mersenne is best-known for his work *L'impieté des déistes* (1631).

[18]Castor of Rhodes (fl. 60 B.C.), a Greek grammarian and orator, wrote a chronicle which was cited by Eusebius, Strabo and Suidas. He is also reputed to have written a work on the river Nile. His work, known as the *Chronological Epitome* "was perhaps the first important attempt in more than two centuries to order the mythologies of the world and attach dates" (Sacks 65). It was also used as a source by Varro in *De gente populi Romani*.

[19]Herbert likely knew of Galileo's *Tres epistolae de maculis solaribus* (1612), in which the great astronomer had described the waxing and waning of Venus as being rather like that of the Moon, which meant that it was sometimes "above" the Sun and sometimes "below" it. This observation contradicted Ptolemy, who believed

to worship the companions of the Sun, and then went on to the rest of the Planets.

Mercury

We have noted before how the Emperor Julian had great esteem for [Mercury], nor was it less venerated by Porphyry.[20] He calls it "the Exhibitor" and "Representer of Reason and Discourse"; that *logos* in the Sun, Porphyry goes on, is actually Mercury, and the one in the Moon is Hecate. He adds that there is a compound word, Ermo-Pan, consisting of a Greek and Egyptian deity. Apuleius, writing of the Egyptians, says that "there was Anubis, whom they called Mercury, and who was represented as having a dog's head, to show us that from him we get wisdom." Diodorus Siculus disagrees, and you may consult him if you like.

It seems that this star was first worshipped in the East, particularly by the Babylonians, who called it Secher, as Hesychius tells us.[21] Mertholis, and then Margenah were other names used by eastern peoples, and amongst the Egyptians, as we find in Cicero, he was called Thoit or Theut (Thoth); the Greeks, as we have seen, called him Hermes or Stilbon, the Romans, Mercurius. That there was great veneration for him may be seen from Seneca, who says that "Mercury was the dispenser of reasons, numbers, order and knowledge." The planet is small compared to the Earth, 19:1 in proportion, as Venus is 6:1, but its influence is very powerful.

The old pagans attributed great virtue and natural phenomena to these inseparable companions of the Sun. I think that the Mercury whom Caesar says was so much respected by the Gauls was an animal god, although what we are told about him seems to agree in a symbolic sense with Mercury, and more so because, as Caesar demonstrates, their worship was not very different from that of other nations. It was he who invented trade and commerce, and who presided over roads; it was the custom to lay a huge pile of stones before his statue, which was placed where roads met, or to

---

that Venus was *below* the Sun both at its inferior conjunction (the bottom of the epicycle) and at the superior conjunction(the top of the epicycle). Galileo pointed out that the diameter of Venus underwent vast variations during its phases, and that the naked-eye observers had made theplanet too large. However, "although he [Galileo] vociferously took others to task for their faulty notions of planetary sizes, only twice . . . did he give an actual measurement of an angular planetary diameter" (van Helmont 68).

[20]Herbert includes a reference to Eusebius, *De praepositiones evangelii*, III. Further information is supplied by Vossius II, xxxii, 470.

[21]For further discussion, see Vossius II, xxii, 470.

put the first fruits [of the harvest] there for the benefit of travellers. This Solomon alludes to in Proverbs 26:8, "As he who binds a stone in Margenah's or Mercury's sling, so he gives honour to a stupid man."

This priestly invention proved very useful, because by it the roads were cleared from stones; if all other rites and ceremonies had been equally useful, the common people would not have been so abused. This custom of piling up stones existed amongst the Indians, Arabians and Saracens, and is still practised by the Mohammedans, as Vossius observes. They paid this honour, or something like it, to Venus, as Vincent [of Beauvais][22] tells us about Mercury's rod, with which, as Vergil says, ". . . pale souls he calls from Orcus / And sends others through the Tartarian walls." As Macrobius notes, by Mercury was understood the Sun, because of some symbolic attribute, and by the same reasoning Cartari proves that Hercules was identical to Mercury, albeit an animal deity.[23] Dionysius of Halicarnassus very clearly explains the opinion of the ancient philosophers about heroes being deified: "There is a certain middle nature between men and gods, a kind of daemon; sometimes they converse with men, other times with gods." But Cicero very cleverly exposes these fictions:

> What? can you say that Apollo, Vulcan, Mercury and the rest are gods, and yet doubt that Hercules, Aesculapius, Bacchus, Castor and Pollux are? As much adoration is paid to them as to the others, and some people venerate them even more. What about Aristaeus, the son of Apollo and inventor of olive-culture, Theseus, the son of Neptune, and many others whose fathers were not gods, why are they ranked amongst the immortals? Why not those whose mothers were goddesses?[24]

In fact, there is a better reason for them — for just as in civil law he whose mother is born free is himself free, so by the law of Nature, he whose mother is a goddess must be a god. Therefore, in the island of Astypalea, Achilles is most religiously worshipped, and if he can be counted divine, so can Orpheus and Rhesus, their mothers being Muses, unless for some reason maritime marriages are more valid than those inland. Cicero does not say this in vain, for from a divine mother and a mortal father, who could the

---

[22] Vincent of Beauvais (c. 1190–1264) was a Dominican friar, encyclopaedist and philosopher. He is famous for having written the *Speculum majus*, which attempted to chronicle all current knowledge, and is particularly useful for its treatment of the controversies arising from Aquinas's ideas on substance. Vincent's work included a discussion of many "pagan" religions as well as a work on the gods, the *Speculum historiale*, which may be characterised as a late Euhemerist work.

[23] See Cartari 501.

[24] Cicero, *NG* III, 38–40 (McGregor 208).

pagans not easily promote? Mercury was called Woden[25] by the Germans, or, as some tell us, Teutatis[26] and Irmensal.[27]

Mars

The planet Mars also received divine worship, although long after the Sun, Moon, Venus and Mercury, for Mars was not known except through a kind of diffusing of its light and its trembling motion, which hinted to the world of its existence. In earliest times there were no accurate observations of the stars, and the courses of Mars, Jupiter and Saturn were not generally known. Names formerly belonging to humans were given to stars when they were discovered, so that the whole story of ancient Saturn, Jove, and Mars is nothing religious, but merely human or fictional; if there was anything religious in it, it was with respect to the Sun, not to those other planets as is generally thought. The religion (or flattery) of the ancients was so prevalent amongst them that they gave the names of stars to heroes, and sometimes gave stars the names of heroes. I do not deny that these stars were known and worshipped before the time of Saturn, Jupiter or Mars, but they would have had other names, and it is unlikely that the first star observed after the death of any hero took his name.

[Mars] was called *Thorras* by the Babylonians, which was the name of the king who succeeded Ninus, but I will not try to determine whether the star was named from the man, or vice versa. The Greeks called him *Ares*, or, according to some authorities, *Puroeis*. Amongst the Romans he was Mars "quod magna vortat," and so the poets called him *Mavors*;[28] to the Sabines he

---

[25]The connexion of *Wodan* with Mercury by the Germans is made correctly by Tacitus in the *Germania*. "Above all other gods," Tacitus says, "they worship Mercury, and count it no sin, on certain feast-days, to include human victims in the sacrifices offered to him" (108).

[26]Teutatis or Tiu is the German war-god.

[27]The modern spelling is *Irminsul*. It is actually a structure known as "the Column of the World" which was destroyed by Charlemagne. It may have been linked with Irmin, a culture-hero of the Hirminones, a western German tribe. He, in turn, might be synonymous with Jormungard, the Midgard Serpent of Old Norse myth, because of derivation from the Old Teutonic word *iormund*, "great." Vossius quotes an inscription from the reign of Louis the Pious (814–40) mentioning Irminsul as "idolum Saxonum." He says further that Irminsul was a statue of Mercury, and supplies a lengthy linguistic derivation to prove this point (II, xxii, 476).

[28]Mavors is an archaic and poetic name for Mars derived from *verto* or *vorto*, "to change around."

was *Momers*, and to the Germans *Hesus*. Lucan[29] writes of "dreadful Hesus with his cruel altars," because the ancient Germans sacrificed their prisoners of war to him. Procopius says "their [the Germans'] greatest sacrifice is the first man they capture in battle, whom they sacrifice to Mars, thought to be their chief god," it being a cruel and absurd opinion amongst the old pagans that nothing but human sacrifice could be acceptable to the greatest god.[30]

There were many different Marses, but the one said to have been born in Thrace was the foremost, of whose birth this amusing story is told: Juno, jealous of Jupiter because he had had a daughter, Minerva, without her assistance, resolved to have a son without him, who was Mars. According to Herodotus, [the Thracians] had an oracle of his amongst them, as did the Egyptians, which delivered prophecies, and could not be exposed as humanly contrived, but was the divine pleasure. This was stage-managed by the crafty priests, for anything they predicted from natural causes unknown to the common people, or when they received information from their spies, they pretended it was not something they knew themselves, but something communicated to them by gods, with whom they were familiar and conversant. Thus they acquired prestige and wealth, being the only people who knew the secret mysteries. What is more, if they cured someone's illness, they credited the cure to the propitiousness of the god, and believed that it was a greater honour to make people recover through prayer than the regular application of medicine. It was to this end, as Herodotus tells us, that the oracles of Apollo, Minerva, Diana, Mars and Jupiter were erected, but these pious frauds were so common to all ages that I could go on forever about them.

Amongst the Scythians, as Herodotus tells us, Mars was worshipped most frequently, although Vesta was their chief deity, and in their language he was called Tabiti. Jupiter was known as Papaeus, the Earth as Apia, Apollo as Erasyrus, Venus Artempasa, and Neptune Thamimasades. They did not erect statues, or build altars and temples to any of these, but only to Mars.

---

[29]Marcus Annaeus Lucanus (39–65), the nephew of Seneca, was the author of the *Pharsalia*, a poem about the great rivalry between Caesar and Pompey. Nero ordered Lucan to commit suidcide. He was very popular in England during the seventeenth century, and there are several translations of his works.

[30] While this phrase "cruel and absurd opinion amongst the old pagans. . . . god" might appear to contradict Herbert's accusations against the priests, I suspect that the condemnation of the priests is implicit, because they were in charge of sacrificial rituals. In any case, Herbert also attacks the priests for having developed their power over centuries so that people obeyed them without thinking.

The Spartans, according to Pausanias, had another custom, which was to bind Mars's statue very tightly, assuming that they could thereby keep him secure amongst them;[31] the Romans are said to have done this to some gods, especially the Tutelar Deities. The priests stood hidden behind them, making them appear to threaten to leave the city at the bidding of an unknown voice.

A winning horse was formerly sacrificed to Mars, and amongst animals the wolf and the dog were sacred to him; amongst birds the vulture and pelican were named "Martial" for him, and, according to some, the cock, into which the soldier Alectrio was changed because he neglected his duty on his watch when Mars and Venus were in bed together. Anyone who wants to know more about his sacred rites may consult Herodotus, who describes the solemn festivals which were held in his honour at Paprimides, a town in Egypt.[32] Jupiter is called *Martialis* or *Areios* by some, which means The Lord of Hosts.

The proportion of Mars to the Earth is 13:1; it is believed to be hot and dry, either because of its own nature or because it passes through the very orb of the Sun. It is 1176 semi-diameters[33] of the Earth distant from us at its nearest, and 8232 when farthest, so that in a short time, that star which is superior to the Sun may be seen under it, as the most accurate astronomers have observed. This could not happen unless Mars passed through and emerged from the vast orb of the Sun very quickly, for which see Kepler[34] and Scheiner[35] about the planet Mars.

---

[31] Pausanias (2, 69) mentions a Spartan sanctuary to Ares at Therapne, but this story is not told there.

[32] Paprimides. The correct version of the name is "Papremis," according to Herodotus (2.59).

[33] According to Nathaniel Carpenter, one of Herbert's sources, "Astronomers measure the magnitude of the Starres by Diameters and Semi-diameters of the Earth" (Carpenter, *Geographia delineata* [1635], I, v, 117).

[34] Kepler had been told by Tycho Brahe to measure the diurnal parallax of Mars. A parallax is a change or alteration in the apparent position of an object (or planet) caused by an actual change in the position of observation. Tycho asked Kepler to measure the *diurnal* parallax of Mars (the parallax of a celestial object observed from opposite points on the Earth's surface) from morning and evening positions, and compare the results with the positions of the Fixed Stars. Tycho's instruments, which were what we would now call "state of the art," could not do this, and the greatest parallax that Kepler got was a mere 4 minutes.

[35] Christoph Scheiner (1575–1650), a Jesuit, was Professor of Mathematics at Inglostadt, Graz, and Rome. He discovered sunspots and invented the pantograph, an instrument for enlarging drawings. His discovery of sunspots (1611) led him into

Jupiter

Jupiter was also much honoured and venerated by the ancients, who thought that it consisted of such a mixed temperament that it was midway between the raging heat of Mars and the cold of Saturn, and so had a very benign influence. Its proportion to the Earth's globe is 14:1; according to the astronomers its greatest distance from the centre of the Earth is 13171 [semi-diameters], its least 8232. But by the name Jupiter the ancient philosophers meant something far more impressive than just a planet or animal deity.

Orpheus terms Jupiter the beginning and end of all things; it existed before time, and will remain after all things that are to come. It inhabits the highest part of the universe, extends to the lowest, and is everywhere. It is Seneca who gives us the best description of Jupiter:

> Wise people do not take for Jupiter that [image] which may be seen in the Capitol, or in any other temple, armed with thunder, but they believe him to be a Mind and a Soul who preserves and administers everything, who made the universe, and governs it by his nod, and he therefore has many divine names. He is properly called Fate, on whom the order of all things in their series of causes depends. He is also Providence, who provides and sees to it that things work as they were designed to, in perpetual uninterrupted causality. He is also Nature, for everything springs from him, and everything that has life lives by him. He may also be called the world, because he is whatever can be seen; he is self-creating, all-encompassing and he fills the universe with his divinity.

This also explains the Stoic belief that the world is God.[36]

The word Jupiter seems to have been derived from Jao or Jah, as we have pointed out; the latter part of the word means "father," as Diespiter in Varro for "the Sun," because he is the father of the day. Also see Horace, "Diespiter, separating the clouds with shining fire." Jao is called Jah by the Hebrews, and not only Strabo, whom I have mentioned before, but Origen (in Sandford's edition)[37] says that when joined together they make the word

---

conflict with his superiors, and he did not publish it until 1615. His *Novum solis elliptici phaenomenon* (1615) defended the static earth theory against Copernicus and Galileo. Herbert owned Scheiner's treatise on optics, *Rosa ursina* (1626). Galileo agreed with Scheiner on the question of sunspots, but not with his theory on how Venus and Mercury orbited the Sun. Herbert, following Vossius, supports Scheiner rather than Galileo about the movement of Venus (see n. 20 above).

[36]For example, cf. Epictetus, "the greatest and most principal and comprehensive of all things is this system, composed of men and God" (*Discourses* IX, 1).

[37]John Sandford (1565–1629) was best-known as a Latin poet, and he also wrote grammars of Latin, French, Italian and Spanish. In 1611 he went to Spain as chaplain to Sir John Digby, and Herbert may well have known him from diplomatic circles.

Jehovah, as Isidore[38] says. Philo Byblius mentions Jevo, a Phoenician god. For the various ways to pronounce this word, according to its letters and language, and how the Tetragrammaton is derived from it, see Sandford's *De descensu dei ad inferos*. I will say more of this later, for it is not my intention here to discuss those humans who were called Jupiter and deified, but only the adoration of the planet with that name.

The ancients believed that this benign planet, together with Venus, made air calm and temperate, and that it settled storms and tempests. In short, [Jupiter] was not only thought of as universally benign, but of such effectiveness that if it were in conjunction with the Moon, we might obtain anything we wanted from God, and Petrus Apianus[39] writes that he himself discovered this to be true.

Saturn

Saturn is the only planet remaining of those that were worshipped by the ancients, for I will not meddle with the stars of the Medici (as Galileo calls them) or [those of the] Bourbons, or any others which have been discovered with the assistance of the telescope. The proportion of this planet to the Earth is 22:1; its nearest distance to the Earth is 13171 semi-diameters, and farthest is 17571. The Chaldaeans and Egyptians knew that it was the remotest planet, and that although it appears to be very slow in motion, finishing its periodic course in little less than thirty years, yet it is really the fastest, because it is so far from Earth.

You must consult the most ancient authors about that Saturn who reigned in Italy, whose era was [known as] the Golden Age and who was afterwards deified, for before his time there was no accurate and intelligible

---

[38]Isidore of Seville [Isidorus Hispanensis] (c. 560–636) was Bishop of Seville from 602. The work Herbert cites is his *Etymologiae, sive origines*, a kind of encyclopaedia of current knowledge which included information on word-derivations and on history. Isidore also wrote a history of the world from the Creation up until his own time. Isidore was a Euhemerist, and attempted to place the gods into the periods of world history. "Drawing by way of Lactantius on Varro, and even on Ennius," Seznec writes, "he reconstructed mythological groups and dynasties . . . he singled out in these primitive ages the heroic figures who, from Prometheus on, had been leaders and pioneers in civilisation" (14).

[39]Petrus Apianus (1495–1522), a German mathematician and scholar, was the author of *Inscriptiones sanctae vetustatis* (1534). It contained many illustrations and representations of Greek deities; Seznec reproduces Apianus's illustration of Mercury (246). Renaissance scholars much admired the engravings in this work.

history.[40] The reason why that in his time, and for ages afterwards, there remained no footprints of truth that we could safely trust is because in those days not only priests, but also philosophers, shrouded whatever learning they possessed in fabulous mysteries. The fact that their opinions were clandestine and obscure does not make them credible; I rather think they dressed them up extravagantly to make them more palatable, yet some of them, I admit, may be sensibly explained. For example, when poets relate that Saturn was bound by Jupiter and thrown headlong down to Tartarus or Hell, mythologists understand that the evil influence of Saturn is restrained and corrected by the goodness of Jupiter; that vast expansion of air where these actions originally took place is Tartarus or Hell.

Saturn was known to Platonists as the author of contemplation, because being next to Heaven he injects that power into the soul, and by this means he calls [men] to their origins, and because of this, sedentary people were considered wisest. Thus Varro says that "a Roman conquers sitting down," and Pythagoras and Numa both asserted that people should worship while seated; [finally, in] 2 Samuel 7:8 "King David went in and sat before the Lord."

Because Saturn was dry and cold, it was believed to preside over those who are afflicted with Melancholy and Black Choler, and when Saturn predominates over other planets at a birth it influences and governs them. [It was also believed] that it presided over Autumn and the seventh day of the week, and our Roger Bacon[41] writes about this that we must not work then, according to Jewish custom, because the dull and slow planet was unlucky. By its influence people were made unfit for business, and because it caused the eight-month birth it was not thought of as healthy; others, however, attribute the cause of those births to the Moon. For the harmonic proportion of planets according to Pythagoras, see Kepler.

---

[40] Saturn and the Golden Age. According to myth and legend, when Saturn (Kronos) ruled, there was no pain and suffering in the world. It was followed by the Iron Age, in which the values it promoted were debased or "inverted." Gianni Guastella gives a lucid and succinct overview of this in a paper entitled "Saturn, Lord of the Golden Age," in M. Ciavolella and A. Iannucci [eds.], *Saturn from Antiquity to the Renaissance* (Ottawa: Dovehouse Editions, 1992), 1–23.

[41] Roger Bacon (c. 1214–94) studied philosophy at Oxford and Paris. He taught at Oxford until 1257, and was then sent to Paris because of his "subversive" views and subsequently confined. In spite of this, he was favoured by Pope Clement IV, and wrote works on grammar, logic, philosophy, mathematics and physics. He is held to be the founder of English philosophy; Bacon insisted that empirical verification was superior to scholastic arguments from authority. He probably invented spectacles and may have known how to make telescopes, although he never accomplished this feat. His great work was the *Opus majus* (c. 1276).

I might here mention those planets that are smaller satellites of the greater [planets], [and I question] especially why anyone should determine positively that those stars known as Erratic, which Nigidius[42] calls *errones*, are no more than they are usually thought to be. He believed that it was possible that other planets might exist, although we could not see them because of either their great distance [from Earth] or their extraordinary brilliance. But I will go no further here, and carry on with my proper argument according to the natural order, passing now to the Fixed Stars.

---

[42]Publius Nigidius Figulus (c. 101–44 B.C.), a Roman Pythagorean philosopher, wrote *De sphaera barbarica et Graecanica*, a work on the geography, history and languages of the European world. He was also a prominent politician and grammarian.

VIII

The Cult of the Fixed Stars

In general, so antiquity assures us, the Stars, fixed or wandering, known or unknown, were thought divine by the pagans. When the ancients lifted up their eyes to the heavens, they saw a constancy and order in the motions and positions of the Stars, which seemed to them united in an eternal league and covenant; they were therefore obliged to attribute divinity to them. When they saw that this [unity] was accurately and constantly kept by the motion of the Fixed Stars, they prayed to them as the causes of anything that was constant and regular in the sublunary world. The pagans had many gods, who were a "militia" [of the Supreme God], but not themselves supreme, so that the Hebrews called all the stars "the Host of Heaven," which (they said metaphorically) fought. Indeed, nothing came more naturally and agreeably to a pagan, when he had properly contemplated the nature of the Stars, than to conclude that the Fixed Stars were the Eternal Law and Book of God, the Planets his Book of Prophecy. By his natural decree, the Supreme God has written his unalterable legal principles both in the Stars and in the hearts of men, with respect to which it is very evident that some things are universal. And, why may not the same God have shown to us the reasons of things present and things future by the Planets, as all sublunary motion originates from theirs? The Stars, then, are the Universal Law and the Prophets of God, which, although they are mute, point at things, like the hands of a clock, with great exactness and accuracy. Wise men observe them and consult them, not with the vain, ridiculous and superstitious forms and maxims of common, ignorant and stupid astrologers, but by observation of events when their motions, conjunctions, oppositions and various aspects are compared with one another.

The Stars certainly act upon inferior bodies, but I do not know whether they are free agents or not, and there are a great many arguments about this. Aristotle thinks that the operation of the Stars is to be thought of as identical to that of animals and planets. The pagans believed that the Signs [of the Zodiac] were the twelve advisers of God, so that if astronomers understood their nature well, they would not be so liable to make mistakes. The things that made the pagans worship the Stars have already been shown to some extent, and I shall now add a few things here.

The pagans first considered the height [of the Stars], which is so enormous that, according to Tycho Brahe,[1] the sphere of the Fixed Stars is 19,000 semi-diameters of the Earth distant from it. Mersenne [fixes it at] 20,000, which space contains 53,961, 647 leagues, or 3 million miles.[2] From this we may infer that if a stone were dropped from that sphere, and moved 1 league per minute, it would be nearly 102 years before it reached the Earth. The height of the sphere may also be inferred from the fact that the Fixed Stars have no discernible parallax from the Earth, whereas the Sun has three minutes' parallax, and the Moon sometimes a whole degree.

Next [they considered] size, the smallest among them being equal to the Moon and Mercury, and the largest to Venus and Mars. Their proportion to the Earth is: a star of the 6th. magnitude, 11:1, and the 1st, 70:1, the rest being mean proportionals. The ancients thought that the number of Fixed Stars that could be counted was 1002, the rest being dim and unobservable, and they were all divided (I have no idea why) into 48 figures or Constellations.

The pagans did not take their arguments for the divinity of the Fixed Stars from the variety of their motions, because they were always at the same distance from each other, at least insofar as our senses could determine. Yet the motion and language of the Planets was thought so wonderful that the pagans, for no other reason, gave them divine status. It was very easy for them to be mistaken about this. If the Fixed Stars remained fixed in respect to one another (which the spaces and distances in shapes formerly ascribed to them by shepherds and sailors seemed to suggest), it is most certain that the Signs move, for this causes the progression of the equinox. The constellation of Aries is sometimes in the place of Taurus, Taurus in that of Gemini, and so on, but after some digression they appear to return to their usual places. Some call this the motion of Access and Recess,

---

[1]Tycho Brahe (1546–1601), the Danish astronomer, discovered the first "fixed star" (1572). His *De nova stella* (1573) "gave Aristotelian cosmology the *coup de grace*" by showing that a comet observed in 1567 was "not a sublunary phenomenon . . . but must be at least six times as far in space as the moon" (Koestler 293). Brahe bequeathed his fine-tuned observations to Kepler. Herbert owned his *Hyperaspites adversus Scipionis Claramontii* (1625) [*FK* 92].

[2]Herbert appears to be misquoting Tycho's measurements. The latter calculated that the sphere of the Fixed Stars was 14,300 Earth radii (or semi-diameters) from the Earth at its greatest distance (van Helden 53). The figures Herbert quotes are closer to those given by the Arab astronomer al-Farghani (c. 800–72), who gives 20,110 e.r. for *Saturn*, not Earth. Magini (see n. 3) favoured larger sizes for the diameters of both Fixed Stars and planets. In fact, he made "[the] actual sizes of planets and Fixed Stars much larger than they had ever been" (van Helden 52).

and others [use the term] "trepidation,"[3] for which see the famous dispute between Joseph Scaliger and Magini.[4]

The speed of the Fixed Stars was another reason why divinity was ascribed to them. The motion of the equinox is so rapid that the stars within it move 376,750 leagues per minute, or 60th part of an hour. If a shell were shot out of the most powerful cannon and carried with a continual, equal force, it would hardly fly around the world in one hundred hours. No, says Vossius, the speed and motion of the Sun are nothing to it, whose circumference is forty times less, so that the Stars next to the Equinoctial must be forty times faster than the Sun, unless, as the Copernican system says, the Earth moves. And this seems improbable, because the dead weight of the Earth, so unfit for movement, would doubly exceed the speed of the cannon-ball. Tycho Brahe proves that the Fixed Stars do not only move longitudinally from the vernal division of the zodiac, but latitudinally also. This, however, is irrelevant here.

Lastly, the pagans considered the power and effect of the Stars, noticing that some brought rain, others heat. But I will not enquire here whether these effects were caused by the impregnation of the Fixed Stars by the Planets, or vice versa. Pisces who, as they say, had sons and grandsons, was also worshipped by the Eastern peoples, especially the Assyrians, according to the interpreter of Germanicus[5] and Hyginus.[6] I suspect that this was the

---

[3]See, for example, John Donne: "Moving of th'earth brings harms and fears,/ Men reckon what it did, and meant,/ But trepidation of the spheres,/ Though greater far, is innocent" ("A Valediction: forbidding Mourning, l. 9–12).

[4]Herbert is referring to a controversy about equinoxes occasioned by the *Confutatio diatribae J. Scaligeri de aequinoctium praecessione* (1617) of the Italian astronomer Giovanni Antonio Magini (1555–1617). The latter was a professor at Bologna who had become disenchanted with astrology, and whom Koestler notes was "Galileo's main academic rival" (374). Herbert owned Magini's *De astrologica ratione ac usu dierum criticorum seu decretoriorum* (1607) and a work concerning the legitimate use of astrology in medicine (*FK* 94).

[5]This is P. Nigidius Figulus (see Chapter VII). Nero Claudius Drusus Germanicus Caesar (15 B.C.–19 A.D.), the adopted son of the Emperor Tiberius, was a soldier, statesman and scholar. He translated and revised the *Phainomena* of Aratus (c. 315–239 B.C.), a work on stellar configurations which was itself a poetic redaction of a treatise by Eudoxus of Cnidos (c. 390–337 B.C.). Germanicus's version is "a more poetic and more independent translation than Cicero's, in which the imperial author corrects some astronomical errors in the original" (*OCD* 76). Germanicus also wrote the *Prognostica*, extant in fragments. Aratus's book was printed in Venice (1499).

[6]Hyginus (2nd century A.D.) wrote on astronomy and mythology, his *Fabularum liber* being printed at Basle (1535). Because of the trend in later Roman times to fuse

sign called *Engonassin*[7] by the Greeks, who paid it divine honours; some believe that Hercules was turned into this Star. So much for the Signs of the Zodiac.

Isidore says that Jupiter Amon was thought to be the Ram in the Zodiac, but Servius says it was Minerva. Manilius[8] says, "Aries takes his own counsel, a princely dignity; / He hears what Libra sees." This alludes to what we said before about the Conciliatory Deities. Gemini, some say, were the Tyndarides, Castor and Pollux, the sons of Leda, the protectors of sailors; some thought they were Hercules and Apollo, others Triptolemus and Jason, or Zethus and Amphion;[9] [still others believed them to be] Samothracian gods. This is hardly strange, because every country at that time added heroes to the number of gods, and pagans, believing that the souls of famous men were immortal, named stars after them.

The Sign Virgo was called Astraea[10] by some; it has been said that "Astraea has left the Earth." By some she was known as Ceres, Atergatis, Fortuna, or Isis, unless you will have the Egyptians' Isis the same as the Romans' Ceres. Others called her Concordia,[11] but it is uncertain whether she was [also] the goddess Panda.[12] Of Pisces, the ancient Syrian gods,

---

astronomy and mythology, this work was of great interest to Renaissance scholars (Seznec 38).

[7]*Engonassin* literally means "kneeling figure," and was used to denote the constellation Hercules (see Aratus 66, 669 [Liddell and Scott 467]).

[8]Marcus Manilius (fl. 20 B.C.–22 A.D.) wrote the *Astronomica*, of which five books remain. It is a verse-treatise on the heavens, and deals with such subjects as the creation and the casting of horoscopes. Its translator was Joseph Scaliger.

[9]The sons of Zeus by Antiope. Abandoned at birth, they were raised by a shepherd. Amphion became a great musician after Hermes gave him a lyre, but Zethus remained an ordinary herdsman. They later built a city-wall for Cadmeia, which they raised by the music of Amphion. For full details see Morford and Lenardon 303–04; Hyginus, *Fabulae* 7–9.

[10]More properly Asteria, sister of Leto and mother of Hecate. Her name means "the starry one," perhaps linked with a myth about her pursuit by Zeus; she leapt into the sea and was turned into a quail, becoming Ortygia, the Island of Quails. This was later renamed Delos, based perhaps on an idea "that the island was originally a falling star" (*OCD* 110).

[11]Concordia was a "goddess" (really, a "personification") of agreement, usually one made between Roman authorities. Livy mentions a temple of hers which was built to mark the peaceful end of an army mutiny, and each town had its own *Concordia*.

[12]Vossius (V, xxvi, 504), following Nonnius and others, thinks that she might have been Ceres. However, there is no goddess Panda: the correct version is *Pandia*.

Germanicus notes in his *Aratus* that ". . . there are two fish-deities of the Syrians,"[13] but there are many opinions about them; as to why they should have been fish, I am perplexed by the matter. The Assyrians believed that they were in heaven above the firmament; do these stars, then, "swim" in the heavens, like fish? Or, as Hyginus suggests, is there some shadowy symbolic meaning? I note also Vossius's opinion that these deities are [actually] Venus and Cupid, as the words of Hyginus's commentary on the *Poetics* infer.[14] The astronomer Rossi says that at one time Venus and Cupid went to the river Euphrates, where they unexpectedly encountered the monster Typhon. Venus and her son threw themselves into the river, and from this act Pisces was formed, so that they managed to escape from the danger. Afterwards the Syrians who lived near the place stopped eating fish and were afraid to catch them.

Another version comes from Nigidius, who says that these fish came from a huge egg in the Euphrates, from which, after a pigeon had sat on it for a few days, the Syrian Goddess was born. She was known as Venus, and from then on the Syrians abstained from eating either fish or pigeons. We have already seen from Hyginus that the Syrians really did avoid catching fish; an anonymous poet in the *Greek Anthology* says that Heliodorus[15] referred to his net as 'the Syrian Goddess,' "[so that] it would be pure for fishing," that is, if fish were caught in such a net the goddess would not be offended. It was also thought that people who ate fish were afflicted by the Syrian Goddess with a swelling, as we can see from Martial, "I swear to you by the Syrian boil," or Persius, "the gods struck their bodies, which inflated," referring to the Syrian Venus and her son Cupid. It can be read in Scaliger's edition of Manilius, and in Saumaise's commentary on Solinus's *Polyhistor*;[16] I have discussed the cult of Atergatis and considered the Syrian

─────────────

She was the daughter of Zeus and Selene, and was possibly the object of festive celebration in the Athenian Pandia, mentioned by Demosthenes. There is, however, a river Panda.

[13]"Annua concludunt, Syriae duo numina, Pisces/ tempora" (Germanicus, *Arati phaenomena* 563–64 [36]). Translation: "the annual cycle ends with the two Syrian deities, the Fish").

[14] Cf. Vossius, "Numina ea sunt Venus et Cupido" (V, xxvi, 504).

[15]The "anonymous" Hellenistic poet is likely referring to the novelist Heliodorus of Emesa (3rd century A.D.) and his romance *Theagenes and Chariclea*.

[16]Herbert correctly gives the title of the work as *Polyhistor*, referring to the second edition of the *Collectanea rerum memorabilium* by Caius Julius Solinus (3rd century A.D.). This work was a geographical description of the ancient world which included Solinus's reflections on customs, religions, wildlife and plants, much of it

Goddess as an animal deity, and I will shortly examine the connexion of the worship of the Moon with the constellation of Pisces.

Even today, amongst modern nations, the Fixed Stars, together with the Sun, Moon and Planets are worshipped, as can be seen from Vossius, nor do I wish to exclude mention of other distinguished scholars in this field. Not only by the Eastern peoples, and through them the Greeks and Romans, were all the stars taken for gods, but amongst other pagans as well, in the same way as the Erratics and before them the Fixed Stars [had been], as other writers have indicated. The most interesting in our day is the honour shown to them amongst the Incas of Peru, who, as Acosta tells us, have a Creator God (in their language known as *Viracocha*,[17] now, after contact with the Spaniards, as *Dios*); they also worship the Sun, Moon, five Erratics, and the rest of the stars, about which the Spanish scholar has this to say:

> Of the stars they invoke [first] *Colcha*, whom we call *Cabrilla* or *Capella*; they add other stars and their functions, too, which they worship singly or in groups. Shepherds pray to *Urchuchillay*, whom they conceive of as a ram of many colours, their *Aries*, to look after their flocks and, it is thought, that star which our astronomers call *Lyra*. Next to this are two others in the same vicinity, *Cachuchillay* and *Urruchillay*. They believe these to be another sheep and a lamb. They also worship a star known as *Machuachuay*, who is in charge of serpents twined around a column, which do his bidding. In a similar manner they venerate a star called *Chuquichinchay*, which means "tiger," who is the appointed guardian of tigers, bears, and leopards. There is no four-footed animal or bird known in the land which is not glorified as a heavenly spirit as well as on the earth.[18]

---

cribbed from Pliny's *Historia naturalis*. The work was edited by Saumaise (1629) and was one of the first Latin books to be printed (Venice, 1473).

[17] Viracocha was the hero of the Inca creation legend. He rose from the depths of Lake Titicaca and created the human race.

[18] Herbert takes this quotation (somewhat modified) from Vossius V, xxvi, 505 (Latin translation from Spanish). The complete text:

> Entre las estrellas comunmente todos adoraban a la que ellos llaman Collca, que llamamos nosotros las Cabrillas. Atribuían a diversas estrellas diversos oficios y adorábanlas los que tenían necesidad de su favor, como los ovojeros hacían veneración y sacrificio a una estrella que ellos llamaban Urcuchillay, que dicen es un carnero de muchos colores, el cual entiende en la conservación del ganado, y se entiende ser la que los astrólogos llaman Lira. Y los mismos adoras otras dos, que andan cerca de ella, que llaman Catuchillay, Urcuchillay, que fingen ser una ovejo con un cordero. Otros adoraban una estrella que llaman Machacuay, a cuyo cargo están las serpientes y culebras, para que no les hagan mal, como a cargo de otra estrella que llamaban Chuquichinchay, que es tigre,

Together with all these various stars there are [deities] called *Charana*, *Topatalca*, *Mamana*, *Mirco*, *Mequiquiray* and many others;[19] above all, they assented with Plato to the notion of Ideas. It can now be seen that the stars, together with the Supreme God, are worshipped amongst the Indians, and this ends our discussion of all the stars, through whose cults the Supreme God was honoured.

---

están los tigres, osos y leones. Y generalmente de todos los animales y aves que hay en la tierra . . . (Acosta, *Historia* V, 4 [221])

[19] Some of Acosta's names (presumably Spanish transcriptions) are difficult to identify with any certainty for one not versed in South American mythology. Colcha probably refers to Mama Cocha, the Inca Mother-Goddess and goddess of the sea. Cachucillay may be Chalchihuitlicne, an Aztec water-goddess, and Mequiquiray may be either Mictlantecuhtli or Mictlancihuatl, the rulers (male and female respectively) of the Aztec hell. Herbert does not distinguish between Incas and Aztecs as a rule; he refers to "the Indians of Peru," "Peruvians," or "Incas."

All these Mexican deities are found in Acosta V, 4, 221–22.

IX

The Cult of Heaven

The pagans proceeded from the worship of the Stars to the veneration of Heaven; their philosophers believed that it was a bodily substance and that the Stars did not move in a vacuum, but were immobile, as Aristotle said. They thought that the Stars acted on inferior bodies by the intervention of the bodily nature of Heaven, and that we cannot know sufficiently through their influences just what their powers and operations are; much has been said on both sides about this, but it is not relevant here, so we shall pass it by.

What was called in Latin Caelum, the Greeks called Aether, to which that verse of Ennius's, often quoted by Cicero, refers: "Look at that sublime brightness, Jove, which all invoke."[1] The following inscription was excavated on the Caelian Hill: "OPTUMUS [sic] MAXIMUS CAELUS ETERNUS," the greatest and best eternal heaven, in which the attribute of "greatest and best," which Cicero says was given only to Jupiter, is here given to Heaven. Some think that Pythagoras favoured this view, that he said God was corporeal, that Heaven was his eyes, the Sun and Moon his testicles, the elements the rest of his limbs, for which also see Epiphanius. This is not likely to have been Pythagoras's opinion, for we find elsewhere that Pythagoras believed in only one God, the maker of the universe, and he says that Heaven was animated by the world-spirit, God himself. Hierocles[2] says "there is only one god, maker of everything, who may be called the God of Gods, the Greatest and Best God." Zoroaster,[3] in Patrizi's edition, [refers to] "the Maker, who by his own power created the world," and, speaking of humans, "the father

---

[1] The exact quotation from Ennius is obscure, but a reference in his surviving fragments comes close, and shows the importance of Jupiter: "Iuppiter hic risit tempestatesque serenae/ Riserunt omnes risu Iouis omnipotentis" (I [?], 446–47 [111]).

[2] Hierocles (2nd century A.D.), a Stoic, wrote a work on the elements of ethics. The first part dealt with self-preservation as a basis for ethics, a subject which Herbert discusses in De veritate. Herbert is quoting from his commentary on the so-called Golden Verses of Pythagoras.

[3] Zoroaster, more properly Zarathustra, has been dated variously from the 6th century B.C. back to 1000 B.C. (Seznec). Modern scholars are rather sceptical of so-called Zoroastrian writings, but both Plato and Eudoxus of Cnidos, to mention two eminent ancient authorities, discuss his doctrines. He was supposed to have written

of Men and Gods, who endowed our Souls with Mind / Our lazy bodies
with a Soul." To conclude, when the Heavens, or all the celestial bodies,
are called by the name of Jupiter, we are not to understand the Eternal God
who rules over everything, but a visible manifestation of him, such as we
find in Herodotus and Strabo. This is how the pagans worshipped [Heaven],
for its immense sublimity, size and circular form, the most perfect form
agreeing with the most perfect body; its brightness is everywhere shining,
adorned with the glittering stars. Lastly, they [adored its] duration and unity,
when they considered its influence over inferior things. These, then, were
the reasons that induced the pagans to believe that Heaven was more than
human, and so they gave it divine attributes.

Amongst learned men there was a question as to whether, although
Heaven was permanent, it was also eternal. They generally agreed that it
attained eternity by a sort of emanation from the Supreme God, although as
inferior to him as light is to the Sun. Indeed, if Heaven were a simple entity,
I would agree that it was the visible image of God, but as it is composed
of matter and form in a miraculous manner, it necessarily follows that we
must explain it by more than a mere emanation. Therefore it is necessary
that something greater and more excellent is needed for making Heaven and
the sublunary world, and it must be the original Maker.[4] Aristotle tells us
that everything necessarily exists, it is necessarily good, and is therefore
a principle, by which he means something that is most excellent and by
means of which all the others exist; he therefore adds that Heaven and Earth
depend on such a principle.[5] According to the most learned philosophers,
[their] production as well as conservation [depends on it, too]. Amongst

---

on science and religion; according to Peter Comestor (fl. 1148–78), Zoroaster was
also credited with the invention of magic and of having "inscribed the seven arts on
four columns" (Seznec 16).

[4] Aristotle specifically does not view God as Creator of the world; he argues
against such a conception of God in *De caelo* (301 ^{b}31). For Aristotle, matter
itself is not created — the world is matter and therefore was not created by anyone.
God could be said to maintain its existence (as Descartes argued later), but again,
Aristotle himself does not say that he did. Herbert might be, by his ambiguous
wording, suggesting that Aristotle was positing a Creator, but it seems more likely
that he was indulging in some philosophical wishful thinking.

[5] Aristotle argues that "where there is a better, there is a best . . . which must
be the divine" (Fr. 1476 ^{b}22–24). Herbert is alluding to this rather less well-known
Aristotelian doctrine, which differs from Aristotle's argument about substance. For
further details see Ross 179–86.

others, Hermes[6] has some very profound thoughts concerning God, calling him "The Preserver of Beings."[7] Aristotle, speaking of [God's] life, says "the length of life according to the degree of the subject: ours is short, his is eternal." Hermes writes to the same effect about the speech of the Mind "Goodness, Beauty, Happiness and Wisdom are the essence of God."[8]

Yet if everything, including even the Originator of all Beings, existed by a fatal necessity (as we suggested earlier) how could we be said to have liberty and free will? How could there then be any divine goodness, when things must be as they are, and not any other way? Where is Divine Wisdom, when Fate is absolute and determinate? How could we pretend to any liberty or freedom of action, when the Originator of all beings himself, the Greatest and Best God, was prescribed and confined under fatal necessity? These opinions, having no grounds in solid reason, ought to be demolished; Fate, or the order of things, comes directly from the most wise Author, who disposes of even the most insignificant things. He is prior to it as a cause is to an effect; the Supreme Deity existed in time before Fate and acted freely according to his pleasure. He united and disposed of the hierarchy of all existing things, as Cicero, amongst others, acknowledged. But more on the subject of Fate later, as we are now proceeding with our argument.

It is well-known that the telescope has revealed many things which the ancients did not know. It has also refuted the errors of those who believed that the Heavens were solid; it is plain that they are airy and porous, because comets either originate or ascend above the sphere of the Moon, Mercury and Venus always move around the Sun, two Planets move around Saturn, and four around Jupiter. There are many spots that rise and set in the Sun, for

---

[6]Hermes Trismegistus was originally the name given by Neoplatonists to the Egyptian god Thoth, who was credited with the authorship of various sacred writings. From the 3rd century onwards his name became associated with Neoplatonic writings, the best-known of which is the *Poimandres*; here, the Divine Intelligence, personified by Poimandres, appears to a sleeper in a dream-vision. Hermes was thought to have been the author of many Neoplatonic works on theology, philosophy and alchemy. The myth that he pre-dated Moses was exploded by Meric Casaubon in the 1660s (as well as the myth of his very existence). According to Jacopo da Bergamo's *Supplementum chronicarum* (Venice, 1483), Hermes also invented astronomy. There is a translation by John D. Chambers, *The Divine Pymander and Other Writings of Hermes Trismegistus* (New York: Weiser, 1975 [first published 1882]), but it is marred by the then-popular pseudo-archaic mode of translation. It is useful because it contains Stobaeus's excerpts and a section of references to Hermes in Justin Martyr and Cyprian.

[7]Hermes Trismegistus, *Poimandres* III and V.

[8]Hermes Trismegistus, *Poimandres* V, 8, 11.

which consult Galileo and, after him, Scheiner.[9] Mars penetrates the Sun's sphere, being sometimes seen above, sometimes below. Vossius adds the roughness and unevenness of the Moon, concluding that it could not move if the Heavens were solid, unless you assume a vacuum or the penetration of bodies.

As the ancients were ignorant of such things, they came to have an exaggerated opinion of the Heavens, and had reason (as they understood it, but we do not) to attribute divinity to them. [These reasons were] sublimity, durability, size, use, and the common notion of the incorruptibility of the Heavens, for they never observed, in any age, any coming into being or corruption in them. This seems as ridiculous to me as to suppose that if there were a Man in the Moon he would conclude that nothing on Earth was liable to corruption because it was not observable at so great a distance, or because to him the Earth is always the same shape and size, he should conclude that the whole thing never underwent alteration. The ancients could have observed something in the Heavens rather like our sublunary generation and corruption, and perhaps more; Pliny, quoting Hipparchus,[10] tells us that a new star was seen at Cyzicenus in the time of Ptolemy II Euergetes and Antiochus II.[11] Another appeared during Emperor Hadrian's[12] time, and one in Cassiopeia in the reign of Otho.[13] Still another [appeared] near the same [constellation] in 1264; another one in Cassiopeia appeared in 1572, disappearing two years later and leaving a chasm; no-one disputed that this one was made up of celestial matter, because observation showed it to be nearly three hundred times the size of Earth. In 1577 one appeared for seven weeks, and in 1600 in the breast of Cygnus; in 1504 there had been

---

[9] See Galileo, *Letters on Sunspots* (1613) [Drake 59–144]. For Scheiner and the controversy over who discovered sunspots first, see Drake 81–83.

[10] Hipparchus of Nicaea (c. 190–110 B.C.), the Greek astronomer, was the first to use trigonometry in his calculations. He improved astronomical instruments and made a catalogue of stars. Hipparchus discovered the procession of the equinoxes, and pioneered the observation of eclipses, solar parallaxes and the size of heavenly bodies (van Helden 10–14).

[11] Herbert has a problem with chronology here. Ptolemy III Euergetes was King of Egypt (246–221 B.C.). These dates do not coincide with those of any Antiochid ruler of Seleucia, although Antiochus II Soter (262–247 B.C.) is close. But the text reads "Antiochorum," which Lewis translates as "the two Antiochuses," which suggests a co-regency that never happened. Antiochus did marry Berenice, Ptolemy II's daughter, which makes him Ptolemy III's brother-in-law.

[12] Publius Aelius Hadrianus reigned 117–38.

[13] Marcus Salvius Otho reigned from January to April, 69.

one in the 18th degree of Sagittarius. An enormous star or comet appeared in 1508, which the most eminent astronomers thought was situated in the Heavens, and for which see Scheiner's *Rosa ursina*.

It is questionable whether the Sun is made of eternally lasting matter, especially if, according to the ancients and to some of the moderns, too, it is fed by vapours. Pedro Mexía[14] says that in Justinian [I]'s[15] time the seasons were very serene and clear one year although the Sun shone so dimly that the Moon provided almost as much light, and it is reported that there was a universal famine in the whole world. Patrizi thinks that the Sun must have been rarefied at the time, and so produced less light and heat. Paul the Deacon[16] tells us that in 790 the Sun went dark, and emitted no rays for seventeen days. A Mexican report that the Sun went out four times and was renewed the same number of times seems improbable to me; I can, as Patrizi does, allow a diminution or rarefication of the Sun's light, but not an extinguishing. Let this be enough to persuade those who think that the Heavens are immutable.

The ancients had other reasons to worship Heaven. For example, they believed it had a soul, as Aristotle states, "the Heavens are alive, and have the principle of Motion."[17] Now, the ancients believed that this principle was self-made, because they thought it was so much nobler than the souls which rule in our bodies, and a first and independent cause should exceed a second, dependent cause. Imagining that the Heavens were twofold in nature, having a formal or animal nature and a bodily or material nature, they made a distinction between right and left, thick and thin parts, and other organs, as we have already mentioned.[18] In the material nature of Heaven,

---

[14]Pedro Mexía [Petrus Mexias] (1496–1552), a Spanish humanist, is most renowned for his version of Aulus Gellius's *Noctes Atticae*, which he entitled *Silva de varia lecion* (1543). He was commissioned by Charles V to write a history of the Roman Empire from the time of Julius Caesar down to Maximilian of Austria (1545), the work to which Herbert alludes here. In spite of its evident lack of conspicuous historical or literary merit, Mexia's history went into several editions.

[15]Flavius Petrus Sabbatius Justinianus was Byzantine Emperor 527–65.

[16]Paul the Deacon [Paulus Diaconus] (c. 730–96), a Lombard historian, lived first at the court of King Rachis and then at Monte Cassino, later ending up at the court of Charlemagne. He wrote *De gestis Longobardorum* and an *Appendix ad Eutropium*, a continuation of Roman history from Valentinian I (364–75) to Justinian I. The former was printed in Lyon (1495), the latter at Basel (1569) and Ingolstadt (1603).

[17]Aristotle says this more than once in his *Physics* (cf. especially 1071 ^{b}12–22).

[18]The word "formal" refers to the Platonic/Aristotelian notion of "form," and the word "animal" is taken from the Latin *anima*, "soul."

they worshipped its soul, and within it God himself. This agrees with Aristotle, who calls the Supreme Soul the chief God, and lower souls the lesser deities. As this opinion was held everywhere, it will not seem so very odd if the pagans worshipped as gods those people who were extraordinary in some way, so that nothing was commoner than the *theanthropos*, or God-Man; Paul and Barnabas, for example, were taken for gods.[19]

It still remains doubtful, however, just what the Soul of Heaven amongst the ancients was. Aristotle allows it intellectual, appetitive and mobile faculties, but not sensitive, although it is one of his own axioms that greater faculties presuppose the lesser ones. He says, however, that this may be understood only of mortals; thus, according to philosophers, the Soul of Heaven does not apply itself to particular objects through the external senses, but only through the intellect, which is the way, we are told, that souls separated from their bodies understand things. I am pretty much in agreement with this, for perfect beings do not need external senses, incapable as those are of understanding anything other than that which is transitory and perishable. The animals have them in order to find food for survival and for avoiding injury, but the Soul of Heaven does not need anything like this, [for] it requires very little food and is very secure from all dangers.

There is another way of exerting the intellect, which is by the mutual sharing of forms, by which I mean that the celestial intelligences mutually know each other as well as whatever else derives from these forms, or passes into all things either here or in heaven. Alexander of Aphrodisias[20] seems to embrace both these opinions, and Terminio explains:

> Heaven understands by receiving what it ought to understand, and not its species, because it is intelligible in itself, and a species is needed only when something is material and is to be understood by the senses.[21]

I shall not enlarge upon the degrees of comparison between intelligences, such as whether the Sun may be more intelligent than the Moon, or, as some say, than the planets, because any such doctrine is based upon pure

---

[19]"And they called Barnabas, Jupiter; and Paul, Mercurius, because he was the chief speaker" (Acts 15:12).

[20]Alexander [of] Aphrodisias (3rd century A.D.) taught in Rome during the reigns of Septimius Severus (193–211) and Caracalla (211–17). He wrote on ethics, metaphysics and the soul, to which he denied immortality. He believed that all our mental faculties were bound together. His commentaries on Aristotle are still highly regarded.

[21]I have tentatively identified Herbert's source, "Termoninus," as the poet and historian Antonio Terminio (c. 1525–80), the city chronicler of Genoa and the author of *Della misera humana* (1599).

conjecture. At the same time, however, I cannot avoid noting the opinion of Simplicius,[22] whom others have followed. He claims that the Prime Mover, according to Aristotle, was not the Supreme God but the chief Intelligence in place and dignity after Him. [Simplicius] attempts to reconcile Plato, who gives God (*summum bonum*) the dignity of first place, then the Mind, as God's offspring and architect of Nature, then Nature, the work of the Mind, with Aristotle. Some believe that Simplicius did not accurately convey Aristotle's opinion, and they prove their assertion by citing the *Physics* and the *Metaphysics*. Even so, they must admit that Aristotle established that there were lesser gods who moved the inferior spheres, besides the Mover of the Supreme Sphere, the cause of diurnal motion. When Aristotle says "the Prime Mover has neither parts nor size," it seems rather difficult to grasp, but I suppose he means that God is infinite and has no parts, which must certainly be true, for if half of infinity were trebled, it would exceed itself, which is completely absurd. Aristotle's words, then, seem to agree with our notion of God, but of course you are quite free to think otherwise.[23]

The Names of Heaven

I will now discuss the names for Heaven that were used by the ancients, first noting the following proposition, "all things happen either by reason or counsel, fortune or chance, fate or necessity." Because of this, Heaven had three names: the first was Minerva, the second Fortuna, the third Parca, the name of one of the Fates. Minerva was called Athenaa or Athena by the Greeks; she presided over study and learning. The Egyptians called her

---

[22] Simplicius (fl. 510–50) was a Neoplatonist philosopher who fled to Persia after Justinian I closed down the School of Athens (529). He is well-known as a commentator on Aristotle and for his interest in older Greek philosophy.

[23] Some clarification is necessary here. Perfect beings can, by their nature, apprehend forms or universals. Imperfect beings, such as human beings, can only apprehend particulars or species, because these may be understood by the external senses. We may know that there are forms and universals, but we cannot know them completely. As Terminio puts it, "a species is needed only when a thing is material and is to be apprehended by sense."

The question of the Prime Mover is rather more complex. Aristotle says that "the [Prime Mover] must be something that is one and eternal" (*Physics* Bk. VIII, 6, 259, 14 [374]), that is, it has neither parts nor size. He considers also that the Prime Mover must not itself move, because movement implies change. The Prime Mover "remains permanently simple and unvarying" (VIII, 6, 260, 16–17 [377]). Herbert assumes that Aristotle equates the Prime Mover with God, a logical deduction for a philosopher writing in the Christian era.

Neith.[24] Cicero mentions five names for her, all of which are those of mortals afterwards deified.[25] Tzetzes, in his commentary on Lycophron, says that there were many Minervas and Venuses, but that by "Minerva" is mystically meant Heaven, or rather its highest part.[26] Macrobius states that "the most careful seekers of truth say that the middle part of the air is Jupiter, the lowest part (the Earth) Juno, and the utmost height of Heaven is Minerva.[27] Pharnutus says that she is called Aetheronia,[28] and St. Augustine notes, "it is said that Minerva possesses the highest part of Heaven, on which account the poets say that she was born from Jupiter's head."[29] Martianus Capella calls her "she who is higher than Jupiter."[30] Some believe, and Phornutus is one of them, that there were temples built to the Minerva of Providence.

----

[24]More properly Net or Nit, this goddess was "one of the oldest of all the Egyptian goddesses" (Budge I, 450). Also known as "the Lady of the West," she appears as a human figure carrying a sceptre or a bow and arrows in one hand, the *ankh* (life-symbol) in the other. She also has various animal forms, in particular that of a cow. She presided over, amongst other things, weaving, which would certainly connect her with Athene and the Arachne-myth.

[25]Cicero, *NG* III, 59–60 [217–18]. The names Cicero gives are "the daughter of Nilus," "the daughter of Jupiter," "the child of Jupiter and Coryphe . . . Koria," "the daughter of Pallas." The fifth, with "grey eyes," is mentioned earlier (I, 83 [103]). Cicero does not advance the theory that they were all once mortals; Herbert could have got this Euhemerist view from a number of sources.

[26]Joannes Tzetzes (12th century), a Byzantine grammarian and poet, was the author of commentaries upon Homer, Hesiod, Lycophron, Aristophanes and Porphyry. He was also the author of a 12,674-line poem, the *Chiliads*, which was printed at Basel (1546). It contains a great deal of miscellaneous information on history and mythology, although its primary subject-matter was supposed to be of a political nature.

[27]Macrobius III, 4 [201].

[28]"Pharnutus" is actually a misspelling of "Phornutus," itself a misprint for [Lucius Annaeus] Cornutus (c. 20–68), a Greek mythographer and philosophy teacher. His name was misprinted on the title-page of the first printed edition of his *Commentarium de natura deorum* (1505), and the error was perpetuated. For further details see Seznec 95ff.

[29]Augustine, *City of God* IV, 10 [147]. Augustine's scorn is evident, but his logic is wanting; since Minerva came from Jupiter's forehead, he asks, "why is she not reputed the queen of the gods on the ground that she is higher than Jupiter?" (147). Since she came out of his forehead, not from the top of his head, the answer should be obvious!

[30]Martianus [Felix] Capella (fl. 410–25) was the author of the *Liber de nuptiis Mercurii et Philologiae*, an allegorical work on education and learning which attained

Heaven was also called Fortune, especially by the Chaldaeans and Geneth-liacs, who predicted events from the disposition of the stars.[31] They also understood more than "chance" or "accident" by the word fortune, and this made them have a particular veneration for the Moon, which they thought was the author of its own change, and ruled all sublunary things. The Moon controlled humidity, upon which death and corruption depended, as well as transubstantiation. Some people, particularly poets, believed that Fortune was a goddess sent down from Heaven; as Juvenal says, "Fortune has no di-vinity, could we but see it: it's we,/ Ourselves, who make her a goddess, and set her in the heavens."[32] Although Fortune was blind, she was considered a great enemy of reason and constancy.

Philosophers thought quite differently about Fortune. Cicero says quite clearly, "Fortune is when anything comes to pass or when anything happens so that it might not come to pass or otherwise happen."[33] Nevertheless, the ancients held Fortune in great esteem, thinking that their prayers would be effective only for those things that were fortuitous in themselves, not where things were governed either by a law of nature or by a universal decree of Fate. This is why Cicero says that fortune should be asked for from God, wisdom acquired by our own efforts. An effigy of this Fortune may be seen on a coin of the Emperor Nerva[34] as a woman crowned in glory and sitting on a throne with a sceptre in her left hand, a pair of shears in her right, with the inscription FORTUNA P.R. Others show her with a cornucopia in her right hand and a rudder in her left. At Praeneste[35] there was a very famous temple to Fortune, where she was worshipped as two sisters; one, very blonde, was known as Good Fortune, and the other, very dark, was Bad Fortune, to whom Cicero tells us there was once an altar on the Esquiline Hill.[36] Cebes in his *Tables* describes her as blind and insane, sitting with her feet on a round stone, which is the commonest way of depicting her to this very

---

great popularity throughout the Middle Ages and the early Renaissance. It was first printed in Vienna (1499).

[31]The Genethliacs were people who made predictions based on the casting of one's nativity. They were not a particular group or sect; the term was simply used for the kind of wise men who performed that action.

[32]Juvenal, Satire X, 365–66 [217].

[33]Cicero, *De divinitate* I [Herbert's textual note].

[34]Marcus Cocceius Nerva (c. 25–98) was Emperor of Rome 96–98, the first of the so-called "Five Good Emperors."

[35]Praeneste is a town about 20 miles south-east of Rome.

[36]Cicero, *De legibus* I [Herbert's textual note].

day.[37] Spartianus relates that two of the best Roman emperors had great respect not only for Fortune herself, but for her image: Septimius Severus, when he was dying, ordered her statue to be placed alternately in the bedrooms of his two sons [Caracalla and Geta], to reinforce the equal division of the empire, and Antoninus Pius, at the point of death, commanded that the statue of Fortune be carried to Marcus Aurelius's room, which was understood to symbolise the transferral of the government to him. Not only were golden statues of Fortune kept in private homes, but were also publicly exhibited.

There is a great deal to be said about the several temples to Fortune amongst the Antiates, Praenestines, Greeks and Romans, but of particular interest is one at Elis, of which Pausanias gives a description. Also, we might say more about her being the same as Isis; according to Apuleius (as we have said before), Isis was certainly the same as the Moon, but I will waive discussion of this at the present time, although I must not omit that after the goddess Fortune, Bonus Eventus was worshipped, and Pliny gives us a description of his statue.[38] Then there is Favor, who was also a god for the Romans,[39] and Felicitas (in Greek, Macaria), a deified daughter of Hercules,[40] who appears on a coin of the Empress Julia Mamaea.[41] The representation of Felicitas here is different from the description given by Cebes, but this will be sufficient evidence to show that in ancient times Fortune stood only for heavenly influences on inferior things, particularly

---

[37]Cebes of Thebes (5th century B.C.) was a pupil of Socrates and makes an appearence in Plato's *Phaedo*. A Pythagorean philosopher of some repute, he is supposed to have written a dialogue. The work to which Herbert refers is spurious, and is also known as *The Picture*. It is a symbolic representation of human life, which modern scholars now assign to a much later date than Cebes.

[38]Bonus Eventus was originally a Roman rustic deity who personified the favourable outcome of matters. Statues show him with a cup in one hand and a sprig of grain (any kind) in the other. See Pliny, *Natural History* XXXV [Herbert's textual note].

[39]Favor was the personification (numen) of good will or support, perhaps also of partiality.

[40]This goddess, or at least the Roman version, is of recent origin, no mention of her appearing before the 2nd century B.C. Julius Caesar planned to build her a temple, but it was built in the end by M. Aemilius Lepidus, the Triumvir and Pontifex Maximus. Felicitas was associated with Honos and Virtus. Her connexions with Macaria, the daughter of Hercules, who offered herself as a sacrifice to save Attica from invasion (Rose 120) is vague.

[41]Julia Mamaea (d. 235) was the sister of the empress Julia Soaemias Bassiana and the mother of the emperor Alexander Severus. She and her son were murdered by Maximinus Thrax, who seized the throne.

on the Moon, and was worshipped for that reason with a cult under her own name.

The Parcae may also be easily shown to be the same as Heaven. There were supposedly three of them; the first governed man's birth, the second his life, the third his death. Clotho carried a distaff, Lachesis spun, and Atropos, or Mors, cut or broke the thread. For these reasons they were known as *Lanificae Sorores*, the wool-managing sisters, and were thought to spin out our lives, or, as Martial puts it, "the cruel goddesses break the fatal thread."[42] Cicero says that they were the daughters of Erebus and Nox, and Plato makes them the daughters of Ananke, placing them on equidistant thrones, clothed in white and crowned, singing the song of the Sirens.[43] Lachesis sings of the past, Clotho of the present, Atropos of the future. Each, together with their mother Ananke, manages a distaff, Clotho with her right hand, Atropos with her left and Lachesis with both. Pausanias quotes an ancient epigram telling us that the first goddess, who presided over birth, was the celestial Venus, as we suggested earlier; she was not that Venus *Libitina* in whose temples funeral decorations were stored, which is what Plutarch informs us. Clement of Alexandria reminds us that the Parcae were allegorically termed "parts of the Moon," i.e. the Thirtieth, the Fifteenth, and the New Moon, but this is inconsistent with what I have already pointed out.[44] I do not want to say too much about the worship of the Parcae except that it is very strange that they should be venerated at all, since they could not possibly be propitiated. Because of this the temple of their mother Ananke (Necessitas), together with that of Violentia,[45] which, Pausanias says, was at Corinth, were kept shut, and it was illegal for anyone to enter them. Mystically, the Parcae represented the celestial influence from which Fate, or the permanent order of things which have their beginning

---

[42]Their names mean, respectively, "the Spinner," "the Lot-giver," and "the Inflexible." They were actually the daughters of Zeus and Themis. A rather more accurate name than "Fates" might be "Allotters" (Rose 16).

[43]Cicero, *NG* III, 46 (212) [Herbert's textual note]. Herbert uses the Latin form of Ananke, Necessitas; Macrobius says that she, together with Fortuna (Tyche) presides over the birth of children. Plato says that Ananke has a spindle of adamant on which the world rotates (*Republic* X, 617c).

[44]Titus Flavius Clemens (c. 150–216) wrote two books in which he attempted to demonstrate the superiority of Christianity to pagan philosophy, the *Protrepticus* and the *Miscellanies*. Both works contain many useful quotations from Stoicism and Platonism. The reference is to Bk. V of the latter work [Herbert's textual note].

[45]Violentia was the goddess of violence. Pausanias does mention a shrine of hers (together with Necessity) at Akrokorinthos (I, 141).

and ending in the sublunary world, originates, passing through several stated changes, vicissitudes and periods.

Allow me to observe here that the ancients did not depict Death as we do, with its skeletal countenance, bony jaws and recessed forehead, but as something pleasant and calm, the image of sleep. They generally said that someone "is gone from us," so that the fear of death might not strike terror into people and that their minds would not become obsessed with the thought that after this life nothing will remain but bones. For this reason they were more valiant and more inclined to practice virtue; death was believed only to be a passage for the good person to a better life. They believed that it was very base and vulgar that nothing of those who had led exemplary lives here should remain after death but their discarded bodies.

Fate or Destiny had yet another role, recorded not only by the ancient poets but by some philosophers as well, notably the Stoics, and to it even Jupiter was subject. The ancients attributed to Fate all those things which were, so they said, beyond the power of God himself. God could not cause his own death, nor could he cause a person who had lived not to have lived; he had no power, except that of oblivion, over the past, and there were many similar things. All this seems to imply nothing more than that it is beyond our understanding to conceive that an eternal and immortal God could be in any way subject to death, or that if something had been done it could be undone. Propositions like these imply contradictions, but their content is irrelevant in that it is contrary to the dictates of common sense that things can both exist and not exist. People ought not, then, express themselves so freely about the greatest and best God, neither should they derogate him, for their vain and ridiculous claims cannot diminish his omnipotence. On the contrary, they expose the ignorance and weakness of human nature in believing that God is subject to Fate. Alexander of Aphrodisias completely destroys the doctrine of Fate by saying that it is nothing but a constant development of Nature, and there are many others who agree with him, including Pliny.[46]

Aristotle includes Fate amongst natural causes, but allows for Divine Providence with respect to them; however, it does not extend beyond [the sphere of] the Moon, for the Stars were thought capable of doing anything except when man's free will predominated. Aristotle denied that God took care of particulars or individuals except when they were included in their species, saying that it was beneath God to bother about them. However, Aristotle is here guilty of great stupidity; he was either ignorant of what

---

[46] Alexander of Aphrodisias, *Lib[er] de Fato* I; Pliny, *[Natural History]* II [Herbert's textual notes].

the mind, or the true nature of God, was, or of in what God took pleasure or delight. This is rather more arrogant than becomes a mere philosopher, and it goes beyond the bounds of right reason. What is worse, this opinion strikes at the very foundations of all religion, for if God did not care about individuals, why should people pray daily to Him? What would religion mean? What is one to make of such impiety? Perhaps Aristotle meant that it would be absurd to think that God takes care of every particular moment or that he had given orders about each one from the very beginning. I will return to this when I come to write about the translation of heroes to Heaven, for they, according to Aristotle, administered these affairs directly under God.

Aristotle's master Plato acknowledges Fate, but [for him] it neither destroys Providence nor excludes free will in man. He aptly connects all of these things together, and with things called *continentia*,[47] so that each has its proper place, especially if the just order of things (Fate) comes from Divine Providence. Now, if man's will determines the proper order of things only within the compass of his power, we may extricate ourselves from the labyrinth of controversy which has so much disturbed modern times. As Chalcidius rightly says, "it is within our power to lead a very evil life, but we are under the fatal necessity of being punished for it."[48]

There was also a kind of mathematical Fate invented, so Sextus Empiricus[49] tells us, by the Chaldaeans, or, as Herodotus says, by the Egyptians.[50] They also had sacred oracles and religious rites, and made altars, images and temples for the gods, that is, the Stars. The same authors tell us that they invented years.[51] Lucretius writes that the Chaldaeans and Babylonians could not agree about the nature of Fate: "That Babylon might disprove Chaldaean doctrine/ She attempted to prove against the astrological arts." It is not clear what "doctrine" was meant; the Babylonian numerology, of

---

[47]Those things which are self-contained, that is, complete in themselves without being attributes of something else.

[48]Chalcidius (fl. c. 330) was a rather obscure commentator on Plato who translated the *Timaeus* into Latin. It is not known whether he was Christian or pagan.

[49]Sextus Empiricus (2nd century A.D.) is usually regarded as the father of scepticism, although he took his doctrines from Pyrrho of Elis (c. 360–270 B.C.). In Herbert's time, sceptics were known as Pyrrhonists. Sextus may have been a doctor, the title "empiricus" denoting a medical practitioner. His chief work is the *Outlines of Pyrrhonism*, an extremely important and influential book whose translation helped spawn the whole tradition of Renaissance scepticism.

[50]Herodotus 2 [Herbert's textual note].

[51]Herodotus 2.4 [132].

which Horace speaks, has no relation to the Stars or to Fate, but only to a certain kind of fortune-telling by numbers.[52] But I will not expand on this as the whole doctrine of Genethliac horoscopes is merely conjectural. Astrologers can never predict anything certain about particular events, although they may about things in general. To predict the happiness or unhappiness of someone's life from a horoscope of his birth is trivial, for, as Ptolemy says, "a person skilful in this art could prevent the operation of the Stars." The Stars only incline — they do not constrain. It is worth noting what Abu Maskar ibn Mohammed has to say, namely, that several religions began in the world at a time when Jupiter was in conjunction with Saturn or another planet. However, he has related some unbelievable stories about the age of some of the religions.[53]

Next we come to the Stoic [conception of] Fate; it also originated in Heaven, but is more severe and rigid than the previous one. Fate and Providence differ, the Stoics say; Fate, in a sense, derives from Providence, so that it is not blind, but wise and clear-sighted. If anyone says that he is under a fatal necessity to sin, they say that he is also under a fatal necessity to be punished, and so by this unalterable law they do not destroy the just and equitable system of things, but reinforce it, establishing virtue above all. Thus the causes of things are not destroyed, but effects are the necessary consequences of them, as Cicero tells us.[54] I am not going to dispute the truth of what the Stoics say here, because I think that the Platonists have done this more than other philosophers; however, I would like to conclude with Seneca's words about God:

> Do you want to call him Fate? You would not be mistaken, for he does determine everything and is the Cause of causes. Providence? You are right also, for it is from his Will that the world comes, remains whole and exerts its power. You would not be wrong to call him Nature, for it is from him that everything

---

[52]Horace, *Odes* Bk. I, 11 [Herbert's textual note]. The reference is as follows: "Do not enquire, we may not know, what end/ The gods will give, Leuconoe, do not attempt/ Babylonian calculations" (79).

[53]Abu Maskar Ja'afar ibn Mohammed [Albumazar] (c. 800–85) was a distinguished Persian astronomer and the author of over fifty books. His main treatise, a work on planetary motion, the *Kitaboul-kironat fi ahkami-n-nodjoum* appeared in the West as *Introductorium in astronomiam Albumacaris Abalachi octo continens libros partiales*, translated by Erhard Ratdolf (Augsburg, 1489).

[54]Particularly in *NG* III, where Cotta makes a strong attack on the Stoics. Lucilius disagrees with him, but the book ends at this point. J.M. Ross appends an interesting "imaginary continuation" of the dialogue (239–51), where the dead Cicero resolves the question of Stoics versus Epicureans as he relaxes in the Elysian Fields.

derives, and by whose spirit we live. The World? He is indeed whatever can be seen, the whole occasioned by his parts, and self-sustaining.[55]

So much for celestial Fate, according to the opinions of the ancient philosophers. I shall not discuss Christian Fate, as Vossius calls it, although in my opinion it differs from the Platonic more in words than in reality, because it is my intention to deal only with those things that are relevant to the religion of the pagans.

---

[55] Sen[eca], *Lib[er] 4 de Benef[iciis]*, 7 [Herbert's marginal note].

X

The Cult of the Four Elements

We have discussed the Stars and Heaven, which, to use Cicero's terms, is what the philosophers call the fifth element, the principle or origin of mixed entities. Fire is the finest and keenest of the elements, the one most adapted for movement. But air is also fine and keen, and second to fire in motion; water, on the other hand, is thick, sluggish, permanent and motionless. Aristotle tells us in his *Metaphysics* that "the elements are said to be the ultimate bodies, into which the others are divided, but they cannot be divided into bodies of a different species."[1] According to Cicero and others, fire and air have the power to move and act, but water and earth are passive.[2] Aristotle claims that air is passive because of humidity, but water is more active than passive because it is cold. But if air is naturally the coldest, as scientists seem to think, this argument is invalid; when it does not receive heat from the sun, it makes everything very cold, congealing the water and turning it into ice. However, the qualities of air and water are so intermingled that it is difficult to say which belongs to each; rarefied water and condensed air differ very little.

The Chinese think that air is not even an element, for what we call air is to them nothing more than "the breath of Mother Earth," which nourishes and feeds us while we live, and weans us at death, setting the soul free to act as it wishes; Mother Earth does not take the breath away from man, but man away from breath. Why should souls need air when they take their flight into the purer regions, where no inferior elements are required? I am not sure how this Chinese philosophy could be tested, but we certainly know that when people climb to the summit of the highest mountains, such as the Andes, they are not only short of breath, but because their lungs cannot function properly by reason of the thin air, they faint and sometimes die, unless someone carries them down to lower levels. This argues that the air we breathe in, which is near the earth, is somewhat thicker. I thought it was worth mentioning this since scholars might like to enquire into this opinion

---

[1] See Aristotle, *Metaphysics* V, 3. " 'Element' means (1) the primary component immanent in a thing, and indivisible in kind into other kinds" (McKeon 754).

[2] See, for example, Balbus's discussion of the roles of the elements in *NG* II, 20–32 (133–35).

of the Chinese; if air is nothing but a thin smoke or exhalation rising from humid matter, and rarefied or exhaled by heat from the bowels of the earth, then there are only three elements.

In order to pursue our discussion, we shall here allow that there are four elements, that which the Pythagoreans call a quaternary, by which they swear as if it were a most holy deity. Hierocles asserted that everything arises from this number, which is the root and foundation. Thus the addition of all numbers from 1 to 4 makes 10, beyond which no language anywhere ever counted without adding unity to it. This number also contains all kinds of numbers, even and odd, square and cube, long and broad, tubal and pyramidical, prime and compound, as George of Trebizond[3] observed in *De harmonia mundi*. The number 4 also contains all musical harmonies, having double, treble, sesquialtera and sesquitertia, from which come diapason, disdiapason, and diapente (diatesseron).[4] Hence it was that agreement and harmony in the symbolic quality of elements was discovered, to which Boethius alludes when he says "you bind the elements with numbers."[5]

In addition to harmonic and arithmetical proportion, the ancients also found geometrical proportion in the elements. Timaeus of Locri,[6] and after him Plato, gave the following shapes to the elements: the Earth was a cube,

---

[3]George of Trebizond (1396–1485) was a Byzantine scholar who, at the invitation of an Italian nobleman, came to Venice as a professor of Greek (1428). He subsequently held posts at other Italian universities, including Rome. His commentaries on Priscian and Cicero were well-regarded, and he wrote a comprehensive study of Plato and Aristotle which was printed in 1523. He also wrote *In Claudii Ptolemaei centum sententiae seu centiloquium commentarius*, printed in 1544.

[4]In music, the *diapason* is the interval of an octave; the *diapente* the interval of a fifth, and the *diatesseron* the interval of a fourth. These terms generally apply to ancient and mediaeval music, as they refer to Greek harmonics. Herbert, a competent musician (he collected a book of lute-music and songs) and occasional composer (for the lute), was attracted to theories concerning musical harmony and the nature of the universe.

[5]Anicius Manlius Severinus Boethius (c. 470–525), Roman philosopher and statesman, put to death by King Theodoric. While in prison he wrote his *De consolatione philosophiae*, which was translated by King Alfred the Great, by Chaucer, and by Queen Elizabeth I, to mention its most illustrious admirers.

[6]Timaeus of Locri (5th century B.C.). There is no hard evidence, aside from Plato's *Timaeus*, that this Pythagorean philosopher ever existed. A work entitled *On the Soul*, ascribed to him, is believed to have been a 1st century A.D. forgery, and is described as "an unintelligent paraphrase of the Timaeus" (*OCD* 909). Freeman confirms the verdict of forgery, noting that "nothing is known of [Timaeus] except from Plato's dialogue" (81).

with 8 angles and 6 sides like a die, because of its stability, weight and lack of motion; Fire was a square pyramid with 4 angles, this [shape] being most natural for ascent; Air was an octahedron, with 8 bases, 6 angles, and 24 solid planes, being, next to fire, that element which most naturally goes up. Water was an icosahedron, with 20 bases and 12 angles, making it very fit, by reason of its flexibility, for motion, and very easily divided. All these shapes derived from the quaternary: the Earth from the first squares, Fire from 4 bases and angles; Air out of 16 (4 × 4) bases, the doubling making it more capable of penetration and fitter for motion, its plane angles 6 x 4; Water out of 20 bases and 12 angles, together making 32, a number made up of two squares whose root is 4. The bases are also 5 quaternaries, the angles 3, making a dodecahedral universe consisting of 12 pentagonal bases, 20 solids and 60 planes, all arising from quaternaries. 12 comes from 3, 20 from 5, 60 from 15. The exact agreement of all these elements may be found in their bases and angles.

The proportion of the bases of Air to those of Fire is double, in angles one and a half, and double also in planes, from which we get the harmony of the double diapason and diapente. The proportion of the bases of Fire to those of Earth is one and a half, and double in angles, which again form a diapason and diapente. With respect to Water, the proportion of bases of Earth is a triple and a third, in angles one and a half, from which arise a diapason, diapente and diatesseron in the bases, and a double-angled diapente, which makes a diapason. But the proportion between Fire and Water is not so exact, because the quality of the proportion which the elements have to each other is completely contradictory when they are placed in order, and where two always agree by a medium which partakes of each, as the ingenious person may observe. This may be seen also in George of Trebizond, *De anima mundi*, Book III. John the Grammarian[7] objects to the octahedron and icosahedron, but Carpenter[8] says that it is certain that the elements receive all the figures in their mixtures, and I therefore think that the controversy will

---

[7]John of Garland [the Grammarian] (d. 1258) was an English alchemist and grammarian who wrote the *Integumenta*, an influential commentary in verse on Ovid's *Metamorphoses*. "The Platonism of . . . John of Garland's *Integumenta Ovidii* sets the tone for commentary [of the 13th century], both in method and content" (Barkan 104).

[8]Nathaniel Carpenter (d. 1635), an Irish prelate, wrote an attack on Aristotle, *Philosophia liberta triplici exercitationum decade proposita* (1621). Carpenter was also an eminent geographer, and produced an important treatise, *Geography delineated forthe into 2 bookes, containing the sphaerical and tropical partes thereof* (1625).

soon be ended, for the Pythagoreans spoke of the proper shape of elements, whilst those who are of the other opinion, which Theodontius[9] teaches in his *Liber de igne*, where the form of fire is said to be pyramidal, are referring to the adventitious [accidental] shape. Amongst the elements Fire was equated with God, as we may read in Deuteronomy, St. Paul or Clement [of Alexandria], as well as whoever wrote the Epistle to the Hebrews, where it is expressly stated that "God is a fire."[10] The ancient Persians were also of the same opinion, but this [similarity] should be examined carefully.

The fact that the elements seemed abstruse or mysterious, and that the reason and proportion of their mixture went beyond human comprehension, that everything derived from them and dissolved into them at death, made the pagans worship them. They found it strange that as the whole world was the sensible image of God, its remotest parts should be venerated, whilst those nearest were despised. For these reasons, and for others which we have already presented, the pagans were very careful to worship the elements; their priests invented many rites and ceremonies by which they enslaved people's minds and forced them to religious observance. At first, they would tell the common people about some very "secret" mysteries which they themselves had invented, opening them and explaning them to the people at random, or else sometimes keeping them concealed. It was absolutely necessary that the ignorant multitude be kept in the dark about those things which neither they themselves nor even the priests could understand, but which they asserted were of divine origin.

I shall begin with Fire, the purest element, which was thought by the pagans to be next to Aether[11] or Heaven.

---

[9]Herbert only has "Theo." as his reference (*DRG* 67); he may be referring to a very obscure Italian grammarian, Theodontius, who was cited many times by Boccaccio (whom Herbert frequently quotes) and other authorities on Ovid. His work is no longer extant. Seznec suggests that he may have been "a philosopher of Campanian origin" (222), who apparently held the belief that a certain Demogorgon was the founder of the race of gods, but this ascription may be due to an error of Boccaccio's. What the *Liber de igne* may have been I do not know, but Seznec does note that Theodontius "furnished Boccaccio with the debris of a very curious and very mixed tradition . . . there are also signs of an syncretist mythology" (222).

[10]See Deuteronomy 32:22 "For a fire is kindled in mine anger, and shall burn unto lowest hell"; Hebrews 12:29 "For our God is a consuming fire." The other reference to St. Paul is too vague to trace.

[11]In Hesiod, *Aither* ($\alpha\acute{\iota}\theta\eta\rho$) is the bright stratosphere (to use the modern term), produced from a union of Night and Erebus: "From Chaos was born Erebos, the

Fire

Ocellus of Lucania, a pupil of Pythagoras, was the first person I know of to have placed elemental Fire under the Moon and above the Air. He was followed by Empedocles and Hippocrates, and then Aristotle, who believed the same but did not credit Ocellus with having said it first. However, most of the learned ancients did not agree with them, and more recent authorities have completely exploded and rejected the theory. The external senses cannot tell us whether this elemental Fire is a burning coal, a flame, or only a light, even though in size it is 800 times larger than the Sun, and 1000 times larger than the Earth. At the same time, it does not consume or devour things, but is mild and gentle in its nature. How, then, does it differ from the Aether? And how can it descend and mix with Earth, Air or Water?

We may observe a fiery power to be present everywhere, [originating] partly from the Sun, partly from the Stars, and even from the bowels of the Earth, which modern writers have shown at length. It would therefore be absurd to suppose that such a great and bright entity as elemental Fire, whose vast thickness, according to some astronomers, is 115,567,000 paces, and which cannot be seen or experienced through effects, should remain undiscovered, when stars, which are so high above it, and reflect the Sun's light, appear so bright and sparkling. I have therefore made the Sun the foundation of that light to which terrestrial and subterranean things are to some degree subordinated, and which exercises its function everywhere as the Sun's vice-regent on Earth. The ancients, then, worshipped the Sun symbolically through fire as they did the Supreme God through the Sun, and they thought it was very stupid not to pay some external tribute to those things which were so obviously derived from the Deity. Moreover, they did not view Fire as simply one element, but as the form, life and motion of all the others. Hippocrates goes even further, calling it a sense: he was convinced that heat could see and hear, that it was indestructible, and that it was so fertile that it reproduced itself by a sudden renovation, shining forth from the confines of the other elements. Other elements were both male and female, but Fire had something superior to either.[12] As Seneca puts it:

---

dark/ and from Night, Aither and Hemera,/ the day, were begotten" (*Theogony* 123–25). Aristotle noted that the ancients considered Aether to be a fifth element, which, "as the primary body of all, suffers neither growth nor diminution, but is ageless, unalterable, and impassive." The name *aither*, he tells us, is derived "from the fact that it 'runs always' [*aei thein* ($\dot{\alpha}\dot{\varepsilon}\iota\ \theta\varepsilon\iota\nu$)]" (Aristotle, *On the Heavens* I, iii).

[12] According to Budge, the oldest gods of Egypt were "invented by people in whose households women held a high position." He notes that there were "pairs" of deities, male and female, who represented "the male and female elements of the

The Egyptians split the elements into two, male and female. In the Air, they said, the wind was male, and that which seemed still or misty was female. Salt water was male, fresh water female. Anything hard on Earth like stones and so on was also male, and that which was soft or could be cultivated was female.

Indeed, if what some botanists say is true, both sexes are found in trees and plants; the Egyptians were also right to think that there might be some imperfect distinction of sex in the elements. Because Fire gathers homogeneous things together, and separates heterogeneous things, it was thought to be the chief agent in the makeup of the world. If we ourselves were not kept alive from day to day by inner heat, our frames would soon disintegrate and the elements would return to their original state; the greater part of the human fabric, then, may be attributed to natural heat.

Amongst the philosophers Parmenides[13] held that Fire was the first principle of the universe, Heraclitus that there was a fiery power, and Hippocrates, so Galen tells us, says that living heat is the author of all nature's works. Hippasus of Metapontinus[14] worshipped fire, and Julius Firmicus Maternus tells us that the Persians and all their Magi valued fire above all the other elements, which is not really strange, because it was worshipped as divine. Because other authors have written a great deal about this, I will leave the reader to consult them himself, only adding here that the Jews (as far as their own writings indicate) have always given their God the title of "consuming" or "devouring" fire; in Leviticus 6:6 they were commanded "to keep a perpetual fire upon the altar," and the same custom prevailed amongst the Greeks, Romans, and Persians.

Amongst the pagans fire was a symbol of divinity, as Vossius tells us; many honours were paid to it and it was worshipped under many different names. Nimrod, also known as Ninus,[15] was the first person to worship fire, and of him it is said that he taught the Assyrians to worship it. From

---

Four Elements" (I, 287–88). They were: Nu/Nut, Heh/Hehut, Kekui/Kekuit, and Ker/Kerhet. This split is what Seneca is alluding to.

[13]Parmenides of Elea (c. 515–435 B.C.) wrote a philosophical poem on the nature of the universe and of human thought. He denied the diverse nature of reality, and stated that whatever is, is not divisible, "since it is all alike: nor is there any more or any less of it in one place which might prevent it from holding together, but all is full of what is" (Fr. 6.11; Robinson 114). For complete translations and discussion of the fragments of Parmenides see Freeman 41–47, Robinson 107–27.

[14]ippasus of Metapontinus (fl. 330 B.C.) was a Pythagorean who held that the world was made of fire and would sometime return to the elemental substance. None of his writings are extant (Freeman 20).

[15]Nimrod and Ninus. Nimrod son of Cush (see Genesis 10) was said to have founded Nineveh, the capital of Assyria. Scholars believe that he might be identified

this, Vossius says, it is probable that the city of Babylon was first called Ur, which is also Urie or Camarina,[16] the Chaldaean priests being known as *Cumerim.* Vossius also believes that Chaldaea[17] used to be known as Orchoa, from Ur; the Latin word *uro,* "I burn," and the Greek *pyr,* "fire," are derived from Ur. He also says that it is likely that Abraham, who was said to have known Chaldaean philosophy, was born in this city, and, according to Genesis 11:31[18] he left it, but his brother died there. It is still not known how far this worship spread amongst the Chaldaeans and Assyrians.[19]

[On the other hand], there is no doubt that the Persians worshipped fire. Herodotus says that they did not burn their dead because they believed that it would be impious to feed the fire-god with a dead body.[20] I believe that from this habit arose the custom of sacrificing human beings, including children, alive. The priests were able to persuade the common people that they were not so much devoured by fire as given to God, or incorporated in Him; this is how widespread was the impiety and cruelty of the priests! Lucian says in his *Tragedy of Jove* that the Persians "sacrificed to fire," and many Greek and Latin fathers also mention this.

The best source for this symbolic cult of God is Maximus of Tyre,[21] from whom Vossius quotes, and whose words I cannot omit here: "all the barbarians equally understood what God is; to them, amongst other signs, there

---

with Sargon of Agade (fl. 2300 B.C.), who may have had other names, "Sargon" being his reign-name, and who, like the Biblical Nimrod, was a great hunter and warrior. Ninus seems to have nothing to do with Nimrod, being a Latin version of the Greek Ninos, itself derived from the Sumerian Nina, a name for the goddess Ishtar.

[16]This reference is obscure. The only Camarina I can locate is in Italy, and hardly fits in here at all.

[17]Chaldaea. The Chaldaeans were originally a semi-nomadic tribe who lived between North Arabia and the Persian Gulf. They settled in Ur, which is often known as "Ur of the Chaldees." The name Chaldaea became used interchangeably with Babylonia, but formerly referred to South Babylonia, where the Chaldaeans lived. A Chaldaean governor, Nabopolassar, became King of Babylon (626 B.C.) and founded a dynasty.

[18]"And Terah took Abram his son, and Lot the son of Haran . . . and Sarai his daughter-in-law . . . and they went forth with them from Ur of the Chaldees, to go into the Land of Canaan."

[19]Vossius II, lxiv, 648.

[20]Herodotus I, 140.

[21]Maximus of Tyre (c. 120–85) was a sophist, and author of several extant lectures, which were collected under the title of *Dialexeis.* His teachings, which were mostly gleaned from Plato, show that he was mainly interested in ethics. Maximus also demonstrates a good knowledge of Cynic philosophy.

was one that lasted, and that was the Persian fire-image, voracious and insatiable." Now Vossius rejects this version, and replaces [the words] ἄγαλμα ἐθέμερον *agalma ethemeron* with *elementum quotidianum*. I agree with the replacing of *imaginem* with *elementum*, and I do not disapprove of the word *quotidianum*, for by that he understands "a fire which is renewed daily." This seems to make the meaning clearer.[22] Now Fire, whether used in solemn processions or, as seems more likely, as a basis for religious rites, was a favourite of the Persian kings in their ceremonies, which the Greeks called *pyreia* or *pyrantheia*. Concerning this, Ammianus Marcellinus writes, "If it may be believed, they [the Persians] bring fire which had fallen from heaven and keep it in perpetually-lit braziers; they say that a small amount is present in each Persian ruler, a mark of favour." It is reasonable that this Persian fire should be thought of as having heavenly origins, for I do not see otherwise how it could be inextinguishable. Diodorus Siculus says that the King could put it out, but we have already exploded this theory; the rest I take to be true, that the priests and Magi served this perennial Fire (although I think they perhaps borrowed it from the Hebrews), and that they were known as *pyrathoi*.

There remains the cult of Fire amongst the Medes and other Asiatic nations, as well as amongst the Sauromatians and others, of which more later. Glycas[23] mentions these cults in his *Annals*, and says that the Persians were named after Perseus, the next king of Assyria after Sardanapalus[24] and thus the Assyrians were known by his name as well. It was during his time

---

[22]Vossius refers (II, lxiv, 648–50) to a translation from Maximus's Lecture 38 (as Herbert's marginal note points out), and the Latin version runs as follows: "Barbari omnes pariter Deum esse intellegunt; constituere interim sibi alia atque alia signa: Ignem Persae imaginem quae una duret diem, vorax quid & insatiabile" (*DRG* 70). Herbert also prints the Greek text, and while Vossius's version is clearer for the argument that Vossius himself is making, there is no reason for him simply to have substituted one word for another to give himself an agreeable source from Maximus! Herbert, following Vossius closely here, agrees with the latter possibly because Vossius had a better command of Greek! Lewis omits the entire passage in his translation.

[23]Michael Glycas (c. 1118–1200), a Byzantine theologian and exegete, wrote a history of the world from creation to the death of the Emperor Alexius I (1118). This is the work to which Herbert alludes. Glycas also wrote the *Kephalaia*, a work on universal theology, in which Herbert was probably interested, as well as political poetry and letters.

[24]The king who succeeded Sardanapalus (Asshur-bani-pal) was Esarhaddon (681–669 B.C.). The story from Glycas seems to be pure conjecture on the part of the latter.

that the Fire fell from heaven, and from that arose a temple and the religious cult of Fire. My authority for the fact that amongst the Persians of today, Fire is still worshipped, is Vossius.[25]

In Egypt, fire was worshipped as the cult of Vulcan, the latter being the son of the Sun.[26] But whether stars were once named for kings, or kings for stars, it is difficult to be certain, and I refer [readers] to Manetho, Diodorus Siculus and Eusebius. There were many Vulcans amongst the Egyptians; they called him Opas,[27] who protected Egypt, as Cicero says,[28] and whose mystic significance, Varro tells us, is natural and powerful Fire; that of Vesta is the fire of ovens[29] and hearths, and that of Pallas the lightest and purest kind. The Egyptians held Vulcan, the Greek Hephaistos, in great respect, and they built a huge temple for him at Memphis which is described by Herodotus; its columns were 75 feet high. In those days the priests of Vulcan had a good reputation, and from their number Sethos was chosen to become King.

Thus we find Tarquinius Priscus, after his victory over the Sabines, dedicating his weapons to Vulcan. Amongst animals, the lion is sacred to this god, on account of his great heat, which, it is said, gives him a perpetual fever. The Romans built many temples to Vulcan, the most ancient one having been constructed by Romulus on the Esquiline Hill outside Rome, for the reason that it was thought that the god would not want his burning symbol in the middle of the city. Sacrifices to Fire were known as "holocausts," and were so hot that nothing was left over from them but ashes. There was another kind of sacrifice where those morsels which fell from the altar, or which were left over from the sacrifice, were distributed by the priests to the people in a dish of food. And there was a further kind of sacrifice, known as the Protervia, where it was the custom, according to Macrobius, if indeed anything remained, to throw it back in the fire; from this action

---

[25] II, lxiv, 650.

[26] Ptah is the Egyptian god generally associated with metalwork, design, sculpture and so forth, all of which the Greeks saw Vulcan controlling. "The Greeks and the Latins," Budge notes, "correctly identified one form of [Ptah] with Hephaistos and Vulcan" (I, 501).

[27] That is, Ptah.

[28] Cicero notes that there were several Vulcans, one of whom "was a son of Nilus [the Nile], whom the Egyptians call Ptah and claim as the guardian of Egypt" (*NG* 214 [III]).

[29] We might note here that the Romans even had a goddess, Fornax, who presided over ovens, and known as "dea fornicalis," the latter word being used by Herbert to denote Vesta's fire. He seems to have borrowed it from Varro.

the sacrifice was known as the Epula.[30] Once Cato, laughing agreeably at Albidius performing the Protervia, said to him, "what good is eating, or eating luxuriously, when in the end it will all be lost in the fire?" We can see from Dionysius how greatly Vulcan was respected by the Romans: their public assemblies met in his temple, and they invoked Vulcan's revenge upon themselves if they did not keep their promises. Any transaction made there was considered more sacred than one made anywhere else. Indeed, in religions where fear was a prevalent factor, Fire was the god that most terrified the pagans. On the other hand, as Fire could do as much good as harm, they could expect greater blessings from it in life.

Vesta[31] was another name for fire amongst the ancients, although some considered that it referred to Earth; to the Greeks it was Hestia. Ovid says: "Vesta, you know, is nothing but a living flame." Dionysius, attempting to synthesise both opinions, says that fire was sacred to Vesta because she was the goddess Tellus,[32] who presided over the middle part of the world: "she herself lights those sublimely-shining fires."

At this point I must venture to disagree with two very learned men, Lipsius[33] and Vossius, who infer from the above that the Earth provides fuel

---

[30]From *epulae*, "dishes of food."

[31]Vesta and the Vestals. Vesta was the Roman equivalent of Hestia, and presided over the hearth. Modern scholars believe that there was a royal hearth-cult in earlier times (*OCD* 943), which led to the building of her round temple, which Herbert accurately describes. There was no statue of Vesta in it, but a fire, which was kept alight, as Herbert says (his references would have been Ovid and Cicero), by the Vestal Virgins. Apparently the cult of Vesta, which does indeed date to the time of Numa Pompilius, was centred in the Forum, not the oldest part of Rome, and there was another similar cult, that of the goddess Caca, on the Palatine, pre-dating that of Vesta. Vestal Virgins were allowed to marry after thirty years (originally five years), but unchastity during their time of service was punished by their being walled up or entombed alive, "an obvious ordeal; Vesta might set [them] free if [they] were innocent" (*OCD* 944). Herbert's remark later on that few of them married is also accurate.

[32]Tellus. There is some confusion here; Tellus was the Roman earth-goddess, whose earliest temple may be dated to 260 B.C., although her cult is much older. Varro notes that she was associated with the gods Tellumo, Altor (the Feeder) and Rusor (the Ploughman). She has no feast-days, but sometimes a pregnant cow was offered to her (see *OCD* 882).

[33]Joost Lips [Lipsius] (1547–1606), a Dutch philosopher who was primarily interested in the revival of ancient philosophical traditions. He was well-known for his work on Stoicism, which was expressed in *Manductio ad Stoicam philosophiam* (1592).

for the celestial fires. I cannot see how they can arrive at this conclusion, for how could the Earth, which itself kindles fires, and which is, compared to many celestial bodies, so small, supply them with fuel? It would be a very small supply anyway, as the vast quantities of vapours ascending to the middle regions of the air are condensed into water, snow, hail, winds, clouds and mists, and either fall down to Earth again or are dissipated in the air. I agree here with Cartari that Vesta is rather the pure fire which gives light to all living things and is therefore distinguished from Vulcan, who represents a baser kind of fire.[34] Some modern scholars agree with Vossius, but I cannot concur; although I know very well that vapours can ascend to a great height, I do not see how they could afford nutriment to the Sun.

The worship of both Vulcan and Vesta in Italy goes back a long way; the Romans got it from the Albans and they, in turn, from Aeneas and the Trojans, as we understand from Ovid, "We see the pledges of Trojan Vesta carried away."[35] There is also evidence from ancient coins which depict a round temple of Vesta with Aeneas carrying his father Anchises on his shoulders. In one hand he bears the Palladium,[36] which, if you can believe it, fell from heaven, and he leads his son Iulus, who also carries sacred objects, with the other. This [account] agrees with what Dionysius and others say. Numa was the first to build a temple to Vesta in Rome, but against this it is believed that before him Romulus made one, from which the Vestal Virgins were recruited and which was on the spot where Romulus was produced by Mars or more likely by one of his priests (Vossius suggests either a warlike or military man, which amounts to the same thing). It is allowed that the Vestal Virgins were introduced by Romulus, as Plutarch, Propertius and Cicero testify. By the will of the Curia[37] I understand that he [Romulus] distributed public altar-fires throughout the entire city, which served as perpetual fires. Next Numa, gathering all the fires into one place,

---

[34]Cartari 203–07. Also cf. Ovid, *Fasti* VI, 291 "nec tu aliud Vestam quam vivam intellege flammam" (Conceive of Vesta as naught but the living flame [Fraser 341]).

[35]This reference is obscure. The Trojan origins and the story of Metellus saving the "pledges" of Vesta is told by Ovid (*Fasti* VI, 417–54), but this line is not there.

[36]The Palladium was an image of Athena (Pallas) which was actually sent down from heaven (it did not fall) by Zeus to Dardanus, the legendary founder of Troy. During the Trojan War it was carried off by Diomedes and Odysseus, which led to the capture of Troy, as the city was no longer protected. The Roman version has Aeneas rescue the Palladium and bring it to Italy, where it ended up in the *penus Vestae* and became the symbol of the safety of Rome. The illustration to which Herbert refers may be found in du Choul (123).

[37]Romulus divided Roman patricians into thirty *curiae*, or divisions. Herbert uses the term *curiatim*, which refers to this. The word later came to be associated

built one common space between the Capitoline and the Palace, of which the first four, then six, Vestal Virgins were in charge. From this number a group of six remained in [Cicero's] time. Plutarch remembered the building of a temple to Vesta; he said that it was believed Numa had surrounded the temple with a perpetual fire of Vesta, and that it was spherical in construction so that it might express not just the Earth (which was like Vesta) but the natural universe, in the middle of which the Pythagoreans recommended that a fire be kept and tended, calling it Vesta and the Unity. There the Pythagoreans paid tribute to Fire.

The cult of Fire was very ancient and universal, and I believe that the common people took it very seriously. There were many other deities, and gods too, that were worshipped amongst the pagans everywhere, but it appears that Fire itself was judged more excellent, because it was quick, present, and unpredictable; it could help or harm just as it felt inclined. Perhaps this is why Pausanias says of the sacrifices that were solemnly performed on Olympus that "they first sacrifice to Hestia, and secondly to Olympian Zeus." And Servius notes that there was no sacrifice without fire, or at which Vesta was not invoked. Ovid provides an example, "from where in prayer/ We say, O Vesta, that you hold the first place."[38] Cicero says, "this is the goddess who presides over hearths and altars. We always make our last prayers and sacrifices to her, for she is the protector of our intimate lives."[39] This perennial fire was kept in Greece and amongst adjacent regions which, it was said, were then known as *Pryzannipides*.

In Italy the Vestals were bound by law not to marry until they had remained pure for thirty years; for the first ten they learned the rites and ceremonies, for the second ten they conducted the sacrifices, and for the final ten years they taught the others. From that time there was nothing stopping them from marrying if they wished to lay down the insignia of their office; but few did so, and those that did [according to Dionysius] were not very happy. These Virgins received great honour from the State, but if they disgraced themselves the punishment was severe. Many Virgins nevertheless remained pure, as no-one was allowed in the temple at night. Amongst them Aemilia and Tatia were said to have performed miracles, as Dionysius relates. Certain holy objects of Vesta were secretly kept in the temple, amongst which was the Palladium mentioned above, and the image whose infamous evil eye the Vestals worshipped so that it might drive away

---

with the meeting-place of the Senate (like the Areopagus in Athens) and then as a word for the Senate itself.

[38]Ovid, *Fasti* VI, 304.

[39]Cicero, *NG* II, 68 (150).

men or hang them by the neck. Taking this even further, they were able to stop fugitives who had not yet left the city, retaining them in their place through prayers and hymns; this strength, Pliny tells us, had been maintained for 830 years. By what means the incestuous Vestal Tatia carried water in a sieve, can also be read in Pliny. There were other interesting events, such as when Q. Caecilius Metellus pulled [the Palladium] out of the flames and presented it to the Capitol.[40]

Pausanias does not refer to any images of Vesta, and Ovid says "there is no image of Vesta or Fire."[41] [However] the image of Vesta appears on several coins; she may be seen in the temple where the Vestals worshipped her, dressed in long, square-cut robes, holding in one hand an incense-box and in the other an earthenware ladle, as an ancient coin depicted in du Choul's book indicates.[42]

From Agelli and Alessandri[43] you may see that the number of Vestals was increased to 20, and that in Ambrose's[44] time 7 more were added, as Lipsius says, although he is in doubt about the exact numbers. The first one, either selected or elected by the Pontifex Maximus, was Amata[45] and the next was called Maxima, as an old inscription of Fl[avia] Manilia

---

[40]Herbert has the wrong Metellus. It was the Pontifex Maximus *Lucius* Caecilius Metellus (d. 221 B.C.) who, according to legend, rescued the Palladium (241 B.C.) from the temple of Vesta (Ovid, *Fasti* VI, 436–54). Metellus was blinded in the accident.

[41]"Long did I foolishly think that there were images of Vesta/ afterwards I learned that there are none under her curved dome./ . . . . there is no effigy of Vesta" (Ovid, *Fasti* VI, 295–98). Ovid explains that as the earth "stands by its own power," so does Vesta.

[42]See du Choul 218. Herbert is correct about Pausanias on Hestia; he notes that in Troizen, "if you go by the sanctuary of Hestia, you find no statue, only an altar . . ." (1, 216).

[43]Alessandro degli Alessandri (1461–1523) was the author of *Dies genialis* (1522), a book describing ancient gods and their attributes. Seznec notes that these descriptions "are by no means the normal ones" (234 n. 3). Herbert also refers to this author as "Alexander of Naples."

[44]St. Ambrose of Trèves (c. 340–97) was the great Bishop of Milan and opponent of the Arians. He may have also been responsible for introducing music into services, and was the author of an exegetical work on the *Song of Songs*, in which he showed that this erotic poem symbolised the union between Christ and the Church.

[45]The only Amata mentioned in Classical sources is the wife of King Latinus and mother of Lavinia. She hanged herself when Turnus, Lavinia's intended, was killed by Aeneas (whom Lavinia married). She does not seem a likely candidate for a Vestal Virgin. I am not sure of Herbert's source for these names of the first Vestals.

attests.[46] The Vestals bound their hair and brought it to the nettle-tree, as Pliny says; this was the sacred tree of Juno, from which she derived her name Lucina;[47] moreover, because the Vestals had renounced marriage they sacrificed to Juno Pronuba and were first chosen for office by the College of Priests. Of their hair being cut, Festus [Avienus] says "the Vestals were shorn when they entered the College of Priests, and they were consecrated with songs." They were prevailed upon to officiate at public sacrifices, and so that the flame did not go out they placed it in a small, deep vessel with firewood, and directed the sun's rays on the centre, as Plutarch tells us. If the flame went out, a public calamity was forecast, and when this happened the whole State suspended the making of treaties or laws, and solemn ceremonies thereupon took place. If it did not go out, it was rekindled during the Kalends of March every year. All the rites associated with Vesta and the Vestals were abolished by Theodosius I,[48] in spite of the eloquence of Symmachus,[49] who said that the harvests would now fail, fields would dry up, and religion itself would be threatened. To him Prudentius[50] replied, describing the Vestals throughout the centuries:[51]

> Now I shall discuss the repute of Vestal virginity
> and the justice of its claim as a standard for the honour paid to purity.
> First, they are taken in early childhood, before the free choice of their wills,
> burning with zeal for the glory and love of the gods,
> can reject the chains of their sex in marriage.
> Their captive purity is turned over to the impersonal altars,
> and in the unfortunate girls desire disappears,

---

[46] See Du Choul 218.

[47] From *lotho*, the nettle-tree.

[48] Flavius Theodosius "the Great," was Emperor of the West 378–95.

[49] Quintus Aurelius Symmachus (c. 340–402) was a distinguished statesman and the last great pagan orator. As prefect of the city (384–85) he engaged in a controversy with Ambrose over the decree by the Emperor Gratian (382) forbidding pagan worship. He was consul several times, and also Proconsul of Africa. Ten books of his letters are preserved, and some fragments of his speeches.

[50] Aurelius Clemens Prudentius (349–after 400), the great Christian Latin poet. His chief works are the *Hamartigenia*, which deals with the origins of sin, and the *Contra Symmachum*, an account of Ambrose's conflict with the latter.

[51] Du Choul also quotes the entire passage (222–23). Cf. Prudentius, *Reply to the Address of Symmachus*, 1064–1108. Herbert's text has been checked with that given by Thomson in the Loeb Classical Library (92–93) and the translation has been modified and corrected from Thomson's somewhat embellished and "cleaned-up" version. Lewis gives no translation of this passage at all.

not voluntarily, but taken from them; their bodies
are intact, but not their minds, and
there is no rest in bed for an unwed woman
who sighs over a secret wound, the loss of marriage;
and then hope remains so the fire does not wholly die
so one day the sleeping torches will be allowed to light up
and over aged figures is thrown the happy bridal veil.
For an appointed time Vesta desires an immaculate body
but in the end she scorns their pure old age.
As long as their swelling breasts made them strong
their flesh was barren; no love made them fertile in motherhood;
but an old woman whose sacred duty's done gets married —
deserting the hearth which was her youth's to serve,
she carries her wrinkles to the bridal bed
and in that cold bed she learns to grow warm.
In the meantime, while the twisted band fastens her straying hair
and the unwed priestess keeps the fatal fire alight,
she is carried through the streets in a public procession,
sitting in a cushioned chariot, and with face uncovered
she obliges the gaping city crowds with the sight of a virgin.
From there to the arena passes this pure and bloodlessly pious figure
to see bloody fights and the death of men; with holy eyes she watches
men suffering wounds to earn their living.
There she sits, conspicuous in her head-bands,
                    enjoying the trainers' products.
O soft, gentle heart! as blows fall she rises
and, as the victor stabs the loser in the throat
she calls him her favourite, and with a flick of her thumb
the pure virgin bids him stab the enemy's breast
so that no life at all remains in his body,
and under deep thrusts he lies in his death-agony.
Is this their function, said to keep continual watch
on the greatness of Latium's Palatine city,
to undertake the preservation of her people's
lives and nobility's well-being,
to let their hair spread elegantly over their necks
or wreathe their brows with dainty ribbons, put braid in their hair
and underground, in presence of the shades cut cattle's throats
in lustral sacrifice, muttering vague prayers?

For further information, see Lipsius, who shows how extensive was the
worship of Vesta, the pure fire (or God in the fire, as I understand it)
grew. It went as far as the East and West Indies, and Leo African-

us[52] claims that it is worshipped amongst the Africans in Libya today, and that they keep it burning according to the Vestal custom.

This is all I have to say about Fire under the names of Vulcan and Vesta; there is no time to describe the temples or the sacred rites, or whether Tubal-Cain was Vulcan, or to insert the opinions of various scholars about the etymology of the word. I have spent long enough on the worship of Fire and the things which are connected with it. I will now move on to Air, leaving the manner of purification by fire used amongst pagans for another place.

Air

After the mysterious operations of Heaven, and the more obvious ones of Fire, nothing has so much sublunary influence as the element of Air. Its composition is so thin, and so adaptable to movement, that it touches, surrounds, and penetrates everything around us, which means that it variously affects us according to its temperature and qualities. It is in this element that the seminal causes of things are stored in Heaven like a vast field, and they, as they come into contact with wind and rain generated in the middle regions, descend upon the Earth. There, clothed in a more substantial body, these seeds produce, with [Heaven's] power and assistance, something visible, and for a number of celestial rotations they continue to function amongst us. After a time, they return to their origin (which, as the old philosophers tell us, is Hades) to operate either there or in a new place. Because they have plastic power, they do not confine their operations to one element only, but, like sculptors, they mould matter into any shape they wish. Wherever they are, they are active, constant, and efficient at performing their natural duties. Heaven and Earth constantly deal with each other in these airy regions as if they were at a fair or a market, receiving some things and sending others down in exchange. As this esoteric doctrine is unlikely to appeal to a mass audience, I will not go any further, but will merely observe with Quintilian that one should not go on too long about things which are neither intelligible nor beneficial.

It should be noted here that the ancients did not consider that there was a great deal of difference between Air and Aether, and in their mystical philosophies Jupiter and Minerva were indiscriminately used for both. Ocellus points out that "Nature and Generation govern everything," and

---

[52]Leo Africanus was the baptismal name of Al-Hasan ibn Mohammed al-Wazzan (c. 1483–1554), a great Arabian traveller and explorer, and the principal source for the West's knowledge of Islam in the 16th and 17th centuries. He wrote (in Italian, which he had learned after being captured by pirates and presented to Pope Leo X, who had him baptised), *Descrittione dell'Africa* (1550; English translation, 1600).

therefore, as common opinion has it, Aether is nobler than Air, but Air is nearer to us and more useful. It cannot be denied, however, that many new things have their beginnings in the Aether, as we have already seen; the *Chronicles of Ferrara*, for example, state that between 7 and 8 o'clock at night a star appeared, which was of such brightness and size that Heaven seemed to be on fire. From this people concluded that Aether and Air were almost the same substance, and that they were both subject to corruption and generation, although this was more frequent in air.[53] Pure Aether is full of energy, but Air is more accessible and agreeable; we breathe it in and out continually, and it is so familiar to us that it approaches our hearts. Neither astronomers nor physicists have been able to determine the size and extent of this element, and although there are mathematical instruments which observe the size and distance of Aether, Air, and the heavenly bodies, they make many mistakes, as I shall point out.

First, astronomers think that the centres of celestial bodies coincide with the centre of the earth, although they are an entire semi-diameter distant from the Earth. Patrizi showed that this mistake was caused by the fact that Earth is not a point in respect of Heaven, but a proportional quantity. A second error arose from assuming that with instruments one can observe half the sky above the horizon, which is impossible when both the sights through which the observations are made and the various positions of the eye are taken into consideration. The density of the lower air, the purity of higher air, and the vast amount of mist and cloud everywhere must cause variations in refraction, so that the thickness and disproportion of the medium can lead to errors as great as the uncertainty of distance. I have discussed these things more fully in *De veritate*, and also in *De causis errorum*, which is not yet published.

I could also use optics here to refute the astronomers, but I will confine myself to explaining the common notions concerning the density of Air. Vitellio[54] thinks that the Earth is nearly 51 miles away from the clouds, and that the Air does not extend above that for more than 200 miles, at which point he says the Aether begins. Aristotle says that Air is 100 times as large as the Earth, to which we should add what some describe as the imaginary extent of the Aether. According to Tycho Brahe, there will be a distance of 52 semi-diameters between the surfaces of the Earth and the Moon, and the Air will therefore be 100 times larger than this globe of earth and water.

Air was considered divine not only by the priests and the ignorant masses, but also by many philosophers such as Anaximenes and Diogenes

---

[53] But for Aristotle's view on aether, see n. 9.

[54] Unidentified.

Apolloniates.[55] Before that, the Assyrians worshipped it, and some Africans, as Firmicus tells us:

> The Assyrians and people in some parts of Africa considered Air as one of the elements, and they worshipped it with imagined veneration. To it they gave the names of both Juno and Venus the Virgin. Minerva was understood by the Egyptians to mean Air.

According to many others, the Greeks and Romans sometimes considered Jupiter to mean Air, sometimes Juno; believing that there were male and female parts of Air, they called the upper part Jupiter and the lower part Juno. They thought that the male air was where the wind was, and that female air was sluggish and cloudy. So much for Air and its adoration as Juno.

Water

The pagans also worshipped Water; they believed that everything came from it, and that it was more capable of condensation and rarification than any other element. Because it varied so much, and because it appeared and disappeared, they venerated it not as an external form or matter, but as a principle with an internal divine power or virtue. Thus Thales, who as Cicero tells us, was the first to examine such matters, designated water as the original substance of all things, and God was the Soul or Mind which formed everything out of it.[56]

The ancients believed that the primary causes of things were to be found in seas, rivers, fountains and lakes, as well as in the air, because the latter contained rainwater. Some people thought that not only lower animals such as horses, cows, pigs, and dogs originated from it, but that humans too, male and female, arose out of the sea. Some fish seem to look human in form or shape, and the explanation was that when they crept out of the sea and got on shore, Nature, by a gradual process, furnished them with appropriate organs for life on land, much as amphibians moving out of one element into another. At last, these offspring of the sea obtained speech and limbs as we have; by degrees their piscine shape changed, and this also happens to other animals, so that they will not seem strange. I would not have mentioned this extraordinary idea except for the fact that ancient

---

[55]Anaximenes wrote "As our soul, being air, holds us togther, so do breath and air surround the whole universe" [Fr. 2] (Freeman 19). Diogenes stated "it seems to me that that which is called Intelligence is called Air by mankind . . . by this all creatures are guided" [Fr. 5] (Freeman 88).

[56]Cicero does not mention Thales by name, at least not in *The Nature of the Gods*. The source for the little that we know about Thales is Aristotle.

philosophy does not give us a satisfactory account of man's origins, yet it is obvious that water contributes a great deal to the flourishing of the human species and to everything else as well. Humidity is required as much, if not more, than heat to make up a complete human being; we more often die for want of moisture than for want of heat. Humidity is an oily or balsamic substance, but it is not watery, because that quality would work against or destroy the heat, whilst the oiliness supports it and feeds it. But worship was paid, under the name of Water, to all kinds of moisture.

When we examine the parts of the elements more closely, the first to spring to mind is the sea, which, as Danskius proves with many solid arguments, encompasses the entire earth, and I refer the reader to him.[57] Granting this hypothesis, I doubt whether there is as great a quantity of subterranean fire as is generally thought. It must be supposed that the earth is full of caverns through which water passes continually. Vossius says that sailors thought the sea rarely more than half an Italian mile deep, with the exception of some whirlpools a mile and a half in depth either near the Flemish Isles or in the Pacific, which cannot be sounded at all. In length and breadth the sea equals, and perhaps exceeds, that of the earth, if we calculate by what we know of the world. Alessandro Piccolomini[58] has written extensively on this subject, so you may consult him.

For the saltiness of the sea, scholars give two particular reasons. First, the rays of the sun draw out the softer freshness of the water, and, secondly, because of this the water becomes harder. If this is the case, the great rivers should be salty; the thinness of the water would be no impediment because the sun's influence would be even more powerful on them. Neither is it too deep, for the nearer water is to the earth, the sooner the thicker parts harden. Also, if this theory were correct, it would mean that the sea was not salty from the beginning, but became so over a period of time, which I cannot see being proved. The only conceivable cause, then, is the Universal Divine Providence, which gave the sea its saline quality and the power to

---

[57]Claudius Dausquius [Danskius] was the author of *Terra et aqua seu terrae fluitantes* (1633). In a Latin note written on the inside of his copy of this book, Herbert calls it "an interesting but puzzling work" (*FK* 88).

[58]Alessandro Piccolomini (1508–78), Professor of Moral Philosophy at the University of Padua from 1540, was one of the earliest commentators on Aristotle's *Poetics* (1575). His work was highly praised by the poet Tasso (Spingarn 87). He also wrote on ancient languages, law and mathematics, and was a dramatist of some repute. Herbert owned a work by him on Aristotle's physics, *In mechanicas quaestiones Aristotelis paraphrasis paulo quidem plenior* (1547), and two works on cosmology, *De la sfera del mondo* (1552) and *Delle stelle fisse* (1552).

ebb and flow in order to adapt it to the nature of the animals which live in it. If that huge expanse of sea-water remained fresh and calm, like lakes, the entire atmosphere would be full of infection. Anyone who wants to know any other reason might as well ask why fire is hot, or why earth is solid and dry, or other such questions. These things are the immediate product of Nature itself, and can be known only through their principles; the ebb and flow of the sea, however, corresponds exactly to the various phases of the Moon, which gives philosophers good reason to conjecture that the motion originated from there as well.

There is nothing stranger than the fact that the sea, in spite of the vast confluence of rivers emptying into it for so many eras, gets neither fresher nor fuller. If, as Aristotle tells us, all rivers go to the sea as a common receptacle, why does it not change in taste or get larger, and why do fountains and rivers remain fresh? It is not good enough to answer that rivers and springs, from all over the world, pass through the Earth's underground caverns and are somehow softened by degrees; rivers rush to the sea with rapid impetuosity; they do not move uncertainly or slowly. There is no correlation between the difficult passage that water has through the narrow pores of the Earth and the precipitous violence of the rivers. Yet inquisitive seekers after knowledge are always trying to find secondary causes for those things which come directly from the wise counsels of God, who established the primaeval perfection of all things.

It is certainly worth observing the impetuous motion of the sea as it lashes against the shores on both sides, rising and falling, and, as Pliny says, "purging itself" every full moon. Modern writers think that the reciprocal motion of the sea is caused by the diurnal motion of the Earth, but there are many objections to this; even allowing for diurnal movement, how could it explain the ebb and flow of the sea seven times a day, or that the tides in different parts of the world are inexplicably inconsistent? To some, like those people at Ausserum in Liburnia,[59] where the tide ebbs and flows more than twenty times a day, the water here must seem stagnant. The theory does not solve the diurnal, weekly, monthly, three monthly, half yearly and annual motions of the sea, for observation has shown that there is such variety. If we try to explain the reciprocal motion of the sea by the Moon, even greater difficulties present themselves, especially as Augustus Caesarius[60] reports

---

[59] The Liburni were one of the peoples who lived in Illyria, modern Yugoslavia and Albania.

[60] Augustus Caesarius (fl. 1210–40) was a Benedictine monk who was abbott of Prum, Germany. He wrote the *Explicatio rerum et verborum* (1222), a polyglot work on etymology which contained a great deal of miscellaneous information.

that when the Moon is south-west or south, the water is high, and when it is east or north-west, the water is low; when the Moon was in the latter, it was high tide in the Mediterranean, and vice versa. No-one has ever been able to explain why this is from observation of the diurnal motions of the Moon and the Earth. Neither, as Aristotle points out, does the exhaling and stirring of many winds by the sun provide an answer, nor does the shape of the shores or seabed, or the direction of the flow of the sea, its circular motion (imitating the heavens) or its casting up of great rocks and stones. Neither the ascension of the Moon to the meridian nor its descent to the West, nor any of its positions and movements, provides a satisfactory explanation.[61]

I will now discuss the saltiness of the sea. When salt water is boiled, it is hotter than other water, and for this reason it is probable that the Caspian Sea, which has no fewer than 80 rivers and 5 lakes running into it and softening its waters, is thus calmed. Another cause may be its being made thin by its flowing in Venilia[62] and being condensed by ebbing in Salacia.[63] I have shown that in many instances the ebbing and flowing of the sea cannot

---

[61]Tides are, of course, caused by the attraction which the Moon exerts on the seas; perhaps it is not so well-known that the Sun does indeed make a contribution as well. When there is a new or full Moon, the tidal force of the Sun is added to that of the Moon, and spring (full) tides are caused. Galileo wrote a paper on tides (1616) in which he said that they were caused by the double motion of the Earth around its axis and around the Sun. But in 1618 he revised the paper and told Archduke Leopold of Austria that the theory was only "ingenious speculation" after all (Galileo 221). Herbert's point with all this discussion of tidal ebb and flow is to show that no modern theory is completely able to cover the reasons why tidal patterns are inconsistent, and, rather naïvely, to claim that as scientists seem unable to come up with secondary (that is, natural) causes, the only answer must be Universal Divine Providence. What Herbert's peculiar stance does indicate is a reluctance to completely swallow new scientific theory and reject Aristotelian science. This attitude may be traced back to his studying with the likes of Cremonini and Liceti in Padua, who were Aristotelians of the old school. No doubt Herbert did not like Tycho Brahe's demolition of the crystalline spheres, either, and there is certainly evidence, both here and in *De veritate*, that he did not wholeheartedly accept the Copernican universe, in spite of having read several of Copernicus's works.

[62]Venilia was a goddess or nymph "of forgotten nature and functions" *(OCD* 940) who was connected somehow with Neptune. Rose notes that she was one of the lovers of Picus (174–75). Herbert's source may have been Varro, who says she is "the water which comes to the shore [*venit*]" (*De lingua Latina* 5.72) or Augustine, who quotes Varro and mocks him (*City of God* VII, 22).

[63]Salacia was, according to Augustine, the wife of Neptune (*City of God* IV, 11; VII, 22). Actually, she was "the cult-partner of Neptunus" (*OCD* 788), the latter being most likely an Italian *numen* of spring-water, not originally the great

come solely from the Moon, for then all its waters would demonstrate the same changes (just as fire burns anything combustible) and that it does not happen everywhere at the same time. It should happen, then, that in the Antipodes, when the Moon does not come out, the greatest tides should be at the new moon, as well as at the full, never at any times between. As the Moon is greater when full than new, we might rationally suppose that she would then be most influential, and these, amongst other arguments, should be sufficient to demonstrate that the Moon is not the sole cause of the sea's ebb and flow, but I cannot go on with this any longer.

The reciprocal motion of the sea has two aspects, one of which was unknown to the ancients because they usually sailed close to the shore and did not put out to sea. The first motion is from north to south, for they sailed sooner from this point to the opposite than the contrary, even though there were good winds both ways.[64] Danes and Norwegians can get to England faster than we can get there; we sail faster to Spain than they do here, as experience proves.[65] Whether this is because of the shallow bottom of the North Sea, or, which is more probable, because of rapid showers of snow and rain in that cold and damp area, I cannot explain here. Now there is a different east-west movement; sailors will tell you that they can get from Spain to America in one month, but take three or four to get home. This might be caused by the winds in the West Indies blowing constantly from the east for a period of time, but from east to west the sea in inclined downwards. This can also be seen in the Mediterranean, the Adriatic Gulf and in the Black Sea; it is much easier to get from any port near Egypt or Phoenicia to Spain than back again. People sail more quickly from the Philippines or Moluccas to the Cape of Good Hope than the reverse, but whether this is caused by inclination of the sea or by the power of rivers flowing from the east and south, the reader may judge. In conclusion, as soon as the ancients discovered a motion of the sea they began to worship it because, as Pliny says, the wonders of Nature were nowhere so obvious.

As for the inhabitants of the sea, they far exceed all other animals in size. They are known as cetaceans, amongst which the whale, grampus, orca,

---

sea-god, although he came to be identified later with Poseidon. Despite the way the name sounds, it probably derives from *salire*, "to jump." Salacia was identified with Amphitrite.

[64] If so, how did they ever get back from where they started?

[65] Herbert cannot resist an allusion to the defeat of the Spanish Armada in 1588, when he was six years old. He may also be referring to Drake's attack on Cadiz a little earlier.

tiburus, pristes and scolopendra marina[66] were known in ancient times, but many more kinds have lately been discovered around Iceland and other parts of the North Sea, and in the Indies as well. As far as I know, the great leviathan[67] was known only to the Jews, but I doubt whether the Rabbis have left us a description of it. There are several reasons why fish should be bigger than other animals: 1. they are made of a moister substance; 2. they always have food near them; 3. they live very long: no-one ever found a fish that died of old age. Galileo gives a good reason why the sea should produce animals of such vast dimensions beyond those on land: on the land, bones sustain flesh, whilst in the sea the opposite is true. If a whale's flesh did not support the ribs and bones like cork, its own weight would sink it. That is why when they are driven ashore by a storm or accidentally get into shallow water, they are helpless, and their huge bulk prevents them from getting free. There were and are many shellfish and crustaceans in the sea that seem to be products of Nature's games, and they deservedly attract the attention of the curious. They seem almost to be fashioned by the power of the sea itself, and this is why pagans believed that the sea deserved great honour.

Miraculous works of Nature are no less evident in fresh water; common water moistens and softens, or hardens chalk and petrifies wood so that a theatre could be built of stones so formed. Some bodies of water appear to be all colours, or all tastes; some extinguish fire and some shine like fire against the rain. Some springs are hot, and others so cold that they quench natural heat. Some slake our thirst, but others, especially those near the sea, increase it. Some are very bland, but others are impregnated not only with the taste, but with the qualities of fossils and minerals. Some can make us urinate and expel bladder-stones, but others may cause them; some have purgative qualities, others stop the flux. They may be good for the eyes, or very bad for them; they can clean and whiten wool, or even give it a new colour. Some trees will flourish near water, but others wither and decay. Mute fish[68] live in some waters, but in others nothing but croaking

---

[66]The *orca* is "a large sea-mammal, probably the grampus" (*OLD* 1265). I have been unable to identify *tiburus*, but it might be a shark of some kind (as suggested by Prof. John Teunissen). The *pristis* is "a large fish . . . identified with the sawfish" (*OLD* 1461) and the *scolopendra marina*, literally "marine centipede," is "a sea-creature . . . perhaps a nereid worm" (*OLD* 1621).

[67]Leviathan is the primeval dragon, and by extension any kind of large sea-monster. The Hebrew word means "the coiled one."

[68]There seems to have been some interest in the fact that fish make no noise, cf. Donne, "Nor will this earth serve him; he sinks the deepe/ Where harmless Fishe monastique silence keepe"("Elegy on Mistress Boulstred," 13–14).

frogs breed. There are waters which make people sober and abstemious, whilst others make them drunk. Some drive people mad, and others restore the senses by removing one of the most serious symptoms, excessive sexual desire, if we may believe what was said of the Fountain of Cyriscus.[69] Some sharpen the wit or improve the memory, others make people stupid or forgetful. Accounts of all these things may be seen in Pliny, Strabo, Vitruvius[70] and others. We may conclude by noting that Nature cannot provide us with anything that Water cannot also produce.

I might say a great deal here about snow and rain-water, but it would be beside the point.[71] I cannot omit, however, what Vossius tells us about why some springs increase and decrease with the sea:

> Water near the sea and which flows from it in direct passage is affected like the sea itself. However, when it meanders for a long way before flowing to the source, and the sea is at high tide, it will then ebb, and if the sea is at low tide, the water may be high.[72]

There are many problems with this. In some parts of the world, notably here, there are springs and wells whose motion corresponds with that of the sea, some rising and falling at the same time. But if the sea had immediate contact through subterranean passages with these springs and wells, I see no reason for their remaining fresh. Likewise, if some springs have this secret contact, why not all of them, or, why should not some of them rise while others fall? With all due respect to so great a scholar, I think that the

---

[69] Herbert does not give a marginal reference to this miraculous fountain, but it is surely the Fountain of Cyzicus mentioned by Mutianus. Mario Equicola mentions it in *Libro de natura de amore* (Venetia: Lorio da Portes, 1525), 153[r]. See also Pausanias, *Description of Greece* "Achaia," ch. 23, Loeb III.306.

[70] M. Vitruvius Pollio (1st century B.C.) was the author of *De architectura*, which book provides us with most of what we know about the theory and practice of Roman architecture. Herbert would have found Book II (the architecture of temples) and Book VIII (on water-supplies) of some interest. *The Ten Books on Architecture* has been translated by M.H. Morgan (New York: Dover Books, 1960). Ovid offers an account of cold water rites to forget love practiced in the temple of Venus on Mount Eryx in *The Remedies of Love*, ll. 551–54 in *The Art of Love and Other Poems*, tr. J.H. Mozley (Cambridge: Harvard UP, 1962), 214.

[71] Actually, most of what Herbert has been saying for the last several pages has been beside the point; indeed, he seems to have quite forgotten what the point was in the first place. However, it does give an fascinating insight into Herbert's fertile brain and his propensity for reading practically anything that came his way, be it scientific explanations of water-systems or a digression on interesting marine life.

[72] Vossius II, lxxiii, 688.

air is disturbed by some unseen pores at the onset of floods, which makes the waters swell, rise, fall and subside by the same degree as the sea itself. However, in those springs and wells whose motion is opposite to that of the sea, I suppose that it would be the other way around; in that case I think that there must be very narrow passages or pores between them and the sea, closed at the end nearest the sea, and so full of air that the water is forced to rise. There may well be, in a straight tube, such a proportion of air to water that can move or expel it. But when the sea rises on a sandy bank, it begins to insinuate itself into the pores, takes over space from the enclosed air, and expels it through the Earth's pores to another, more remote area, so that the water, hitherto supported by the air, falls by degrees. As the sea recedes, the air returns to where it was, and the water rises by the same number of degrees. Several pneumatic experiments show this to be the case, but I will not presume to elaborate on so arcane a subject. I simply wanted to show that there seem to be so many wonderful things about water, and that it was so useful and ubiquitous an element that the ancients gave it divine attributes.

Athanasius,[73] himself an Egyptian, tells us that they were the first to worship Water as a god, although others worshipped rivers or fountains. They venerated the Nile, as Firmicus says, "worshipped it, prayed to it and petitioned it." They held many aquatic animals sacred, amongst them a sort of scaly fish, and eels, according to Herodotus.[74] The mystic name of water amongst them was Osiris or Siris. Osiris, the First Principle of Good, was the Sun in heaven and Water on earth, particularly the Nile. This is not strange, for, as Cartari tells us, the same god can stand for different things, or different names be applied to the same thing. I think that this originated with the priests explaining their various mysteries according to their own interests and whims, or for making them intelligible to the common people; we ought to bear this in mind at all times, or it will be impossible to understand ancient theology. Canopus was once a sailor, but after death was translated to the heavens as a star; to the Egyptians he stands for

---

[73] St. Athanasius (296–373) was Bishop of Alexandria from 328. Expelled by the Arian emperor, Constantius II, he lived in the desert until the emperor died in 361. Cardinal Newman called him "a principle instrument after the Apostles by which the sacred truths of Christianity have been conveyed and secured to the world" (Attwater 50). Herbert's passage comes from the *Oratio contra gentes*, one of Athanasius's many tracts against Arianism.

[74] There was an Egyptian fish-god, Remi (Budge I, 303), but he only occurs once, in the *Book of the Dead*. The Nile-god was Hapi, with whom Osiris was indeed identified in later Egyptian times (see Budge II, 40ff).

Water.[75] Rufinus[76] tells us about the priest of Canopus, who by his cleverness was not thoroughly subjugated, and who destroyed the gods of the Chaldaeans and the Persians. When the fire came, they threw the great god on it in front of a large crowd of people, filled it with water and produced a watery deity under which his rivals, sure of their victory, made a fire. The wax soon melted, the water ran out, and presently put out the fire. Whether this all ended in a joke, or had great religious significance, we are not told, but we do know that the Magi held both Fire and Water as the principles of all things. Vitruvius says that according to the traditions of the Egyptian priests, everything came from water. They cover an urn full of it and carry it to the temple with the deepest imaginable reverence, falling flat on the ground and lifting their hands up to the skies as they give thanks for all the products of the divine mercy.

They also had a great veneration for the sea under the name of Typho, and would not use salt at the table because it was his foam. Neither would they salt any fish, because they were his people and they might incur his anger by doing so; they even shunned sailors because they used the seas, but whether this was because they were afraid of floods or for any other reason, I will not enquire about here. The Egyptians believed this deity was the Neptune of the Greeks, whom their Libyan neighbours worship under the name Pelasgus,[77] but they did not worship Neptune because they believed that the merciless sea, like inexorable fate, could not be supplicated, although both were divine.

Herodotus, Strabo, Clement of Alexandria and Arnobius all mention the Persians as paying divine honours to water as well. They believed it was impious to urinate, spit, throw anything dirty into water, or even to wash their hands in a running stream, as I mentioned before. Tacitus says it was considered very irreligious to spit into the sea or contaminate it with anything, however humanly necessary it might have been. If sailors on long voyages were to observe this custom, there would be great mortality amongst them, because nothing helps preserve their health more than cleanliness. The Persians sacrificed horses, especially white ones, to water, which I assume was done in Neptune's honour, but I will discuss it later.

---

[75]See Cartari (249).

[76]Rufinus (after 400) wrote a Latin paraphrase of Eusebius's history. Herbert may be using it because of his lack of confidence in Greek, but in his favour it must be noted that Eusebius, according to his modern translator, "is by no means easy . . . some of his words have meanings not met with in Classical Greek," and there are stylistic problems as well (Williamson 17).

[77]In the Near East, this deity is known as Baal-Saphon (Teixidor 43).

The Atergatis of the Assyrians, so Vossius tells us, was associated with water, but this seems rather contrived because not long before that he tells us that Atergatis was associated with the power of the Sun.[78] From this he concludes that the Sun influences the Moon, and the Moon the Water, which means that Atergatis might have reference to the latter. This is a very weak argument, for it may also be applied to the Air and Earth as well as to other things under the Sun's influence, such as Water. He adds as proof the fact that Atergatis is depicted as a woman above and a fish below, and that the name refers to a great and powerful fish. In the presence of the goddess the priests eat broiled fish to honour her. In spite of her being half woman and half fish, there is no evidence that she must therefore stand for Water, or have anything to do with its veneration. If he had said that although the woman was not worshipped, the fish was, he might have made more sense, if he wanted to prove that Atergatis was a great fish. Also, if Atergatis had been a fish, it is strange that the priests would eat fish in her presence; it would be difficult to find any pagans who ever cooked and ate their gods, pretending by it to honour them. I am more inclined to believe Macrobius, who says that Atergatis was neither water nor a wonderful fish, but, as his description of her images confirms, the Earth. I also believe it because the Assyrians, as Vossius himself notes, were so far from eating fish that they refused even to catch them. The most likely explanation may be this: Atergatis, a queen of Syria, issued an edict saying that no-one was allowed to eat fish except her. Because she loved them so much herself, her priests, afterwards, in imitation of her, ate boiled or grilled fish before her statue, while hungry people looked on! However it really was, I cannot easily see how these contradictions in Vossius may be resolved. But enough of this.

I do not dispute that the Assyrians worshipped Water, as well as other elements, but not by the name Atergatis. Neither is Vossius very successful at trying to prove that by Dagon the people of Palestine meant Water.[79] This image, too, was supposed to be half man, half fish, but it does not follow from this that water was worshipped. I think that there was a story behind this worship: Atergatis, or, as some call her, Derceto, threw herself into a lake near Ascalon which was full of fish. They looked after her, and eventually she metamorphosed into one. It is not in the least improbable that the wicked priests imposed a story like this about their Dagon on the common people, as can be seen from Selden's *De diis Syris*, for example. I shall leave others to decide whether Euronyme, the daughter of Oceanus, who had a statue like that of Atergatis or Derceto, or the Sirens, may contribute anything to

[78] Vossius II, lxxvi, 699–700.

[79] Vossius I, xxiii, 165.

the clarification of this matter. Some, such as Pausanias, thought Atergatis was Diana; he notes that this deity was worshipped by the Pitigalenses, who lived in Arcadia.[80] Her temple was open every day and public as well as private worship was paid to her.

At one time Water had both masculine and feminine names; for the better understanding of their history it is necessary to note here that this was usual practice for all deities. In Joshua 46:8[81] the God of the Hebrews seems to take the feminine gender, concerning which, amongst others, you may consult Liceti in his book *De quaesitis per epistolas*.[82]

Amongst the various names given to Water, Oceanus is the principal; the ancients considered him as Father of the Gods. Homer refers to "Oceanus the Father of the gods and Tethys the Mother." Moses says that Water was created on the first day.[83] The images of Oceanus and Neptune were quite similar, but Oceanus was considered, as Neptune's grandfather, the elder. Vossius says that Oceanus stood for the exterior sea, and Neptune the interior, or watery humours in general.[84] Justin Martyr mentions the worship of the ocean: "when Alexander had captured the city, he returned to his ships and offered a sacrifice to the Ocean, praying for a safe return to his country." The Greeks called the sea Poseidon, the Romans Neptunus. Herodotus relates how sacrifices were offered to "Poseidon the Deliverer," and mentions temples to him amongst the Patidaeatae and the Carians.[85] Pliny tells us that the Romans celebrated the Neptunalia on the tenth day of the Kalends of August. The entire month of February was sacred to Neptune, either to make him favourable to sailors in spring and summer, or because any expiatory purgations made during that month were never done without water. Soothsayers dedicated galls to Neptune, believing that something bitter would be acceptable to a bitter god. It was Neptune who first tamed

---

[80]Pitigalenses. This reference is obscure. Pausanias mentions a sanctuary of Artemis in Phigalia (2, 471), which is in Arcadia, but I can find nothing closer; the inhabitants may have been called "Phigalenses" by the Romans.

[81]The Book of Joshua does not have 46 chapters, and I cannot locate this reference anywhere in the text.

[82]Fortunato Liceti (1581–1657) was Professor of Philosophy at Padua, and had known Herbert since the latter's visit to Italy in 1609. Liceti presented Herbert with several copies of his works (*FK* 88–89). Rossi notes that he was "smiled upon by Galileo" because of his prodigious memory and industry (I, 223), although he was an old-school Aristotelian.

[83]Genesis 1:3.

[84]Vossius II, lxxvii, 702.

[85]I can find no mention of this in Herodotus.

horses and taught riding; he is even said to have been finally changed into a horse himself. There was an incredible temple to him in the land of Atlantis: he was seated in a large chariot, with a bridle in his hand and his head touching the very roof of the huge temple, although Herodotus says that his statue was only seven cubits high and made of brass.[86] Thus it was that the Circensian Games were sacred to Neptunus Hyppius, but Livy says that they were instituted by Romulus in commemoration of the rape of the Sabine women. The Romans called these games the Consualia and the Arcadians the Hippocratia, during which time horses and mules were exempt from work and were crowned with flowers, according to an underground altar either erected, or found near the Circus Maximus. Whether Consualia derives from the name of the god Consus,[87] consult either Plutarch or Dionysius of Halicarnassus. Some think that the idea of great counsels being kept secret originated with this, which is why the passage to his altar was never open except at such times, and this seems to suggest that Neptune and Consus were the same. Pausanias adds that because people at those Games were frightened by the horses, the god was called Neptunus Taraxippus, and they supplicated him to avoid the fear. Dionysius tells a different story, and you may consult him at your leisure; for [Neptune's] trident, the huge shell like a chariot in which he rode, his princely retinue and triumphal procession, you should read the poets. Another male name for a sea-god is Nereus, who had fifty beautiful daughters, the Nereids, by Doris.[88]

---

[86]The mythical island of Atlantis (or Island of Atlas) was supposed to have been located off the Straits of Gibraltar. "Its kings," the *OCD* states, "were defeated by the pre-historic Athenians" (116). Atlantis is mentioned in Plato, *Timaeus* 24e, and described as "larger than Libya and Asia put together . . . pre-eminent in courage and military skill" (Hamilton and Cairns 1159). Plato also describes the destruction of Atlantis, not by the Athenians, but by natural disasters. See Phyllis Young Forsyth, *Atlantis: The Making of Myth* (Montreal: McGill-Queen's UP, 1980).

I find no mention of Atlantis in Herodotus, although he does write of a "seven-cubit bronze Poseidon" (9.81) which was made by King Pausanias of Sparta after his defeat of the Persians.

[87]Consus had his festivals when the harvest ended and when autumn sowing was over. His name probably derives from the verb *condere*, and "he is the god of the store-bin or other receptacle for the garnered grain" (*OCD* 232). Livy identifies him with Neptunus Hyppius (*History of Rome* 43 [I.9.6]), and also mentions the celebration of the Consualia by Romulus (43 [I.9.8]).

[88]Nereus and Doris. Doris was an Oceanid. One of Nereus's daughters was Thetis, who became the mother of Achilles. Nereus was known for his wisdom. Herbert is wrong to make Thetis the daughter of Doris and Oceanus.

Feminine names which belong to the sea include Thetis, the daughter of Oceanus and Doris, and the nymph Tethys, one of the Nereids.[89] To these we may add the Napaea, or Naïads, the nymphs of the fountains, the Hydriades and Ephydriades. The term nymph refers particularly to those who preside over fresh water, and not to the Nereids. Theodorus of Gaza says that he once saw one of them in the Peloponessus, and she had a beautiful face.

Then there were the Sirens, daughters of Achelous and the Muse Calliope; one of them sang, the second played a flute, and the third a harp.[90] They made such melodious harmony that they enchanted poor admiring sailors, who were wrecked upon the rocks of Sicily. Ulysses, sailing that way, tied himself fast to the mast of his ship, and his crew put wax in their ears, so that the Sirens, deprived of the prey, threw themselves into the sea, where their lower bodies were changed into fish. But Servius thinks they were part bird, and not fish at all; this opinion is supported by Ovid and by Claudian.[91] Boccaccio says that the Sirens lived in pleasant fields with the bones of the dead scattered around them, but Xenophon writes that the Sirens sang the praises to people of conspicuous merit whose virtues had gained them universal approbation. Aristotle, in his *De admirabilibus*, says that there were some islands off the far coast of Sicily called the Siren Islands where the people worshipped them, building temples and erecting altars to them. Their names were Parthenope, Leucosia, and Ligeia, but that is enough about them.

It was not simply that the sea, rivers and fountains in general were worshipped, but some were revered beyond others. For example, the Messenians[92] adored the river Pamirus, the Phrygians the Maeander and Marsyas. The Umbrians called the Clitumnus by the name Jovis Clitumnus, putting that title on the temple-porch, perhaps because when cattle drank its waters they became white, as Claudian tells us in one of his *Panegyrics*.

---

[89]Tethys was not a Nereid. According to Hesiod, she was the daughter of Earth and Heaven, and sister to Oceanus (*Theogony* 136 [131]). She became mother to the rivers and 3000 Oceanids.

[90]The Sirens are often considered as the daughters of the Earth (*OCD* 842). Achelous was a river-god (Rose 118) of one of the longest Greek rivers, but I find no connection between him and the Sirens. The Island of the Sirens was located near Scylla and Charybdis.

[91]Claudius Claudianus (c. 355–408) was the official poet of the Emperor Honorius (395–423). He composed panegyrics on the Imperial family, verses on Stilicho's Gothic victories, and a mythological epic, *De raptu Proserpinae*, from which Herbert quotes here. Claudian was a skilled allegorist and tended to write rather elaborately.

[92]Messenia is the south-west region of the Peloponessus.

Amongst the female names of the nymphs that presided over fountains and the goddesses who ruled rivers and lakes, some of the former were Hippocrene and Salmacis in Halicarnassus, whose waters are supposed to feminise those who drink them. There is Arethusa the Fugitive,[93] and the Fons Camenarum[94] in Rome, from which the Vestals, whose duty was to keep water as well as fire, took the water they purified themselves with. Amongst the Sabines there was the Fountain of Blandusia, and Aristotle speaks of a fountain in Cappadocia whose waters were very cold, but yet seemed hot. People suspected of perjury were brought to it, and if a person were innocent the water would remain calm; if not, it would rage, swell and foam so strongly that it would not only spray on his feet and hands, but dash into his face as if it were the arbiter of justice. This went on until he had confessed the truth and asked forgiveness for his offence; if he kept on doing evil, he would get oedema, or vomit a great quantity of filthy blood. It was, therefore, known as the Fons Jovis Perjuri, and we need have no doubt that this fountain merited divine honours.

You may consult other scholars about the river nymphs such as the Ismenides, Ionides, Pactolides, Amigrides and Tiberiades,[95] or about Anna Perenna[96] of the Romans, whose sacred rites were performed in March, or about Juturna[97] and Naïs,[98] the glory of rivers. I should not omit that the Styx, Acheron, Periphlegethon, and Cocytus were excluded from the upper earth by the ancients and banished to the underworld. Cassander,[99]

---

[93] So-called because the nymph Arethusa, being pursued by Alpheus (the river-god), was turned into a stream by Artemis, who made a place for it to run. It flowed underground and united with the waters of Alpheus to form the fountain Arethusa when it emerged from the ground at Syracuse in Sicily (Morford and Lenardon 456).

[94] From Camenae, the old Latin goddesses of poetry. They were later fused or identified with the Greek Muses.

[95] The Ismenides were the nymphs of the river Ismenus in Boeotia; the Ionides of the rivers in Ionia; the Pactolides of the river Pactolus in Lydia, which had golden sand in it; the Tiberiades are the nymphs of Tiber. The Amigrides are obscure, although the name translates as "emigrants."

[96] Anna Perenna was an ancient Italian goddess whose feast-day was March 15th.

[97] Juturna [more properly Iuturna], a water-nymph, was the sister of Turnus of Rutilia, a great warrior killed by Aeneas.

[98] The word "Naïs" simply means "a water-nymph," or Naïad.

[99] George Cassander [Casant] (1513–66), who taught literature at Ghent and Bruges and theology at the Academy of Duisberg, was attacked vehemently by both Catholics and Protestants for "excessive tolerance" (New Catholic Encyclopaedia 3,

quoting Lycophron,[100] places these three rivers in that part of Italy known as Ausonia.[101] Other writers mention a Cocytus in Italy and another in Epirus; Pausanias says that there is a Styx in Arcadia, and that it is a cold spring full of mercury and sulphur, and so acidic that nothing can stand it except the hooves of an Indian horse, mule, or donkey. It is commonly said that Alexander the Great was poisoned with its water.[102] The name Styx is derived from *stigus*, which means sorrow; this seems more plausible than deriving it from *setika*, silence. As it was a horribly sulphurous and poisonous fountain, lake or river in either Arcadia or Italy, it is incorrect to derive the name from the Oriental languages. The gods, it is said, always swore by this infernal stream, because as they enjoyed eternal good in heaven, people thought that they swore by what they did not know, for the stream encompassed hell, a place of extreme horror and distress.

The Platonists, I know, explain this another way, saying that this world is the *infernum* (hell), into which the soul descends when it joins a mortal body. The first thing it meets with is the river Lethe (actually in Africa, near Bernices, but, like the former, said to be in hell), and, having drunk from it, forgets the past. Then it drinks from other rivers which bring grief and sorrow, and this fable symbolises the state of the soul in this world.[103]

Let us pass by these delirious dreams, proceeding now with the oaths of the gods, and the punishments which attended their violation, one of which was to be deprived of life and motion for an entire year. Servius, following Orpheus, extends the time, saying that gods who swear by Styx and perjure themselves are punished for nine thousand years. The poets invented these myths so that oaths might be considered sacred and unbreakable because

---

180). The work to which Herbert is referring, as it does deal to a degree with water, is probably *De baptismo infantium* (1563).

[100]Lycophron of Chalcis (b. c. 320 B.C.) was a poet, dramatist and librarian of Alexandria. Suidas and Tzetzes mention his tragedies, but Herbert is citing the *Alexandra*, a dramatic monologue containing a great deal of history and legend. The *OCD* comments that this work's "obscurity . . . exceeds that of any other Greek poem. This is due to the recondite material and the blending of inconsistent myths, but above all to the language" (521).

[101]Ausonia, usually known as Campania, extends from the Apennines to the Tyrrhenian Sea.

[102]Pausanias 2.18 [1–6] (414–16). He says that he has heard the story about Alexander the Great, but that there is no proof.

[103]See Plato, *Republic* III, 387c (Hamilton and Cairns 632), where the Styx is described as "abhorred Styx, the flood of deadly hate." It is also mentioned by Socrates when he discusses the rivers of the Underworld in *Phaedo* 113b (Hamilton and Cairns 93).

even the gods themselves were not immune from punishment. Indeed, much in pagan religion depended upon the validity of oaths: they swore oaths in particular temples wearing particular clothes before the altars, holding a sword or knife upright as the sacrifices burned, and they had a great many other religious ceremonies to strike terror into perjurers. Jupiter Horcius, who presided over oaths amongst the Greeks, was portrayed with a thunderbolt in his hand, and Deus Fidius,[104] the Jupiter of the Romans, is represented with the masculine image of Honour on one side and the feminine image of Truth on the other. According to Dionysius of Halicarnassus there was a great temple dedicated to him, and with good reason; nothing is more treacherous and wicked than perjury, and unless God avenges it, it always goes unpunished, for no-one is secure against it.

Lake Avernus, because it had a foetid and sulphurous smell, was also translated to the lower regions, and it was of such a nature that it killed any birds which tried to fly over it. However, the Emperor Augustus, by an edict, caused the woods to be cut down [around it] where they grew thickest, and it became healthy and pleasant, as Servius informs us in Book 3 of his commentary on the *Aeneid*. Yet it was not only these rivers and Lake Avernus which were thrust underground by the pagans; Gehenna[105] itself, which used to be a valley near Jerusalem where the Jews offered up children to Moloch, was banished by the Hebrews, and King Josiah, that he might defile the place as much as possible, ordered rotting carcasses and all sorts of filth to be brought and dumped there. As St. Jerome tells us, this is how it got its name, which signified a place of torment for evildoers.

Water was worshipped by the Greeks and Romans as well as by the Eastern peoples, under different names, and not only the Scythians, Celts and others, but by the people of America today. The Scythians called Vesta *Tabiti*, Jupiter *Papaeus*, Earth *Apia*, Apollo *Octosyrus*, Venus *Artempasa* or the Celestial One, and Neptune *Thamimasides*. Bishop Willibald of Eichstett[106] in Germany says that before his time people used to sacrifice to Water. José de Acosta tells us that in America the sea (called Mammacocha),

---

[104]Deus Fidius. Herbert is probably referring to Semo Sancus Dius Fidius (Ovid, *Fasti* VI, 213), who was a sky and lightning god (hence the connexion with Jupiter), and whose temple had a hole in the roof so that people could see the sky. See Frazer's note on Dius Fidius in Ovid (429–30). See Joseph Plescia, *The Oath and Pergury in Ancient Greece* (Tallahassee: Florida State UP, 1970).

[105]Another Hebrew word for Hell.

[106]St. Willibald (700–86), Bishop of Eichstätt after 740, was born of a noble Anglo-Saxon family. He went to Rome at age 22, travelled to the Near East on a lengthy pilgrimage, and later became a monk at Monte Cassino before being sent

springs, and fountains are considered divine. I do not question that those countries, according to the ordinary ancient concept of God amongst them, deified Water in general as they did the Stars and Elements, considering it the most useful element, although it was sometimes harmful. All religious worship derives either from love or fear.

Earth

Amongst the gods of the pagans we must add the densest one of all, the Earth, which was always worshipped as Universal Nature by them. As Heaven dispensed the seminal virtue of things to the various elements through the air, so Earth was the warehouse that received it and distributed it like a steward, for which reason the pagans held it to be the most obvious and pleasant testament for divinity. Without its help, the secret principles of things would have no external dress, and could never be seen by us. It was for this reason that the ancients invented a sort of marriage between Heaven and Earth, making Heaven the man, Earth the woman, from whom came the vast progeny of life on the earth. It was not only because Earth produced things that she was worshipped, but because she poised and supported herself in space by a miraculous way. And to this we may add her diurnal motion, which was not the discovery of modern philosophers.

For these, and for many other reasons, probable or superstitious, the Earth was profoundly venerated, especially because no other element received man and the other animals into its bosom after their allotted time. As this element was thought to be the originator of all, she would not let mortals be abandoned after death. In order to show their grateful dependence on her, people laid children on her as soon as they were born and commended them to her care. Afterwards, they lifted them up and put them in the care of the goddess Levana, then Cunina, who protected them in the cradle and prevented bewitchment. Then they were taken care of by the god Vagitanus, who stopped crying, the goddess Paventia, who banished childish fears, and lastly to Edusa and Potina, who looked after food and drink.[107]

---

as a missionary to Franconia by Pope Gregory III. He was venerated during his own lifetime.

[107]The nature of these "tiny gods," as Augustine rather unkindly calls them, is as follows:

Levana: lifting children is always rather risky, so a goddess was needed, presumably so that babies were not dropped.

Cunina: Herbert is quite correct about this goddess.

Vagitanus: for some reason, Augustine calls him "Vaticanus" (*City of God* IV, 8 [143–44]). He presides over the wails of babies.

The Earth was not regarded merely as the mother of humans, but also of the gods and of those who through conspicuous deeds had become immortal — it is for this reason that she is called the Magna Mater, or Great Mother. I shall discuss later whether she was called Cybele from a cube, the figure which Pythagoras, taught by the Egyptians, gave to the Earth. She has many other names, such as Isis, Ops, Rhea, Vesta, Ceres, Proserpina, Bona Dea, Flora and Pales; many other deities are also of the earth, signifying some power or attribute belonging to it.

Isis, though she is actually the moon-goddess, as I have indicated, has some connexion with the Earth. As Osiris, the active principle of Goodness, was known as the Sun in Heaven, so Isis, as the passive principle, was known by the Egyptians as the Moon in Heaven and Earth here, as will be seen from the following. Servius says that Isis in the Egyptian language is the Earth, and Macrobius states:

> Isis was worshipped in a double capacity as the Earth or the Nature of all Sublunary Beings. All things increase through the sustenance of this goddess's breasts, as they are nourished by the Earth or Universal Nature.

This is confirmed by Julius Firmicus. We may also include Ceres here: Herodotus tells us that Isis is the Egyptian equivalent of Ceres, and Apollodorus[108] mentions not only that their rites are the same, of which more later, but that these rites came from Egypt to Greece, which is confirmed by Clement of Alexandria.

Amongst the Phoenicians and Syrians, Rhea, the Syrian or Hierapolitan goddess, signified the Earth, and Lucian claims that he was told of this by a very reliable source. The worship of Rhea and the Hierapolitan goddess had the same ceremonies, and went as far as the severity, unheard of in our times, of castrating the priests in imitation of Atys. I really believe that these sacred rites were the invention of the *rex sacrorum* rather than of the priests themselves. A tower-like crown was placed on the heads of these goddesses, and their chariots were drawn by lions with drums beating before them, as we learn from Lucian.

Macrobius proves that the Atergatis of the Assyrians also signified the Earth as well as the Moon, and all Nature is subject to the influence of the Sun. From the Egyptians, Phoenicians and Syrians, I will proceed to the Phrygians, who worshipped the Earth under the names of Rhea, Cybele, and many others. In every account of pagan religion some things relate

---

Paventia: Herbert's definition is accurate.

Edusa and Potina: Herbert's description is correct.

[108] Apollodorus of Athens (fl. 140 B.C.) was a Greek grammarian and the author of the *Bibliotheca*, the work cited by Herbert. It was printed in 1555.

to historical actions, and others apply mystically to the nature of things. According to Vossius, Rhea can be considered in three ways: first, as Rhea, the common mother of all, or Evah, mother of all living things and wife of Adam, who was, if we take the word to mean a man and not nature, the most ancient version of Saturn. Secondly, she was the wife of Noah, who is also called Saturn. Thirdly, she was a queen of the ancient Phrygians, in love with Attis, a ploughman; after her death she was called the common mother of all things and so had the same honour and veneration paid to her as the Earth. As Great Mother, Rhea had a variety of names according to where she was worshipped. The Romans, who inherited worship of her from the Phrygians, called her Mater Phrygia Cybele, from Mount Cybelus, which was in Phrygia, or, as some said, in Bithynia. She was also known as Dyndamena, from Phrygian mountains of that name, Idaea, from Mount Idus in Phrygia; Pessinuntia, from Pesinus in Galatia, near its border with Phrygia; Mygdonia, from a place in Phrygia, Agdistus from a mountain, and also Pylene. Even the Cimmerians worshipped her under the name of the Great Mother; Hesychius says that the Cimmerians called the Mother of Gods Cybele, and that she brought an insanity to men which the Greeks called *cybebein* and that those men were known as *cibici*, inspired and protected by the Mother of Gods as were the priests of Cybele.

St. Augustine, quoting Varro, says that Mother Earth had many names and styles, denoting her as a goddess.[109] The Earth was known as Ops, because it could be improved by work, as Mater, because it was plentiful and productive, Great, because it brought forth all kinds of food, Proserpina, because it produced vegetables, Vesta, clothed with herbs and flowers, and other goddesses, without absurdity, were absorbed into it. Amongst the pagans Tellumo was the male seminal power, Tellus the female, though, in common understanding, Tellus stood for both. Amongst other Romans, Tullus [Hostilius] made vows to Ops or the Earth; as Dionysius of Halicarnassus says,

> Tullus, lifting his hands to heaven, made a vow to the gods that if the Romans defeated the Sabines that day, he would afterwards decree festivals to Saturn and Ops, which the Romans later publicly celebrated every year after harvest, and doubled the number of Salii.

I do not doubt that by Saturn and Ops, heaven and earth are understood; Tatius built them a temple and consecrated altars by the names of Saturn

---

[109] Augustine, *City of God* VII, 23 (280–83). Varro is attacked in a long passage for indulging in "natural theology," a discussion of the World-Soul, of which the Earth (Tellus) is a part.

and Rhea. Pliny mentions a temple built for Tellus in Spurius Cassius's courtyard, and Varro says that she had a small chapel in the palace, into which only Vestals and public priests were allowed.

Let us now consider how the Great Mother was portrayed, and what sort of worship was paid to the Earth. St. Augustine, citing Varro, says that the Great Mother has drums, which mean that she is the Earth's sphere, towers on her head, which represent towns, and chairs around her, because everything moved but her. Capons were held sacred to her, which suggested that those things which had no seminal faculty of their own should serve the Earth, as everything could be found in her. Those who worshipped her were not allowed to sit down, because there were always things for them to do. The noise of cymbals and clashing weapons represent her — the weapons were made of brass because she had been worshipped before iron had been discovered. Tame lions were loose about her to show that there was nowhere in the world either so remote or so savage that it could not be civilized or cultivated. Ovid gives another reason, to which I would refer the reader.[110] Also, there was a certain sacred stone, which the Phrygians called the Great Mother; how it came to be taken to Rome, placed in the Temple of Victory, and had funeral banquets and games instituted in its honour called the Megalesia, consult Livy, Cicero, and Quintilian.[111]

So much for her representations. Now we come to her worship, which I am not sure whether to call "mystical" or "crazy." I wish we had that book by Proclus Licius which Suidas mentions; Proclus, he says, "wrote a book about the Great Mother of the Gods, which, if anyone studied, he could find by inspiration all the theology of that goddess," but the book has perished in the ruins of time. The Curetes were the most eminent priests, made up especially of Aetolians, Cretans and Phrygians; they were called Curetes[112] from *cura*, shaving, and, on the contrary, Acarnanes, unshaved. Vossius gives a reason for this, but it is not one I can agree with; I understand that the customs of the order of priests of the Great Mother came from certain religious rites rather than a military or accidental reason because of a similarity between the rites of Isis and of the Great Mother, as mentioned above. The priests of Isis, amongst other common ceremonies, shaved their heads, made wailing noises, beat their breasts and tore at their arms. I also think

---

[110]Ovid, *Fasti* IV, 215ff. (204–06).

[111]The Megalesia, which took place on April 4, were named for Megale ('The Great One'), an alternative name for Cybele.

[112]According to Cornford, these were "mystical societies" who claimed to be able to control the forces of Nature, "on whose behaviour all life depends" (94). See Jane Harrison, *Themis*, for a full treatment and further information.

that there were other orders of priests belonging to this goddess, such as mentioned by Strabo, the Corybantes, Cabiri, Idaei, Dactyli, and Telchines. The Corybantes were so-called because they danced at the sacred rites of the Great Mother, the Cabiri were named after a mountain in Berecynthia at whose foot they lived, the Dactyli because there were only five of them and represented the number of fingers on the hand. The Telchines numbered nine, and accompanied Rhea from Rhodes to Crete, which latter was named Telchinia after them. Strabo will tell you about many more opinions which the ancients had on this subject. Cybele's priests, all castrated, were called Galli, not to reproach the Gauls for setting Rome on fire, as St. Jerome thought, but from the river Gallus in Phrygia, as Herodian says. The Phrygians of old celebrated the Orgyia near the river Gallus, and it is from this that the eunuch priests took their names. It was reliably reported that anyone who drank its water went mad, and, if this is true, it is not surprising that people assisting at the celebration of the rites ran up and down like lunatics. Ovid refers to this in the lines "between green Cybele and high Celaenae/ A river of mad water, which we call the Gallus, runs."[113] People who imitated the madness of the Galli were said to "be gallant" (*gallare*); thus Varro says in the Eumenides, "how can people who gallant like that be beautiful?" With their weapons held before them, they tossed their heads and waved their weapons around. As Lucretius writes, "They carry arms, the sign of violent rage, before them." Also they beat their drums, not, I think, to make themselves more frightening, because the way they carried themselves, if not their entire bodies, showed that they were soft and tender. Their hair was scented with the richest perfumes and ointments, their faces covered with white silk veils. The chief amongst them were known as Archigalli, of whom Tertullian says "the holiest offers up his most impure blood." They let out such howls and dismal noise that the fable the priests invented about their Great Mother's lover Atys could not be better represented. Then they beg, for which they were nicknamed "the Great Mother's con-men," and this was done in many places, particularly in Carthage at the time of St. Augustine. They were not allowed to beg in Rome except on certain special days, so that, as Cicero says, that their minds might not be filled with superstitions.

Allow me here to quote an excellent passage from Dionysius of Halicarnassus which will show how the Romans felt about exotic religions:

> Although people from all countries live in this city, and it is convenient for them all to worship as they do in their own countries, no foreign religious rites are allowed in public, which is the same in many other cities. If, at the command of an Oracle, they are introduced from other countries, the citizens worship them

---

[113]Ovid, *Fasti* IV, 363–64 (214).

in their own way, rejecting any ridiculous and absurd fables. This is done in the worship of the Idaean Mother, to whom the emperors sacrifice and institute yearly games after the Roman fashion. Yet the Phrygians perform the priestly offices: they carry[the goddess] through the city, gathering money for her and beating their breasts. Others follow, playing songs of praise to her on pipes and drumming. But no native Romans ever gathered money with them in the streets, and by Senate decree they are forbidden to celebrate the Phrygian *orgyia*, so much aversion is there to all foreign ceremonies and indecorous madness.

No-one will imagine, I suppose, that I am ignorant of the good that some Greek myths have done mankind, either instructing them in the ways of Nature through allegory, or comforting and supporting them in times of human need, freeing their souls from terror, discomfort and delusion, or some other benificent action. I know this as well as anyone else does, but I am passing it by with reverent caution, only approving the Roman theology, knowing that very little good can accrue from these Greek myths. They are useful only to the few who examine them carefully and understand their scope and design; few people are masters of such judgment and wisdom. The common people and those who are ignorant of philosophy make ill use of them, for they either become contemptuous of God, who seems subject to so many misfortunes, or give themselves up to immorality, seeing that God does the same thing. However, I will leave these things to the consideration of those who study speculative philosophy.

The sacred rites were called Megalensia, but afterwards the letter N was omitted, and they became Megalesia. They were begun by M. Junius Brutus,[114] who, as Livy relates, dedicated a temple to the Great Mother in the palace. I question whether her sacred rites were known as Materoa; I know that Dionysius mentions the Matroamela, which I take to be a poem composed in the goddess's honour, but there is no evidence that her sacred mysteries were named Materoa, as Vossius thinks. The games were celebrated in April, and servants were forbidden to attend them, as Alessandri tells us. Afterwards feasts were given in her honour, where they were very careful about expenses, and at which no foreign wine was served; these feasts were held in the presence of the Great Goddess, and only the principal people of the city were present. These sacred rites were first instituted by Dardanus, and the sacrifices consisted of a ram and a bull, with a pine tree also being cut down in a pine grove sacred to Cybele, because it is said that Attis was changed into a pine; Vergil alludes to this in his line

---

[114]M. Junius Brutus (d. 76 B.C.) was tribune of the plebs (83) and commander against Pompey's forces in Cisalpine Gaul. In 77 he surrendered to Pompey, and was killed later.

where the Mother of the Gods says "The pine wood has for many years been my delight." And Ovid, in Book X of the *Metamorphoses*, says "Cybaean Attis/ Put off his human form for that of a tree."[115] Lastly, there is Martial's line about the pine-nuts, "We are Cybele's apples."

The oak tree was also dedicated to Mother Idea, and Apollodorus says that it was the first tree that offered food and shelter to animals. The musical instruments used in the rites of the Great Goddess were brass cymbals, pipes of boxwood, drums, small bells, and the horn. Dempster, quoting de Jonghe,[116] mentions bells and *nolae*,[117] smaller bells, as being used in Cybele's rites, but in my opinion these were rather brass cymbals and *crotala* (castanets); those learned in such matters know that bells and *nolae* were invented long afterwards. At the feast, the rites having been performed, the guests poured wine out of a drum, and drank out of a cymbal, by which means they were inspired with the mysteries of the religion. Julius Firmicus says that spears, torches, platters and sheep-hooks were present, but I do not know what they signified.

I shall now conclude this description, as fables are being interwoven with mysteries: some things are to be understood morally and some mystically, although I cannot see that much can be gathered from them. Many specious arguments might be brought forward for the adoration of the Earth, but I cannot conceive how Proclus could have justified the ridiculous rites invented by the priests, although I wish his book had come down to us.

It is thus evident that not only the Sun and Moon, the other Planets and fixed Stars, the Heaven and superior Elements were paid divine honours, but the Earth also, which, while it appears to be the lowest and most vulgar part of the world, yet sustains itself as well as any of the elements or Heaven itself.

In a more special manner the Stars perfect their operations on it, and their power and effectiveness end here. Of what great value our globe is we may see from this: suppose it could be paved all over with the most valuable jewels in a mosaic, we would rather throw them to the bottom of the sea than be without the land to plant a garden on, for three acres of ground is more

---

[115]This reference is confusing. Ovid tells the story of Cybele turning Hippomenes and Atalanta into lions, and of Venus transforming the dying Adonis, but there is no mention of Attis in Book X. It is to be found rather in the *Fasti* IV. 221ff.

[116]Adriaan de Jonghe [Hadrianus Junius] (1511–75) was a Dutch doctor and emblematist. He wrote a detailed analysis of all the attributes of Mercury in *Insignia Mercurii quid?* (1565). He showed how each attribute could be interpreted in the light of a wise saying or hidden symbolic meaning.

[117]The word *nolae* first appeared in 1102 (Latham 314), which makes Herbert's late date accurate.

useful to mankind than thirty acres of diamonds. To conclude, I would only like to mention a few more things, as I intend to treat them in more detail in *De causis errorum circa religionem*.

The old pagans not only worshipped the World in its universal extension and size, but its very parts also; they thought that it was very impious to worship only the most obvious parts of the deity, but pass by others with neglect. If we should pretend to revere the breast of a great Monarch, yet neglect his worthier parts, or any part without regard to the whole, or appear to admire his eyes or nose at the expense of other organs, or praise all his body except the nose and eyes, would he not believe himself to have been outrageously insulted? Thus the pagans believed it was vulgar, even irreligious, to give divine honour to this or that star or element while despising other parts of the world as vile and unworthy of praise. As they believed they were worshipping the entire World through the Stars, Heaven, and four Elements, its integral parts, and that these parts, of which the World was composed, best represented the deity, so they thought that they worshipped the Supreme God by paying external worship to an external deity, internal to an internal one, but I shall handle this subject later with more freedom, God willing, and others, if they like, may do the same. In the meantime, I have lost nothing by showing that those names which the common people, in their ignorance, thought belonged only to humans, now refer mystically, thanks to the words and deeds of the more cultivated pagans, to the stars, the heavens and the elements. If nothing more were to be understood by Jupiter, Juno, Mars, Apollo, Diana, Venus, Saturn, Rhea and the rest of the deities than the fictions reported of them by poets, we would conclude that the pagans had been most ridiculous and absurd. I now intend to show whether it was from priestly invention, princely tyranny, or the servile and ignorant flattery of the common people that the adoration of human beings insinuated itself into the world.

XI

The Special and Symbolic
Worship of Heroes

After the veneration of the Supreme Godhead, and the World with its parts, a lesser form of adoration, that of heroes, offers itself to our examination. This would not have seemed at all inharmonious or absurd if those to whom religious and sacred rites were entrusted had kept themselves within reasonable bounds, or if human authority had not formerly become so powerful that it could make innovations in even the purest religion. But what contributed to the profanation of religion at that time was the fact that even divine worship itself was instituted or performed for certain people who had led exemplary lives. The pagans did not only elevate their heroes to heaven, but enrolled their names amongst the gods, for the most part worshipping them under the names of stars, the names serving interchangeably for one another. Thus it is not easy to determine whether the old myths are to be applied mystically to the stars, or morally to people. Here the poets, the Muses' favourites, have made extensive use of their licence, so that it is difficult to know which they refer to, and I expect that their scabrous ribaldry may be the effect of ignorance or petulance. Was there nothing so obscene, base or irreligious that first Greek, then Roman poets, would not invent and relate about people who had deserved well of their countries or of mankind in general? I can only call what the early poets have handed down to us fiction, for there is not one prose writer I know of who ever credited any of them with telling the truth. We must therefore be wary of the poets in any study of ethnic theology, for not only have they mixed the true history of ancient heroes with mythical fiction, but they have made it questionable, almost completely improbable to even the most credulous. They have mixed their romantic stories with mystical doctrines of the Heavens, Stars, and Elements, using this way of writing to conceal or explain their meaning, and have left nothing whole or perfect in either history or religion.

The origin of these fables was something like this. There were, over many ages, many Jupiters, Marses, Venuses and Bacchuses in different parts of the world. At that time, some humans became numbered with the gods; people in favour of their own country's gods ridiculed those of other people, and they, in turn, felt free to requite them. They fell to mocking each other, and the "secret memorials" of their gods consisted of nothing but stories about adultery and other such crimes; the more modern Greek and Roman poets have built such fabulous tales that they have managed to make it impossible any more to tell true history from false.

Romulus, to rectify this situation and so that humans might have a clearer view of the gods, ordered a great reformation of religion. According to Dionysius of Halicarnassus, Romulus thought that any myths handed down from our ancestors which contained things that were either scandalous or criminal were useless and indecent, and that they were not fit either for the superior gods or for good men. So he ordered that these myths be put aside, and instructed his people to think and speak about the gods with reverence and respect, ignoring anything that was unworthy of the divine nature. No Romans, then, tell the story of Coelus being deposed by his children, nor Saturn fearfully destroying his own family because he thought they wanted to kill him. There is nothing about Jupiter deposing his father Saturn and shutting him up in hell, no wars between gods, nothing of their wounding, capture or servitude. There were no cruel festivals of lamentation where women were put to death to propitiate the gods by their cries, no performing, in Greek fashion, of the rape of Proserpina or the downfall of Bacchus, and other similar matters. In spite of this, Greek myths were prevalent amongst the Romans, and some came from the East. Yet even superstition itself would have been acceptable if the Greeks had attributed no more to their deified heroes than to their Amadis,[1] whose actions were virtuous and modest — nothing like the sordid debaucheries of the pagan heroes.

The way the pagans venerated their heroes was to erect statues adorned with military insignia, with candles lit around them and cinnamon and frankincense burning; their noble deeds were sung in Saliarian Hymns. Mamurius,[2] Verrarius,[3] and Volumnia,[4] amongst others, were honoured like this, according to Varro, but I have not found that hero-worship extended

---

[1] Herbert is not referring here to *Amadis de Gaula*, the Spanish or Portuguese romance written by Johan (1261–1325) or Vasco de Lobeira (d. 1403), but to *Amadis of Greece*, a continuation of Book XI of *Amadis de Gaula* by one Feliciano de Silva, written in the 16th century. The hero of this work is not Amadis at all, but his son Lisuarte of Greece. No English translation of either work was available until Southey's abridged version (1803), but Herbert may have known the French version of Herberay des Essart (1540).

[2] The mythical maker of the ancilia, the sacred shield kept by the Salii.

[3] I have been unable to identify Verrarius.

[4] Lucia Volumnia was the mother of Cnaeus Magnus Coriolanus (d. 491 B.C.), a Volscian hero and the subject of Shakespeare's *Coriolanus*. Volumnia was said

beyond this point. Plato, in his Laws, says that heroes should not be worshipped after death, but that their statues should be adorned and honoured — temples, altars and sacrifices were appropriate only to divine worship. Plutarch tells us what some of the ways of worship were; the people of Lampsacus, for example, first paid honours to their heroes, but afterwards sacrificed to them as gods, upon which it was decreed that blood-sacrifices should only be made to the gods.

Even if heroes did not have temples and altars dedicated to them, they did at least have shrines. According to Dionysius of Halicarnassus and Plato, heroes have a middle status between gods and men, who sometimes interacted with one another and from whom sprung a race of heroes. Such heroes amongst the Romans were Curius,[5] Fabricius,[6] Coruncanius,[7] Duilius,[8] Metellus,[9] Lutatius,[10] Fabius,[11] Marcellus,[12]

to have saved Rome by persuading her son to turn his army back, and a temple to Fortuna Muliebris was erected on the spot where Coriolanus met his mother.

[5]Manius Curius Dentatus, a plebeian statesman, held the consulship four times between 290 and 274 B.C. He defeated the Samnites and built Rome's second aqueduct.

[6]Gaius Fabricius Luscinus was consul in 282 and 275 B.C. He was the hero of the war against King Pyrrhus of Epirus, and is often mentioned by Cicero, together with Manius Curius, as an example of old Roman virtue.

[7]Tiberius Coruncanius, consul in 280 B.C., defeated the Etruscans and organised the defence of Rome against Pyrrhus. He was the first pleb to become Pontifex Maximus (253).

[8]Gaius Duilius was a Roman admiral. Consul in 263 B.C., he defeated the Carthaginians at Mylae (the battle mentioned by T.S. Eliot in *The Waste Land*). From the spoils of his victory Duilius built a temple to Janus.

[9]Quintus Caecilius Metellus Numidicus (d. 91 B.C.), consul in 109, fought against King Jugurtha of Numidia and was noted for political integrity. The latter caused his downfall, disgrace, and possible murder by poison.

[10]There are two eminent Romans of this name, and Herbert does not specify which one he means. Quintus Lutatius Catulus (d. 87 B.C.) was a soldier, poet and philosopher whom Cicero has as one of the participants in *De oratore*. Q. Lutatius Catulus (d. 61/60 B.C.) was consul in 78, and is praised by Cicero for his integrity as leader of the "conservatives" in the Senate.

[11]Herbert does not specify which Fabius he means. Paullus Fabius Maximus (46 B.C.–14 A.D.), friend to Augustus and patron of Ovid and Horace, was consul in 11 B.C. and Governor of Asia (3–2 B.C.). Quintus Fabius Maximus Verrucosus "Cunctator" (c. 280–203 B.C.) who kept Hannibal at bay with his delaying tactics (hence the nickname) was often held up as an example of Roman virtue.

[12]M. Claudius Marcellus (d. 208 B.C.), four times consul, defeated Hannibal

the Scipios,[13] Paullus,[14] the Gracchi,[15] the Catos,[16] Laelius[17] and many others. Although they did not have divine help, there had never been anyone else like them, as Cicero tells us in The Nature of the Gods. Amongst the Greeks we have Ulysses, Diomedes, Agamemnon and Achilles, whom, according to Homer, the gods accompanied in their greatest need, which implies a notion of divine grace going with heroism. Cicero mentions three classes of gods to whom divine honour and worship was paid: first, those who lived in heaven; secondly, those whose deeds have elevated them to heaven, and thirdly, those whose assistance is necessary to obtaining divinity. He calls the latter Mind, Virtue, Piety, and Faith. I will reserve discussion of this for later, as it will very well illustrate the religion of the ancients.

---

several times and was noted for piety and culture. He built temples to Honos and Virtus, and was a great collector of Greek art.

[13]Publius Cornelius Scipio Africanus (236–184 B.C.) defeated the Carthaginians and established Roman hegemony in Spain. Like Marcellus, he was known for his deep interest in Greek art and culture. Scipio Aemilianus Africanus Numantinus (185–129 B.C.) was a soldier and statesman, the natural son of L. Aemilius Paullus (see n. 14) and the adopted son of P. Cornelius Scipio. A Stoic of liberal views, he was a political opponent of the Gracchi (see n. 15), in spite of being married to their sister Sempronia.

[14]Lucius Aemilius Paullus Macedonicus (d. 160 B.C.), soldier and statesman, defeated King Perseus of Macedon and governed Greece during the subsequent occupation. He was celebrated for his humanity and learning.

[15]Tiberius Sempronius Gracchus (d. 133 B.C.) and Gaius Sempronius Gracchus (d. 123 B.C.) were two reforming statesman who happened to be brothers. They were both murdered after taking part in constitutional changes and upheavals which led to violence and rioting.

[16]M. Porcius Cato "the Censor" (234–149 B.C.) and his grandson, M. Porcius Cato Uticensis (95–46 B.C.) were considered the supreme examples of Roman virtue and uprightness. Cato Uticensis, however, was a very stern and unbending Stoic, hardly an attractive character at all.

[17]Gaius Laelius Sapiens, consul in 140 B.C. served as a soldier under Scipio Africanus and opposed the Gracchi. His surname was bestowed upon him because of his attachment to Stoicism.

The Indigent Deities[18]

As I have already discussed those gods who always live in heaven, I would like now to examine the second group, who attain heaven after death. They were known as *dii indigetes*, according to Servius, or, as others say, *dii minorum gentium*; Scaliger tells us that in an old list they were termed *hemitheoi curetes* (the company of demi-gods), and included Hercules, Faunus, Carmento, Evander, Castor, Pollux, Aesculapius, Acca Laurentia, Quirinus and others. Festus [Avienus] says that it was impious to invoke them or call upon them, lest some should be worshipped before others. Amongst them also are the Lares[19] and the Novensides,[20] as Livy has noted. There was a register of Indigetes, which Vossius calls the *Hieratica biblia*,[21] and the Romans *Indigitamenta*; it contained the names of these deities and their origins, very much like our calendar or rubric. The heroes that we have mentioned were probably called Indigetes from this book, rather than because of having any special or tender regard for humans, to whom they were closely related.

The ancients exempted the Supreme God — who was infinitely and perfectly happy — from all administration. Cicero quotes a passage from Sophocles concerning this, that when a very valuable cup was stolen from the temple of Hercules, he appeared [to Sophocles] in a dream, and described the thief. He did this several times, but Sophocles ignored it, but after being

---

[18]There are problems with the precise meaning of the word *Indigetes*. They are a group of gods, and as Herbert states, there is a list or register of them (the *Indigitamenta*). Some scholars believe that they are relatively unimportant as deities, including amongst them goddesses like Cunina, whom Herbert mentions in Chapter X as the guardian of babies' cradles. Others think they were "native" gods or even deified ancestors. The word *indiges* certainly means "native," but it also means "needy," if it is derived from the verb *indigeo*. Herbert may have been alluding to this when he writes "quasi dii agentes" ("as if they were effective gods"), perhaps intending an untranslatable pun. Lewis has "as if they prevailed upon gods" (165), which does not make much sense. I have therefore omitted the phrase altogether.

[19]The Lares were originally farmland deities, but later came to have associations with the dead and were kept in the house. Ovid says that they were the offspring of Mercury and Lara, but as there are no other known references to "Lara" he probably invented the myth. The cult of the *lar familiaris* was widespread in the Roman world.

[20]The Novensides are very mysterious deities, and their purpose or function remains unknown. As Herbert suggests, they might have been associated with the Indigetes, but in what capacity no-one knows. Herbert spells the word "Novensiles," which is "Livy's characteristic Italian variation of *d* and *l*" (*OCD* 612).

[21]Full detials of the nature and function of these may be found in Vossius I, xii, 85–98. He cites the Greek term *anthropodaimones* as covering all of these various deities, including the Lares and Novensides.

admonished several times, he went to the Areopagus and told the story. When the person named by Sophocles was interrogated, he confessed, and returned the cup, from which time the temple was called that of Hercules Indicis. There are more examples like this one of Cicero's. Lucretius and others give the etymologies of the Indigetes, and everyone may come to his own conclusions about them. I will now discuss Hercules and others, from which it will be shown that the pagans did not only attribute immortality to their heroes (and at that time they never questioned the immortality of the soul), but happiness also, which conferred divinity itself on famous persons.

Hercules

There were many people called Hercules; Varro, for example, lists forty-four. Amongst these the best-known were Hercules Margusanus, Hercules Ogmius,[22] the symbol of eloquence amongst the Gauls, Hercules Pollens, Hercules Thebanus or Alcides, Hercules Tyrius, or the Egyptian Hercules. There were actually two of the latter: the elder was Melicarthus[23] or Esau, the founder of Tyre, and the younger, who overcame Geryon,[24] was worshipped at Sidon in Spain. The Phoenicians tell stories of their Hercules that are similar to those deeds of Joshua in Canaan. I strongly suspect, moreover, that from the killing of the lion and other things, that Samson and Hercules were identical, but for this see Vossius, who has much to say on this subject.[25] In short, it seems that all brave men used the name Hercules, and the most famous was the one who defeated so many tyrants; the Hercules mentioned by Dionysius of Halicarnassus, however, was no less remarkable for his piety. The pagans used to offer human sacrifices to Saturn, but Hercules, in order to abolish this savage custom, built an altar on the Saturnian Hill in Rome, ordering that the sacrifices be made with pure fire. They used to bind men hand and foot and throw them into the Tiber to appease the anger of the god, but he had them make do with a dressed-up puppet, and the

---

[22]Hercules Ogmius, or the Gallic Hercules, made an interesting comeback during Herbert's own time. In 1600 Henri IV of France marries Marie de'Medicis, and the king was saluted by the Jesuits of Avignon as the Gallic Hercules. They noted that "l'illustre maison de Navarre a prins sa source de l'antien Hercule, fils d'Osiris" (Seznec 26). Alcides is the name usually given to the Theban Heracles, and most of the other names are self-explanatory.

[23]Melicarthus is usually known as Melqart, who had a shrine at Gadeira (now Cadiz). This area of the Mediterranean was under the Carthaginian sphere of influence, and Melqart was a Semitic deity (see *OCD* 414b).

[24]Geryon was a giant defeated by Hercules in one of his Twelve Labours.

[25]Vossius I, xxii, 169.

custom continued until Dionysius's time. Diodorus Siculus writes that tenths were dedicated to Hercules, and that people who offered them were most fortunate, Hercules having promised them [fortune] before he was deified; reference may also be made to Plutarch, Aurelius Victor,[26] Macrobius, Servius and others. Some of his surnames are Cubans,[27] Defensor, Magnus, Triumphalis, Sylvanus, Vector Musarum and Musagetes.[28] On his medals may be seen the titles Pacificus, Invictus and Olivarius, and under these names many temples and statues of him were erected in Rome and elsewhere, for no other hero was so universally revered as Hercules.

Faunus[29]

There were two kings of the Aborigines[30] whose names were Faunus; the first is said by some chronologers to have lived in about 1520 A.M. The other, the son of Picus,[31] first dedicated buildings and groves to certain gods, from which, so Probus[32] tells us, they are called fana; from him some people

---

[26]Sextus Aurelius Victor (4th century A.D.) was governor of Pannonia Secunda (361) and held other political offices in Rome. He wrote a history of the emperors from Augustus to Constantius II (337–61), but *De viris illustribus*, a biography of Republican heroes to which Herbert is quoting is now thought not to be his. In this work the author shows an interest in the supernatural, which is why Herbert alludes to it here.

[27]Literally, "the Recliner." He was thus the protector of bedrooms.

[28]Both titles mean the same, i.e. "Leader (or Director) of the Muses." Whilst these titles are more often associated with Apollo, Hercules seems to have been more than just brawn; he was an accomplished musician, and played on a lyre given him by Hermes (Peck 793).

[29]Faunus was a deity often identified with Pan, and his festivals were celebrated with dancing and singing. He seems to have been thought of as being connected with the strange noises one hears in forests, and was also the god of herdsmen. It is noted that he had a dark side also, being linked with Incubo, a deity associated with nightmares (*OCD* 358).

[30]The Aborigines. Not an esoteric prophecy about the undiscovered (in 1645) inhabitants of Australia, but a reference to the mythical ancestors of the Latins. They are mentioned by Cicero.

[31]Picus was an early Italian (Aborigine) king whom Diodorus Siculus identified with Zeus. The *OCD* states that Picus is the woodpecker, a bird sacred to Mars, and that Ovid might have invented the myth that King Picus was turned into a woodpecker (692).

[32]Valerius Probus (d. 88 A.D.) was a Roman scholar who commented on Terence, Lucretius, Horace and Vergil. Apparently he did not write anything, "but communicated his learning in conversation with friends" (*OCD* 732). Herbert would have

derive the origin of fauns and satyrs. He was a contemporary of Hercules, from whom he received his wife; after his death he used to frighten people with his terrible voice, excite panic in them, and scare them with apparitions. He was therefore elevated to the Indigetes, sacred honours were paid to him and verses written in his praise. Vossius says that Faunus was not a king of the Aborigines, but I do not agree with him, for Dionysius is positive that Faunus held the kingdom and inherited it from his ancestors; I will not worry about the other Faunus, who, as some writers say, was king of the Aborigines in 2724 A.M. Faunus and Picus, gods of the Aventine mountain, are said to have enticed Jupiter down from heaven to answer whatever questions they asked him. As Ovid writes in the *Fasti*, "The minor gods lured you, Jupiter, from Heaven / And now men celebrate you, calling you Elicius."[33] Apuleius, being guilty of the same detestable deed, should have suffered the severest punishment.

Carmenta[34]

Carmenta, daughter of Mercury and mother of Evander, was named Nicostrata, but she was called Carmenta from carmen, which means "oracle." Others derive carmen from Carmenta; she was believed to be a prophetess, and Plutarch describes her as not looking like someone in her right mind when she delivered her predictions, but raging. The Romans, especially middle-aged women, worshipped her devoutly, and they dedicated altars to her at the Carmental Gate under the Capitol, where they sacrificed to her. She had a temple in the eighth quarter of the city, and was entitled to heroic honours.

---

been referring to a 15th century "invention" known as "the Younger Probus," to whom a number of works claimed to be by Probus were ascribed because scholars had noted, from Suetonius, that the historical Probus had written nothing.

[33]The name Elicius is based on an untranslatable pun made with the verb elicio, "to lure or entice." The lines read, in Latin, "Eliciunt caelo te Iuppiter, unde minores/ Nunc quoque te celebrant, Eliciumque vocant" (Ovid, *Fasti* I, 3). Lewis's translation is, as usual, inaccurate.

[34]Herbert is mostly correct about Carmenta, except that he neglects to note that she taught the Aborigines to write, and that she is more commonly a he, Carmentis. The feminine variant "is found in Greek authors and very rarely in Latin" (*OCD* 167). There are actually two Carmentae (or Carmentes), Prorsa and Postverta (see Varro and Gellius) who are water-nymphs and may also have had some association with birth.

Evander

Son of Carmenta and Mercury and living at about the time that Hercules was in Italy, he was more powerful in his authority than Arcas the King of the Aborigines. He was an ingenious inventor; besides inventing musical instruments such as the lyre, he originated ball games and the Greek alphabet. He also established laws; his unrivalled learning and wisdom led to his being paid not only heroic honours but being offered annual sacrifices.

Castor and Pollux

They were called the Dioscuri, the sons or children of Jupiter and brothers of Helen, and often were seen aiding the Romans in battle, fighting on horseback. They were demigods, as Dionysius says, descendants of a divine parent, for which they were made divine, had temples built, sacred rites performed to them, a fountain dedicated and annual sports decreed. They also had a splendid horse-parade on the Ides of July, the day the Romans are said to have won a victory with their help.

Aesculapius[35]

Cicero, in *On the Nature of the Gods*, mentions three people of this name; the first was Apollo's son, the second Mercury's father, and the third the son of Arsippus and Arsinoë. All of them were eminent doctors, especially the son of Apollo. The Romans brought him (actually a snake that the Greeks worshipped as him) from his temple in Epidaurus, and put him into a new temple built for him on the island of Tiber. There sick people used to lie all night, expecting that way to recover their health. He was first received as a god at Epidaurus, and afterwards in Greece, Carthage and Rome, having all the honour due to a hero paid to him.

---

[35] Herbert is confused about the parentage of this god. In Epidaurus he was the son of Apollo and Coronis (see Hesiod, *Theogony*; Pindar, *Odes*); in Messenia, of Apollo and Arsinoë, and in Arcadia, of Arsippus (Herbert has *Archippus*, which has been duly emended) and Arsinoë. In mediaeval times and up to the Renaissance, scholars believed that Aesculapius had lived; Jacopo da Bergamo (1434-1520), who compiled a *Supplementum chronicarum*, places him in a list of "viri disciplinis excellentes," which also included Faunus (see n. 29).

Acca Larentia[36]

Acca Larentia was the wife of Faustulus;[37] she was very beautiful and grew very rich by prostitution. She was nurse to Romulus and Remus, who were said to have sucked a wolf because they sucked *lupa*, which also means "prostitute," and from which name comes *lupanar*, a brothel. As she left all her money to the people of Rome, they thought that she deserved public sacrifices and a day of honour. Romulus himself established her festivals, which were called Larentalia. He did this not only because she had been his nurse, but because after he had killed his brother Remus and was going to kill himself, she prevented him, and by her advice his spirits were raised.

Quirinus[38]

Some people derive Quirinus from the Sabine word *cuis*, which means "spear," or from the *genius aborigines* of a certain place. In the time of the Aborigines, a young girl was dancing in the temple of Engolus, and, seeming to be in a sacred rapture, she threw herself into a chancel where the god made love to her and had a hero by her. When Romulus became elevated to divinity, he told the Romans to call him Quirinus, saying, as Plutarch tells us, "I am Quirinus." And Quirinus, without doubt, was indeed Romulus, although the name is sometimes used by Mars, and refers to brave and valiant men in general; the Romans, especially the soldiers, were known as Quirites from him. Varro mentions a shrine for Romulus or Quirinus called the Quirinal Tomb, and Dionysius states that Tatius built a temple and altar to Quirinus. So much for the Indigetes.

Now, although some of these people had adoration paid to them beyond the normal honours accorded heroes, this was either the effect of flattery or of the superstition of the times; the worship properly belonging to heroes

---

[36] Acca Larentia. Herbert spells the name Laurentia, but there is no justification for this variant. An even less correct version is Larentina (*OCD* 2). Hercules was responsible for her having obtained great wealth.

[37] Herbert's source for Faustulus, the husband of Acca Larentia, is Licinius Macer (d. 66 A.D.), the Roman annalist. He tells us that Faustulus was a herdsman, and Macer also makes the connexion between the two meanings of *lupa*. Faustulus was probably a by-product of Faunus; "if a deity *favet*, he is *faustus*" (*OCD* 358).

[38] Quirinus. The first thing that should be noted is that Herbert was wrong about addressing soldiers as "Quirites," at least if he thought that it was complimentary to do so! Both Tacitus and Suetonius tell us that if a general did this, he was reproaching the troops, because the word referred *only* to civilians. Herbert is quite correct about the Sabine etymology, however; the Sabine word for spear is *quiris* or *curis* (Simpson 497), and the god's connexion with Mars is also accurately described.

was not that extensive. For example, when Alexander had mourned the death of his friend Hephaestion[39] for a long time, he erected a tomb for him that cost twelve thousand talents and commanded him to be worshipped as a god, as a consequence of which it became most sacred to swear by his name. Because he could not trust his own authority, Alexander asked the Oracle of Amon whether it was lawful to place Hephaestion amongst the gods. The Oracle commanded that he should be honoured and revered as a hero; it is obvious that the Oracle distinguished between the two, although in the passing of years superstition increased, and the pagans paid more adoration to heroes.

The solemnity of ceremony, the antiquity of the myth, and the craftiness of priests, whose sole design is to enslave the people in all religions has a tremendous influence on people who are prone to credulity. As priestly authority increased, the honours paid to heroes turned into religious worship. Another reason may be that the pagans, believing that the Supreme God committed the care of particular things to heroes, and being prone to superstition anyway, paid them divine honours to make them become favourable faster.

The Caesars[40]

After his death, Julius Caesar was deified by Augustus, and, as Manilius wrote, "Now he is made a god and sent to the stars / And through Augustus he grows famous in the heavenly kingdom." The title of divus was given to him, and Pliny says that Tiberius placed him in heaven "to introduce the notion of majesty." Tacitus notes, "the funeral ceremonies being over, temples and divine honours were accorded him." According to Dio Cassius, Numerius Atticus said that he saw Augustus ascending into heaven, for which Livia gave him ten sestertii.

Pliny tells us that Claudius was deified by Nero as a joke, Vespasian by Titus, Titus by Domitian; the latter were deified so that one might have a god for a father, the other for a brother. Pliny also says, later on, [to Trajan] "you have exalted your father Nerva amongst the stars." These honours were not only paid to emperors by their successors, but sometimes by the vote of the Senate. Julius Capitolinus tells us that Antoninus Pius "was voted divus

---

[39]Hephaestion (c. 356–324 B.C.), one of Alexander the Great's commanders, was appointed *chiliarch*, the highest office next to the king (324), but soon afterwards died of a fever.

[40]The Caesars. Livia (58 B.C.–29 A.D.) was the wife of Augustus. The dates for the emperors are as follows: Tiberius [I] 14-37, Claudius [I] 41–54, Nero 54–68, Vespasian 69–79, Titus 79–81, Nerva 96–98.

with universal consent, everyone being for his admission," and likewise Marcus Aurelius.[41] The Emperor Pertinax[42] was placed amongst the gods by Senate and people. Herodian gives us a description of the apotheosis of the emperors and how the Romans deified them. After the celebration of the ceremonies, a wax image of the emperor in repose was placed on an ivory bed in the palace porch, covered and adorned with cloth of gold. The senators in black and middle-aged ladies in white visited for a week, and the doctor stood by the bedside looking at the image as if it were a sick person, saying every now and then that he is getting worse and worse. Then, on the appointed day of death, young men from the ranks of senators and knights lifted the bed on their shoulders and carried it along the Via Sacra to the Old Market, where Roman magistrates used to resign their power. Hymns and paeans were sung in the dead man's praise by a chorus of patrician boys and women of quality; then he was carried to the Field of Mars, where a square stage of wood was erected and filled with inflammable matter rising to a point. He was then divested of his rich clothes, ivory images and pictures, while incense was put in position and the knights, in their armour, danced around the pyre. After this the successor to the Empire took a lighted torch in his hand and set fire to the place where the bed was put; at the same time the spectators threw fire on it until the whole structure went up in flames and the incense was consumed with a fragrant odour. After that an eagle was let loose, which, it was believed, carried the Emperor's soul to heaven, where he was worshipped with the other gods; the pagans believed they had the right to vote in Heaven itself, as they were citizens of the same universe, and that the gods would not deny admission to someone whom they had unanimously judged as worthy of deification.

It will hardly seem strange, then, that those gods whom the pagans thought most benign and ready to answer prayers were the men that they themselves had deified. Yet they still adored the Supreme God as the author of all happiness — they believed him to be happy because, although he governed everything with justice and prudence before order was established, now he had excluded himself from looking after particulars, unless they were

---

[41] Marcus Aurelius Antoninus (121–80), emperor (161–80) and Stoic philosopher, author of the Greek *Meditations*. He held that we must obey the divine law, which is within us, and which teaches us that wisdom is superior to sense-experience, death inevitable. The work was first printed in 1550 from an MS which has since been lost. Herbert's friend Meric Casaubon translated it into English (1642).

[42] Publius Helvius [not Aelius] Pertinax (c. 119–93), was Roman emperor January–March 193. He was murdered by the Praetorians, who then put the Empire up for sale. It was bought by Didius Julianus.

concerned with the general situation of the universe or eternal laws. But more of this later.[43] The custom of consecrating emperors was not quite gone even by the time of Constantine the Great, as may be seen by an ancient coin, on which his soul (covered with linen and the rest naked) is being carried to heaven in a chariot. His arm is outstretched and is being received by another arm from heaven; under this is written "CONS." Perhaps his successors thought it odd that these honours and rewards should be given to a Christian emperor as they had been conferred on some of the worst heathen emperors, because there is a difference. The eagle which carried the pagan emperors to heaven was not present, and Constantine was carried in a chariot; he could not have attained heaven without the assistance of the extended arm, which symbolises the grace of God.

Famous women, too, had divine honours paid them. Thus Livia, the wife of Augustus Caesar was deified, not by her son Tiberius, but by her grandson Claudius, with the additional honour that women should swear in her name. She was consecrated as Juno, so that Juno and whatever Juno mystically represented might be worshipped in her. Prudentius writes "Rites were added, and Livia made into Juno." There is an inscription in the Capitol honouring Faustina,[44] the wife of Marcus Aurelius the philosopher, "Congratulations to Faustina deified by the Senate." Gaius Caligula[45] commanded that his sister Drusilla should have divine honours paid to her in all cities, and a certain senator, Livius Geminius, swore that he saw her ascending into Heaven and speaking to the gods. He called down destruction on himself and his family if what he had said was false, and he asked the gods, including Drusilla herself, to bear witness. Besides Numerius Atticus, whom I mentioned before, and Julius Proculus, who swore he saw

---

[43]"It will . . . later." This is a clear statement not so much about ancient beliefs, but about the kind of deism that Herbert promotes in this work. He is arguing, using historical justification, that the view of a once-benevolent though now remote God is based on logical deductions made long ago by the ancients. Heroes and demigods are part of an established order of things; God does not need to be directly concerned with the government of the world, although he may be in a *general* sense.

[44]Anna Galeria Faustina (d. 141) was the wife of Marcus Aurelius, who, in spite of rumours about her faithfulness and virtue, deified her after her death.

[45]Gaius Caligula reigned 37–41. His sister Julia Drusilla (c. 16–38) was his favourite, and it is possible that they were lovers. The inscription, which was written by one of the Mummius or Memmius family, may be linked to P. Memmius Regulus (d. 61), Governor of Moesia (35–43). In 38 Caligula ordered him to divorce his wife Lollia Paulina so that he himself could marry her; it was generally prudent to comply with Caligula's requests.

Romulus ascending into Heaven, here was a third person daring to aver improbable things with the most dire imprecations, but he deserved, or at least received, the ten sestertii. Dionysius says that Drusilla, dressed as Venus, was deified by the name of Panthea,[46] and Justus Lipsius mentions an ancient inscription, "VENERI CELESTAE AUGUSTAE SAC. MUMMIA C.P. DORCAS S.P.F.C." Julia Maesa,[47] [Septimius] Severus's wife and grandmother of two emperors, was also deified.

Some men from the imperial family were ranked amongst the gods, although they were not actually deified themselves. There was Geta,[48] of whom his brother Bassianus [Caracalla] said "he may become a god, provided that he is no longer alive." Antinous,[49] the Emperor Hadrian's lover, had divine honours granted to him after his death, and an Oracle was set up of which Aelius Spartianus tells wonderful things.[50]

The Worship of the Greek Heroes

Although the Greeks elevated their heroes to the status of gods, they still acknowledged a most Great and Good God, far superior to these, who was worshipped by all nations and to whom only they paid service. They called the gods whom they believed the Supreme God had placed to preside over them, or who had been admitted to the celestial society after this life, *dii* or *numina*. The latter included heroes who had deserved well of their countries or of mankind in general, people who were believed worthy of immortality

---

[46]Presumably Drusilla was being compared to Panthea, the heroine of one of the stories in an historical romance which was supposedly written by Xenophon, the *Cyropaedia*. It may well be "the first Greek love-story in prose" (Peck 1168). If this is the case, it certainly reflect's Caligula's strange state of mind.

[47]Julia Maesa (d. 222) was not the wife of Septimius Severus, but of Julius Avitus. She was the mother of the Empresses Julia Mamaea and Julia Soaemias Bassiana, who have already been mentioned. The wife of Severus was Julia Domna (d. 217), the sister of Julia Maesa.

[48]Lucius Septimius Geta (184–212), the brother of the Emperor Caracalla, was made Caesar in 198 by his father Septimius Severus, and became Augustus in 209. He was murdered by Caracalla in 212, having shared the throne with him as co-emperor for one year. Caracalla's witticism doesn't work in English; the Latin reads "sit divus dummodo non sit vivus," a very nasty play on words indeed.

[49]Antinous (c. 109–30) was taken by Hadrian to Egypt, where he subsequently drowned in the Nile. Hadrian built a city, Antinoopolis, in his memory. It is the modern Sheikh Abadeh.

[50]For illustrations of coins and medals of Antinous issued by Hadrian after the former's death, see du Choul 212–13.

and a more blessed life. When deities of this order occur in Greek authors, we may understand by them the mystic meaning of the Stars, Heaven and Elements, or that they were human beings who, by general consent, had been deified. This attempt at plumbing the occult secrets of the Supreme God might have been very presumptuous and daring, but it made a great contribution to the establishment of virtue. I am aware that the Church Fathers bitterly reproach the pagans for worshipping deified mortals, but they are here imposing a different sense of the word god on their readers than the pagans understood by it, as I have already indicated.

I believe that deified humans amongst the pagans meant no more than makarites, or Saints, amongst the Fathers, unless the latter can be said to enjoy a more abstract, or, as they call it, spiritual happiness. This is a stupid opinion, unworthy of a pious person, but it is not only in vogue amongst the Mohammedans and most Indians now, but was an older and more universal doctrine than is generally supposed. The Pythagoreans[51] were alluding to this with their transmigration of souls into new bodies, as does the mystic divinity of the ancient poets, and the opinions of the Brahmans and Punga in India about the future state of souls. According to them, people who have conducted themselves well in this life are afterwards clothed with more glorious bodies and enjoy pleasures and delights far in excess of ours; the souls of those who have not are transmigrated into animals. In his commentaries on Abraham and Lazarus,

---

[51]"Pythagoreans . . . Brahmins and Punga." Pythagoras (fl. 530 B.C.) left no written works. Herodotus says that the doctrine of transmigration originated in Egypt, which is wrong, but the legend that Pythagoras travelled to the East may well be true (Robinson 61). Xenophanes, a later contemporary of Pythagoras, tells the following story: "They say that once, when a puppy was being whipped, Pythagoras, passing by, took pity on it and said, "Stop! don't beat it! It's the soul of a friend; I recognise his voice" (Fr. 4.11). Pythagoras was inferring that as all souls are transmigrated into animals, all living things are our relations. Like modern Hindus, Pythagoras forbade the eating of meat.

Herbert's reference to the 'divinity' of poets is a Renaissance commonplace. He could have found it in Aristotle's *Poetics* or in his cousin Sir Philip Sidney's *Apologie for Poesie* (1576).

Professor Terence Day identifies Herbert's "bongi" as the modern *punga*, "skyclad" (i.e. naked) Jains of India. Herbert might have heard about them from another cousin, Sir Thomas Herbert, who travelled to Delhi and spent two years at the Moghul court. (See Herbert, *Religio laici* 1–2; Butler, *Lord Herbert of Chirbury* 376, n.30.)

Heinsius[52] learnedly discusses the many aspects of this subject.

I have already sufficiently proved that the pagans believed the gods to have had bodies, because if the human soul, separated from its body, should lose its plastic power, it would become idle and spend ages in mere contemplation, totally incapable of performing its former functions. It could not even so much as attempt to do the many good and useful things which it used to do with the help of the body. Amongst the pagans it was a question whether the soul was more perfect in its own nature, or when it was corporeal; this is why they gave bodies to the gods, because neither a soulless body nor a bodiless soul could operate properly. I admit that there are many horrible things told about the pagan gods, but they were either fictions invented by poets to discredit other peoples' gods, or else things the gods were supposed to have done on earth. If they were lecherous or exceeded the bounds of modesty after they became immortal, the pagans held that everything was lawful for the gods, and by that means heroes appeared. Far exceeding our weak and feeble nature, they came into this world to do great deeds as men and then became gods themselves. These were some of the arguments that the priests offered to vindicate their immoral deities; some may pass as pleasant stories, but others are so ridiculous that they not only exposed the weaknesses of the gods but seemed somehow designed to cover and conceal the adulterous crimes of people themselves.

I will now add a few things that may help to understand ancient theology better. Cicero, in Book 3 of *The Nature of the Gods*, says "they now have in Greece a number of humans who have been translated into gods, such as Alabandus of Alabanda,[53] Leucothoë,[54] who was Ino, and her son Palaemon;[55] all Greece has a Hercules, Aesculapius, and the Tydarides.[56]

---

[52] Daniel Heinsius (1580–1655), an eminent Dutch scholar and pupil of Joseph Scaliger, was the first to produce a definitive edition of Aristotle's *Poetics*. He was also the author of many treatises on philosophy and literature, including *De tragoediae constitutione* (1611), perhaps his best-known work, and *Aristarchus sacer, Sise ad Nonnis in Johannem metaphrasion exercitationes* (1627), which Herbert had in his library (*FK* 99).

[53] Alabanda was a city in Caria, known all over the ancient world for its luxury and opulence.

[54] Leucothoë or Leucothea was a sea-goddess usually identified with Ino, the sister of Semele and daughter of Cadmus. The name translates as "the white goddess."

[55] Palaemon was the son of Ino and Athamas, his name being changed from Melicertes when he was deified.

[56] The Tyndarides were the children of Leda and Tyndareus, king of Sparta. They included Helen, Clytaemnestra (the wife of Agamemnon) and the Dioscuri (Castor and Pollux).

From this it may be deduced that some heroes and gods were worshipped in cities or provinces which were strangers to neighbouring nations. But there were also others whom universal consent of the people had deified, and Cicero tells us who they were. Persaeus,[57] a disciple of Zeno, said that those who had invented things useful to human life were called gods. This is also reported by Maximus of Tyre.

The Greeks also sacrificed to good men, and celebrated the memory of their virtue. They preceded the Romans in this kind of worship, and the Egyptians came before them, for it was in their workshop that the religious worship of mortals was invented. Isis and Osiris were nothing more before they were deified and had stars named after them — it is for this reason that I disagree with Sallust,[58] who says "the Cretans were the first to invent religion." Religion sprung neither from a Jupiter of Crete, nor one from any other island in the entire world, for if by religion we mean the internal adoration of the Supreme God, it could not have originated in Crete, because it is written in the hearts of men. If we mean by it external rites, ceremonies, and particular ways of praying to acquired deities, or the priestly inventions which seem to be the genuine sense of the word, they did not come from Crete either, but from Egypt and Greece, as I have proved.

I shall now, following Vossius, who has made a great effort to collect them, briefly say something of deified humans like the Balacides of Sicily and perhaps Marcellus, for mention is made of the Marcelleis in his honour. Castor and Pollux, the Tyndarides, were first in the Peleponessus, afterwards all over Greece, but not only them, as Cicero tells us in *The Nature of the Gods*.[59] There were also the Anakes,[60] but whether Anac, Aenac, or the Anakim of the Jews are related to them I will not discuss here.

---

[57]Persaeus of Citium (c. 306–243 B.C.), soldier and Stoic philosopher. His particular forte was the expounding of Plato's doctrine of the philosopher-king. After he lost the city of Acrocorinthos to Ptolemy II Philadelphus's forces, Persaeus committed suicide. Herbert is correct in saying that his philosophical master was Zeno of Citium (335–263 B.C.), the founder of Stoicism.

[58]Gaius Sallustius Crispus (86–35 B.C.), Roman soldier and historian, quaestor and Governor of Numidia under Julius Caesar. He is noted for having written the *Bellum Jugurthinum*, an account of the war against Numidia, the *Historiae* (covering 78–67 B.C.), and a work on the conspiracy of Catiline against the Roman state.

[59]Cicero 197–98.

[60]The form is, more correctly, Anaktes. The name means "lords," and usually refered to the Dioscuri, but Cicero (*NG* 3.35) says it was a name for the Tritopatores, an obscure group of wind-gods from Attica. Pausanias says that they were gods from Amphissar.

The Spartans had a hero named Hyacinthus,[61] whose rites were celebrated at festivals of Apollo; actually Apollo was venerated under his name and there was a procession with garlands of ivy like that of Bacchus. Agamemnon, Menelaus and Helen were worshipped, and Helen with her husband had divine honours paid to her, as Isocrates[62] says in his *Encomium*, although not as gods, but as heroes, thus making the distinction between worship of heroes and gods more evident. The Spartans dedicated a temple to Lycurgus,[63] Leonidas,[64] and Barsidas. The Messenians worshipped Polycaeon the son of Lalage, Glaucus,[65] and others, although the Parentalia[66] were performed only for Eurytus.[67] This, as I see it, is the third and last degree of honour paid to people after this life, but Cicero says that it was often mixed with supplications. The Arcadians raised Arcas and Calisto to the stars, and deified Aristaeus[68] because he taught them beekeeping, according to Servius. The citizens of Mantinea in Arcadia instituted annual

---

[61]Hyacinthus was killed accidentally by a discus, and from his blood grew up the iris. He was "a pre-Hellenic god worshipped at Amyclae" (*OCD* 443). He is often associated with Apollo, supposed to have been his lover.

[62]Isocrates (436–338 B.C.), Athenian orator, statesman and educator. He wrote works against the Stoics, and his *Encomium of Helen*, which Herbert cites, was intended to serve as an example of how to treat legendary subjects.

[63]Lycurgus, the legendary lawgiver of Sparta, was supposed to have been the son of Eunomus (Harvey 497). If he existed at all, no-one is certain when, the dates ranging from 1100 to 600 B.C. (*OCD* 521). As he is first mentioned by Herodotus, scholars do not think that he was that early. There are two gods of the name, to add to the confusion, one at Nemea (Rose 123), another in Thrace (Rose 48).

[64]Leonidas II (d. 480 B.C.) became King of Sparta in 487. He fell with his entire army at Thermopylae, fighting against Xerxes of Persia.

[65]Glaucus of Anthedon became immortal through a magic herb. He then leaped into the sea and assumed the duties of a sea-god (Ovid, *Metamorphoses* 13.290ff).

[66]The Parentalia may be equated with the feast of All Souls, taking place 13–21 February, the week being known as *dies parentales*. The last day was a public festival, but the others were used for private family rites. *Parentalia* (1626), was the title given by George Herbert to a collection of poems to the memory of his (and Lord Herbert's) mother.

[67]Eurytus (Moliones) was the son of Poseidon and Molione. A mortal, he was killed by Hercules because he and his brother had attacked Hercules's men.

[68]Aristaeus was the son of Apollo and Cyrene, and the protector of cattle and fruit-trees. He was chasing Eurydice when she was bitten by a snake and died, for which Aristaeus was punished by the death of all his bees. Vergil invokes him in Book IV (315ff) of the *Georgics*, and Cicero (*NG* III, 211) says that Aristaeus discovered the olive.

rites and the games held every five years in honour of Antinous, whom I have mentioned before, and divine honours were paid to Anius or Elius, founder of Eleusis. The Argives made Perseus into a constellation, and then worshipped him as a god. A shrine was built for Lyncaeus and Hypermnestra[69] and a temple outside the city of Epidaurus for Aesculapius; there were others at Ambracia and Rome. It was perhaps thought dangerous to bring a god of medicine into a city in case he increased the number of sick people so that there would be more opportunities of gaining worship! These people are the most remarkable, but I shall add some more who gained either divine honours or hero-worship; I distinguish between them and those to whom divine worship (cultus) was paid by the pagans.

Amphilochus,[70] according to Aristides,[71] also was venerated in the Attic or Beotic Orepus as well as Athens itself, where Cecrops,[72] who was said to have been changed into the zodiacal sign Aquarius, and his daughters were worshipped. There were Ceneus,[73] Triptolemus[74] the inventor of the plough, Amphitryon[75] who became the constellation Heniochus or Auriga because he invented the chariot, Icarius who was shown by Bacchus how to make wine,

---

[69]Lyncaeus, gifted with extraordinary sight, was the brother of Idas, the sworn enemy of the Dioscuri. Hympermnestra, more properly Hypermestra, was his wife and the youngest of the Danaides, the 50 daughters of Danaus. She was the only one who did not kill her husband.

[70]Amphilochus was a Trojan prophet and warrior; he was killed by Apollo.

[71]Aristides of Miletus (c. 100 B.C.) is "credited, probably falsely, with several . . . works, including *Italike*, pseudo-historical anecdotes with a novelistic tendency" (*OCD* 90). Petronius quotes his *Milesiaka*, a collection of obscene stories, in the *Satyricon*. He is mentioned by Plutarch and Lucian.

[72]Cecrops was the first mythical king of Athens.

[73]Caenis or Caeneus of Thessaly (Herbert has Ceneus). In Book XII of Ovid's *Metamorphoses*, Nestor mentions that he once saw Caeneus "enduring a thousand blows without any injury to his person" (272). He was once the maiden Caenis, who was seduced by Neptune and asked what she would like as a reward; she replied that she would like a sex change, "that I might never be able to undergo such an injury again" (273).

[74]Triptolemus, a citizen of Eleusis, was chosen by Demeter to teach agriculture. The Eleusinian Mysteries, which may have pre-dated Demeter, were concerned with crops and fertilty, and, because of Triptolemus, Eleusis was considered the centre of farming knowledge.

[75]Amphitryon (Herbert has "Amphyction") was the son of Alcaeus, who accidentally killed his brother Electryon and was exiled. Hesiod tells their story.

Erigone,[76] who for her exemplary love of her father became the constellation Virgo, though some think this was a different Erigone, and there was Erechtheus[77] and his daughters who loved their country, Perdix,[78] Aeacus,[79] and Alcmene,[80] Androgeus[81] and Theseus had many shrines in Athens, as did Connidas, Theseus's tutor, and Hercules, his companion. There was Hebe, Hercules's wife, as well as Iolaus,[82] Menestheus[83] and Codrus,[84] who, having given his life for his country, was deservedly raised to heroic status. St. Augustine says in his *City of God* that sacrifices were offered to Polynaeus. There were some people who achieved heroic or divine honour under the Archons.[85] These included Toxaris the Scythian[86] and the Attic hero

[76]Erigone was the daughter of Icarius and beloved by Dionysus. Finding her father dead, she hanged herself, and Hyginus tells us (*Fabulae* 30) that young women emulated her until her spirit was propitiated.

[77]Erechtheus was a legendary king of Athens, raised by Athene. Homer mentions his cult (*Iliad* II, 547ff). He sacrificed his daughter to obtain a victory over Thrace, and all her sisters thereupon killed themselves as well.

[78]Perdix was the sister of Daedalus. She was held to have invented implements associated with wood, such as the saw and chisel. She is sometimes confused with her son Talos and made masculine, which confusion credits her or him with inventing the compasses and the potter's wheel as well.

[79]Aeacus, the son of Zeus and Aegina. He was celebrated for piety, and was called upon to judge between the gods. He also started building the walls of Troy. He was rewarded after death by being made a Judge of the Dead.

[80]Alcmene was the wife of Amphitryon. Seduced by Zeus, she became the mother of Hercules. When she died, a stone was put in place of her body and she was taken to the Isles of the Blessed.

[81]Androgeus was the son of Minos of Crete, and was sent by King Aegeus of Athens to fight the Bull of Marathon. He lost, and Minos attacked Athens, demanding the tribute of seven youths and seven maidens for the Minotaur.

[82]Iolaus was the son of Hercules's brother Iphicles, and accompanied the hero on several of his exploits.

[83]Menestheus, a legendary king of Athens, contributed 50 ships to the Greek side during the Trojan War. Pausanias mentions a famous depiction of the Trojan horse with Menestheus climbing down from it (I, 66–67).

[84]Codrus was an early, possibly historical king of Athens. When the Dorians invaded, they were told that they would win if they spared the king; Codrus disguised himself, started a fight with some Dorians, and was killed, thus saving Athens.

[85]The Archons were ancient rulers of Athens, usually nine in number. The most famous period of their rule was from 800 to 487 B.C.

[86]Toxaris was a Scythian doctor who became a hero after saving Athens from the plague, having received the cure in a dream.

Pelops,[87] who had, according to Hesychius, a shrine, a fountain, and a statue. There was a shrine of Amphiaraus,[88] who was first deified by the people of Oropius in Boeotia; the Adelphians worshipped Neoptolemus,[89] and the Boeotians also had other deities such as Ino, Melicerta, and the Theban Hercules, the friend of Theseus whom Homer describes and in whose honour festivals and sports were held. There was also Trophonius,[90] famous for his cave; Democrates,[91] Cyclaeus[92] and Leucus[93] were also worshipped. Aeneas was worshipped in Macedonia, Aristotle amongst the Stagyrites, and Ammonius[94] mentions his festival in his life, unless he means Philopoemen,[95] although Vossius believes that divine honours were paid to Aristotle. In Macedonia Philip, Amyntas, and Alexander the Great[96] were worshipped, although Justin Martyr is dubious about this. The inhabitants

---

[87] Pelops was the son of Tantalus, who cooked and ate him, for which he was punished after death. Pelops was restored to life (Ovid *Metamorphoses*, 255–57).

[88] Amphiaraus was a seer who prophesied the expedition of the Seven against Thebes (see play by Euripides). Knowing that he would die, he nevertheless went to Thebes at the urging of his wife Eriphyle and was duly killed by a thunderbold. A shrine arose on the spot (Cicero, *NG* 125).

[89] Neoptolemus (Pyrrhus) was the son of Achilles, and is depicted in Homer as a vicious thug, his main exploit being the killing of the aged King Priam of Troy. He himself was killed in a brawl with some servants.

[90] Trophonius built the temple of Apollo at Delphi. Cotta asks Balbus in *NG*, "Is Amphiaraus then to be a god, and Trophonius" (213).

[91] I have been unable to identify Democrates.

[92] Cyclaeus was a legendary Carian who founded the settlements on the Cyclades Islands.

[93] Pausanias mentions a statue of Leucas, an Athenian hero (I, 429), and there is a river Leucas as well. I can trace no legends associated with either.

[94] Herbert is probably referring to Ammonius (2nd century B.C.), a philosopher and commentator on Homer and Pindar. He also wrote a work about Aristophanes and the Old Comedy.

[95] Philopoemen of Megalopolis (c. 252–183 B.C.) was the general of the Achaean League against Sparta. He was eventually poisoned by the Messenians, who had changed sides. He is one of the very few genuinely heroic figures of this late period of Greek history.

[96] Philip II was King of Macedon 359–336 B.C. and was the father of Alexander III "the Great," who reigned 336–323 B.C. Herbert does not specify which Amyntas he means, but it was probably Philip's father Amyntas II (r. 399–370 B.C.), who had a statue in the Sanctuary of Philip at Olympia (see Pausanias II, 258–59).

of the Chersonese worshipped Miltaides,[97] and in Leuce there is a temple of Achilles famous for its anathemas. Theaginas the wrestler was venerated in Thebes, and it has not been determined whether the Lesbians worshipped the nine Muses or someone called Mysa, educated by them according to the directions of the Muses. Aristaeus was worshipped at Chios, and Drimachus, the commander of the fugitives. The Samians venerated Lysander,[98] the people of Tenedos adored Callistagoras, the Naxians Ariadne and the inhabitants of Salamis paid divine honour to Ajax, the son of Telamon. Aeacus had the same in Aeginum, Homer was worshipped on Ios, one of the Cyclades, which led Varro to think that he must have been from there, and in Astypalaea they worshipped Cleomedes, a wrestler. The Cretans adored Europa, her brother Cadmus and the two grandchildren of Minos, Idomeneus and Molone; they sacrificed to them and invoked them during wartime. Lastly, we have Epimenides,[99] and Theognetes the boxer.

I could wish that the lives and careers of all these people had come down to us, because if the ancients thought them worthy of divine or heroic honours they cannot be judged unworthy by history. Vossius has done some work in this direction, but it is not sufficient to display their virtues, which have been covered by the wounds of time. This is enough of the Indigetes and others whom the pagans called *dii minorum gentium*.

---

[97]Miltaides (c. 550–489 B.C.), Athenian general and statesman, is probably best-known for his victory over the Persians at Marathon (490). He later fell into disgrace.

[98]Lysander (d. 395 B.C.), Spartan statesman and soldier. He defeated the Athenians at Aegispotami and conducted the surrender of Athens, imposing the Thirty Tyrants upon the city. Arrogant and unpopular, he was eventually disowned by his own government.

[99]Epimenides (c. 500 B.C.) was a Cretan religious teacher and prophet. He was credited with out-of-body experiences and miracles, and is said to have remained asleep for 50 years. Freeman notes that "he was sometimes included in the list of the Seven Sages," and that he may have written epic poetry and an Orphic cosmogony (9). St. Paul mentions him by name in Titus 1:12.

XII

The Olympian Gods
and Other Major Deities[1]

There was such a great number of gods amongst the pagans that not only did every region and province have its country deities, but every island and almost all rivers, however small, had their rustic deities as well, so that they should not be outdone by their neighbours, and eventually they began to argue about the priority of worship. The Romans and others, to end the dispute, decided that some gods should be established as *dii maiorum gentium*, far superior in power to the *dii minorum gentium*, the heroes, demigods and *semones*. Fulgentius Planciades says "there were some deities that the ancients did not think worthy of heaven as they were of little merit, but because of their virtues they could not be returned to earth."[2] These were the *semones*, or *semi-homines*, as distinguished from the *semidei*. Varro divided them into two groups, the *dii certi* and the *incerti*; the *certi* were the ones to whom the Romans had built temples and other public buildings in which they had erected statues, and the *incerti* were those about whom nothing much was known. Cicero, as we have mentioned, divided them in a different way: those who lived in heaven he called *dii maiorum gentium*, and those whose merits had advanced them to deification were known as *semidei* or *indigetes*. A third class included those by whose assistance humans may get into heaven, such as Mind, Virtue, Piety, Faith and Hope, and each will be discussed in place.

It will be very useful in elucidating ethnic theology to determine who the *dii maiorum gentium* were, and which were known particularly as *consentes*, "allowed by common consent." Ennius lists them as Juno, Vesta, Minerva,

---

[1] The *Dii Consentes*, strictly speaking, were those Roman gods whose statues were erected in the Forum.

[2] Fabius Fulgentius Planciades (5th–6th century), perhaps Bishop of Ruspe, wrote on mythology and was a commentator on the *Aeneid* in dialogue form. In his *Mythologiae* Fulgentius supplies symbolic meanings for episodes in Greek mythology which could be held consistent with Christian beliefs and ethics. His *Fulgentii episcopi Carthaginensis mythologiarum ad Catum presbyterum Carthaginensum* was printed, together with Hyginus, in Basel (1535).

Ceres, Diana, Venus, Mars, Mercury, Jupiter, Neptune, Vulcan, and Apollo.[3] To these twelve (six male, six female) some authors add eight more, making the number twenty (twelve male, eight female); these are Janus, Saturn, Genius, the Sun [Sol], Orcus, Bacchus [Liber Pater], the Earth [Tellus], and the Moon [Luna]. The *dii consentes* were those who made up Jupiter's "privy council," where momentous affairs were debated, and they had golden statues set up in the Forum. The rest of the *dii maiorum gentium* were the "nobility" of the heavenly kingdom. The rest, including the *indigetes*, were inferior to these, and there were even "plebeian" deities, as the poet tells us, of whom more later.

Although I have spoken of these gods before, I should like to add something here, the better to explain their mystic theology. Because their history or mythology seems elaborated so much by poets and priests, or even perhaps by grandparents telling them to children, it is almost impossible to uncover the truth which is mixed in with the myths, so obscure and inconsistent are these stories. I hope that readers will be content if I try to collect information about these gods from the best authors whose works remain.

The *dii consentes*, or *selecti*, were those whom the pagans had elevated to deity through their merits, and had adoration of several kinds paid to them such as prayers and vows made to them. The pagans did not only believe that men such as kings and magistrates ruled over them by the appointment of the Supreme God, but that the heroes in heaven were responsible for directing and managing human affairs. The Supreme God allowed them to do this so that he could be free from care and trouble — it was sufficient for him to have originated the law and order of things at the beginning, by which things would be forever governed, leaving administration and management to the heroes, who (like us) were rewarded and punished by divine law. This was necessary so that they did not become idle and lazy in heaven or uninterested in human affairs. Although the overall management was ultimately reserved for the Supreme God, this principle allowed the pagans to transfer the worship of a univerally-acknowledged Supreme God to the secondary deities. Their priests learned how to amuse the people's minds with strange, conflicting stories, which, as they explained, were full of mystery, containing so much that was above the comprehension of common people. Arrogantly they pretended that these were all confirmed by the oracle of that god whose priests they were, but more of this in its proper place.

---

[3]Ennius 190. Herbert quotes the list directly.

Saturn

We will start with Saturn because he is the most ancient of the pagan gods; although Janus was thought of as the God of gods, Saturn is understood mystically as all Time, present and future.

The plentiful issue of the divine race was said to originate from Saturn and Ops whom Tertullian calls "the breeding sow" of the gods. Amongst the ancients it is ambiguous whether his name or surname was Saturn, but as Jupiter under the name of Pater Iuvans[4] was a common name, it is probable that Saturn, whose name, Joseph Scaliger tells us, means "concealed," may be applicable to several personages. Those deities with whom people on Earth were familiar originated from some god who lay concealed. This may be confirmed by the great number of Saturns and Jupiters; *De aequivocis*, supposedly by Xenophon, states that the Saturns were the first kingly or noble family who built cities. Vossius thinks that Saturn was Adam; others believe that he was Noah, or that Abraham was worshipped under that name. Cristoforo de Castro[5] says that Moloch and Saturn were identical, and Sanchuniathon shows him with two faces; if Saturn was Noah, then he must also have been Janus, which is why he had the two faces. Vergil gives the best account of the origins of Saturn:[6]

> First from Olympian heaven came Saturn,
> Fleeing, an exile from the weapons of Jove.
> Mankind was then dispersed on high mountains;
> He brought them together, taught them law
> And chose the name Latium, for there he was safe:
> Under his government came the Golden Age,
> The people were content and he reigned in peace.
>
> (*Aeneid* VI, 794–800 [252])

Saturn was shown with a sickle in his hand, either for reaping, or because

---

[4]Literally the "Helping Father" of the gods.

[5]Cristoforo de Castro (1551–1615) was a Jesuit scholar and theologian who taught at the universities of Alcala and Salamanca. The work to which Herbert refers is probably his *Commentarium in duodecim prophetas minores* (1592).

[6]Indeed. Herbert may have thought Vergil's the best account, but the origins of Saturn are shrouded in mystery and were not clear to the ancients themselves. Herbert usually cites Cicero on the origins of various gods, but he may have realised that both Cicero and Varro, the other authority, were far off the mark. Modern scholarship confirms Scaliger's thesis (1581) that Saturn was actually of Etruscan origins, and as Herbert cites Scaliger he must have known this. For further details, see Giuseppe Pucci, "Roman Saturn: The Shady Side," in Ciavolella and Ianucci (38–40).

he was the inventor of agriculture and the use of manure, or else from his mystic name Kronos, Time, which like a sickle mows everything down. There is hardly a writer who has not told the story of how Saturn ate his own children, of whom Jupiter, Juno, Neptune and Pluto survived, and to whom mythologists (as I have shown) gave power and rule over the elements, even though they could not abolish or destroy those elements.

In ancient times it was the Carthaginians and Gauls who paid particularly profound worship to Saturn, but many other Western countries propitiated him with human sacrifice. Thus Dionysius of Halicarnassus tells us how Hercules abolished this custom and built an altar on Saturn's Hill, where holy sacrifices were made with pure fire. The Greeks called these *thymata hagia*; the *thymata*, as the commentator on Thucydides tells us, were loaves baked in the shape of animals and offered up to the gods. Dionysius says that they "looked like people," and Ovid tells us of similar things made of straw or rushes, "the citizens throw straw images into the water," and, later on in the *Fasti*, "an image of rushes is thrown into Father Tiber." This was done by a virgin from a bridge, according to the same author, or perhaps by men over sixty, called *depontani*. There were small figures called *oscillae* offered to Saturn, and his shrines were all over Italy, with cities, rocks and tombs named for him, as Dionysius tells us. [King] Tatius built a temple to Saturn and ordered public feasts and sacrifices in his honour to be held yearly, as A. Sempronius Atratinus and M. Minucius Felix did when they were consuls.[7] Macrobius relates how Tullus Hostilius, carrying out a vow, dedicated a temple to him, and first instituted the Saturnalia in Rome.[8] Saturn's temple was on the Capitoline Hill. P. Valerius Publicola, because there were no thefts committed in his time, made it, or another temple of Saturn, the public treasury.[9] Any ambassadors coming to Rome went there, and all the records of contracts, or whatever parents promised their children, together with the names of every Roman citizen, were written down and preserved there in the Elephantine Books.[10] Finally, Suetonius mentions

---

[7] Aulus Sempronius Atratinus and Marcus [Quintus] Minucius Rufus were consuls in 110 B.C. See Dionysius of Halicarnassus II, 50 [455].

[8] Macrobius I, 8 [63].

[9] Publius Valerius Publicola [Poplicola] was traditionally thought to have been one of the first Roman consuls (509 B.C.). He held office many times during the earliest years of Republican Rome.

[10] The connexion between the temple of Saturn and the Elephantine Books seems odd. Elephantine Island lies just below the first cataract of the Nile, and was used as a customs station, military installation and a religious centre. The *OCD* mentions

two temples built by Munatius Plancus.[11]

Sacrifices to Saturn were made bare-headed, but covered to all other deities; there are not a few reasons for this, but I willingly pass them by. Saturn's statues were always chained, being untied on festivals to commemorate the security and prosperity people had enjoyed under his rule. Arnobius says that Saturn was bound for being a parricide, and only set free on days devoted to him. I will not go over all the incredible myths that exist of Saturn and his children; the older a god is, the more stories are told about him, and it was neither safe nor easy to convince people otherwise. As Cicero says, "it is very difficult not to believe things that claim divine origin, even though there may not be any reason to do so."[12] He adds that these things came from Ocean and the lust of Heaven, generated by the conceptive power of Earth. Amongst them were Phorcys, Saturn, and Ops, but who Phorcys was, I have no idea, unless he was the father of Medusa and was poetically meant to represent the power of petrification.[13]

Ops

Ops was the sister and wife of Saturn known as Magna Mater and Berecynthia,[14] as we see in Vergil, *Aeneid* VI: "Mother Berecynthia/ Crowned by the cities of Phrygia, advances,/ Propitiously bringing a hundred grandson gods."[15] Ops, Cybele, Vesta, Rhea, Ceres and others were goddesses in the same sense: they either represented the Earth or things that it produced. Homer calls her *zodoron*, "life-giver," and Hesiod *eurysternon*, "broad-breasted." She rode in a chariot drawn by lionesses, who were formerly Hippomenes and Atalanta, metamorphosed into lionesses for insulting the

---

that"many *ostraca*, chiefly customs receipts, have been found" there (312), but this still does not explain what Herbert means, unless they somehow ended up in Rome.

[11] L. Munatius [Munacius] Plancus (d. after 20 B.C.) was one of Caesar's generals. Later he fought for Octavian, and proposed (in 27 B.C.) that the latter be given the title of Augustus. He was consul in 42, censor in 22.

[12] I cannot find the exact quotation in Cicero. However, Cotta says that the philosopher Carneades (c. 213–123 B.C.), whilst not denying the gods existed, "which would ill become a philosopher," said that the Stoics could not demonstrate that they did, either (*NG* III, 42–44 [210]).

[13] It is strange that Herbert claims ignorance of this mythological figure. According to Hesiod (*Theogony* 237), Phorcys was the son of Nereus and Gaia. He married his own sister and became father of the Gorgons.

[14] The name is taken from Mt. Berecynthus in Phrygia, one of Cybele's sacred mountains.

[15] Vergil, *Aeneid* VI, 784–86 [252].

goddess.[16] The chariot was covered with cloth, and it was blasphemy for anyone but the priest to touch it, as he alone knew whether the goddess was there. She carried a key, symbolising her power to allow or stop the growth of all things on earth. Pigs, because they were the most fruitful animals, were sacrificed to her. Tacitus says that the Germans honoured her in groves, as they had neither temples not statues of her. Herodotus mentions the burning of Cybele's temple, and Dionysius describes a temple of the Earth. I will omit the trivial story of Claudia drawing the goddess with a rope, but Dionysius mentions a wonderful cave, sacred to her, into which no-one but her priest dared go.[17] I have already discussed her surnames.

Jupiter

Poets tell us that we should begin with Jupiter, because while Saturn was the oldest god, Jupiter was senior in rank to all the gods. This is in spite of his being represented as an infant, greedily sucking a breast together with [his sister] Juno as they sat in Fortune's lap. Yet married women in Rome had great veneration for him, according to Cicero; I think, however, that he was the first god crying in a cradle that the pagans adored, and they could hardly have been very attached to such a snivelling deity before he had done any noble deeds![18]

There are historical, mythic, and moral stories told about [Jupiter]; the priests made no distinction between them, believing that it was more expedient that people should come to them for explanation. It was also the policy of those in authority that common people should be kept in a kind of limbo, not troubled too much with superstitious ceremony, because their minds might be deflected from observing the law. The authorities did not care that something doubtful, uncertain, or merely having a veneer of truth, not to mention some monstrous lies, should all be mixed up with the religion. They knew how ignorant people venerated the oracles pronounced by the priest, and so they were maintained unless they had something in them that

---

[16]Hippomenes, usually known as Melanion, won the race with Atalanta and married her. The metamorphosis occurred because they had sex in a place sacred to Aphrodite without first offering the goddess a sacrifice.

[17]Claudia Quinta (fl. 204 B.C.) was a Roman lady (sometimes erroneously called a Vestal Virgin) who was able, through her purity, to unstick a ship carrying a statue of Cybele when it ran aground. She thus gave the lie to those who impugned her chastity, because Cybele would not otherwise have permitted the miracle to happen.

[18]See the Introduction concerning the controversy over this passage. Lewis assumed that Herbert was mocking pagan religion, but he failed to see the importance of the word "first."

might discredit religion's luxuriant flowering. Absurd and false as it was, religion gained a great influence over people's minds. The priests seemed to think that iron as well as steel was needed to forge a good sword; a proper mixture would produce the best religious temperature and make a better edge. Thus inconsistencies were foisted upon religion because they made it look dark and mysterious: if something were perfect it would not need interpretation. How badly these heterodox notions distorted true religion I shall discuss later.

There were many Jupiters amongst the ancients: Varro says that he found three hundred of them in one place or another. We are told that there was no era before the Trojan War which did not have its Jupiter. The best-known was Jupiter *Cretensis*, of whom, although he was younger than Jupiter *Argivus*, Diodorus Siculus writes:[19]

> This god surpassed the others in strength and virtue. Coming to power after Saturn, he introduced many things that were useful for human life; first, he ordered people to maintain justice amongst each other and to refrain from injury and oppression. He prevented strife by these judicial means, and he encouraged whatever was conducive to quiet and happy life; he supported the virtue of good people, and restrained the wicked through threats or punishment. He travelled all over the world fighting against blasphemous robbers, introducing law and justice.

This particular Jupiter, who, some say, was cared for by the Curetes as an infant, flourished at about the time of Isaac and Jacob.

There was another Jupiter *Cretensis*, known as Asterius,[20] who raped Europa and had Minos, Rhadamanthus, and Sarpedon by her. The eldest, Minos, retired to a cave on Mount Ida, and said that Jupiter communicated his laws to him there; Numa Pompilius was later to boast that he had had his laws communicated to him by the nymph Egeria. It was insufficient merely to enact just and good laws unless they were sanctioned by the authority of some deity. This way of introducing laws was the custom amongst the Indian peoples, as their writers testify, not to mention the angel Gibreel of Mohammed.[21] There were two Jupiters known as the Argivi, and I refer you to Vossius, who has recorded all the Jupiters collected out of the most famous authors extant.

---

[19]These two names mean, respectively, the "Cretan" Jupiter and the "Greek" Jupiter.

[20]The Starry One.

[21]The angel Gibreel (Gabriel) directed Mohammed to start reciting *The Quran*.

Hercules built an altar to Jupiter *Inventor*, after he had discovered Cacus's oxen and had atoned for their slaughter with river water. Dionysius of Halicarnassus mentions a temple of Jupiter *Feretrius*, fifteen feet long, built by Romulus;[22] Livy says that this was the first temple consecrated in Rome, and that Augustus repaired it when time had practically ruined it.[23] The Romans would swear by his sceptre and strike with his flint to ratify treaties. Dionysius gives us the historical and moral sense of the word *feretrius*; Romulus dedicated the weapons of the Caesenians,[24] whom he had conquered, to Jupiter Feretrius (possibly derived from the Greek *hyperpheretren*) because as he takes in the nature and motion of all things, he has pre-eminence over them.

Romulus built a temple to Jupiter *Stator* for the following reason. The Sabines having defeated the Romans, Romulus amongst them, he lifted his hands to heaven and begged this god's help; he made a vow to build him a temple, saying, "O Jupiter, you commanded through your birds that I found this city on the Palatine; now the Sabines, through treachery, have taken the Tower. Let the Romans be inspired with courage to resist, and I swear that I will build a temple to you as Stator." After he had prayed, the Romans held their ground, and, so Dionysius says, conducted themselves most bravely. Seneca provides a mystic meaning, saying that Jupiter was called "Stator" because by his power everything stood still. In this temple, Cicero tells us, the Senate sometimes met and made laws.[25] Jupiter *Elicius*, whom I have mentioned before, also had a temple; he was thus named because, with priestly assistance, he answered questions there. Arnobius records a friendly dialogue between Jupiter and King Numa, which Plutarch has also written about. Livy tells how Tullus Hostilius and all his family were struck by lightning for neglecting to perform his sacred ceremonies.[26]

The most venerated was Jupiter *Capitolinus*; he was called Best and Greatest, with *optimus* coming before *maximus*. One signified his generosity, the other his power. He got his name from the Capitoline Hill, which

[22]Dionysius of Halicarnassus II, 34 [411].

[23]Livy 1.9 [44].

[24]Caesenians. Herbert probably meant the people of Casinum, a town in Latium.

[25]Velleius says that Chrysippus the Stoic "identifies Jupiter with the power of eternal and immutable law, which guides our lives and directs our efforts" (Cicero, *NG* I, 38–41 [86]).

[26]The above-mentioned surnames may be explained as follows:
Inventor: the Finder.
Feretrius: the Striker.
Stator: the Upholder.

was formerly covered with trees and where a temple was built for him and divine worship established. Tarquinius Priscus dedicated this temple during the Sabine War, but Servius Tullius and after him Tarquinius Superbus completed it by using plunder from their enemies. After the expulsion of the kings, Horatius Pulvillus rededicated it with such magnificence that the Roman people afterwards spent more money adorning it than expanding it. After 415 years, during the consulship of Julius Scipio and Caius Norbanus, the temple burned down and was rebuilt in the same way. This one remained until the time of Vitellius, when it was utterly destroyed in that time of rebellion and sedition. Vespasian rebuilt it again, but after his death it was burned down. Domitian rebuilt it a fourth time, its pillars and gilding costing twelve thousand talents. It covered an area of eight acres; two golden crowns were kept in it, one dedicated by the Gauls, the other by the Carthaginians to Jupiter Best and Greatest.[27]   The Sybilline Books,[28] thought of by the Romans as having great authority and always consulted by them in difficult times, were most sincerely venerated, and the future divined or guessed from them. When emperors went to war, they swore vows here, and if they returned victorious they proceeded there in triumph to perform sacrifices to Jupiter. It was for this reason (I think) that the statue of Jupiter *Imperator* stood there, and that the Senate met there on occasion. People often spent the whole night there for religious reasons or for the interpretation of their dreams, a custom I have mentioned already. Jupiter was portrayed with a thunderbolt in his hand, which he was believed to hurl. I might add more about the mystical worship of this Jupiter, but I have only described this as preparation for enlarging on the argument in a chapter on the Supreme God. Allow me to point out that the pagans never used Jupiter for a name, but only as a cognomen meaning *iuvans pater*, "helping father"; as I have mentioned before, some derive it from *Jao*, and I shall add more later.

---

[27]The chronology for the Capitoline Temple is as follows. M. Horatius Pulvillus was consul in 509 B.C. As early republican dates are largely conjectural, the history of the temple before 83 B.C. need not be repeated here. Julius Scipio and Gaius Norbanus Flaccus were consuls in 83 B.C. Q. Lutatius Catulus rebuilt the temple in 69 B.C. but it burnt down during the reign of Vitellius (69 A.D.), as Herbert records. The temple built by Vespasian lasted only until 80, and Domitian rebuilt it in 82. This one survived until 455, when it was flattened by King Gaiseric of the Vandals.

[28]These were the collected prophecies of the Cumaean Sybil, supposedly sold to King Tarquinius Priscus, who put a college of priests in charge of them. In times of crisis, the Senate could order them opened, and after the destruction of the capital in 83 B.C. a new compilation was made. In 363 A.D. the Emperor Julian ordered the last consultation of them, as Ammianus Marcellinus tells us (256), and they were destroyed by order of the Emperor Honorius Flavius (395–423 A.D.).

Tarquinius Superbus built a temple sacred to Jupiter *Latialis*;[29] for those times it was a magnificent structure erected wisely and prudently for foreigners living nearby who had different religious customs, especially the Latins, Volscians and Hernici.[30] Tarquin, as King of Latium, sent envoys to the Volscians and Hernici asking for their friendship and co-operation, and he proposed, amongst other things, that a temple common to all of them might be built where they could have a solemn meeting every year to perform sacred rites. They accepted, and the temple to Jupiter Latialis was built almost in the middle of the area where those people lived. Dionysius tells us that Tarquin also began the building of a temple in the city to Dios *Pisithos*, but Spurius Postumius[31] later dedicated it to Jupiter *Fidei* or *Sponsor*.[32]

Cartari refers to this when he mentions Jupiter *Horcius* of the Greeks,[33] and Jupiter *Lapis* is also linked with it because when treaties were ratified they held a flint in their hands and pronounced these words: "If I knowingly lie, may Diespiter [Father of the Gods] throw me out of here and out from the society of decent people as I throw this stone." A temple to Jupiter *Victor* was erected on the Palatine Hill, and there was also Jupiter *Lucetius*, named for the light he provided, and without doubt he is the Sun. Agelli and Servius say that *Diespiter* is the same, and P. Victor built a temple to him in the tenth quarter of the city. In all probability Jupiter is the same as the Sun, or Sol Heliogabalus, for which see Saumaise's[34] notes on the Emperor Heliogabalus, or Fuller[35] following Porphyry, who identifies Elagabalus or Heliogabalus with Sol Opifex, the "Maker of the Universe." The Syriac

---

[29]That is, of Latium, the district in which Rome was situated. An alternative form is Latiaris.

[30]The Hernici were one of the local peoples of Latium who predated the Romans. Note how Herbert makes sure that he commends the toleration of the Romans towards others' beliefs.

[31]Spurius Postumius Albinus (d. after 109 B.C.) was consul in 110, and played a minor part in the war against King Jugurtha of Numidia.

[32]Dios Pisithos is a puzzle. The old Epic word *pisos* means "meadow," which would give something like "Jupiter of the Meadow." Sponsor: the Guarantor.

[33]Derived from *horkos*, "an object by which one swears."

[34]Claude de Saumaise [Salmasius] (1588–1653), Professor of Greek at the University of Leyden. He is best-known to English readers for his controversy with Milton over monarchical government in 1649–51. In 1607 Saumaise discovered the 10th century manuscript of *The Greek Anthology* in the Palatine Library at Heidelberg.

[35]Thomas Fuller (1608–61), theologian and historian, was Rector of Broadwindsor and Canon of the Savoy. His works include *The Holy State and the Profane*

word *gabal* and the Arabic *gabil* mean "builder," which agrees with the Sun being called *ktises t'oikomenes*[36] on the great obelisk which Constantine the Great commanded to be carried to Rome. Some maintain that Elagabalus is only a mountain-god or a deified mountain, from the Arabic word *gebel*, but I do not give this much credit.[37]

Augustus built a temple to Jupiter *Tonans*[38] in the Capitol, about which Suetonius tells us. There was another to Jupiter *Genetius*, so-called from a mountain or river of that name nearby, which is mentioned by the Scholiast on Apollonius Rhodius[39] and Strabo in Book VI. There was a temple to Jupiter *Ultor*,[40] called the Pantheon ("of all gods"); it was dedicated by Agrippa[41] and is now named All Saints' Church or Santa Maria Rotunda from its circular form. It was first built for Cybele. I saw it when I was in Rome; the pillars that were in front of the porch had sunk deep into the ground because of earthquakes. There used to be twelve steps up to this church; now, as [Ammianus] Marcellinus says, you have to go down as many. Fabricius[42] gives a very elegant description of it and says that Agrippa would have placed a statue of Augustus there and given him the credit for the building, but Augustus refused, so Agrippa placed Julius Caesar's statue in the Pantheon and Augustus's in the porch.

Domitian first built a small chapel in the Capitol to Jupiter *Custos*, and afterwards a huge temple to Jupiter *Conservator*, and he consecrated himself

---

State (1642) and his best-known book, *The Worthies of England* (1662). He was personally known to Lord Herbert.

[36]Founder (builder) and Regulator. This quotation comes from Vossius, who Latinizes it to *conditor universi*, "the Builder of the Universe" (II, v, 232–33).

[37]The Sun was actually worshipped in a coastal town of Aradus called Gabala (Teixidor 49). Much information about Elagabalus comes from Aelius Lampridius in *The Lives of the Later Caesars* (290–316).

[38]The Thunderer.

[39]Apollonius Rhodius of Alexandria (after 247 B.C.) was a poet and librarian. His most extensive extant work is an epic poem, the *Argonautica*.

[40]The Avenger.

[41]Marcus Vipsanius Agrippa (c. 65–12 B.C.), Roman admiral and right-hand man of Octavian during the latter's struggle with Antony. Agrippa wrote a work on geography which often cited by Strabo, and an autobiography. Both works are now lost.

[42]Georg Fabricius (1516–71) was a German philologist and the Director of the College of Meissen from 1553. For years his *Antiquitatis monumenta insignia per eundem collecta et magna occasione iam auctoritate* (1550) was the standard work on the subject. His description of ancient Rome appeared in A. Thysius, *Roma illustrata* (1657).

in the bosom of the god, as Tacitus tells us. On some of Diocletian's coins Jupiter can be seen holding out victory in his right hand, and an upright spear in his left, with the inscription "IOVI CONSERVATORI ORBIS," "to Jupiter, Preserver of the World." Jupiter *Arbitrator* had a temple in the tenth quarter of the city, and an ancient inscription to Jupiter *Propugnans* appears in the Palace. In Dionysius we read also of a Jupiter *Faunus*, and Suidas mentions Jupiter *Hercaeus*,[43] which Budé[44] renders as *Septitius*. There was an altar to him built in the courtyard or halls of some private houses, and whoever had Jupiter *Hercaeus* had the right of a citizen. Ricchieri[45] says that he is depicted as having three eyes, and explains why. Plutarch tells us that many great honours were paid to Jupiter *Hospitales*.

Divine honours were also paid to Jupiter *Terminalis*. Numa established a *lex Terminalis* which stated that the Romans should be content with their own laws and not covet those of other nations, and Dionysius gives an account of the punishments inflicted on those who violated this law.[46] Jupiter Praedator also had a temple, and part of all plunder was owed to him. There was the temple of Jupiter Olympius, to which a great pilgrimage was made from Greece, people competing to bring the noblest offerings. For Jupiter Ammon, see Vossius.[47] Jupiter had many more surnames, all of which,

---

[43]The names listed here are as follows:
Custos: the Guardian.
Conservator: the Preserver.
Propugnans: the Defender.
Hercaeus: a title of Jupiter as a household god.

[44]Guillaume Budé [Budaeus] (1467–1540), French scholar and critic, secretary to Francis I and the founder of the Collège de France. Henry Peacham, in his *Great Assizes holden in Parnassus* (1645) makes him one of the "Lords of Parnassus," together with Heinsius, Vossius, Isaac Casaubon, J.C. Scaliger, Selden and Grotius, to mention only those known or cited by Herbert (Spingarn 197). Herbert owned Budé's *De studio literarum recte et commode instituendo* (1533) and *De philologia libri duo* (FK 110).

[45]Ludovico Ricchieri [Caelius Rhodiginus] (1450–1520), Italian humanist and scholar, was the author of *Lectionum antiquarum libri XXX* (1516), an extensive study of the mystical and symbolic interpretation of the old gods, pagan vestiges of the Trinity, and speculations on Egyptian hieroglyphics.

[46]Dionysius of Halicarnassus II, 74 [531].

[47]The names listed here are as follows:
Terminalis: derived from the same root as the name of Terminus, the god of boundaries, and has to do with setting the limits of Roman law.
Praedator: the Plunderer.

St. Augustine tells us, were attributed to the different causal powers of one God, for which further see Vives.[48]

The eagle was sacred to Jupiter for two reasons: mystically, because it can look right into the Sun, and poetically, because it is said to have brought Jupiter his weapons in his battle with the Titans. The oak and the olive trees were sacred to him, the oak also being sacred to Bacchus, Rhea, and Ceres. Sacrifices consisted of a she-goat, two lambs and a white bull with gilded horns, but the Romans sometimes sacrificed nothing but corn, salt and frankincense to him. The Athenians sacrificed an ox only, with the silliest ceremonies, as you may see from Pausanias.

It is impossible to enumerate everything mythical, historical or poetic about Jupiter. Suffice it to have shown that some pagans venerated him as the Original and Father of Gods and Men, related to the Sun, although by Jupiter some mean the aether only; generally, however, he was thought of as the Supreme God, superior to the Sun, who administered and governed all things on earth, and dispensed good to humanity. By this he is distinguished from *Vejupiter* (whom Martianus Capella calls *Vedios* also), who only has power to harm.[49] Just as people worshipped some gods in order to receive blessings from them, so they tried to appease or pacify others to stop them

---

Ammon: Am[m]on was the Greek version of the Egyptian Amen, the great god of Imperial Egypt. The Greeks apparently discovered his cult through contact with the small community of Siwa, which they acquired when they conquered Cyrene in the 6th century B.C. The oracle of Amon became identified with that of Zeus, and was so famous that it was consulted by Alexander the Great. When Zeus became Jupiter, his Amon-identity went along with him; the earliest mention of Zeus Ammon is in the fragment of a hymn by Pindar (Pausanias I, 339 n. 75; Vossius II, xi [361]).

[48] Juan Luis Vives (1492–1540), Spanish philosopher and humanist, the spiritual mentor of Katherine of Aragon. He deserves his place in intellectual history for his "rejection of any slavish adherence to the scientific, medical or mathematical ideas of Aristotle" (Copleston 3, ii, 23). Carlos Noreña states: "Like Erasmus, Vives was much more interested in the ethical dimensions of religion than in its revelatory or institutional character. Vives's name deserves much more to be linked to that of Grotius or Herbert of Cherbury than to that of Ignatius Loyola" (291). This is not surprising when one realises that Vives actually saw "the fundamental truths of God's existence and the immortality of the soul" as "common notions . . . which human reason can reach with a degree of prudent persuasion sufficient to base upon them a firm moral decision" (Noreña 293). Another source of Vives's appeal to Herbert was likely his severe criticism of the priesthood in *De veritate fidei Christianae*, posthumously published in 1543.

[49] Vejupiter [Veiuppiter], originally an Etruscan underworld deity, was imported by the Romans. Modern scholars agree with Herbert's interpretation of him. "Non-

from inflicting injury. The god Vejupiter was so called because he had no power to help, the particle *ve* being negative. His temple was between the Tower and the Capitol, where his image stood holding arrows ready for doing harm, and nearby was the figure of a goat, his sacrificial animal. Agelli says that some people thought he was Apollo, and Martianus makes him Pluto, but whoever he was, it was believed that he hurt only people who were wicked or perjured.

I will speak more of this subject when I come to examine the principle of good and evil amongst the pagans, and I shall also show what they thought about the Supreme God, mystically disguised by the name Jupiter.

Juno

Jupiter's wife comes next, even though the ancients have shown Jupiter himself, his head bound, groaning like a woman amongst the goddesses who helped him as he laboured to give birth to *Liber Pater* or Bacchus. Juno is known as Jupiter's wife, but she is also his sister. It is not strange that Jupiter should give birth, for both Eastern and Western people attributed bisexuality to their gods. Like Jupiter's, Juno's name is derived from *iuvando*, "assisting." As his sister, she symbolises the near relationship and conjunction between Aether and Air, according to the Stoics. The commentator on Theocritus has a story of how Jupiter, in the form of a cuckoo, flew into Juno's lap, returned to his own shape and promised marriage, as this line of Vergil symbolically suggests, "He descends with joy into his wife's lap."[50]

Her statue, as Cartari tells us, did not represent one goddess, but many, for it is possible to see in it something of Pallas, Venus, Diana, Nemesis, the Parcae and others. She sat on two lions, a sceptre in one hand, a shuttle in the other, a halo around her head, and surrounded by things that belonged also to other deities, from which Lucian shows that she was worshipped and adored under different names.[51] Others describe her statue as having a rainbow about its head. Iris (the rainbow) the daughter of

---

helper" is perhaps the most accurate rendering of his name and function. Herbert's reference is Martianus Capella II, 41G [69].

[50]This story tells how Zeus ambushed Hera during a thunderstorm on "Cuckoo Mountain" disguised as a cuckoo, and sheltered under her dress! After confirming Pausanias's source (a commentator on Theocritus), Peter Levi explains that the story originated in a history of Hermione written perhaps by Aristotle, but more likely by Aristokles, although Hera's "connection with cuckoos is independent of it." Levi further points out that the cuckoo is "famous as a secret lover in English and Latin" (Pausanias I, 218, n. 208).

[51]Cartari 179–81.

Thaumas,[52] was said to be Juno's messenger, or the air, and was the sign of good weather after clouds and rain.

The peacock was held sacred to Juno; the Emperor Hadrian once offered her a gold peacock, covered all over with splendid jewels. There was a sort of hawk, or vulture, held sacred to her by the Egyptians, according to Aelian;[53] they crowned Isis with the feathers of this bird, and she included many deities whom the Greeks and Romans worshipped separately. Geese were also sacred to Juno, and the Romans, grateful for the saving of the Capitol, kept some at public expense, carrying one every year in pomp on a richly-adorned throne. At the same time they ran a dog through with an elder-stake to symbolise punishment for lax guardianship of the Tower.

The Greeks called Juno [H]era, which is Aer[54] if you transpose the letters, as Athenagoras[55] observes. It is probable that she received her name Sospita[56] from this, because different effects proceed from the different temperatures of the air, and even illnesses, as experience tells us without our having to consult Hippocrates or Galen. Juno had many surnames. Juno *Regina*'s statue was brought from Veii when Camillus[57] was dictator, and dedicated by married women on the Aventine Hill. Livy and Plutarch tell a pleasant story about this, and how she answered prayers in a very serious manner. They also state that this statue was so sacred that no-one dared touch it except the priest of a particular country. Camillus afterwards dedicated a temple to her on the Aventine Hill, and during his war with the Ligures, Flaminius established another in the Capitol. Juno was also called *Caprotina*, from the fig-tree where some servant-girls once gave a signal by which the Romans overcame some enemies, as you can read in

---

[52]Herbert has Thaumantia, which is incorrect. Iris was the daughter of Thaumas, son of Pontus (the Sea) and Gaia (the Earth).

[53]Claudius Aelianus (c. 170–235), a priest of Praeneste, wrote a treatise on animals and the *Varia historia*, a work on human history. A Stoic, Aelian believed that reason demonstrated itself through the creation of the animal world.

[54]Cicero says that this belief was held in particular by the Stoics. "The air, however, as the Stoics argue, being interposed between the sea and sky, is worshipped under the name belonging to Juno" (*NG* 149).

[55]Athenagoras of Athens (fl. 170 A.D.) wrote *A Plea for the Christians*, an eirenic work which he addressed to Marcus Aurelius. He was a disciple of Justin Martyr (Chadwick 79).

[56]The Saviour. It also connotes "lucky" or "favourable."

[57]M. Furius Camillus (fl. 400–370 B.C.) saved Rome after the Gallic invasion of 387. He is often known as "Rome's second founder."

Macrobius.[58] She is known as *Moneta*, from *monendo*, "advising," according to Cicero and Livy, whom I consider better authorities than Suidas.[59] There were books called *Lintei*,[60] said to contain the fate of the Roman Empire, preserved in her temple. Juno *Sospita*, whom we have mentioned, had three temples, one at Lanuvium, two at Rome, and her statue had a goatskin on it, a spear, a small shield, and small shoes. At their coming into office the Consuls scarificed to her, as Cicero says in his *Pro Murena*.

There was Juno *Lucina*, who gave light to newly-born babies, according to some, but others say the name came from *lucus*, "a grove," where her temple was built. Lucius Piso,[61] in Book I of the *Annales*, says that Servius Tullius, in order to find out the number of people in Rome, the births, deaths and comings of age, decreed how much money everyone should bring for births to the treasury of Eilythia (Lucina), burials to that of Venus (Libitina), and coming of age to that of Iuventus (Youth). She was also called Juno *Juga* because, according to ancient custom, people who were marrying were tied together, from which comes the word *coniunx*, "wife"; there was an altar to her in a street named Iugarius. She was called *Sororia Julia* and *Martialis*, and there were temples and altars dedicated to her under those names. Brides and bridegrooms used to sacrifice to Juno *Pronuba*, removing the gall-bladder and throwing it behind the altar. Her sacrifices were a small pig or a lamb; the Queen (wife of the priest of the sacrifice the King) performed the rites. This was because during the time of the kings of Rome, they performed these ceremonies themselves; when they were expelled, the priest took over, but he was inferior to the Pontifex Maximus (High Priest), so that his name did not suggest absolute power. Because she presided over marriages and punished immoral women, Juno had several names, such as *Domiduca*, *Unxia*, and *Cinxia*. She was known as *Gamelia* or *Zugia* by the

---

[58]Caprotinus means "goat-footed." The Latin for "fig-tree" is *caprificus*, and Herbert may have intended Caprotina to read "Caprifica" (125). Juno, however, has some connexion with goats, as Herbert describes the statue of Juno Sospita wearing a goatskin.

[59]Literally, "the Adviser." However, the name became associated with money because the Romans minted money (*moneta*) in the temple of Juno Moneta. See Livy 4.7.12 [278].

[60]The *libri lintei* were books written on linen; they were the archives of the ancient Roman kings, and are no longer extant.

[61]Lucius Calpurnius Piso (d. after 120 B.C.), Roman statesman and historian, consul in 133, censor in 120. His *Annales* span the period from Rome's foundation to his own day, and he is cited by Cicero, Varro, Livy and Dionysius of Halicarnassus as an authority on mythology, although no book of his on that subject remains.

Greeks, who invoked her at marriages. Because she was worshipped and invoked during the Kalends, the ancients called her Calendaris. The priests worshipped Juno *Novella* in the Kalends of February, and she was also called *Februata*, because her sacred rites were celebrated in that month. Dionysius of Halicarnassus gives an account of Juno *Quiritia* and the banquets held for her in courtyards, and you may read Pliny for an account of the temple of Juno *Ardia*, renowned for its paintings, or the altar of Juno *Locinia*, where the ashes never blew away even in the strongest wind. She was known as Juno *Populonia* for the frequent pleading of the people, *Opulonia* and *Fluonia* by women, but especially by women in labour, both before and after delivery.[62]

Apollo

Cicero, in *The Nature of the Gods*, tells us that there were four Apollos, the most ancient, according to Vossius, being Jubal, the Father of the Canaanites, a relative of Tubal-Cain unless, as I rather think, he lived in an earlier time. He was a great singer and had a matchless voice;[63]

---

[62]These names are explained as follows:

Iuga: the Yoker. The *Iugarius vicus* was near the Forum.

Sororia Julia: Juno gave special protection to the Julian family.

Martialis: the martial Juno.

Domiduca: she who governs the household.

Unxia: the Anointer.

Cinxia: the Girdled One. This refers to the way female garments were worn at religious festivals, or, generally, to "girdle oneself," that is, dress.

Gamelia: derived either from *gamos*, a wedding, or from *gameleuma*, "of a wedding."

Zugia: from *zugon*, "a yoke," or, more likely, from the ver-form, hence, the Joiner (see Iuga above).

Calendaris: literally "of the Kalends," the day in the month when the times for Nones and festivals were proclaimed. The Kalends of February, incidentally, were sacred to Juno Lucina (see also Juna Februata).

Novella: the young Juno.

Ardia: the Shining One.

Locinia: she who unites in matrimony.

Opulonia: the Splendid One, or the Enricher.

Fluonia: she who causes water to flow, referring, presumably, to the breaking of a woman's waters just before birth.

[63]Jubal, son of Lamech, "was the father of all those who play the lyre and pipe" (Genesis 4:21), hence the inventor of music. Cf. Dryden, "When Jubal struck the corded shell,/ His listening brethren stood around,/ And wondering, on their faces

Timagenes[64] says that music was the oldest study of all. The other Apollos were related to some deities, notably the Sun, but whether Jubal achieved this honour or not is unknown. Osiris's brother [Set], who accompanied him in his wars, is a very ancient Apollo, recorded by Diodorus Siculus. Also there is Apollo *Delius*, Diana's brother and the son of Jupiter and Latona;[65] as Macrobius has it, he was worshipped together with Jupiter and had rites performed every fifth year in Delos. From this he was called *Deliacus*, because he delivered oracles there all summer; the priests said that he had gone somewhere else in winter, but it was really because they would have found it difficult to invent stories all year round so that people who came for answers should not discover the fraud. From Delphos he was known as Apollo *Delphicus*, where he had a temple famous for its oracles, which Livy calls the Common Oracle of Mankind and the Navel of the World. The Scythians had their Apollo *Hyperboraeus*,[66] and for the intricate altar of Apollo Genitor, once thought of as one of the seven wonders of the world, see Plutarch, Callimachus,[67] Ovid and others.

The Greeks and Romans venerated Apollo Delius in particular as the god of music and the inventor of medicine; he was called *Iaculator*, *Sagittarius*, *Pythius* and *Vates*, "the god of prophecy." Amongst the Greeks his surnames were *Agyieus*, *Akersocomes*, *Krysocomes*, *Loxias*, *Lykios*, *Nomios* and *Thyraieos*, and to the Romans he was *Caelispex*, *Medicus*, *Capitolinus* (this one came to Rome from the Thracian Bosphorus), and *Palatinus* who

---

fell/ To worship that celestial sound" ("A Song for St. Cecilia's Day" [1687], 17–20). Tubal-Cain was actually Jubal's half-brother through Lamech's union with Zillah, described as "an instructor of every artificer in brass or iron" (Genesis 4:22).

[64]Timagenes of Alexandria (d. after 45 B.C.) was a teacher of rhetoric in Rome, where he lived at the house of Asinius Pollio (see Chapter X). His *Historia regum* is quoted by Pompeius Trogus, who is Herbert's source here.

[65]Latona (Greek Leto) was a Titaness who bore Apollo whilst leaning against Mount Cynthus in Delos, hence her son's association with the area as the "Delphic" Apollo.

[66]The Hyperboreans were a legendary people who worshipped Apollo. Herodotus mentions that offerings purporting to come from them arrived regularly at Delos (4.32–36 [290–92]), but there is no agreement amongst modern scholars about their origins.

[67]Callimachus of Alexandria (c. 305–240 B.C.), librarian and poet. Having declared that epic poetry was passé, he promptly wrote an epic poem, the *Aetia*, which ran to over 3000 lines. He was an outstanding lyricist, and thanks to a marvellous new translation by Stanley Lombardo and Diane Raynor (Baltimore, 1988) his poetry may soon be more widely-appreciated.

is also known as *Actiacus, Novalis* or *Parcetonius*.[68] Octavian, after he had defeated Antony, erected a temple to this Apollo on the Palatine Hill and decorated it with statues made of silver and gold. It was most magnificently built, and scholars tell us that it possessed an excellent Greek and Latin library as well as its immense treasures. Lawyers would meet there to decide difficult or dubious cases, and Propertius[69] gives a description of it, and Pliny mentions how famous it was. Apollo was also known as *Choragus*, or "Captain of the Muses."

Because of the diverse images and statues representing him, such as the one the Spartans had of him with four ears and as many hands, he came to have many further surnames such as *Sandalarius, Sosianus, Tortor, Thuscianus*, and *Diadematus*.[70] There are many more in ancient inscriptions,

---

[68]This group of names may be explained as follows:

Iaculator: the Thrower or Hurler.

Pythius: from Python, the monster guarding Delphi which was killed by Apollo.

Agyeius: the name of a road-god, whose function Apollo sometimes usurped.

Akersocomes: Ever-young, or "Unshorn." Cf. Herrick, "Get up, get up for shame, the Blooming Morne/ Upon her wings presents the god unshorne" ("Corinna's Going a-Maying" [1648], 1–2).

Krysocomes: Golden-haired.

Loxias: this name is thought to refer to "the difficult and devious nature of [Apollo's] replies" at his Delphic oracle (Morford and Lenardon 163).

Lykios: Lycian.

Nomios: a Greek word meaning "pertaining to shepherds." There is a reference in Callimachus to Apollo as the "shepherd of Adonis" ("Hymn to Apollo," 47). On the other hand, *nomos* means a lyre, also applicable to Apollo as god of music, although the spelling is different.

Thyraieos: named for the coastal plain around Astros in Argos (Pausanias I, 223).

Medicus: the Physician.

Actiacus: Apollo was worshipped at Actium, the site of Octavian's victory over Antony and Cleopatra.

Novalis: the Protector of Unploughed Land, from *novalis*, "fallow land."

Parcetonius: refers to Apollo's connexion with the Parcae.

[69]Sextus Propertius (c. 64–2 B.C.), the Roman elegiac poet. He wrote chiefly on love, although he frequently digresses into other topics. His four extant books show a sensitive, learned and attractive talent at work.

[70]The final group of Apollo's names:

Choragus: a *choregus* was a sort of Master of Ceremonies at poetic and dramatic festivals, as well as the leader of the dithryambic chorus of boys. Cf. Pausanias, "Apollo is called the Dance-leader of the Muses" (I, 15).

and also many temples. Porphyry has collected many of Apollo's mystical surnames and their mythical interpretations in his book on the Sun, out of which Servius has borrowed.

Four-footed animals sacred to Apollo include the wolf, being voracious like time; amongst insects the grasshopper, and amongst birds the swan, crow, cock and hawk. The Egyptians, however, understood by the hawk Osiris, who is for them the Sun; they also honoured the hawk because in ancient times it had brought a book written in red letters to the priests of Thebes (Egypt's main city) from an unknown region. It contained all the sacred rites, and that is why theologians amongst them wear red caps with hawk's wings on them.[71] Anyone who knows the history, however, knows that these fictions were invented by priests so that their laws, rites and ceremonies might have more effect. Amongst trees, the laurel was sacred to Apollo, and people made predictions by it; if, when it was thrown on a fire, it burnt noisily, the ancients believed it to be a good omen, but if it did not burn very much, it was an evil one. Anyone who bound laurel around his temples when he went to sleep would see whatever he wanted to know in his dreams. Hesiod said, "the laurel promotes the health of the nation." It was not only the symbol of poets, but of triumph too, the Romans placing it in the lap of Jupiter Optimus Maximus as an acknowledgement that victory came from him. The Emperor Julian says that the palm was sacred to the Sun or to Apollo, although Libanius[72] unaccountably says that it came *from* Apollo.

Sandalarius: more accurately Sandaliarius, the Sandalled One. The sandal-makers in Rome erected a statue of Apollo in their street.

Sosianus: unknown.

Tortor: the Torturer. Apparently there was a temple of Apollo in that district of Rome where torturers used to live. Cf. Juvenal, *Satires* 6, 480.

Thuscianus: either from *thus*, a variant of *tus*, "frankincense," or from *Tuscianus*, "the Etruscan."

Diadematus: the Crowned One.

[71] Herbert is wrong. Osiris was never portrayed as a hawk, but as "a mummy, wearing a beard with the White Crown upon his head, and the Menat, an amulet associated with virility and fecundity, hanging from his neck" (Mercatante 115). His son Horus, however, is always depicted as hawk-headed.

[72] Libanius (415–96) was a rhetorician and orator. His chief fame is as the teacher of St. John Chrysostom. Herbert is probably quoting his *Pro templis gentilium non exscindendis oratio* (Geneva, 1634). He also owned Libanius's *Parasitus ob coenam occisam se ipsum deferens* (Paris, 1601) [*FK* 99, 112].

Diana

Cicero lists three Dianas; the best-known is the mother of the winged Cupid, daughter of Jupiter and Latona, and sister to Apollo as the Moon was sister to the Sun.[73] I have dealt with her etymology already, but do not agree that she was called Diana from *deviana*, "wandering in the woods," or in heaven itself.[74]

She is shown as the strictest and most chaste of all the gods and goddesses. Because of her aversion to pleasure, rather than hatred for humanity, she could only be propitiated with human sacrifices, even though she allowed a hind to take the place of Iphigenia on the condition that the latter became her priestess for the future. Men were generally sacrificed, especially in Tauris, whose people sacrificed all strangers, particularly Greeks, to her. Pausanias says that the people of Patrae sacrificed the handsomest boy and a young virgin every year to Diana.[75] But Iphigenia, who would not sacrifice her brother Orestes when he was captured, hid the goddess's image in a pile of wood, then carried it to Aricia, a town not far from Rome. There the custom of sacrificing strangers continued for some time, but after a while this barbarity displeased the Romans, even though only servants had been offered up, so they sent the image to the Spartans, who only whipped the boys and sprinkled the altars with their blood. Later only harts and hinds were sacrificed to Diana, and their horns were hung up in all her temples. The poets, particularly Claudian, write of her chariot being drawn by yoked deer. I have discussed this at length to expose the cruel and impious sacrifices of the priests, which they invented under the name of religion to persuade people that some deities could only be placated with human blood and that those who were offered up were being honoured by representing everyone else! Diana also presided over women in labour, and they dedicated their

---

[73]The curious juxtaposition of Diana and Venus is borne out by Renaissance portraits. Wind, for example, describes a portrait of Giovanna Tornabuoni in which Diana and Venus (chastity and love) are shown joined by beauty. The origin of this symbolic synthesis is apparently Vergil, although Wind doubts that the Roman poet's intentions were quite the same as Renaissance iconographers understood them. Vergil does mention "virginis armata," for whom see Venus Armata below. For further detail, see Wind 77ff.

[74]Herbert was right to doubt the origins of the name. The name Diana is derived from *di*, meaning "bright one," as in Diespiter (Jupiter). Diana certainly became associated with woods, as her most famous place of worship, the grove of Nemi, indicates.

[75]Patrae was a town in Achaia near the Gulf of Corinth. It was founded by Patreus, son of Preugenes (Pausanias II, 12).

clothes to her, from which she is called *Chitone*. Not only deer, but sterile cows were offered up to Diana, and her statue was carried by one of the latter, which was sometimes white, sometimes black.

Her statues show her as large and tall, clothed down to her ankles; her face is youthful and girlish, she carries a lighted torch in her right hand, a bow in her left, and a quiver hanging over her shoulder. By some she is known as *Britomartis* or *Dictynna*, by Orpheus she is called *Cynegetus*, and by Callimachus *Theretira*, "she who presides over hunting." She was herself a great huntress, and all groves and forests were sacred to her. The Egyptians called her *Bubastis* after a famous city of that name, and her sacred rites were known as Bubasta.[76]   She had a temple in Crete, and another was built on the Aventine Hill in Rome. There are also temples at Caeliola and Suburra.[77] The oldest ones are in Spain and Aulis, but the best-known is at Ephesus, much mentioned by authors, and is in the Acts of the Apostles.[78]

I should perhaps mention something further about the Sun and Moon, who are said to be the children of Rhea, or the Great Mother, and Hyperion,[79] as Diodorus says, but I will leave this to others.

Mercury

Cicero lists five Mercuries, amongst whom the most famous was the son of Jupiter and Maia.[80] The ancients joined him with Minerva not by marriage,

---

[76]The names of Diana:

    Britomartis: originally a Cretan woman who jumped into the sea to avoid the attentions of King Minos, she became entangled in a fisherman's net, from which she got the name Dictynna (*diktuon*, "a net") and escaped to Aegina, where she took sanctuary in a grove sacred to Artemis. In Aegina she was worshipped as Aphaea, not as Artemis herself, although the goddesses are so similar they are often taken as the same. Pausanias, speaking of the sanctuary of "Issorian Artemis," notes that "she is not really Artemis, but the Cretan Britomartis" (II, 47).

    Cynegetus: possibly derived from *cyne*, "dog," but may also be connected with *cynegeta*, which are books about the training of hunting-dogs.

    Bubastis: both a town and a goddess. She is the cat-headed goddess Bast who presides over fire.

[77]Caeliola is in the district of Mt. Caelius, south of the Palatine and east of the Aventine. Suburra was a rather seedy district of Rome, although Julius Caesar lived there and there was a Jewish synagogue.

[78]Cf. Acts 19:28, 34: "Great is Diana of the Ephesians" and other references.

[79]Hyperion was a Titan, but his name is often given to Apollo or Helios, the Sun-god.

[80]Maia, daughter of Atlas, was the mother of Hermes by Zeus.

but in mutual attachment; he was said to be the messenger of the gods, and the inventor of writing, music, wrestling and geometry. He also taught rhetoric, especially to the Egyptians, who, as we have said, worshipped him under the name Anubis. The ancient Germans held him in great awe, and it was lawful to offer him human sacrifices on certain days. He was called *Deus Communus*, "the common god," and it was the custom that whenever something was found on a road, he would be invoked because he knew what was found and was believed to preside over roads. Statues were erected at crossroads of cities, or where three roads met, which the ancients called *Hermae*, and the Athenians had them in their houses in front of the doors. I will not elaborate as this is too well-known.[81] Pliny mentions a statue of Hermes in Ethiopia, and he had two temples, as many chapels and an altar in Rome. He is called *Cyllenius* and *Camillus*, "servant of the gods," and *Trophonius*, or "the Subterranean."[82]

Minerva

Cicero mentions five Minervas, the most remarkable being the one who is said to have sprung out of Jupiter's head. She was the goddess of prudence and war, and, some say, invented armed dancing, clothmaking, and wool-dyeing amongst many other things. Workers pray to her, from which she is known as the goddess of skills, together with Mercury, their altars and statues being common to both, and known as *Hermathena*.[83]

---

[81] Hermae, or Herms, were pillars with a bust of Hermes on them, often with male genitals added to them. Sometimes they represented other gods and even goddesses (with the necessary anatomical changes). Plotinus apparently thought that the phalli on Herms could be represented symbolically as an idea that all generation derived from the mind. "This, I think, is why the Sages of old . . . exhibit the ancient Hermes with the generative organ always in active posture . . . the Intellectual Reason-Principle" (*Enneads* III, 6, 19 [212]).

[82] The names of Mercury:

Cyllenius: from Mt. Cyllene, Hermes's birthplace.

Camillus: the Latin word denotes an acolyte in the cult of a god.

Trophonius: literally "the Feeder." He was an oracular god whose cult originated in Boeotia; when people consulted him they were taken underground. His oracle was at Lebadeia (Pausanias I, 392ff).

[83] Hybrid gods appeared in the Orphic hymns, and philosophers translated their nature to the idea of coincidence of opposites. Wind notes that Renaissance writers were inclined to make too much of an occasional reference to these hybrids in classical writers, and soon they began to attach mystical meanings to them which never existed (199–200). Wind further notes that Cicero did not make much of

Her oldest temple was built in Orvinius's tower; Herodotus mentions a temple of Minerva *Assessia*, but it was burnt down, as was the one at Palleni in the land of the Tageates.[84] He also speaks of many other temples dedicated to her in many other places; she had one in Landum, a Rhodian island, and another in Elis. There was a shrine in the Capitol, and in Rome there were temples to Minerva *Medica*, *Flaviana*, *Chalcidina*, and *Catuliana*. In the temple dedicated to Minerva by Pompey the Great were kept records of all that he had accomplished in the East.

She was also known as *Pallas*, and the famous Palladium that was said to have fallen from heaven was her statue; it brandished a spear and moved its eyes, but nobody was allowed to see it except the Vestal Virgins, who looked after it. There was a very ancient temple to her on the Aventine Hill. Cicero privately worshipped Minerva *Custos* at home, but when he went into exile, he took her to the Capitol and dedicated her.[85] Her sacrifices were clean, such as white lambs, white bulls, or a wild heifer with gilded horns. The owl was amongst the birds sacred to her, so that her image hardly ever appears on a coin without an owl sitting on her helmet and the inscription "ATHENE," the name the poets called her, as in Homer's "white-throated Athene." She carried a Medusa's head on her shield or breastplate to symbolise victory; as Pausanias notes, in Attica the sculptured head of Medusa on her breastplate signified the Athenian Victory. Every schoolboy knows who Medusa was. The olive, which she is said to have invented, was her sacred tree; Herodotus remarks that "for a long time, no-one had olives but the Athenians."

Mars

As Minerva was said to have been born without a mother, so Mars was produced without a father. Juno, jealous of Jupiter because he had a daughter

---

obtaining a Hermathena, and that Vergil mentions the Venus-Diana combination only once (203). The most obvious of these gods was Janus, about whom Herbert himself, following Vossius, writes quite extensively. In the case of Hermathena, Renaissance writers would have recognised a combination of eloquence and steadfast wisdom.

[84]Palleni [Pallene] was a city in Thrace (Pausanias II, 62).

[85]The names of Minerva:
   Medica: the Healer.   She was patroness of all arts, including the art of medicine.
   Flaviana: protectress of the Flavians.
   Chalcidina: this could be a misspelling or misprint of Chalcioecus, itself a Latinised version of Chalkioikos, "with the house of brass," a name for Athene. Simpson lists it as being used by Livy to denote a temple of Minerva (101).
   Catuliana: may derive from *catulus*, "a young animal," because, as Herbert notes, lambs and heifers were sacrificed to her.

without her, had a great desire to have a son without him, so she made use of some flowers which had been shown to her by Flora, as Ovid tells us.[86] Juno gave birth to Mars in Thrace, where the people venerate him greatly. Some authors mention another Mars, son of Jupiter and Enyo.[87]

Acinacis was the true Mars of the Thracians and Scythians, as Herodotus says in Book VII.[88] The Northern people swore by him, and the people of Arabia Petraea, who venerated him just as much, depicted him in the following way. They cut a square black stone of four feet high and two feet across, with nothing on it. Others describe him as looking armed and terrifying, a spear and flail in his hand, his chariot drawn by two horses, one of which is called Terror and the other Timor, with Fama going before them blowing a trumpet. The Romans thought Romulus was the son of Mars (more likely of his priest!) and that is why they paid him great adoration.

His oldest temple was in the Campus Martius, from which the place had its name; it was there that the *comitia centuriata* met[89] and the army paraded, as Dionysius explains, and he also mentions a very old temple of Mars in the city of Suna, as well as an oracle in Tiora. I have already mentioned his oracle in Egypt. There was a temple of Mars in the Circus Flaminius and another in the Capitol; the largest was built by Augustus and dedicated to Mars *Ultor*, and Ovid celebrates its magnificence in his *Fasti*. A second temple to Mars Ultor (or, more accurately, Bis Ultor) was erected by Augustus in the Capitol for a victory which he gained over the Parthians, and their standards were hung there. A very large, elaborate temple was erected to Mars *Gradivus*[90] outside the city on the Appian Way, which P. Victor[91] calls *Mars Extramuraneum*, "Mars outside the walls."

---

[86]Cf. Ovid, *Fasti* V, 193–214. Flora, one of the oldest Roman deities, was the herald of spring and goddess of flowers. Ovid tells us how the nymph Chloris was transformed into Flora as she tried to escape from Zephyrus, the West Wind. For Flora as an important symbol in Western art, see Wind, Chapter VII.

[87]Enyo was a Greek war-goddess, identified with Bellona; however, the name is also that of one of the Graiae, sisters of the Gorgons, which may fit better here.

[88]Actually, Herodotus discusses the worship of Ares amongst the Scythians in Book 4.59–62 [302–03].

[89]This is the assembly of the "centuries," 193 divisions of 100 people each into which Servius Tullius divided the Roman populace.

[90]Gradivus: he who walks in battle, from *gradior*, "to step, walk."

[91]Piero Vettori [P. Victorius] (1499–1585) was a Greek scholar, translator and editor who held the post of Professor of Greek and Roman Rhetoric at the University of Florence from 1538. He produced scholarly editions of Cicero, Varro, Aristotle, Dionysius of Halicarnassus and Sophocles, to list only some. He wrote

Bellona

After Mars comes Bellona, his sister, wife, or both. Her temple was in the Circus Flaminius, and there the senators received foreign ambassadors whom the Romans would not admit into the city. Her priests, Tertullian says, were called *Bellonarii*; to propitiate their deity they cut and slashed themselves with knives, for no other blood would work. After this they went into a strange rage or fury, and then they prophesied. Statius says that she drove Mars's chariot: ". . . she drives the black team,/Bellona with the bloody hands." Caesar writes that the Cappadocians venerated her so much that her priests were next in honour to the king. Some say that she is the same as Minerva, which seems more probable than Apuleius's making Diana, Juno, Venus and Bellona all the same, or of a certain learned person who tries to make the Moon and Bellona the same.

In front of Bellona's shrine there were some fairly small pillars which the Romans called *Bellica Columna*; when they were at war with anyone, and had opened the gates of Janus's temple, one of the consuls threw a spear in the direction of the enemy and from that time war was declared. At the same time, they sent a herald to the enemy camp; he declared the reasons for going to war and ceremoniously threw his spear towards the camp.

In later pagan times Pausus, the opposite to Bellona, was considered a god, and his aid was implored when they had suffered through a war. The ancients do not mention Pausus anywhere, insofar as I know.

Bellona was depicted with flowing hair, armed with a torch, carrying a sickle in one hand and a shield in the other.

Victoria

Victory was raised with Minerva, and became a goddess at the same time. The Romans paid her great devotion and she was depicted as a winged virgin, offering a crown or a palm. Her image was carried in procession around the Circus [Maximus], and she had an altar in the Senate House that could be moved anywhere the Senate went, as Dempster[92] tells us. She had

---

a pioneering critical assessment of classical literature, the *Variorum lectionum libri XXXVIII* (1582).

[92]Thomas Dempster (c. 1578–1625) was a Scottish biographer, Latin poet, historian, scholar and eccentric. He was Professor of Civil Law at the University of Pisa (1616–19) and of Humanities at Bologna (1620–25). His autobiography, according to the *DNB*, is "clearly-marked by the same habit of grotesquely-exaggerated falsehood which appears in some of his other writing" (V, 785). His *Antiquitatem Romanorum corpus absolutissimum* (1613), however, was a work that, according to the same source, "displays extraordinary diligence and learning" (V, 790). Herbert

three temples in Rome, two chapels, a grove (like most other deities) and an altar. Her oldest temple was on the Aventine Hill as it was the most convenient place to pitch tents, and she had others in Rome itself as well. Cicero tells us that Victory at Capua would sweat, like Apollo at Cumae did, when evil was foreseen.

Nemesis

When the Romans went to war they sacrificed to Nemesis, the daughter of Justice, and put on a public show of gladiators, as Pomponius Laetus[93] relates. Another Nemesis stood for the power of fortune; P. Victor says that she was worshipped in the Capitol and had a temple in the city. This concludes what I have to say about the gods who presided over war with Mars, or were his auxiliaries.

Venus

At one time, so Cicero tells us, there were four Venuses, but her name is modern; Cincius[94] and Varro, quoted by Macrobius, state that in the era of the kings it was neither a Greek nor a Latin word. I have already given you Selden's thoughts upon this subject.

The ancients worshipped her as the goddess of generation, sexual pleasure and external beauty, which she could give or take away as she pleased. It is from these attributes that Plutarch gives her history, or rather myth, of originating in the sea, so that he could prove the generative power of salt, and for many other reasons. The Platonists posited two aspects of Venus: one was *Urania*, "the celestial or divine love," the other *Terrestris*, "earthly love," who was later deified.[95]

---

owned Dempster's *De iuramento libri iii: locus ex antiquitate Romanae retractus* (1623) [*FK* 110].

[93] Junius Pomponius Laetus (1425–97), Italian philologist and Neoplatonist. He lost his position at the Roman College for alleged plotting against Pope Paul II and was tortured, but he was reinstated by Sixtus IV. When Alexander VI was crowned (1498), Laetus compared the Borgia pope to Julius Caesar: "the other [Caesar] was only a man; this is a god" (Seznec 137). Such useful praise ensured his survival. His books include the *Compendium historiae Romanae*, a digest of Roman history from Gordian III (238–44) to Justin II (565–78) and *De legibus et antiquitatis urbis Romae* (published 1521). He also edited the works of Varro.

[94] Lucius Cincius Alimentus (fl. 220–195 B.C.), praetor of Sicily (210–209), was the author of a history of Rome, which for some reason he wrote in Greek. He fixed the date of Rome's foundation at 729 B.C. and is very informative about the Second Punic War, having himself been a prisoner of Hannibal.

[95] Platonists (see particularly Plato, *Symposium* 180 d–e) make a distinction

Some mythologists make Venus the same as Juno, the Moon, Proserpina, Diana or some other goddess, but these names only illustrate the diversity of her attributes, and I have written of these interpretations already. Venus had a statue in Paphos; it was not human in form, but conic, with a broad, round base, gradually terminating to a point at the top.[96] Many ancient statues were like this one of Venus, not always human in form. In other places she is depicted as a beautiful young girl, naked, standing in a shell, as if she had just risen from the sea. Augustus dedicated Apelles's[97] painting of Venus *Anadyomene*, "emerging from the sea," in the temple of Julius Caesar.

Venus was also called *Thalatta*, "marine," to whom a certain island was sacred, and had a temple built on it. The most ancient of her temples, according to Herodotus, was that of Venus Urania in the city of Ascalon, Palestine, which, as I have said, the Scythians demolished. Enraged, the goddess sent a sickness to their women, but Herodotus does not say what it was, nor does it much matter here.[98] I have already mentioned her being known by the Assyrians as *Mylitta*, *Alitta* by the Arabians, and *Metra* by the Persians. Herodotus mentions a temple of hers amongst the Aterbechi,

---

between Aphrodite Pandemos (sexual love) and Aphrodite Urania (divine love). Neoplatonists such as Pico della Mirandola, following Plotinus, interpreted this as "the distinction between a celestial and an earthly vision of beauty" (Wind 138). Herbert's note that the earthly part was "later deified" may refer to the Neoplatonists' tendency to oversimplify the distinction between the two Venuses and somehow claim that the "earthly" one was not deified. Herbert also observes at the end of the section on Venus that she was worshipped by prostitutes and respectable women alike; he thus recognised that the ancients saw Venus in the two roles. In the Renaissance, Venus's dual role was symbolised by her being depicted both naked and clothed.

[96]Pausanias mentions the sanctuary of Aphrodite at Old Paphos (II, 379), but he does not say anything about its odd shape, neither does Peter Levi in his note, although he does remark that "in spite of recent excavations we still know far too little about the most important aspects of this crucial site" (II, 379 n. 29).

[97]Apelles (4th century B.C.) was perhaps the greatest of Greek painters. He may also have written a treatise on painting, no longer extant. The dedication refers to Julius Caesar's claim that he was descended from Venus.

Wind has an interesting note on the Botticelli painting of the same name; the artist, he says, "aimed at recapturing the spirit of the lost *Venus Anadyomene* of Apelles, which was known from ancient descriptions" (132).

[98]The answer is to be found in Hippocrates *Of Airs, Waters and Places*. See *Oeuvres complètes*, ed. Littré, vol. II, p. 79 (Amsterdam: A. Hakkart, 1978). The "female" sickness was an affliction of men who became *ehareis*, or effeminiate. This may be related to their practice of cutting the veins behind the ears, that would, in Hippocrates' view, render them sterile.

and a chapel of Venus *Hospes* in the temple of Proteus, as well as Venus Urania, worshipped by the Scythians under the name of *Artempasa*.[99] The first thing that Aeneas and the Trojans did when they arrived in Italy was build a temple to Venus. She had a temple among the Zacynthi,[100] near what was then called the Bridge of Anchises,[101] and also amongst the Leucadians and Actienses.[102]

While we know that the worship of Venus Urania was the oldest, we do not know whether she represented Celestial Love, the power of Celestial Fortune, the Queen of Heaven, or the star named after her. This Venus was worshipped not only by prostitutes, but by respectable women as well, so that she would endow them with grace and beauty, making them attractive to all. Widows also worshipped her so that their second marriages might be happy; the festivals of Venus were regularly observed by all kinds of women.

Her surnames included *Acidalia*, either because she causes disagreeable things, or from the fountain of that name in which the Graces, sacred to her, bathe. She is called *Cluacina*, from *cluere*, which was the old word meaning "to fight." King Titus Tatius built her a temple, and her temples and chapels are mentioned by Onufrio.[103] She was known as *Libitina*, as we have said, because the pagans believed that she presided over births and deaths; funeral equipment was sold in her temples, and young girls, when they matured, dedicated their dolls, the symbols of their infancy, to her. Alma Venus, holy and beautiful, also known as *Verticordia*, encouraged women to be chaste. Amongst the Greeks, Harmonia, the wife of Cadmus, called her *Antistrophia*, because she discouraged wickedness and evil thoughts. Another name was *Erycina*, from Mount Eryce in Sicily, where Aeneas built a temple to his mother, and Q. Fabius Maximus dedicated a temple to her when he was dictator. Venus Erycina had a temple at the Colline Gate, and there was a temple on the Via Sacra to Venus *Romana*, the Comfort of Rome, about which Prudentius says "incense is burnt to the twin goddesses."

---

[99]Herodotus gives the name as "Heavenly Aphrodite Argimpasa" (4, 59 [302]). The "marine" Venus would have some affiliation with Proteus, "the Old Man of the Sea," and Venus "Hospes" (the guest) in his temple is appropriate enough.

[100]The island of Zacynthus (Zante) is situated in the sea near Mt. Cyllene in Epirus (Pausanias II, 155).

[101]Anchises was the lover of Venus and father of Aeneas.

[102]The inhabitants of Leucas, an island in the Ionian Sea. The inhabitants of Actium.

[103]Onofrio Panvinio [Onuphrius] (1529–68), an Italian scholar and theologian, specialised in the study of mythology and its application to the art of his own time. He is cited by Vasari in *The Lives of the Artists*.

Ammianus mentions this temple as particularly deserving of admiration. There was also Venus *Calva*, known as "bald" because when the Gauls were besieging Rome, the women cut their hair off to make ropes for defence machines. The Cyprians had a statue of Venus *Barbata*, or "bearded," as Alessandri informs us; Suidas says that Venus was sometimes depicted with a beard and comb because once a terrible itch broke out amongst the Romans which made their hair fall out, so they did not need combs. The women prayed to Venus, and she heard them and restored everyone's hair. They represented her with a comb and beard because the goddess who presided over reproduction should be both male and female; the upper half of her body as far as her girdle was male, and the lower half was female. Almost all other deities were bisexual, too, so that they might not be thought lacking in anything, and this was extended by the Egyptians to include the elements as well.

The Spartans dedicated a temple to Venus *Armata*, who was first described by Lactantius, and of whom Ausonius[104] writes,

> Pallas saw the armed Venus in Sparta;
>   "Now," she said, "let Paris judge who wins."
> To which Venus replied, "Isn't it rash to attack me now,
>   When I beat you naked once?"

Pompey dedicated a temple to Venus *Victrix*, "the Conqueror," during his second consulship; the Greeks, Pausanias says, call her *Nicephora*. On some of Faustina's coins Venus is shown holding out victory in her right hand, and the inscription is "VENERI VICTRICI." Postumius Tubertus,[105] the first to triumph easily with a bloodless victory, entered Rome crowned with the myrtle of Venus Victrix, as Pliny tells us. Julius Caesar built a temple to Venus *Genetrix* after the battle of Pharsalus, and dedicated the plunder to her; amongst other things there was a breastplate made of British pearls. Augustus erected a brass statue of the deified Julius in this temple, with a blazing star shining over his head like that which appeared at his death, for which see Dionysius and Appian.[106] Venus *Placida* had a chapel, and

---

[104] Decimus Magnus Ausonius (c. 310–95), Christian philosopher, poet, rhetorician and tutor to the Emperor Gratian (368–83). The best product of his muse was the *Mosella*, a long poem about the Moselle river. Herbert quotes from his "Epigram 64," a translation of a poem from *The Greek Anthology* (cf. Wind 93 n. 39).

[105] Aulus Postumius Tubertus, who defeated the Aequi at the Battle of the Algidus River, was dictator in 431 B.C.

[106] Appian of Alexandria (2nd century A.D.) wrote an ethnographic history of Rome in 25 books. He moved to Rome some time after 117 and became a Roman knight, surviving to the reign of Antoninus Pius (138–61).

Suetonius mentions Venus *Capitolina*.[107]

The ancients held the myrtle-tree and the rose sacred to Venus, and Vergil mentions "the myrtle of beautiful Venus" in *Eclogue* 7. Some believed it had the capability of gaining and securing love. From Euripides's *Electra* we learn that the Greeks placed myrtle crowns on the heads of the dead, perhaps because Venus Libitina took care of the dead. Venus used to be known as *Myrtia* or *Myrtaea* from the myrtle. The rose, sacred to Venus, is analogous to external beauty; nothing is as graceful and fragrant, and nothing less permanent. The poets tell us about a white rose dyed purple with Venus's blood.

Cupid

Cicero lists three Cupids. One was the son of Mercury and Diana, the second and best-known was the son of Mercury and Venus, and the third, Anteros,

---

[107]The surnames of Venus:

Acidalia: the first meeting Herbert gives may derive from the river Akidos, which joins the Anigros, but it is the latter which Pausanias says has the "filthy smell" and whose fish are inedible. The Akidos itself cannot be identified with certainty, and there is no river Anigros (Pausanias II, 208, and Levi's note, 209).

Cluacina: the etymology is incorrect. The verb means "to clean," not "to fight." The more accurate name is Cloacina, from *cloaca*, "drain or sewer." King Titus Tatius built the temple to commemorate his success is clearing and filling the lake in the valley near the Capital and building the Forum (cf. Ovid, *Fasti* [Appendix] 436–37).

Libitina: perhaps a confusion between Libitina, a Roman burial-goddess, with Lubentina, the proper form of the surname. Lubentina is a variation of Libidina, which carries the meaning of "sexual desire."

Alma: the Nourishing One.

Verticordia: Turner of Hearts.

Antistrophia: One who Turns around.

Armata: in this guise, Venus symbolises "love-as-war." Wind elaborates, "she is a compound of attraction and rejection, fostering her gracious aims by cruel methods" (93). Naturally Pallas is not pleased with Venus's usurpation of her role; for some reason, poets and orators were especially devoted to this Venus.

Victrix: that is, "victorious" the wars of love (see *Greek Anthology* XVI, 173). Nicephora is the Greek equivalent.

Genetrix: Venus was worshipped by the Imperial family (due to Caesar's claim, for which see above). Suetonius quotes a rude remark of Cicero's about the "descendent of Venus" and Caesar's homosexual deflowering by King Nicomedes of Bithynia (35).

Placida: the Quiet or Gentle One.

the son of Mars and Venus. It is not relevant here to restate what the poets say in praise of Cupid, nor need I enlarge upon that divine or celestial love which the Platonists hold so dear, and of which Marsilio Ficino has written so much.[108] Some believed that if Cupid favoured and helped love, Anteros opposed it, but others, such as Porphyry, saw Anteros as mutual love:

> When the infant Cupid did not grow, Venus consulted the goddess Themis, who told her that Anteros was necessary to Cupid so that they could alternate, each mutually assisting the other. So Anteros was conceived, and as soon as he was born Cupid began to grow and spread his wings; when Anteros was with him he always grew in height and girth, but in his absence he pined and wasted away.

Is there anyone who doesn't understand that?[109]

Philostratus[110] mentions a great many Amores, or loves, the sons of nymphs; Apuleius depicts them as handsome boys either descending from heaven or rising from the sea. Orpheus says that there are two gates to Heaven, through one of which souls descend below, and the other through which they ascend.[111] I need not discuss what Cupid looks like, as this is too well known, although the ancients had several kinds of images for him as well as for his mother Venus. I know of no temples of his, except the ones found in hearts.[112]

---

[108]Herbert refers to Ficino's *De amore* (1490). The patient reader of these notes may wish to know that Ficino, following Pico, explains Cupid's blindness as a means to intuit a higher form of love, divine love, which corresponds quite handily to Herbert's common notions, in that it requires no formal intellectual input. The spiritually-enlightened need no eyes. For details, see Wind 139ff.

[109]Two of Herbert's most valuable unacknowledged probable sources are involved here, for both tell this *mutual* version of Eros and Anteros in the Renaissance, both crediting Porphyry, but both actually using Themostius' version. Celio Calcagnini, *Anteros sive de mutuo amore* (Basileae: Froben, 1544) 436ff. and Lelio Gregorio Giraldi, *De deis gentium libri sive syntagmata* XVII, Syntagma XII (Lugduni: J. Junctae, 1565). Source: Themostius, *Orationes*, ed. W. Dindorf (Hildesheim: G. Olms, 1961), orat. 24, pp. 367ff.

[110]Philostratus, son of Nervianus (b. 190 A.D.), a sophist, often called the "father of art criticism." His *Imagines*, written as lectures and rhetorical exercises, contains many desccriptions of ancient paintings.

[111]This rather obscure passage must refer to Ficino's division of the Amores into either "sacred" or "profane," and is an example of Herbert's evident attraction to Neoplatonism.

[112]Herbert is correct that there were no known temples to Eros in 1645. However, Pausanias mentions one near Baiae either built or restored by Hadrian, a fact that was confirmed by an inscription found in 1842 (Pausanias I, 364 n. 144).

The Graces

They were, some say, the daughters of Bacchus and Venus; others make them daughters of Jupiter and Erymone,[113] and still others the daughters of Juno. Chrysippus[114] tells us that the Graces were a little younger and more beautiful than the Hours, which is why they were thought of as companions of Venus. Others believe that the Hours were the same as the Graces. Their purpose was to foster friendship and to make people grateful for whatever benefits they had received. Pausanias says that the Spartans had only two Graces, but the Athenians three. Hesiod supplies their names: *Euphrosyne*, "cheerfulness"; *Aglaia*, "majesty and gracefulness"; *Thalia*, "joyful flourishing"; Homer adds a fourth, *Pasithea*, to these, and says that one of them was Vulcan's wife.[115] Seneca mentions only three, and describes their statues; Athenaeus mentions a temple dedicated to the Hours, in which there was an altar to Bacchus.[116] Alessandri, citing Aristotle, says that a temple to the Graces was built in the middle of a road to remind people everywhere of benefits received. The Greeks called them *Charites*. Servius says that they were depicted as naked, to show that they were not devious, and joined together because they were inseparable in their nature. The reason why they are shown with one looking away from us and two towards us is because when we do a good deed it doubles in the returning.[117]

Adonis

Servius says that Adonis was Venus's assistant, and the ancients gave all the gods assistants with less power and authority, such as Virbia to Diana and so forth.[118]

---

[113]More properly Eurynome, an Oceanid nymph (see Hesiod, *Theogony*, l. 358).

[114]Chrysippus (c. 280–207 B.C.) succeeded Cleanthes as head of the Stoic School in 232. Probably the greatest of the early Stoics, his doctrines being taken as the epitome of Stoic ethics, he wrote a now-lost work on liberality in which he joined the actions of offering, accepting and returning gifts to the Graces.

[115]Other sources mention Auxo (the Grower), Kale (the Beautiful) and Peitho (Persuasion), the last being an invention of the poet Hermesianax of Colophon (fl. 300 B.C.). Herbert is partially correct about the number of Graces, which was not fixed until Hesiod.

[116]Seneca quoted the lost work of Chrysippus mentioned above; he explained that there were three Graces with symbolic interpretations. Herbert agrees with Seneca's idea that the Graces must always operate together (see Seneca, *De beneficiis* I, iii; Wind 28).

[117]See Servius, *In Vergilii Aeneidem* I, 720.

[118]The myth of Adonis is well-known (cf. Frazer 441–48; Kirk 234ff). Zeus

Bacchus

There are, Cicero tells us, five Bacchuses or Dionysii. The first was Jupiter's son by Proserpina, the second of Nilus who perished on Nysa, the third the son of Caper, who was King of Asia and had the Sabazia made sacred to him, the fourth the son of Jupiter and Luna, to whom the rites of Orpheus were paid, and the last was the son of Nisus and Thione, from whom it was thought that the Trieterides were established.[119] Poets call him the son of Jupiter and Semele, as do Diodorus and Eusebius. The word Dionysus is said to be a compound of Jupiter and Nysa, but just which [Mount] Nysa is meant is uncertain, as there were several. Diodorus places it between Phoenicia and Egypt, a place where the Muses raised Bacchus in a cave. Not only was he the inventor of wine and vineyards, but of a barley drink which some people call *zithum*. He travelled all over the world with an army of men and women, more of women than of men, punishing criminals as he went.[120]

Vossius thinks that the earliest Bacchus was Noah, but he is sometimes Osiris, sometimes the Liber who led an expedition to the Indies, or, more properly, to Arabia. The ancients called all land beyond the Mediterranean India, whether it was beyond the Ganges or not. This Arabian Bacchus was, as Sandford and Vossius after him assert, the same as Moses. I will clarify this point with reference to both authors. We know Moses as the famous lawgiver, but Orpheus calls Liber *Misen*, and it does not matter that the word means "proclaimed queen," for Dionysus or Liber was

---

allowed Adonis to spend part of the year on Earth with Venus, the other half with Proserpina in Hades. This raised Adonis to the status of a fertility-god worshipped at Byblos and Amathus in Cyprus. In Athens he was identified with Eros.

[119]Herbert, following Cicero, misquotes him. The passage actually reads: "First there is the son of Jupiter and Proserpine. Then a second, who is a son of Nilus, and figures in legend as the destroyer of Nysa" (*NG* 217). Nisus was a king of Megara with a lock of red hair, which, if cut off, led to the fall of the city and his death. His loving daughter Scylla performed the operation, and King Minos of Crete took Megara. Nisus was turned into a sea-eagle, Scylla into a small bird which the eagle pursues. Sabazius, whom Herbert has already discussed, was often identified with Dionysus, but to the Phrygians he was known as Zeus Sabazius. Cicero mentions the "Trieterid festival" (217), celebrated every three years. Lewis mistranslated "a quo Trieterides constituti putantur" (*DRG* 137) to suggest that the Trieterides were some kind of "offspring" of Nisus and Thione.

[120]Herbert might have mentioned that the Orphics counted no fewer than nine Bacchuses, and their names and attributes were listed by Ficino, one of Herbert's sources (*Theologica Platonica* IV, i). They are paired with the nine Muses so that each Bacchus could have a spiritual as well as "Bacchic" side (Wind 278 n. 4).

bisexual,[121] and Alexander Polyhistor says that there was a woman called Mosa who gave the Jews their laws. Sometimes the ancients dressed Bacchus as a female, as may be seen from Philostratus's description of the image of Ariadne,[122] but Eusebius, quoting Porphyry, thinks that Bacchus was horned as well, to express the two-fold nature of male and female that exists in plants. Bacchus is known as *Bimater*, "having two mothers," and the daughter of Pharoah was thought to have been a second mother to Moses (Exodus 2:10). In Acts 7 it is written that Moses was taught all the learning and wisdom of the Egyptians. Diodorus praises Bacchus's wonderful handsomeness, and Josephus says the same of Moses.[123] Liber was brought up on Nysa, a mountain in Arabia, and Nyssus in the *Alexandrian Chronicle* is Sinai in Arabia, where Moses received the law and where, after forty years' exile in Egypt, he returned. Plutarch, in his work on Isis and Osiris, speaks of Liber's exile, as does Theodoret.[124] After forty years' captivity Moses brought the Israelites out of Egypt; Nonnius[125] says "With trembling step the traveller flees/To the yellow banks of the Red Sea." When Moses had passed over this sea, he fought many battles with the Arabians and with neighbouring rulers; Liber, too, as Dionysius tells us, citing

---

[121] Herbert is correct. Mise is called bisexual in the *Orphic Hymns*, and is identified with both Dionysus and Demeter.

[122] Herbert's reference: "It is easy for anyone to paint Ariadne as beautiful . . . and look at Ariadne, or rather at her sleep; for her bosom is bare to the waist, her neck is bent back and her delicate throat, and all her right armpit is visible" (Philostratus, *Imagines* I, 15, 64–65).

[123] "For his beauty, there was nobody so unpolite as, when they saw Moses, they were not greatly surprised at the beauty of his countenance" (Josephus, *Works* 57). Also see Acts 7:22 "And Moses was learned in all the wisdom of the Egyptians . . . "

[124] The exact location of Mt. Sinai is unknown. F.C. Fensham says that the most likely location is Gebel Musa (Moses's Mount) in Saudi Arabia, and the claim for this site "is so ancient [about 1500 years] and the granite formation so imposing that it is quite probably Mt. Sinai" (*IBD* III, 1461). Theodoret of Antioch (386–458), a Byzantine theologian, was Bishop of Cyrrhus from 423. He was first an ally then an enemy of Cyril in his conflict with the Nestorians. Theodoret wrote an ecclesiastical history from the years 324 to 429, of which a French translation appeared in 1544. No English translation was made until 1854.

[125] Nonnius Marcellus (4th century A.D.) was a lexicographer and grammarian, author of *De compendios doctrina*, a work on grammar which contained a great deal of other information. It also includes the only known poem by Varro. Herbert gives the source as "Nonnius in 20 Dionysiac" (138).

Antimirus,[126] came with a following of men and women to Arabia. Moses of course had all the people of Israel with him, men, women, and children.

Orpheus calls Dionysus *Thesmorphoron*;[127] Moses was the Jewish legislator to whom Orpheus attributes *displaca thesmon*, because of the Ten Commandments. Liber, or Dionysius in his hymns, is called *Taurometopus*, "having the forehead of a bull," and *Corniger*, "horned like a bull." The Vulgate renders the rays that shone from Moses's face, which represent sunbeams, as "the face of Moses was horned" (Exodus 34:29). Moses in the wilderness struck a rock with his staff and water gushed out, which also happened in the *orgii* of Liber, and Euripides, in the *Bacchae*, writes, "Taking a thyrsus he then struck a certain rock,/ From which a stream of pure cold water sprang."[128] God sent fiery snakes amongst the Israelites which killed many of them, but when they repented, Moses, by God's command, set up a brass snake, and whoever looked at it was cured. Bacchus-worshippers tied snakes around their heads, as may be seen from Euripides, Catullus, Clement of Alexandria and Arnobius. The Bible makes mention of Caleb, a most loyal companion of Moses;[129] *keleb* in Hebrew means "dog," and Liber had a dog as a companion, who was afterwards received into heaven. Nonnius [of Panopolis] portrays him talking to his dog:

> . . . for all your work I give you
> Thanks, and next to Sirius, the star of Maera,
> I will make you a citizen of Heaven, and with many shining stars
> Near the first Dog you will ripen the grape,
> And the branches will receive your splendour. (*Dionysiaca*, Bk. 15)

As Moses brought his people to a land flowing with milk and honey, so in the *Bacchae* of Euripides it may be read: "And the ground is flowing with white milk and flowing with red/ Wine and flowing with nectar of bees,/ While a smoke as of Syrian incense falls. . . . "[130] I have said enough on

---

[126]Antimeiros of Mende (c. 450 B.C.) was a rather obscure Thracian sophist. He is believed to have been a pupil of Protagoras of Abdera and is mentioned by Plato in the *Protagoras* as "the most eminent of Protagoras's pupils" (315a [314]).

[127]The Law-giving. Actually, this is an epithet of Demeter and Persephone as well as of Dionysus, who is only saluted as such in the Orphic hymns (42, i). The Thesmophoria, held in Athens and other cities, were a festival for women in honour of Demeter (for more details, see below, n. 143).

[128]Euripides, *The Bacchae* 707–08 [34].

[129]Caleb ben Jephunneh remained faithful to Moses when the Israelites rebelled at Kadesh, andwas rewarded by exemption from God's curse (Numbers 14:24).

[130]Euripides, *The Bacchae* 143–46 [8].

this subject; these Greek stories are not reliable, neither is anything cited by those whose truthfulness we have reason to suspect. For the difference between the Egyptian Bacchus, whom some call Osiris,[131] and the one in Thebes, whose sacred rites were like those in Egypt, see Vossius in *De idololatria*.

The name Bacchus comes from a Greek word *bacchien*, "to howl." His surnames were Iacchus *Lycaeus*, *Lenaeus*, and *Licnotes*; of these Ausonius says:

> Ogygia calls me Bacchus,
> Egypt knows me as Osiris;
> The Mystae call me Phanaces,
> And in India I am Dionysos.
> To holy Rome I am Liber,
> Adonis to the people of Arabia,
> And to a Lucanian I am Pantheus.   (Epigram 29)

Those who would like more should read Ovid's *Metamorphoses*, Book IV, although there is no mention of Bacchus *Eleutherius*, who was named that way for freeing the Boeotians.[132] Scaliger notes that there was an altar common to Bacchus and Proserpina, and Artemidorus counts him as one of the gods of the Underworld.[133] Ancient historians, St. Augustine in his *City of God*, and the poets, especially Catullus, have described his crazy rites known as the Bacchanalia; Catullus, amongst other things, writes about "the orgies which in vain the wicked desire to hear." The Scythians, as Herodotus says, would not allow the Bacchanalia because they thought it stupid that there could be a god who wanted to make people leave their senses.[134] In Italy, too, to a degree, they were abolished, but some things were retained; Dionysius of Halicarnassus says that there were some productive aspects

---

[131]Pico della Mirandola identifies Bacchus with Osiris (*Oration on the Dignity of Man* [116]), following Herodotus 2.48.

[132]The names of Bacchus:
Iacchus: the name of a god worshipped at Eleusis who was associated with wine and thereafter subsumed by Dionysus.
Lyaeus: the Releaser from Care.
Lenaeus: pertaining to the wine-press (Greek *lenaios*).
Licnotes: Bearer of the Winnowing-fan (Greek *liknos*).
Phanaces: Bringer of Light (Greek *phanos*).
Pantheus: the All-embracing God.

[133]Artemidorus of Ephesus (2nd century A.D.) wrote eleven works on geography and was the first person to attempt to measure the length and breadth of the earth.

[134]Herodotus 4.79 (309–10). The Scythians disliked foreign ways.

of the festivals of Bacchus, and perhaps I should describe them, but the craziness and obscenity of the rites in general will not allow it. That is why they took place outside the cities, as Herodotus says, and amongst others Suidas mentions the Phallus.[135]

Herodotus mentions a shrine of Bacchus inscribed with Assyrian writing, and a temple at Samos; Pliny says that there was a temple of Bacchus in the Second Quarter of Rome, and a chapel of Liber Pater in the Sixth. He was depicted as a young boy, or a man, or an old man. A panther was always nearby, his sacred animal, also a donkey or bull. Pliny tells us that he was, like Apollo, in command of the Muses, and poets were crowned with ivy as well as with bays. Ivy in Greek is *kissos*, which comes from *kissan*, "to lust," and it was sacred to Bacchus.[136]

The ancients say that Bacchus was the first to ride in triumph on an elephant. Cartari says that the magpie, amongst birds, was sacred to him, because it was acceptable for anyone to disparage a person triumphing. I doubt this, as the chattering of that bird is more applicable to drunkards at a party than it is to people insulting a triumphant person. Suidas says that Bacchus and Priapus were the same, and others that Bacchus was his father.[137] I will discuss Bacchus's winnowing-fan later when I speak about penitence amongst the ancients. Bacchus's companions were the Sileni, Bacchae, Lenae, Thyiae, Mimellones, Naïades, Satyrae, Bassarides and Nymphae.[138]

---

[135]The Phallus was a model of a penis used in the rites of Dionysus. There was also a *daimon*, Phales, who personified the penis. Lewis omits the entire passage.

[136]Herbert is correct about *kissos*, but the verb *kissao* (the only one in Liddell and Scott resembling what Herbert cites [955]) means "to crave for strange food," and is associated with pregnant women.

[137]The general consensus, in spite of Suidas, is that Priapus was the son of Bacchus and Venus. He ended up as a garden-god, "where his statue (a misshapen little man with enormous genitals) was a sort of combined scarecrow and guardian deity" (*OCD* 729).

[138]The followers of Bacchus:

> Sileni: the same as Satyrae, but only because classical authors mixed them up. The former are old and have horses' ears, and the latter are part-goat, led by Silenus, "an elder and slightly more sober kind of satyr" (Rose 24).
>
> Lenae: those who took part in the Lenaea, a festival which took place in January. *Lene* is another name for maenad.
>
> Thyiae: from the Thuia, the festival of Dionysus at Elis.
>
> Mimellones: actually Mimallones, the Macedonian version of Bacchantes.
>
> Bassarides: Thracian maenads, female followers of Dionysus. The *bassara* was a dress made from fox-skins.

Ceres [and Proserpina]

The daughter of Saturn and Ops, Ceres was worshipped not only by the Greeks, but by the Romans also, and Vergil wrote of her, "It was Ceres who first instituted the ploughing/ Of the earth." Similarly, we find in Ovid, "Ceres first moved the earth with a hooked plough,/ She first gave fruit and produce to the land,/ And was first to give laws: everything is the bread of Ceres." According to some, she was called *Libera*,[139] but Herodian contradicts this by noting that Postumius made a vow to build a temple to Ceres, Liber, and Kore, which is translated as Libera. According to Cicero, Libera was Proserpina, but she certainly was not Ceres, and he also says [in *The Nature of the Gods*] that "our ancestors celebrated Ceres very solemnly and reverently with Liber and Libera."[140] Some people think that this Libera was Venus, but I will agree with Cicero until I have better reasons not to.

Ceres's surnames were *Panda*, becamuse she gave us bread, as Varro, quoted by Nonnius, says, "those who take refuge with Ceres have bread given them." Others say that Panda is the goddess of peace.[141] She is described as *Alma* because she feeds us, and, as Dionysius says, "the Egyptians say that Ceres and Isis are the same, and that she first taught them to sow seed." The rites of Ceres used in Athens are much the same as those of Isis. Herodotus says that she and Liber ruled over the Underworld, which is why the winnowing-fan of the purgation of the soul, or repentance, was associated with Bacchus. The same author mentions temples built in Plataea and Eleusa as well as orgies of Ceres *Aetheria*.[142] Ceres *Legisera* was worshipped by women, and Dionysius says that the rituals of Ceres and Proserpina were observed every year by the Athenians. Servius, in his commentary on Book IV of the *Aeneid*, tells us why she was known as Legisera. "Ceres supposedly invented laws," he says, "for her sacred rites were called Thesmophoria, which means the introduction of laws." This must be fiction, because before Ceres invented the sowing of corn, humans ranged freely over the world and were not subject to laws; this uncivilised behaviour ceased after land became property, from which laws arose.

---

[139]They would argue, presumably, as Ovid does, that Bacchus raised Ariadne to heaven as Libera. "As you have shared my bed," he tells her honourably, "so you will share my name" (*Fasti* III, 512).

[140]Cicero, *NG* 148.

[141]The first version comes from *panis*, "bread," and *dare*, "to give." The second may be a compound of *pax* and the same verb.

[142]For Demeter at Eleusis, see Herodotus 6.75 (438); for Plataea and other locations, 9.16–88 *passim*.

The Syracusans sacrificed to Ceres and her daughter Proserpina, but in a more modest manner than the people of Eleusis. Of the latter, Athenaeus says:

> Heraclides of Syracuse has written about the old established customs; he says that the Syracusans at their Thesmophoria made images of women's pudenda out of Indian wheat and honey. These were known as *mylloi* throughout Sicily, and carried in honour of the goddesses.

Of this Vossius adds,

> This was a disgraceful custom, even if it was symbolic; just as a man's penis was carried about at the sacred rites of Bacchus and Osiris to symbolise the active power of generation, so in the Thesmophoria of Syracuse female pudenda are displayed to symbolise the passive principle.[143]

Dionysius mentions a temple of Ceres where chaste rites were performed by priestesses after the Greek manner up until his own time, but the law stated that women only could assist at these sacred rites. Estates of people who killed, struck, or opposed the authority of a tribune, were confiscated and given to Ceres; there is a temple of Ceres in the Circus Maximus above the prisons. She had others, too, of whom P. Victor says that in her Eleusinian rites the priestesses ran through the dark with torches, the one in front continually shouting "Get back, get back, you impious people!"[144]

Nobody could be admitted to Ceres's presence without being initiated and atoning for any crimes committed. We read about Nero that he was

---

[143]The Thesmophoria "celebrates [women's] relationship with one another and their affinity with the productiveness of nature" (Dowden 162). Burkert says that these festivals "give an impression of extraordinary antiquity," perhaps dating back as far as the Stone Age (13). They are, he continues, "the most widespread Greek festival and the principal form of the Demeter cult" (242). Men were excluded from the Thesmophoria, and the women could "enter into contact with the subterranean, with death and decay, whilst at the same time phalloi, snakes, and fir-cones, sexuality and fertility, are present" (243). In Athens, pigs were sacrificed at the Thesmophorion on the Pnyx hill. For further details, see Burkert 242–46.

The connexion with law is a later interpretation. Demeter was said to have brought such "law-like" concepts as marriage and civilisation to humanity (see Diodorus Siculus 5.5.2; Servius, *In Vergilii Aeneiadum* IV, 58), but lawgivers are people, not gods. Demeter gave mankind "the civilising gift of corn; the land can now be dominated by human activity" (Dowden 123).

The displaying of female pudenda is mentioned by Theodoret in *Graecarum affectionum curatio* (3.84). This is the likely source for both Vossius and Herbert.

[144]For details of the Eleusinian Mysteries, a "secret which was open to thousands every year" and which "drew men and women from all of Greece and later from the whole of the Roman Empire," see Burkert 285–90.

never at these ceremonies because he was well aware of his own criminality, but the Emperor Antoninus [Pius], as proof of his honesty, was initiated into the sacred rites of Ceres Eleusina. Her annual rites were known as *Initia Maiora*, or "Greater Initiation"; at this time it was publicly broadcast out of mysterious books what was going to be done at this sacred ceremony. These books were hidden under a heap of stones, and Pausanias tells us that when the Pheneans[145] took oaths on matters of great importance, they went there. He also says that the image of Ceres *Cidonia* was kept there, and that the priest, on certain days, dressed up like it and chastised people in a fatherly manner with rods.

Ceres had many other rites and customs. Initiates were to put on clean shirts, which they never took off until they were completely worn out, after which they carefully kept the pieces to make girdles for their children. No-one knew what was carried in the ceremonial parades of Ceres *Eleusina*, and it was thought impious to ask; sacred objects were carried in a closed chest, in complete silence, which is why the young girls who carried them were called *Canophorae*. People who revealed the mysteries were rebuked in their dreams, if you can believe it, and told that their taking such a liberty was displeasing to the goddesses Ceres and Proserpina. Pausanias says that he intended to describe these rites, but was prevented by a ghost;[146] he mentions nothing more than the temple of Triptolemus, to whom Ceres taught agriculture, and brass cows with gilt horns, decorated with flowers, which were sacrificed to her. The Arcadians venerated Ceres and Proserpina greatly, and religiously kept a fire burning constantly in their temples.

Ceres had a huge marble statue; her daughter Proserpina was depicted clothed, because as all seeds were covered with rind or bark, so she was not as visible as her mother Ceres. Hercules was placed at her feet, and in her sacrifices, unlike those of the other deities, no wine was used; the sacrifices were called *nuptiae*, or "marriages." Sows, because they ate the corn, were her particular sacrifice; the pagans were so strict in their religion that they did not believe they had the power to kill animals, but as sows were a menace when they destroyed the harvest, it was thought lawful to sacrifice them. Ceres was also known as Demetrus, Erinnys, Lysia, and Melaina, whose name is explained by Pausanias. She is shown seated on a stone, all of her a woman except her head, which is like a mare with a mane, and there

---

[145]The Pheneans lived in the city of Phenos in Arcadia. Levi notes that it "has not been found" (Pausanias II, 408 and n.).

[146]"The dream forbids me to write what lies within the sanctuary wall, and what the uninitiated are not allowed to see they obviously ought not to know about" (Pausanias I, 108).

are snakes and other creatures playing about her head. The rest of her body, down to the soles of her feet, is covered with a long garment; in one hand she holds a dolphin, and in the other a dove, which symbolise the animals of the elements. I will not trouble my reader with the story of how Ceres was turned into a mare and Neptune was later changed into a horse.[147]

Vulcan

Cicero mentions four Vulcans, amongst whom is the one said to have been the son of Jupiter and Juno. Both Hesiod and Lucian write or report stories that he was conceived without the assistance of god or man, but this only means that fire may sometimes be generated by air alone. Jupiter's throwing him head first down to the island of Lemnos and making him lame refers, some say, to thunderbolts.

The Egyptians believed he was the inventor of fire, which is, I think, why he was deified and why he symbolises fire for the ancients. Nothing which has been discovered since the world began is as quick and wonderful in its effects than fire, and nothing is more useful and advantageous. Vulcan was thus thought of by the ancients as some deity making himself visible as an emblem of the sun, as I have already said. His most famous temple was at Memphis — I have described his colossus, 75 feet long, lying on its back by the temple, as well as the priests who were picked to celebrate his mysteries. Amongst these Herodotus mentions a king who had a stone statue in Vulcan's temple, and who held a mouse in commemoration of a victory gained with the help of this little animal over Sennacherib of Assyria. It has the inscription, "Look on me, all of you, and be pious."[148] Dionysius tells us that Tatius built a temple to Vulcan, that Romulus dedicated four bronze horses to him and that speeches were made in front of and inside the temple. Pliny says that the Romans established festivals for him; it is

---

[147]The surnames of Ceres:

Aetheria: literally "of the upper air," hence "heavenly."

Legifera: Bearer of the Law.

Cidonia: the Kidarian Demeter. Levi tells us that the *kidaris* was "a special head-dress, or, more appropriately here, a special dance" (Pausanias II, 409 n. 112).

Demetrus: more accurately Demetros, a variant on Demeter.

Erinos: the Furious. See Callimachus, Frag. 207.

Lusia: Releaser or Deliverer from sin.

Melaina: the Black. Pausanias says that she was so-called because she was dressed in black (II, 476–79).

[148]The full story of the mouse is in Herodotus 2.141 [192–93].

not material here whether he made weapons for the gods or whether he was Venus's husband, whom Cincius [Alimentus] calls Maia and [Lucius] Piso calls Maiestas.

Vesta

The name of Vesta in Greek is Hestia, but it may well come from the Hebrew *eschia*, which means "fire of God." Some think that the custom of worshipping fire came from the Jews and remained with the gentiles after being mixed with other newly-invented rites. The goddess Vesta was a daughter of Saturn (according to Diodorus Siculus and Apollodorus), and, as Quintus Fabius Pictor says, the wife of Janus.[149]

It is possible, as Castor notes, that the ancient Romans began their sacrifices to other gods by invoking Janus and Vesta, Janus first because he was the first to build a temple in Italy and to institute sacred rites, according to Macrobius. The hearth was sacred to Vesta because no sacrifice could be made without fire; it was known as *lar*, and the Lares were worshipped there. The word *vestibulum* comes from Vesta, because the entrance to the house was sacred to her. On some old coins she is shown as a woman sitting, holding a drum.

It is said that the Scythians worshipped Vesta as fire under the name of *Tabetis*;[150] fire was usually worshipped as Vulcan both in the East and West, except in Italy, where Vesta was held in great veneration. Livy says that the Romans got the worship of Vesta from the Albans.[151] Sacred rites were also performed at Athens, Delphos and other places in Greece. Dionysius mentions a temple of Vesta built by Numa Pompilius, and says that her priests were chosen from the noblest families. For the sacred objects kept in her temple, such as the Palladium, consult Dionysius and Plutarch, and especially Luis Vives's commentary on Bk. II of Augustine's *City of God*. Pliny tells us that it was burned down, which, as Plutarch remarks, was not surprising, because it was surrounded with perpetual fire. Some think that Vesta refers to either the Earth or the action of an internal power of the Earth. This is enough for Vesta and Vulcan, deities who represent both pure celestial fire and earthly elemental fire.

---

[149]Quintus Fabius Pictor (fl. 280 B.C.), soldier and scholar, wrote a history of Rome in Greek, and was particularly interested in the possibility that Aeneas was the founder of Rome. He set the date for Rome's foundation at 747 B.C.

[150]More accurately, *Tabiti*. Herodotus writes that "in the Scythian language, Hestia is called Tabiti" (302).

[151]"He [Numa] further appointed virgin priestesses for the services of Vesta, a cult which originated in Alba . . . " (Livy, *Early History of Rome* 1.20 [55]).

Neptune

He was the son of Saturn by Ops or Rhea, and presided over the sea because he had invented navigation. Cicero says that he was "an intelligent mind moving over the sea,"[152] and sailors sacrificed to him. Pliny writes about a temple sacred to him in Caria. Some ancient coins mention Neptune *Redux*, to whom there was a temple in the ninth quarter of Rome, and another of which P. Victor speaks.

Neptune, because he also taught horsemanship, was called *Hippios*, *Seisichthor* and *Poseidon* by the Greeks because he shook the Earth with his feet, or the hoofs of his horses did. In Vergil's *Aeneid* we find that "The sound of hoofs shakes the yielding fields," and in the *Georgics*, "His hoofs echo like the solid horn."[153] People who raced horses always swore by Neptune that they would not cheat. Pausanias says that Hippios was the best-known of Neptune's names in all countries, and the Circenses were games sacred to Neptune, played on horseback. He was also called *Taxarippus*, because, as Pausanias tells us, horses are sometimes frightened and taken with a sudden trembling near his altar. Festus [Avienus] reports that four horses were always sacrificed to this Neptune every ninth year. There are two coins, one of Vespasian's and the other of Hadrian's, which beautifully depict Neptune in both his aspects. He is shown standing naked, a cloak over his left shoulder, holding a triple-lashed whip in his right hand, and an upright trident in his left.[154]

Servius tells us that amongst the ancients, gates were sacred to Juno, towers to Minerva, walls and foundations to Neptune. Statues of Neptune and Oceanus were so similar that they could hardly be told apart; the ancients called Oceanus the Father of the Gods, but symbolically the name only meant that primaeval humidity from which all things grow.

---

[152]This idea was further developed by Ridewall in his *Fulgentius metaforalis*, where Neptune is identified with the virtue Intelligentia (Seznec 94).

[153]Vergil, *Aeneid* VIII, 596. Herbert gives neither book nor line references for his quotations from the *Georgics*.

[154]The names of Neptune:

Redux: the Restorer, also a surname of Jupiter.

Hippios: "of the horse." Neptune created horses; he did not teach horsemanship.

Seisichthor: the Earth-shaker. This is the epithet most frequently used by Homer.

Taxarippus: Handler of Horses.

Portumnus

I must not leave out Portumnus or Portunus, a deity who presided over gates. However, I shall not waste time enquiring whether he was the same as Palaemon and Melicertes. He had two temples in Rome, both in the twelfth quarter of the city.[155]

Genius

There is no agreement amongst the ancients what Genius is, or how it became an animal deity. In my opinion, Servius explains it best: "Genius is the natural god of every place, person, or thing." We have ancient inscriptions "LOCI HUIUS GENIO," "to the Genius of this place," and Arnobius mentions the Genius of cities. There is an inscription at Puteoli, "DEO MAGNO GENIO PUTEOLANORUM & PATRIAE SUAE," "to the great god, the Genius of the people of Puteoli and his own country." Claudian, in his *Epistle to Severus*, makes Genius the preserver of the Empire, and Symmachus, in his *Letter to Valentinian, Theodosius and Arcadius*, says, "Just as those who are born receive souls, so do the people receive destiny." These words may be seen on an inscription of Hadrian, "GENIO P.R." "to the Genius of the Roman people." There is a military figure, clothed to the knees, with a shallow dish in his right hand, such as is used by an officiating priest, while in his left hand is a cornucopia. These things were also associated with Nemestinus, the god of groves, or with Collina and Vallina, goddesses of hills and valleys.[156]

St. Augustine quotes Varro as saying that every rational creature had a genius; the ancients took the word genius this way when they made it an animal deity. Censorinus says, "Genius watches so carefully over us that it never leaves us for a minute, attending us from our birth to our last breath."[157] The ancients believed there were two: one, like our Good Angel,

---

[155]Portumnus was the god of harbours and is, indeed, identified with Palaemon, son of Athamas and Ino. Herbert has already mentioned Melicertes, deified as Palaemon when Hera drove his parents mad because they had looked after Dionysus (see Ovid, *Fasti* VI, 547). In fact, this god is more interesting than Herbert allows; there was a dispute over whether he was a harbour-god or a gate-god, *portus*, "harbour," and *porta*, "gate," being similar. Ovid says it was the former, together with Vergil, Cicero and Servius. Festus Avienus is in favour of the second meaning. Portumnus had a temple near the Aemilian bridge, but the second temple ascribed to him by Herbert is now identified as one to Mater Matuta. Both are now churches.

[156]Collina and Vallina are found only in Augustine, *City of God* IV, 9 (145), where they occur as Collatina and Vallonia.

[157]Censorinus (3rd century A.D.) wrote one extant work, *De die natali volumen illustre*, which deals with the effect that the stars and planets have on human life. It

was a protector; the other was like the Devil, trying to make us sin. Those who believe this say that man received his Genius from the Stars when he received his soul; after preserving and guarding him here, it brings him after this life either to a state of happiness or turns him over to punishment. Horace writes of "Genius, our comrade who directs our birth-star,/ The god of human nature," and describes him later as having a face either black or white, so that he could be an overseer of human actions as well as an observer. The ancients were prompted in their opinion by a belief that God did not concern himself with the government of the world, and that it was thereby necessary for each person to have a particular guiding spirit. The Greatest and Best God, they thought, could not have an accurate account of people's thoughts and actions unless every person from birth had a Genius. People who concern themselves with women allow them a Juno instead of a Genius.

There were many ancient depictions of Genius. As a snake, he symbolised regeneration, while others showed him having a vase of flowers in his right hand, which he places on an altar, while in his left hand is a flail or something similar. Some depict him as a boy, others as a youth, and still others as an old man; you may consult Pausanias about Genius in the form of a boy and as a snake. The Elians erected an altar to him in thanks for a victory obtained with his help. Pausanias also mentions the evil Genius who met Euthymus and overcame him.[158]

There was great similarity between the Genii and the Lares, which led the Romans to set up and worship the most important of them at crossroads, or where three roads met. Everyone worshipped his own genius separately, but especially on his birthday. At that time, people who celebrated with happiness and joy were said to *indulgere Genio*, or, at the opposite extreme, *Genium defraudare*, namely "depriving themselves of pleasure." A birthday Ovid calls a *festum Geniale*; Claudian, in *The Rape of Proserpina*, refers to "the couch of Genius"; Vergil in the *Aeneid* writes of "the throne of Genius,"

---

was edited by Louis Carrion (1583) under the title *Fragmentum Censorini*.

[158]There is some confusion here. Polites, one of Odysseus's crew, was killed by the Temesans for rape. His ghost had to placated by the sacrifice of a young girl every year, a rather strange outcome of a crime. Euthymus, a boxer, fell in love with one of the destined victims, beat up the ghost, and rescued the girl (see Pausanias II, 301–04). Levi notes that Callimachus tells the story in the *Aetia* (98–99), and that it is also found in Aelian, another of Herbert's sources.

Herbert's Latin is ambiguous here, and reads as follows: "De *malo* etiam *Genio* cum Euthymo congrediente, illumque vicente" (147). It should probably read *illoque*. Lewis follows the mistake, translating "an Evil Genius that encounter'd Euthymus, and overcame him" (237).

A wedding-day, or any day for mirth or pleasure was known as *Genialis*; Juvenal says "that day/ Will be known as genial."

The Genius of rulers was taken very seriously; for example, anyone who swore by a ruler's genius and violated his oath would be punished as much as a notorious perjurer. Suetonius tells us that the Emperor Caligula used to punish people who never swore by his genius because he thought they must despise him. People offered wine and flowers to Genius on their birthdays, but they did not perform blood-sacrifices, believing it impious to take away the life of anything on the day they had received their own lives. Censorinus adds that when these sacred rites were performed to a Genius, no-one might eat before the person that was the host. Scholars say that the plane-tree was sacred to Genius, and that he was crowned with it, perhaps because, as Aelian suggests, an owl would not come near a plane-tree. Sometimes, according to Tibullus, he was crowned with flowers: "Genius will be seen at his own rites,/ Flowery garlands decorating his head." Plutarch sets out to prove, in his book *Why Oracles are no longer Consulted*, that one Genius may have more virtue, wisdom, or power than another. In the description of the [fourteen] districts of Rome, mention is made of temples dedicated to the Genii of children and to the Genii of the Lares in the sixth district; there is a small chapel of the Genii Sangi[159] in the seventh district, but as their private worship was so widespread, I have not come across mention of any more public temples or chapels.

Penates

They are so called from being the nearest and *penetissimi*, "most inward," deities. Dionysius calls them Mychioi, from *mychios*, which means "an inner chamber," and we also find them known as *ktesioi*, in Latin *Quaestuarii* or *Fortunatores*, names also applied to Jupiter and Mercury. Others know them as *Penates* from *patrous* or *patrios*, still others as *Genethlioi, Natalitii*, or *Herchioi*, because they are confined within the limits of the house.[160]

---

[159]Probably a misprint for *Sani*. If so, it refers to the Genius of Health.

[160]Names for the Penates:

Mychioi: Herbert's translation of the Greek is correct. The name also applied to Aphrodite Mychia.

Quaestuarii: the Gainful Ones.

Fortunatores: Ones who bless.

Patrous: the Fatherly Ones.

Genethlioi: Those who preside over birth. The Roman counterparts were the Natalitii.

Herchioi: those in the courtyard.

Dionysius also mentions temples with their images, and thinks that the first letter of their name was originally D, not P. Cicero says that they were called *Penates* from *penus*, which means "store of food," or because *penitus insident*, "they dwell inwardly," for which reason the poets call them *Penetrales*.[161] They presided not only over the head of the household, but over his guests also; Cicero and Ovid both note that it was a most heinous crime to murder a stranger in their presence.

They were depicted as young men in armour, with spears in their hands; some say they are Apollo and Neptune, others that they are Castor and Pollux, while still others maintain that the Penates are deities in their own right. They were worshipped in the innermost part of the house, before the householder conducted any business. So Terence has Demipho say, "He was going home to worship his Penates before returning to the Forum to do business." When the Penates were angry, sacrifices were made to them; Horace speaks of appeasing them in this way. Dictators and magistrates in Rome always sacrificed to the Penates and to Vesta on the day they [vacated] office.[162]

Lares

Some believe that the Lares and Genii are the same, and that the Penates are not much different from them. Apuleius in his book *On the God of Socrates*, says that the Lares were formerly known as Lemures or Spectres, but Lar certainly has a benevolent meaning. The Lemures or *Lar[v]ae* punished the wicked, but the Lares were kind, domestic, family gods, worshipped within the house.[163] The hearth, known as the *focus Laris*, was sacred to them.

---

[161]Cicero, *NG* 151. The name Penetrales signifies "the dwellers within." Grant confirms the link with *penus*, "store-house," and relates the tradition that Aeneas brought the Penates from Troy. Herbert is mistaken, however, about the officials sacrificing to them on the day they entered into office ("die dignitatem inibant" [149]), for the sacrifice was made when they *vacated* their office (Grant, *RM* 81).

[162]Modern scholarship confirms the obscure origin of the Penates. "It is enough to remember," Rose says, "that they were generally considered to be Trojan deities brought with him by Aeneas" (175).

[163]Lemures were, literally, "ghosts." They had their own festival, the Lemuria, which was held in May, with the object of expelling them (Ovid, *Fasti* V, 421).

Larae is a mispelling of Laruae (Larvae), another word for "ghost" or "spectre."

According to Michael Grant, *lar* means "a dead and revered ancestor" (*RM* 81). As Herbert points out, while they did become household gods, the Lares retained their connexion with rural areas and crossroads, as the quotation from Propertius indicates, and which is confirmed by Grant (82).

Near the Forum stood the Lararium, where Lares were kept. Lampridius writes that Emperor Alexander Severus had two Lararia, in one of which he kept the images of Christ, Abraham, Orpheus and Apollonius, in another the busts of Cicero and Vergil.

The Lares were thought of as the guardians of fields and the entire city as well as of private homes. Festus tells us that balls and the effigies of men and women were hung up at crossroads and that feast-days were celebrated there. Varro says that the Compitalia were the days devoted to the Lares, but Cicero refers to them as *dies Compitalii*, and mentions sports used at them. Balls representing the heads of servants and effigies of children were made so that the Lares would spare the living and be content with them instead. Pliny tells us how Servius Tullius introduced the Compitalia and games; the king, lying down, felt a burning in his head, and thus believed he was the son of the familiar Lar. But Varro says that Titus Tatius, king of the Sabines, was the first to make vows and build temples to the Lares. Plutarch says that the proper name of the Lares was Praestites,[164] and that their role was to assist the dog. They were dressed in dog-skin because as the care and custody of the house was in their charge, they should be tame and friendly towards the family yet terrifying to all others, like a dog.[165] In Plautus's play *Aulularia*, the Lar himself describes the rites which were performed to him: "He has an only daughter, who every day to me/ With frankincense, wine, or something similar/ Sacrifices, and gives me a garland." According to Ovid, they also had a woollen ribbon given them. The meat that was offered to them from the table was burned, because it was blasphemous for anyone to eat it. Propertius describes the sacrifice offered to them at a crossroads, "they expiated themselves with a small, fattened-up pig," Sheep were also sacrificed to the Lares.

It was commonly thought that the Lares presided singly over families, and together they protected entire cities. Propertius credits them with Hannibal's defeat, and Festus says that people sacrificed to the warlike Lares because they imagined they had defeated their enemies. There was a temple in the eighth district of Rome, as well as a grove and chapel. L. Aemilius Regillus[166] made vows to the Lares of the sea so that they would assist his naval campaigns. Curtius dedicated an altar to the Lares Praestites who

---

[164]Those who stand before.

[165]Cartari describes the Lares as having "the shape of two young men clothed in dogskins" (448).

[166]Lucius Aemilius Regillus was an admiral and statesman, praetor in 190 B.C. The text reads "Regulus," an error which Lewis repeats, but this name fits neither the occasion nor the *praenomina*.

preserved the city walls, and Cicero reports that they were very angry when a temple to Licentia[167] was rebuilt in their area. I will not trouble you with stories of the word being derived from *lara* or *larunda*. The Greeks called them *heroes kat'iokian* or *Katoikidioi*,[168] the former name suggesting that the souls of some heroes became Lares.

Pluto

The son of Saturn and Ops, brother of Jupiter and Neptune, Pluto was believed to govern the underworld. Diodorus Siculus says the reason was that he invented funeral rites and parental obsequies.

He was known as Orcus or Horcus from an oath which the ancients swore, and by this name he is included amongst the major deities. Poets report that he ruled over Hell as Jupiter rules over Heaven and Neptune over the sea, so everything below, especially that which was subterranean, was under Pluto's direction. The jurisdictions of the brothers were not so distinct that they did not sometimes interfere with one another. Pluto was called the god of riches, for *plutos*, the origin of his name, means "wealth."[169] By Latin people he is also called Dis, from *ditare*, "to enrich." This is actually applied to the Pluto who rules the inner Earth from which metals are mined, for as god of hell he did not confer wealth, but distributed rewards and punishments. After this life, according to the poets and philosophers, there was a field, the Field of Truth, which had two paths in it, one leading to the Blessed Isles and the other to the place of punishment. It was said that there were three judges, Aeacus, Rhadamanthus, and Minos, who knew everything that people had done in their lives on Earth. Rhadamanthus and Aeacus held rods in their hands while they judged, and Minos sat by himself, a golden sceptre in his hand, deliberating every single case. The souls stood naked, divested of their bodies and stripped from earthly covers, so that the judges could see into their most secret and intimate thoughts and make a just judgment on their important actions.[170]

---

[167]Licentia is the goddess of (sexual) license.

[168]Literally, "the heroes of the home," or "those in the dwelling-place."

[169]Herbert is not quite accurate here. The god Plutus (Plutos) is connected with Pluto[n] (Hades) "in idea" (*OCD* 707), but is also associated with an Oceanid nymph, "ox-eyed Plouto" (Hesiod, *Theogony* l. 355). Plutos was sent by Demeter and Kore (Persephone) to people they favoured, who would then become rich. This god also stands for the prosperity of crops. The confusion arose from the Greek Plutos (Plutus) with Pluton (Pluto).

[170]Aeacus was a legendary king of Aegina, famous during his lifetime for his justice, but also for raping the nymph Psamathe. Rhadamanthus was the brother

Plato and his disciples explain the symbolism of these stories by asserting unanimously that there are rewards and punishments for souls after this life, or else the dictates of conscience would serve no purpose if there was no other state of happiness or misery. Eusebius gives another interpretation from Plato, saying that Porphyrius represented the Sun. He spends little time with us during the winter and more with our Antipodes, and is said to govern the underworld, hardly giving any light to our hemisphere. Proserpina's detention by Pluto means that Pluto, or the Sun, preserves the generative power (symbolised by Proserpina) either in himself, or in the husk which contains the seed; this needs no further explanation.[171] The poets show him presiding over the spirits and reigning as king in Hell. Claudian writes, "Leaning on his black sceptre/ He sits enthroned in awful majesty, while horrible filth/ Extends over his domains."[172] Martianus Capella gives him an ebony crown and sceptre because he was king of the underworld. Homer, Plato, and Hyginus write that he carried a helmet which, if anyone wore it, he became invisible although he could see everyone. This may symbolise the occult power of the Sun when it is not seen by us. It was with the help of this helmet which Minerva had borrowed from Pluto that Perseus overcame Medusa. According to Fulgentius, Cerberus lies at his master's feet, his three heads signifying that three things are necessary for seed to be productive: it must be spread on the ground, be covered with earth, and sprout when covered.[173]

---

of Minos, the King of Crete, and is "specially associated with Elysium and the Isles of the Blessed" (Kirk 265). Minos was turned by Boccaccio (one of Herbert's sources) into "human reason, which governs the soul and leads it along the right path" (Boccaccio, *Genealogia deorum* IV, 10, quoted by Seznec 224).

[171]I disagree. It does need some explanation. Porphyrius is derived from *porphura*, "purple" (dye, fish, cloth) and is also the colour associated with death. The association of Hades with Apollo (as the Sun) is more plausible in the light of the curious linkage, in the Renaissance, of Cerberus, the three-headed guardian of the Underworld, with Apollo, which the music theorist Francini Gafurio makes in his *Practica musice* (1496), for which see below.

The generative power of Proserpina, who returns from Hades to earth, scattering flowers to usher in the spring, is alluded to rather aptly by Herbert himself in a poem: "Having interr'd her Infant-birth,/ The wat'ry ground that late did mourn,/ Was strew'd with flow'rs for the return/ Of the wish'd Bridegroom of the earth" ("Ode upon a Question moved, whether Love should continue for ever?" l. 1–4).

[172]Claudian, *De raptu Proserpinae* I, 276–88 [136–37]. Pluto is getting ready to ascend to the upper world.

[173]It is actually Ridewall in his *Fulgentius metaforalis* who describes Cerberus this way, and links the dog with Cupiditas, the personification of insatiable desire

Pindar describes Pluto having a rod in his hand, which he uses to drive souls down to Hell, either to keep them there or to dismiss them, as he thinks fit. The ancients have him in a chariot drawn by four black horses who blow fire out of their nostrils. Orcus or Pluto used to be known as Agesilaus[174] because he drives everyone, and, according to Cyril,[175] he is also known as Adoneus, king of Molossus.[176] Orcus also means Hell itself; Pluto may also be called Summanus, i.e. *summus manium*, "the overseer of the spirits," but according to others Summanus was only the god of the night, and Ovid is doubtful about him in the *Fasti*.[177] Another one of his names was *Allor*, from *alo*, because everything receives nourishment from the earth,[178] yet another *Rursor*, because all things return to him, and finally *Februus*, because the Februa and other purification ceremonies had reference to the life to come in the Underworld, of which he was

---

(Seznec 94). Gafurio, in the work mentioned above, makes the following statement: "the earthly sphere, because motionless, is silent, which is indicated by the triple-headed Cerberus" (Seznec 141), and shows him lying at Apollo's feet. For details about Gafurio's theory of the harmony of the spheres, see Wind 265ff. Curiously, the amateur musician Herbert makes no use of these ideas.

[174]The Leader of the People.

[175]Cyril of Alexandria (c. 373–444), Patriarch of Alexandria from 412, best-known for his controversy with the Nestorians over the divinity of Christ and the function of the Virgin Mary. He was also the implacable enemy of the pagan philosopher Hypatia, whose murder he connived at, if he did not initiate it. See Niceaphorus Collistus, *L'histoire ecclesiastique* (Paris: Antoine le Blanc, 1587), 764–65. This is Nicephorus of Constantinople, c. 1256–c. 1335.

[176]The name Adoneus is similar to Aidoneus, a name interchangeable with Hades or Dis.

[177]Ovid mentions "a temple . . . said to have been dedicated to Summanus, whoever he may be [*quisquis is est*]" (*Fasti* VI, 731). Frazer adds a note on this line that Summanus was "a sort of Jupiter, god of the nightly sky . . . a hurler of thunderbolts" (376 n.*a*). Modern scholars, unlike Herbert, think that comparing him to Hades is "fanciful" (*OCD* 867), but Herbert also used Festus Avienus as a source, who specifically says that Summanus used thunderbolts. Furthermore his name means "he who lives in high places" (Herbert's derivation is incorrect), another reason to support Frazer's idea.

[178]It was sometimes held that the "nourishment" which came froPluto was spiritual. In Plato's *Cratylus* he is described as a god of supreme intelligence, and Plutarch extended this role to picture the terrible Hades as "a benign sovereign delighting his subjects with supercelestial discourse" (Wind 280). Renaissance writers such as Pico and Pierino Valeriano, both cited by Herbert, saw Hades also as a god of secret counsels and hidden things.

god.[179] There was a temple of Orcus in the tenth district of Rome; Summanus had one in the eighth and another in the sixth, which, according to Varro, Titus Tatius dedicated.

Parcae and Furies

The Parcae (Destinies) and Furies were thought of as the ministers of Pluto. Of the former I shall speak later. I shall here discuss the Furies briefly: their names were Alecto, Tisiphone, and Megaera, and some add a fourth, Lissa. The real Furies are within us, such as inordinate desire, anger, and lust. Cicero calls them "mental distress" instead of Furies. As ministers of Pluto, they sometimes left Hell to punish mortals, and they were worshipped like the *dii Averrunci*,[180] so that they might not inflict harm and so that they could deflect impending misfortune. Pausanias says that it was for this reason that the Greeks sacrificed to them.

The Furies, like other deities, had rites and altars. Cicero says that they saw and punished all wickedness.[181] The Sicyonians[182] offered newly-hatched eggs to them, I believe, under the name of *Eumenides*, which means "the mild ones." They used to offer wine mixed with honey, and wreaths of flowers as well. The Eumenides had shrines in both Achaia and Athens, so Cicero tells us;[183] they brandished torches and had grey hair in which snakes were entwined. They were not only at Pluto's beck and call, but Jupiter, Juno and Hecate used them together with the rest of the infernal attendants such as war, hunger and disease, or any other disasters to be inflicted on the human race.

---

[179]The words *februus* and *februa* refer to "anything used in a ceremony of purification" (*OCD* 359), and there is no particular association with Pluto, neither are the Februa (held on 15 February) connected with that god, February being held by the Romans as the "cleaning month."

[180]Literally, "the turning-away gods." There was also a minor god, Averruncus, whose function was to avert evil.

[181]"They must be goddesses too . . . no doubt as observers of human conduct and the avengers of crime and evil-doing" (Cicero, *NG* 212).

[182]They lived in Sicyon, a town near Corinth famous for its art and culture.

[183]I am not sure whether Herbert is correcting Cicero's speaker (Cotta) here, but the text reads "and they have a shrine at Athens and at Rome too, I believe, in the grove which is named after them" (*NG* 212). McGregor's note points out that Cotta is confusing the phrase *lucus Furinale* as "the grove of the Furies," when in fact it refers to the grove of the goddess Furina, who was not at all baleful. She was a river-deity who had a sacred grove on the Janiculum hill. See also Herbert's discussion of the Harpies.

The Harpies

Like the Furies, but with the faces of young girls, they were sent from Hell
to punish the wicked. There are descriptions of them in Ovid, Vergil, and
Statius, but I will not insert them here. The Lamiae and Styges, and some
think also the Sphynges, belong to the same group.[184] Cicero mentions a
goddess Furinna and her sacred grove in Rome. I will not elaborate on all of
these because ancient religion was so mixed with fiction that it is impossible
to tell what was invented by priests or poets.

Janus

I shall finish my list of gods with Janus, whom some authorities call the first
of the *dii selecti*, but the subsequent offspring of the gods made it preferable
that I begin with Jupiter.

Janus was a very ancient king of Latium, the son of Caelum and Hecate,
and he was elevated to divine honour through his merit. Some people think
that he was the same as Ogyges[185] or even Noah; others believe that he was
Japhet, Noah's son, or Javan.[186] We are told that he hospitably entertained
Saturn during the latter's exile, and that he was the first to instruct humans
in agriculture, by which they came to live in a more orderly fashion and
learned to mint money for trade and commerce. Janus was said to have
been the first to erect altars and to establish religious rites and ceremonies,
which is why he is mentioned at the beginning of every sacrifice; corn and
wine are offered to him, and he is invoked as "Father." He invented folding
doors, locks and keys for the security of houses; a door is called *ianua* from

---

[184] A Lamia was a rather unpleasant spirit whose function was to steal babies from
their cradles. Originally there was only one, Lamia, the daughter of Belus and Libya.
Stryges is another name for Harpies, and Sphynges is merely the plural of Sphinx.
Pico della Mirandola noted, interestingly enough, that it was the sphinxes "carved
on the temples of the Egyptians" who "warned that the mystic doctrines be kept
inviolate from the profane multitude by means of riddles" (*Oration on the Dignity
of Man*, 10). Pico's sphinxes and Herbert's obfuscatory priests, it seems, had the
same idea.

[185] Ogygus was said by Pausanias to have been an ancient Theban king (I, 108).
The connexion with Noah was made by Eusebius, who wrote about a deluge which
happened in Ogygus's time.

[186] Javan was the son of Japhet (Genesis 10:2), the reputed founder of some tribes
who lived in north and west regions of the Middle East. "It is generally accepted,"
T.C. Mitchell writes, "that this name [Heb. *yawan*] is to be identified with the Greek
'Iones,' which appears as Iaones . . . in Homer [*Iliad* 13.685]" (*IDB* 2, 735). There
is no connexion, however, of Javan with Janus.

Janus, and the first month is named for him. He blessed the fields and altars
of farmers, and gave each one who was newly starting out a rod made of
whitethorn, known as *ianalis*, as well as *fasces*, "bundles of sticks."

Janus is shown with a rod, a key, and twelve altars for the twelve months
positioned under his feet. Macrobius and Pliny tell us of an image of him
in the Capitol which was so made that with the fingers of its right hand it
expressed 300, and with those of its left, 65, to show the length of the year.
Ricchieri developed a method of counting from this. [Janus] is said to have
invented ships, bridges, and crowns. On some coins he is shown with two
faces on one side, and on the other the stern of a ship; those who show him
thus say that he, like Noah, observed two worlds.[187] Others give him four
faces, with reference to the four seasons, [which is] as he is in his temple.
Cicero says he is called Janus from Eanus,[188] but Vossius derives the name
from the Hebrew *jain*, which means "wine," and says that Italy, which was
once called Oenotria,[189] was called after him also. Janus (or Noah) came
after the flood to Italy, but not, it seems, in an ark. Cyril calls him *Xyluthius*
and adds that the Assyrian word is derived from *ziz* or *zus*, meaning "posts"
or "thresholds," so that this Janus, too, was Noah.[190]

Now, is it possible to produce some light from this ancient darkness, so
that some part resembling truth may come from all of it? We shall attempt to
deal with the important parts. [First], he [Janus] did not preside over earthly

---

[187]Herbert may be thinking of Neoplatonist interpretations here. Pico, for example,
interprets Janus as looking at the material and spiritual worlds simultaneously, the
idea being that both should be equally taken care of (see Wind 200–01).

[188]Cicero says nothing of the sort. He writes: "they [Stoics] held that Janus is
the leader in every sacrifice, and derived the name from *ire* (to go)" (*NG* 150). A
reference by Frazer gives ii, 27.1 in Cicero as a reference, but there is no mention
of Janus there at all. Ovid himself (*Fasti* I, 127) seems to say the same: "praesideo
foribus caeli cum mitibus Horis:/ it, redit officio Iuppiter ipse meo,/ inde vocor
Ianus," but Frazer cautions us that "Ovid has a craze for derivations, which are
mostly wrong" (10 n.*a*).

[189]Oenotria was a name for southwest Italy employed by Latin poets contemporary
with Vergil. The Greek *oinos* does mean "wine."

[190]The name Xyluthius looks rather like a Latinisation of the Greek Xithouthros,
itself a Hellenisation of a Babylonian flood-hero or king's name. It may be found in
an account of the flood by one Berossos (*IBD* 2, 1093), who is Cyril's source. Cyril's
derivation may be from the name of the Babylonian hero Ziusuddu (in Akkadian,
Utnapishtim) in the Sumerian version of the flood-story. Berossos (fl. 290 B.C.) was
a priest of Bel and the author of a history of Babylon, in which Book I deals with
the flood. The likely source for both Vossius and Herbert for this somewhat garbled
myth would have been Athenaeus.

doors only, but those in Heaven as well. According to Homer, when the doors were shut to prayers, he would hold out his hand and support [the prayers], thus obtaining their admission into Heaven.[191] Janus was believed to hold the powers of peace and war, from which came the ceremony of opening and shutting the folding-doors in his temple, and the names Patuleius, Clusius and Clusinus have reference to this.[192] Vergil very elegantly describes, in Book VII of his *Aeneid*, how the temple was opened when war was declared, and Servius tells us that it remained closed only three times, the Romans being so continually at war: in Numa's time, after the First Punic War, and after the Battle of Actium by Augustus, even though there was a civil war at the same time.[193] Consuls were inaugurated in Janus's temple, and began the [consular] year from there; there were two or three Januses in the Forum at Rome, the traditional meeting-place for merchants. Money-lenders could be found there, too, and Ovid mentions someone "who fears returning months, the judge, and Janus." Janus sometimes stood symbolically for the Sun, and universal nature itself. Septimius [Serenus][194] sums up what can be said about Janus in these lines:

Father Janus, Janus the patron, two-faced god,
O wise Originator of things, first amongst gods;
Whose doors move often, whose thresholds are trodden,
To whom the golden secrets of the world are known,
To you the Sacellan Aborigine raises his ancient altar.

I have mentioned some of Janus's names before; others include *Junonius*, because the Kalends come from Juno, *Consevius* from *conserendo*, "sowing," because he taught it to mankind, and *Quirinus*, "powerful in war." Portumnus was also known as Janus because he was a gate-god and held keys in his hand. In the *Salian Hymn* he was known as the God of gods.[195]

---

[191] Homer is unlikely to have made such a statement, for, as Rose points out, "Janus is one of the few deities for whom no Greek equivalent could be found" (166).

[192] Patuleius, more accurately Patulcius, means "the Opener," and both the other epithets mean "the Shutter." Ovid writes, "When the priest offers me a barley-cake/ ... on his sacrificial lips I'm now Patulcius and now Clusius called" (*Fasti* I, 129–30).

[193] Numa Pompilius, who traditionally reigned from 715 to 673 B.C., was known as a peaceful ruler.

[194] Septimius Serenus (2nd century A.D.) was an obscure Roman poet whose works have rural themes. Very little is known about him.

[195] The *Carmen Saliare* is a very obscure and fragmentary piece of a ritual hymn of the Saliar priests, "already unintelligible in Republican times to the priests themselves" (*OCD* 167). The Salii were variously connected with Mars and Quirinus;

The first temple to Janus was built by Romulus, or, according to some, by Numa; another that Duilius built after the First Punic War was restored by Tiberius. A third one in rectangular form, very grand indeed, was dedicated by Augustus. Horatius built a temple to Janus Curiatius to commememorate the famous fight in which he killed Curiatius. We might also mention [the temple of] Janus *Septimanius*, but it is so obscure that I cannot say anything certain about it. Procopius says that Janus had a chapel made of bronze in the middle of the Forum, near the Capitol, and Varro says that there were forts sacred to Janus all over the city. About Janus *Medius*, you may consult Brodeau,[196] the books of the Magi, or Pliny.

Fauns, Sylvans, Satyrs, and Pan

As we have now examined the nobles and councillors in this celestial republic of the pagans, I will now look at the "commons," who are not dissimilar to our own. Ovid, first invoking the higher class of gods, then speaks of "You common gods, Lares, Fauns, and Satyrs/ Rivers, Nymphs and demigods." Vergil makes Faunus, whom Aurelius Victor[197] says is the same as Sylvanus and Pan, the father of the Fauns, Satyrs and other rustic gods. The Fauns, Sylvans and Satyrs were shown almost alike; they had short tails and their lower bodies were rough and hairy. Lucian says that the Satyrs had pointed ears, were bald, and had two horns on their foreheads; Philostratus gives them a human face and goats' feet, which [characteristics] Pliny says made them very quick, extremely oversexed and prone to getting drunk, for which they became the companions of Bacchus. Pausanias reports that when they got old they were known as Sileni. Silenus, who rode a donkey, was Bacchus's companion, and some say his teacher; he had a temple in Elis.

Pan, also a country-god, was both man and goat, and what I said above [about the Satyrs] applies to him, too. He was the Father of the Fauns and Satyrs, and the stories about him, his pipes, and his love for the nymph Echo, I will leave for others to tell. Mystically, Pan stands for universal

---

their name derives from *salire*, "to dance," and the source is Ovid (*Fasti* III, 260). If any reader has read this many notes and wishes to check further, there is a lengthy explanation by Frazer (398–401).

[196] Jean Brodeau (1500–63), was "one of the most distinguished intellectuals of the sixteenth century" (*NBG* 7–8, 467). Amongst his many works we find a commentary on the *Greek Anthology* (1549) and commentaries on Euripides and Martial.

[197] Sextus Aurelius Victor (d. after 390 A.D.) was a soldier, politician and historian. Herbert cites his *Origo gentis Romanae*, which modern scholars have since demonstrated is not by Victor. His only authenticated work now is the *Caesares*, a history of Rome from Augustus to Constantius II (d. 361).

nature,[198] but surely this cannot be the same Pan who, as the poets tell us, was just a rural god. Vergil calls him "Pan, keeper of the sheep," and sudden scares are called "panics;" the ancients used the same word as we do today for the fear that seizes men when they go into battle. This mystical Pan was depicted like Jupiter Lycaeus, part of his body being covered with a goatskin, the rest naked. Justin[199] describes a temple that was built to him at the foot of the Palatine Hill. The Egyptians and the Arcadians worshipped Pan with the same ceremonies used for major gods; a fire was kept burning in his temple and oracles were delivered there by the nymph Erato. The Athenians believed that he often appeared to help them in war, making their enemies panic, and they built him a temple in the Parthenian woods. They thought that he was responsible for apparations and strange sounds.

Faunus, also known as Pan, had many names:[200] *Inuus* or *Incubus* because he had sex with animals; *Aegipan*, because he was half-goat, *Ephialtes*, *Fatuus* and *Fatuelis*. More on this can be found in Schott's annotations on Dionysius [of Halicarnassus]. For other interpretations, see Boccaccio and other mythographers, and about his sacred pine, see Emperor Constantine VII in his *Geoponica*.[201]

---

[198]Pan, whose name means "all," is the god who unites all opposites and dichotomies in himself or the universe. He is often linked with Proteus (the Old Man of the Sea), who can transform himself into anything and who symbolises human mutability.

[199]Marcus Junianus Justinus (3rd century A.D.) wrote the *Historiae Philippicae*, an epitome of Pompeius Trogus.

[200]The names of Pan:

Inuus: from *inire*, "to go in." Livy mentions a god Inuus who was worshipped by the Luperci, and links him with Pan Lycaeus (38), as did the Greeks (Frazer, in Ovid 392).

Faunus: in his own right, Faunus was the god of cattle fecundity. Ovid, together with many others, identifies him with Pan (*Fasti* II, 268).

Incubus: more accurately, Incubo, a deity associated with nightmares. His name means "he who lies upon."

Ephialtes: in his own right, another nightmare deity (Rose 57).

Fatuus and Fatuelis: both names mean "the Speaker" and refer to strange sounds heard in woods and forests.

[201]Constantine VII Porphyrogenitus (905–59) was Byzantine emperor from 912 to 959. Retiring and learned, he compiled and wrote several encyclopaedic works, including the *Geoponica*, based on a treatise written by Cassianus Bassus in the 6th century A.D. His *Hippiatrica*, a work on horses, was printed in 1530, and *De virtutibus et vitiis*, a kind of dictionary of virtue and vice, was printed in Paris in 1634.

Other Minor Deities

There were other rural deities, too; for example Pales,[202] to whom the Palilia or Parilia were dedicated, and Flora, to whom the Florilia were consecrated. In the latter, women, particularly prostitutes, fought like gladiators, ran, and danced stark naked. There was Pomona, the goddess of fruit, and Vortumnus,[203] supposed to preside over contracts and whose festivals were known as Vortumnalia. Some people thought he governed men's minds, and even the year itself, and that he assumed various shapes according to the seasons, for which see Propertius. He had a statue in the Tuscan Street. There were the protective deities Tutanus[204] and Tutelina,[205] and those who presided over grain: Seia, goddess of sowers, Nodotus, Volutina, Patelena, Segesta, Hostilina, Lacturtia, Lactens, Matuta and Runtina.[206] They worshipped Frutesca, who guarded fruit; Spinensis, who warded off thorns;

---

[202]Pales: a bisexual deity, [s]he was responsible for the well-being of flocks and herds. Ovid gives a detailed account of Pales's rites and festivals (the Parilia) in the *Fasti* (IV, 721ff). The Parilia took place on April 21. Ovid, Vergil, Tibullus, and Festus Avienus are for the female version; Varro, Arnobius, and Martianus Capella are for the male (see Frazer in Ovid, 411–13).

[203] Flora: see note 86 above.

Pomona: wooed and won by Vertumnus, a goddess associated with fruit, especially apples.

Vertumnus: originally an Etruscan deity from Volsinii. Frazer tells us that his reputation as shape-changer was derived from the mistaken etymology of his name (from *vertere*, "to turn"), and that the mistake originated with Propertius, whom Ovid is following here.

[204]Tutanus: identified with Rediculus (!), an unknown "power" that made Hannibal go back from raising the seige of Capua (*OCD* 756). He had a shrine near Porta Capena. Herbert may be confusing him with Tutelina, who oversaw the safe storage of grain (Augustine, *City of God* 144).

[205]She presided over the corn while it was still underground. She and Segesta had a statue in the Circus Maximus. Herbert's source is given as Pliny, *Natural History* 18.8.

[206] Seia: presided over the corn whilst it was underground (Augustine 144).

Segesta: after Seia had finished her work this goddess took over "as soon as the shoots came above the ground and began to form the grain [*seges*]" (144). Augustine calls her Segetia.

Nodotus: "looked after the nodes and joints on the [corn] stalks" (144).

Volutina: "saw to the envelopes [*involumenta*] of the follicles" (144).

Patelena: mentioned by Arnobius (*Adversus gentium* IV, 7) and by Augustine, who says that she presided over the time "when the follicles opened [*patescunt*]" (144).

Robigus, who protected corn from mildew;[207] Fulgora, who protected people from lightning; and Populonia, goddess of population. The bakers venerated great adoration to Pilumnus, who invented baking,[208] and Picumnus and Stercutius, who taught people how to manure the ground. We have Bubona, Hippona and Mellona, who protect cattle, horses, and bees; we might add Iugatinus, the god of mountain-tops, Collina and Vallina, goddesses of hills and valleys. Rusina managed country life, and Terminus, consecrated either by Tatius or Numa, was worshipped as the preserver of boundaries. When King Tarquin wanted to pull down temples of other gods so that he could build a very spacious one to Jupiter, it is amusingly reported by Dionysius, Livy, Ovid and St. Augustine, amongst others, that Terminus and Iuventus[209] would not allow it!

This is enough about rustic deities. Amongst many others, who cannot exactly be classified, we find Fortuna, who will be considered here as she has a cult amonst the Romans.

Fortuna

Fortuna has many surnames, and splendid temples were built to her, especially by Servius Tullus, who established [temples] to Fortuna *Primigenia*, *Obsequens*, *Privata*, *Viscosa*, *Parva*, *Macula*, *Barbata* (of whom he had

---

Hostilina: Augustine states that "when the crops were evenly eared, then came the turn of the goddess Hostilina [the old word for "make even" was *hostire*]" (144). She is not mentioned elsewhere.

Lacturtia and Lactens: "sucking milk," these deities are concerned with mother's milk. Augustine also mentions a god Lacturnus, who was there "when the crops became milky" (144).

[Mater] Matuta: goddess of mothers, whose June festival was known as the Matralia. Often identified with Ino, the mother of Melikertes, although this is incorrect (see Ovid, *Fasti* VI, 545). Her temple in Rome is now the Church of Sta. Maria Egiziaca.

Runtina: probably a misprint for Runcina, whom Augustine says presided over the time "when crops were plucked up [*runcantur*]" (144).

[207]Robigus: also known as Robigo, another bisexual deity who personified mildew. [S]he even had a festival, the Robigalia (April 25) at which sacrifices were offered and games held. [S]he is mentioned by Servius, Festus Avienus, Augustine, Varro, Columella, Lactantius and Tertullian, to name only authors who are referred to by Herbert.

[208]Pilumnus: originally the god of pestles, but also invoked when babies were delivered so that he could drive Silvanus away (*OCD* 692).

[209] Terminus: god of boundaries. His story is told by Ovid (*Fasti* II, 61, 64).
Iuventus: the genius of Youth.

a temple in the palace grounds), *Bona Spes*, *Averrunca*, *Blanda*, *Plebeia*, *Convertenta*, and *Virgo*. Ancus Marcius dedicated a temple to Fortuna *Virili*, and there was also one to Fortuna *Muliebris*, where it was said that Fortune was placed for priests and old women. Q. Fulvius Flaccus erected a most magnificent temple to Fortuna *Equestri*; the goddess Fors Fortuna was honoured by those who wished to live without working, and a notable temple to her was built by Servius Tullius.[210] Q. [Lutatius] Catulus dedicated a temple to Fortune of the Present Day. Pliny tells us that the Emperor Nero erected one in Cappadocia to Fortuna *Seia*, built of hard, white, translucent marble, which also had yellowish-brown veins cut into it, from which it was known as *Phengites*; from this [marble] Servius Tullius had built a temple to Fortuna *Seia*, the golden house complex. It was closed twice daily by folding doors, on which account during the day there was no light enclosed there which did not pass through a window-pane. There was a shrine to Fortuna

---

[210]These surnames need some explanation:

Primigenia: "original" Fortune, hence "of the first-born."

Obsequens: compliant or favourable Fortune.

Privata: private or personal Fortune.

Viscosa: inmost Fortune (from *viscus*, "entrails").

Parva: "small" Fortune, perhaps that of children or the poor.

Mascula: courageous Fortune.

Barbata: bearded Fortune. Augustine has some rude things to say about this one (150).

Bona Spei: the Fortune of good hope.

Averrunca: "turning-away" Fortune.

Blanda: literally "caressing" Fortune.

Convertens: see Averrunca.

Muliebris: "if Fortuna speaks," Augustine states, "then it would have been better to have the Fortune of Men [Fortuna Virili] speaking, not the Fortune of Women, for then it would not be suspected that this impressive miracle was a piece of female gossip" (158).

Equestris: the Fortune who protected knights. In the Renaissance this one became associated with "the *immoderatus impetus* of the Platonic horse" (Wind 147 n.24). Cartari calls her *Fortuna a cavallo*, constantly galloping away and needing to be caught.

Fors: chance or luck. Fors Fortuna is mentioned frequently by Livy, and Ovid describes the festival of Fors Fortuna (*Fasti* VI, 773).

Dubia: doubtful or wavering Fortune.

Regia: royal Fortune, whose temple was at Praeneste. "Throughout his reign, Domitian had made a practice of commending each new year to the Goddess Fortune at Praeneste" (Suetonius 310).

Mammosa: big-breasted Fortune.

Mammosa at the head of the Via Nova, and in the neighbourhood another to Fortuna *Dubia*. Domitian built a temple to Fortuna *Reducis*, and there was an altar also consecrated to the return of Augustus, known as Fortuna *Regia*, together with a temple of Hera, one at Praeneste torgether with a temple of Hercules, and of Fortuna *Prospera* together with *Fides*, of which we may mention that it had a very appropriate dedication: where faith was not served, good fortune could not be expected for anyone. Whether they concealed this goddess for these reasons, or lost sight of her, it was believed that she exerted her strength. Amongst the Romans especially there was a cult [of Fortune], but no mention of it is made in Homer, as Sponde[211] correctly observes, and the cult is not found amongst the Greeks or in the East, unless in a certain way Venus Urania supplies the need; on both sides it was believed that happiness was granted to humanity from above. So much for Fortuna.

In the meantime for rustic gods, urban gods, or the rest of the hotchpotch, consider Cloacina, Fugia, Rediculus or Ridiculus, and Minutius; for hostile deities, consider Pavor, Pallor, Febris, Tempestas; for speaking gods, there is always Aius Locutius and others invented by the priests; there are Nuptiales, Parturientes, and Infantes. I say that all these gods and goddesses or Indigitamenta may be freely left to our scholars, for we have already spent much time on the major deities, and more on the inferior ones would indeed be tedious.[212]

---

[211]Henri de Sponde [Spondanus] (1568–1643), French Protestant scholar who converted to Catholicism and became Bishop of Pamiers. Amongst his many works Herbert may have found some use in *Annales sacri a mundi creatione ad eiusdem redemptionem* (1637) and his continuation of Baronius, *Annalium Baronii continuatio ab anno 1127 ad ann. 1622* (1639).

[212]The absolute last list of obscure deities in this chapter:

Fugia: goddess of flight and exile.

Minutius: the god who makes things get smaller.

Pavor: god of trembling.

Pallor: god of pallor.

Febris: goddess of fever. Rome boasted three temples to her.

Tempestas: god of bad weather.

Aius Locutius: a deified disembodied voice which warned the Romans about the impending arrival of the Gauls, who were defeated at the Battle of the Allia. What it subsequently said I do not know.

Nuptiales: marriage-deities.

Parturientes: deities of birth-pains and labour.

XIII

The Supreme God

As I have explained the universally-held constitution of the members of the celestial kingdom according to paganism, it remains for us now to discuss the Head which presided over them, and then at last to speak about what principles allow us to ascend to Heaven and to be admitted. It is clear beyond all dispute that this can only be the Supreme God who is, has been, and will be through all eternity. Although as I shall show the pagans argued about the attributes of God, I maintain that neither educated nor ignorant people ever questioned that there was always, and is now, one Supreme God. What was controversial was whether God's eternity was self-generated, so that the world co-existed with him or whether God first came in order, dignity, and power yet not in time, and so made and formed matter in the way we understand it now. Or did God first create matter itself, and out of it make the world?

Those people who think of God as an Eternal Principle, but at the same time deny that he made the world, are being over-simplistic; no-one could be so stupid as to imagine that the world was produced without a cause (any cause at all) or could hope to find a cause more appropriate than the Supreme God himself. There is a second opinion, that God did not only form the world out of chaos but is continually doing so, ridiculously implying that this lump of matter we call the world is co-eternal [with God], a confusion of cause and effect.[1]

There were many amongst the ancients who held a third opinion, or something like it, that the world was created in time. Patrizi supplies a long list of them; from the time of Ocellus, and Aristotle after him, nobody asserted that the world was eternal (if Patrizi is correct), but that it was still being made and shaped. This belief had many adherents, because only

---

[1] This was, essentially, the view of Herbert's contemporary (and friendly critic), Descartes. The argument claims that "it does not follow from the fact that I existed a little while ago that I must exist now, unless there is some cause which creates me afresh at this moment — that is, which preserves me." Descartes asserts that this proposition can be easily known through our reason; after all, "it is quite clear to anyone who attentively considers the nature of time that the same power and action are needed to preserve . . . as would be required to create all things anew" (Descartes, "Third Meditation," *Philosophical Writings* II, 33).

the Jews and Christians believed that the world had been made in six days, and even amongst them there are many who interpret the entire story of the creation as an allegory. Cicero, for example, is quite clear about who made the world; he says "God made and formed the world," and again, in *The Nature of the Gods*, he writes "the world was made in the beginning for the gods and for men."[2] We cannot infer from these phrases, however, whether matter was made first and then the world. See Proclus or John of Garland on this subject; the latter discusses it beautifully in his book *On the Eternity of the World*, and he presents all that can be said on both sides. It is not certain whether or not Proclus followed Plato; as Ficino tells us in his edition of the Timaeus:

> If you consult the interpretations of Severus Atticus,[3] Plutarch, and many others whom Proclus mentions, you would conclude that Plato thought the world was not eternal. However, if you look at Crantor,[4] Plotinus, Porphyry, Iamblichus, Proclus himself, and many others, you would think he thought the opposite, that it was eternal, continually coming from God, whom, if we assume existed before the beginning of time, we must conclude that the world was not made. However, if it proceeds continually from God, it is being produced daily, and depends on God as much as it would if it had received its origin at once from him.

Plato (or, as some say, Pythagoras, whom Plato follows in the *Timaeus*) argues very clearly that sense-objects have a beginning, and since these are objects in the world, it follows that the world itself must have had its origin from God. Some Epicureans say that the world is made up entirely of atoms and that all visible objects derive from the chance configuration of them,[5]

---

[2]This is the gist of Balbus's position in Book II of *The Nature of the Gods*. However, it is not necessarily that of Cicero, who claims merely to be stating the non-Stoic view of the relationship between God, man, and the universe.

[3]The Severus Atticus mentioned by Ficino is obscure, but may be Sulpicius Severus (c. 350–421), lawyer, theologian and monk. He wrote a *Chronica* which went from the Creation to his own times.

[4]Crantor (fl. 300 B.C.) was a philosopher and a pupil of Xenocrates. He did write commentaries, but unlike many of his contemporaries Crantor concentrated on practical philosophy, psychology, and consolation. His work on the latter was cited by Diogenes Laertius, Cicero, Plutarch and Apollonius.

[5]Cf. Epicurus, "Each world was formed by being separated from its own whirling mass, and will be dissolved again." The number of worlds so formed, he claims, is infinite, and consists of "an earth and heavenly bodies associated with it" (Epicurus, "Letter to Herodotus," *Letters, Principal Doctrines, and Vatican Sayings*, 28). Of the atoms themselves, Epicurus notes that they are "infinite" and that they make up "sensible objects" (10).

so that God could not be involved; for example, Lucretius writes: "By no means are the origins of nature divine, / The nature of the world is such that sin is already provided."[6] Other Epicureans attribute everything to chance or fortune, but if that were true I cannot understand how there could be any species or kinds of things, let alone a hierarchy of any kind amongst them. If you look at a watch (and you have not lost your wits), which shows the time exactly for 24 hours, you will conclude that it is the product of skill and work. So, how much more would someone who contemplates the vast machine of this world, which so regularly goes through its motions not just for 24 hours, but for so many ages, claim that it came from an all-wise and all-powerful Author? Those who advance this theory have used a great deal of ingenuity and skill to support the absurdity that reason and order were not present in things as well as in words, or that [things] were endowed with an intellectual faculty but that chance should rule everything else. In several places Cicero refutes this error.

These opinions about the origin of the world circulated only amongst the philosophers, and they went beyond the understanding of common people. The latter were happy in knowing that everything had been organised from the beginning of time so that they could live comfortably here if they worked hard enough. They cared about nothing else, unless they were thinking that some internal Force or Deity operating in the world might have the power to take either their blessings from them, or them from their blessings. They readily acknowledged that this latent power had started everything, but they did not know why, and all their seekings and attempts to get a clearer knowledge of it proved unsuccessful. They could discover nothing more than the fact that in all ages everything derived from the Supreme Principle, on whose pleasure it depended whether things remained as they always had been, or continued in the same way.

Presently they decided that this God should be requested to divert evil from them, or to look favourably on them, and that they should therefore pay respect to his chief ministers. When they meditated on these matters, they either invented a kind of religious worship based on notions that they already had of God or derived from some internal impulse, or they received it from the priests. Everyone claimed that his own God was the Best and Greatest, putting Best before Greatest because they thought it inconsistent for a God who was not the Best to be the Greatest, and because God's goodness was necessarily antecedent to his power.

---

[6] A more characteristic passage, expressing the same belief, suggests that "all life is a struggle in the dark. As children in blank darkness tremble and start at everything, so we in broad daylight are oppressed at times by fears as baseless" (Lucretius, II, 61).

Now that God had been acknowledged Best and Greatest, they began to wonder whether he could have other attributes; they did allow him others, but only such as were derivative from those [he already possessed]. If we understand these attributes which all the [theological] schools have added, they are either contained in the original [attributes] or are only those which the human mind can confidently assert. So if we call God "just," "merciful," or "wise,""omnipotent" or "infinite," we will find [these attributes] all together in the first one [Best], or included in both. As Best, God provided for everything, which means that in so doing he must be just, merciful and generous; as Greatest, nothing is impossible for him, nor can he be limited; as both Best and Greatest he is the wisest and most prudent maker of all things, their preserver and their governor. He justly rewards the virtuous and punishes the wicked. These attributes have been given to God throughout the ages, and will continue through eternity, because they contain all that can be known of the Supreme God through the use of reason.

Now, I have to admit that God's condemnation of some to eternal damnation at his mere pleasure, and for his honour or glory, is not consistent with these attributes. But it is impious to think of the Supreme God in this way; his counsels are secret, and closed to us, so that it is impossible for mortals to comprehend them. It will have to be sufficient for us that we be sure that he cannot and will not depart from his attributes of Best and Greatest. Let me try and make this a little clearer. Imagine a man of great natural intelligence who has received no information from tradition, revelation and so forth. I think that he would have the same thoughts about the world after he has carefully observed it as he would if he saw a strange musical instrument which was not put together by blind chance, or which had such a complexity of parts that it was self-productive. When he hears a skilled musician play it, he will admire both the ingenuity of its maker and the great art of the master who plays it so beautifully; he will conclude that everything was put together for this end. He will not likely conclude that there are two makers, but that both the instrument and the music originated from the same source.

We could object that because there are so many things in the universe, and so many causes of them, that there must necessarily be a plurality of gods, because there is too much for one to do, or because it would be impossible for him to do so many different things. Therefore the world could not have been made so perfect and complete, but would be very defective. To this I answer: the worse the instrument is, the more skill the player needs to produce beautiful melodies with out-of-tune or poor quality strings. Yet the "instrument" in question was not made in a hurry, but with careful forethought. In short, the more diversity there is in the nature of things, or even contradiction and contention, the sooner we need recourse to a Supreme

God or Deity who regulates things and keeps them in working order. It is quite rational to suppose that some less-important matters might be the result of chance or randomness, but it is ridiculous to think the same of the world, which is so huge, beautiful and sublime, and so regularly ordered in all its parts, that we can neither see nor imagine anything that could compare with it. Even if one of the elements could be removed from its proper place for one day, we could hardly imagine what a commotion and a disturbance the whole fabric of the universe would undergo.[7] The aversion that the [fabric of the universe] has to a vacuum is a sufficient demonstration.[8]

Perhaps it might be said that there is no particular order in the universe: the stars are not placed in any mathematical order, and the elements seem jumbled and mixed up together. I answer, if someone who knows nothing about music should see any book with musical notation, he would think it meant nothing. Yet if he were to hear the harmony that can be made [from it], he would soon change his opinion and conclude that there is a great deal of skill and study in composition. And it is the same with the stars and elements; although parts of the world seem confused and disorderly, when we consider the exact constancy that goes along with all the revolutions, periods and returns, we can agree with Pliny, who says that harmonious reason only makes nature seem more consistent. What appeared confused and disorderly will be found to have been the product of insufficient wisdom and judgment. Proportion, for us, is either arithmetical, geometrical or harmonic, but that which God uses far transcends these; it

---

[7]Compare Donne, "Moving of th'earth brings harms and fears,/ Men reckon what it did and meant,/ But trepidation of the spheres,/ Though greater far, is innocent" ("A Valediction: Forbidding Mourning," Donne 84).

[8]A nice example of *petitio principii*; Herbert is doing here what he always accuses the priests of doing, namely resorting to mysticism and obfuscation. We have to assume that God is not self-contradictory, but the argument from analogy which follows is not at all convincing. Why would someone "of great intelligence" *necessarily* make that conclusion? Could he not conclude that there was both a composer and a performer who may well have originated "from the same source," but protest that we were not talking about the origin of the participants, but of the melody. Of course, Herbert may be arguing here that the very conception of the divine, however it is conceived, is enough, that a created thing could not ever represent the infinite, but for any conception or representation to exist at all, it must be of something, therefore the divine exists. This was the view of Nicolas Malebranche (1638–1715), but whether we have a presaging of Malebranche or not is a moot point. However, see Malebranche, *The Search after Truth*, T.M. Lennon and P.J. Olscamp, tr. (Columbus: Ohio University Press, 1980), 237. What seems missing in the analogy is the person who actually made the instrument.

exceeds not only our senses, but also our understanding. Therefore, what to us may seem lacking in proportion, when compared to other things which are not apprehendable by the senses but which are known to God, will appear as being established with the greatest of symmetry and proportion.[9]

A pagan might say that he cannot see himself under obligation to an obscure and unknowable deity to the extent of offending or neglecting those beneficent and eternal deities, the Stars and Heaven. If there were any such God, his goodness would surely not think it evil that a human being should give thanks to those superior powers which are his great benefactors, or pay that worship which is justly due to such great causes. What is more, this would not get in the way of the worship of a transcendent or pre-eminent deity whenever the latter showed himself willing to appear, or to shower benefits upon the human race. People who argue this way are like a person who says that only the instrument makes the music, paying no attention to the player who tuned it and made it play so beautifully. We might compare the world to the instrument, and the stars shining in the sky to the strings; if no-one touched the strings and made the sharps and flats sound in proportion, thereby producing a melody, Nature would either be completely dumb, or her voice would be awful. The instrument itself would be useless, as it would have no prior cause to make agreeable and pleasant sounds. Therefore chief honour and praise should be paid to God; it is the highest indignity imaginable to offer any sort of inferior praise to either the Stars or to Heaven which does not end directly with the advancement of the Best and Greatest God's glory.

A god who so evidently and continually shows himself in all his works cannot be said to be hidden or obscure; indeed he demonstrates through the tiniest animals and insects that he is the greatest Maker. Here I shall not only be attacked by pagans but also by some sects amongst us. If the Best and Greatest God is the primary cause of everything, why does he allow such

---

[9]Herbert gives a version of the argument from design because he thinks that it is the only valid proof of God's existence and participation that allows for reasoning to take place. Our reason, so we are told, can see the design, and therefore posits a designer. But, as Herbert notes, we might object that it does not necessarily point to there being only one Designer, or whether it was the only attempt to make a world, or whether making the world bears any relation to the divinity or omnipotence of the Designer. Herbert does not agree with Descartes about continual creation, and none of this actually proves God's benevolence. Herbert does not like to face the fact that both Designer and design must exist in time, which in effect means that the Designer must be shown to have existed antecedently to the instant at which he produced the design. A self-creating Designer, of course, would not do.

terrible calamities as famine, plague, and war to infect the world? Surely the Best and Greatest God cannot be the Author of these dreadful devastations?

It will be impossible to understand how not only different but contrary effects should come from the same cause without establishing the two principles of good and evil. [The pagans] thought both principles worthy of adoration, [praying to] the one to be kind and benign, the other not to hurt them. Plutarch tells us that the Egyptians called the evil principle Typhon[10] and the Persians, especially the Magi, know him as Ahriman; others call him Vejupiter, and some Indians [in South America], the Tapujans, believe in this principle today. Yet, according to this notion, they do not think that the evil principle has equal power with the Supreme God, but is inferior, as we say that darkness is inferior to light. Thus the principle of good is God, but that of evil is not, as Pliny notes. The Persians had a tradition that the principle of good, which they called Ormuzd, would subdue and utterly destroy the evil Ahriman.[11] Philosophers seem to agree that evil is not the highest power. The pagans thought that the principle of evil could only be appeased with blood, for which see Labeo, Porphyry, Augustine and others, but they adored the good principle with praises, honours and other rites which encouraged mirth and happiness. This Persian notion of a principle of evil appeared in Christian times; St. Augustine says that the pagans got it from Marcus Cerdon[12] and Apelles,[13] but others, including Vossius, say that St. Paul was hinting at it in 2 Corinthians 4:4, when he says "The God of this world hath blinded the eyes of the faithful." Christians themselves claim that Adam, after the Fall, became the principle of evil on earth, and that all sin originated from him, mankind being infected with his guilt. But if they

---

[10]This is the Egyptian god Set. As the monster Typhon in Greek myth and the personification of utter mayhem and disorder, he was defeated in battle by Zeus.

[11]These are the principles of good and evil in the Zoroastrian religion; as far as it goes, Herbert's information is accurate. Zoroaster himself claimed to have been sent by Ormuzd as a prophet, and he founded the sect of the Magi. Ormuzd created man with free will, but the conflict between Ormuzd (Ahura-Mazda) and Ahriman centres in man. Zoroastrians believe in an afterlife and in rewards and punishments after death.

[12][Marcus] Cerdon (c. 100 A.D.) was a Christian dissident philosopher, attacked for heresy by Epiphanius, Irenaeus and Augustine. All we know about him comes from Irenaeus; Cerdon believed "the God whom Moses and the Prophets preached is not the Father of Jesus Christ; the one is knowable, the other not, the one merely just, the other good" (*Adversus haereses* I. 27.1 in Jonas 136).

[13]Apelles (c. 110–90) was a Gnostic and a disciple of Marcion. He is mentioned by Augustine as being a follower of the [false] prophetess Philumena, who performed miracles.

made the Devil himself, the Cacodemons, and all his infernal followers, who tempt and entrap us in this age, the cause of all evils, it would still be a weak argument.

In ancient times many thought there were two principles, one good, the other evil, that the influence of some stars was good, that of others was bad, that some daemons were friendly, others hostile to man. To explain this: there are two kinds of evil, that of crime and that of punishment. The evil of punishment (famine, plague, war) are the just, though obscure, judgments of God. When any of these happen to good people, the Best and Greatest God gives them a better life; when he sends them amongst the impious or wicked, it is vengeance. Death, then, is a reward for one, a punishment for the other. As for the evil of crime, this comes solely from free will, implanted in everyone from birth, and which God has given us as the greatest blessing. It distinguishes us from the animals more than even reason does, but it is doubtful and unstable, and sometimes inclines to either side, or is overpowered and so slides into evil. Still, free will is a divine blessing, and of such great importance that we cannot do any good without it, and it cannot be proved that we did so unless we had the power to act against it. The source of evil is that spontaneous inclination and swerving of the soul towards what is wicked and depraved, without restraint or compulsion.

As these things are so obviously true, there is no reason for establishing a principle of evil, or for venerating it. Evil, whether it is that of crime, flowing out of our own vicious inclinations, or that of punishment, the consequence of the former comes from ourselves. To worship and adore it is to act like schoolboys guilty of something and kissing the cane that beats them. When people suffer God's just judgment, they should submit to it with thankfulness, as it is either a correction or a reward; they should hope thereby to avoid heavier punishments, but it is not my purpose here to enlarge on this now.

I shall leave it to the theologians to deal with the principle of evil and its derivation from the Fall. It is not very evident to ordinary understanding how the soul of Adam could have been made in the image of God if he were altogether ignorant of good and evil before his fall, or how he had committed so terrible a crime, fatal to himself and all his posterity, by eating the fruit of the tree that gave him such knowledge. If, before he had eaten it, he had been ignorant of good and evil, how could he understand that it was forbidden, and think it just and equitable that he should by this means commit such a dreadful crime by which his innocent posterity should suffer eternal punishments, even though they were not involved in anything? And why, after so many ages, could nothing less than human sacrifice appease

God? Let the theologians explain these questions so that they may be clearly understood, and set out so that lay people may understand them.

I assert nothing here except that the principle of evil cannot be derived from Adam. All our sins and transgressions are voluntary acts, and divine goodness never necessarily determined any human being to do any evil which might be avoided. As for the demons, and the Devil himself, he ought not to be seen as so evil; he is only a public hangman and executioner, who cannot be blamed for carrying out God's just judgments. In their own natures, none of these can be seen as principles of evil. Ancient philosophers, according to the number and influence of the stars, thought that demons were either benevolent or malicious, and they gave them the power of being able to affect bodily things.[14] As Ficino says, "they love good men, but they hate the wicked," and so they are more concerned in earthly matters, especially in human affairs. But they, too, have their affections, and are governed by free will just as we are, which is apparently why pagan religions instituted rites and sacrifices to propitiate them. Now if these demons had simply been essentially evil in themselves, the pagans would hardly have imagined that any worship or veneration could have influenced them. They did not deny that there were two sorts of demons, some inclined to good, others to evil; but this could not have been the case, because they could decide any way they wanted. Ibn Sina[15] tries to prove that one demon came from another, as man comes from man, or animal from animal. But to pass by those things which are beyond sense-experience; all that can be said is that the principle of evil cannot be inferred from "demons." See also Epiphanius, *Adversus haereses*, and Augustine's writings against Faustus and the Manichaeans. Further information about the principle of evil amongst the pagans may be found in Vossius.

---

[14]Cf. Milton, *Paradise Lost* II, when Beelzebub counsels the devils "to learn / What creatures there inhabit, of what mould,/ Or substance, how endu'd, and what thir Power" (356–58). "Substance" is the important part of man, because that is where he is most open to corruption.

[15]Abu ibn Sina [Avicenna] (980–1037), the eminent Persian physician, philosopher, and commentator on Aristotle. He was "the real creator of a scholastic system in the Islamic world" (Copleston 2, I, 215). For him, God is absolute Goodness, which leads to a tendency to diffuse goodness, therefore God creates. Every attribute of God is necessary, and creation itself is from eternity. Herbert seems to be referring to his doctrine of the ten Intelligences, of which the tenth is known as "giver of forms" (Copleston 218), a kind of pure potentiality which thus has no form and may well be evil. It is also, not surprisingly, the active intellect in man. The *Avicennae operae* were published in Venice (1495–1546).

I am now going to prove that the Supreme God amongst the pagans was the same one that we acknowledge, which is evident from the words of Paul in Romans 1:19, Acts 10, 17, 28 and 29, as Vossius proves by many arguments. The "unknown God" of the Athenians seems to agree with what Paul says about the God of the Jews, and his will and pleasure about Christ in Acts 17:23, "Whom you ignorantly worship, him declare I unto you," and Lucan mentions "the unknown God of the Jews." Epimenides speaks of altars raised to the Unknown God; in his time there were three of them in Athens, called "the nameless altars," and in all likelihood St. Paul saw one of them when he was preaching to the Athenians. For other information on these altars to the Unknown God, you may consult Pausanias, Philostratus and Agelli. The latter writes:

> The altar which Epimenides erected because of the epidemic to the "appropriate God" [deo conveniente] I am sure is not the same as the former [altars to the Unknown God]; it means no more than that Epimenides, not knowing which God to sacrifice to, did this to propitiate all of them.

Indeed, it does seem a little far-fetched to make this god the God of the Jews, but the instances quoted from the Scriptures do suggest that the [Supreme] God of the pagans might be the same as the common God of all. However, it is very plain to me that this "Unknown God" of the Athenians was quite different and that they erected an altar to him only so that no deity whatsoever might be deprived of worship; the Apostle cleverly seized upon the notion to teach them.

I cannot dispute that the pagans, taught by Nature's book, acknowledged and worshipped a Supreme God; as he appears in his works, so they venerate him, and I hold as a certain truth that pagans today, taught in the same way, such as the Indians and others who inhabit this world, do exactly the same and arrive at a conception of the Supreme God. I would sooner doubt that the sun shone in remote parts of the world than that they did not know of God, because he is so conspicuously evident in all things, even in the sphere of the sun itself. I shall not pursue this line of argument any further, because most scholars are of this opinion, including Bullinger.[16]

---

[16][Herbert's marginal note]: *De origine cultus dei* VIII. Heinrich Bullinger (1500–75) succeeded Zwingli as chief pastor of the Old Minster at Zurich in 1531. He wrote a series of social sermons, the *Decades*, which became the required reading of junior clergy in the Church of England, and by 1585 had already been three times translated into English. A friend of the Marian exiles, Bullinger maintained a vast and interesting correspondence with European religious leaders, even co-operating with Ramus in a work about the Last Supper (1570).

The pagans' notions of the Supreme God were rather vague and imperfect because of the wickedness or insanity of priests, who led them astray from knowledge of true principles to lead them to God, greatly influencing them and boasting that only they themselves knew the mysteries of religion, that there was no way but through them to reach God, and that without their help He could never be propitiated. This spread a dark cloud over the minds of the common people; it intercepted the rays of light and shrouded the people in such ignorance that they hardly dared stir or move a foot unless the priest led them by the hand or directed them with his words. I could go on for a long time about this, but many distinguished scholars, especially Platonists, have done so already, and I would just be repeating what they said.

Now we will look at the worship of the Supreme God under his attributes of Best and Greatest. The conclusion is, naturally, to whom else should reverence and adoration be paid other than to the Greatest, and who else deserves more love than the Best? And what worship is more reasonable than that which comes from reverence and love? When these are truly present, nothing else is needed, for when God is worshipped in his might with due reverence, this is justly called the beginning of wisdom; the Supreme God will not be offended by crime and man will attain Heaven through the path of virtue. He will admit that he is unfit for glory and eternal happiness when his soul is contaminated with guilt, and therefore he will be thought unfit and unworthy to be in the company of the Best and Greatest God. When the perfect love of God is established in the human mind, all wickedness and conflict will be overcome, and there will be the hope of and belief in a better life. It is upon these things that the whole of religion rests; however, it is extremely unfortunate that weak-minded superstitions and profane rites or ceremonies were coined in the priestly mint and mixed with the pure gold of religion. Had they remained firmly on the former basis, the pagans would not have wasted so much time.

XIV

An Inquiry into
the Origins of Pagan Religion

I will now attempt an investigation of the value of pagan religion and its first causes, because any religion which was so universally held must have been established for some great and noble end. I have therefore derived these causes from philosophical schools, from legal writings, and from the practices of the priests themselves as they have been handed down to us from history. I compared them, understood them, and redacted them, after which I thought that I should present my own thoughts on the subject rather than simply summarise. If anyone does not like what I have to say, let him publish his own interpretation.

I must lay down one established truth, namely that ancient pagan religion was not as absurd and stupid as it is generally thought to have been. It was accepted for many ages by the most learned philosophers, the greatest lawgivers, and the bravest heroes, as well as being believed by the common people, although in spite of this it was still full of grossly serious errors. After the pagans had established the idea of a Supreme God, as I have mentioned, there sprang up that race of clever priests who, thinking that it was not sufficient to have one God in the universe, decided that it would be in their interest to associate some other [gods] with the Supreme God, although there was no doubt than that the Best and Greatest God should be pre-eminent. But this was not the only purpose they had for introducing these gods; they thought that they could dazzle peoples' minds more easily with a company of gods than with just one, however great he might have been, and more so after they had invented a special mode of worship for each one of them. They also expected to get more profit and larger allowances for themselves from the various rites, ceremonies, and sacred mysteries which they invented and explained rather than from people performing duties of piety and worship. The latter was the true way of worshipping the Supreme God, [by it] their country was safe from enemies, and the citizens all lived together in friendship and peace. Yet there was nothing in this to the particular of private advantage [of the priests], so they mixed the truth with what was probable, possible, or absolutely false,[1] and with such arguments they gained first the confidence of, and then control over, the populace.

"Nothing is more certain" [they said] "and beyond a doubt than that there is a Supreme God, and that he is the First Cause. But this does not prove that he is solitary and alone; surely from the beginning he either found or created some companions either in Heaven or on Earth? And is God capable of no other happiness than self-contemplation throughout all the ages of man, or indeed eternity? Self-contemplation is unworthy in a woman looking in a mirror, so it must be even more unworthy of the Supreme God. We must rationally conclude, then, that God has companions who share his blessed state, and [even] that some people, through the ages, are received into Heaven; everything that deserves praise or merit is not already done, but is still being done daily, and will continue to be done forever. There must be, then, some self-existent Beings, produced by God's eternal decree, either co-eternal with Him or contemporary with the world. These beings, who live in Heaven for ever, may deserve to be known as gods. I do not mean the Sun, Moon, or Stars, which move in Heaven, but whatever else exists in infinite space and enjoys the eternally blessed state amongst the gods. We should, then, worship them as being next to the Supreme God. Another kind of respect is due to consuls, senators, tribunes, quaestors or archons; they will not allow insults or disobedience to go unpunished, and therefore we should try to avoid giving them the least displeasure, which we can do only by paying them the adoration that is their due. It is unlikely that God will be displeased with our doing so, because [all praise] ultimately ends in that of the Supreme God, the author and maker of everything. That is why the lesser gods or secondary deities should be worshipped, even if they were not there eternally, but had a beginning; more so, if they were self-existent and co-eternal with the Supreme God, as many philosophers argue forcefully."

---

[1]Herbert alludes here to those chapters in *De veritate* where the probable is distinguished from the possible, and the possible from the false. "All tradition and history, everything in short that concerns the past, whether it be true or false, good or evil, possesses for us only probability, since it depends on the authority of the narrator" (314). Herbert goes on to note that probability, as defined here, can yield truth when it occurs under "the necessary conditions by which the proper faculties could have been brought into conformity with their objects," that is, on the part of whoever is recording the "probable" event. As for Herbert "probability . . . signifies the past," so "possibility [signifies] the future, and both refer to what is uncertain and unknown" (323). Falsity, he asserts, "is simply that which cannot correctly be described as probability or possibility, but is yet so completely opposed to truth . . . as to imply contradiction of it" (332).

"If this is true, then, they ought to be worshipped, but with less veneration than is paid to the Supreme God. They must have the sole administration of some affairs both in Heaven and on Earth, especially concerning those which are foreign to the nature of the Best and Greatest God, as many things in this world are. But supposing they had created the world, as some think, this creation being seemingly unworthy of the Supreme God, where the inhabitants are disgracefully lacking in everything, where other animals are savage and miserable, where Heaven itself appears extreme and immoderate, and where the best people value nothing above unless it rewards them, nothing below unless it brings some profit or advantage? If this is the case, then these deities, whether they are self-creating, whether they created the world, whether every one of them has his own duties, whether they were created by God and carry out his will and pleasure, or whether they, like human beings, act in the world as they please, should have some adoration paid to them and some rites instituted. How small a matter it is to pay some veneration to them, to make them propitious, for they will immediately give you their favour, or from whom, when they are angry, you will have a real fear of retribution. If you suppose that you can ever worship the Supreme God sufficiently either in himself or in his works, or in whatever exists in the universe, you are entertaining very insulting thoughts of Him."

After the greater part of the human population had swallowed these empty notions and opinions, they made little distinction between what was true, probable, possible or false, but had implicit faith in priestly guidance; by degrees they gave themselves completely up [to the priests]. The maxim of eternal truth, "all deities may be worshipped in the Supreme God," no longer prevailed. Instead, they asked the priests who the gods were, and how they should worship them, because they did not wish to appear ungrateful for all the favours they had received from them and wished the priests to show them how it was done. It was quite obvious that everything good came from Heaven, but from what god, star, power, or influence they did not know, unless they were told, and this gave the priests a fine opportunity to manage them.

"It is very difficult," [they said] "for us to inform you who these gods, that you are so keen to know about, are. They are not only supra-sensory, but above our understanding, too, for they are not governed by the same conditions which govern matter or those objects which we perceive. Neither is it easy to say much about their worship, as nothing certain has yet been revealed to mankind in general. It is universally acknowledged that a Supreme God exists, and that there are inferior deities or daemons as well. It would be very ridiculous to imagine that only Earth was inhabited, and that the vast expanse of Air, Aether and Celestial Bodies, not to mention the immense space above them, had no-one living in them.

Philosophers have divided [the beings who inhabit these spaces] into three groups: the Supercelestial, the Celestial, and the Subcelestial. The first are very remote from us, and they are concerned only with what is necessary to their own nature; they are in harmony with the Supreme God and do not pay much attention to human affairs. They do not spare a moment from their celestial existence to worry about them at all, and there is no reason that they should meddle in the affairs of the world. The Supreme God, from all eternity, has established laws and regulations concerning everything to do with the heavens, the stars, and the nature of things. Some of these laws are, for example, that everything here should be in a constant flux; that whatever begins here will, after an allotted time, pass out of existence, and that in spite of this, things should be concerned with self-preservation; that prosperity should be the result of hard work; and that our consciences should tell us that some things are good, others bad. That the strict worship of God, and moral virtue, are the most important good actions, whilst the important wicked ones are irreligion and vice. That humans might exercise free will, and that through the proper means they would always get what they wanted. If people behaved themselves, they would be rewarded both here and afterwards; if they were evil and vicious, they would be punished. God gave the Celestial Deities the power over these laws and over many others which would take too long to list. A kind of Fate, or Order, should be perceived in the world and made manifest in [these deities], so that humans would not remain ignorant of the causes of the things from which they so much benefited.[2]

The Supreme God, then, was hidden, together with the Supercelestials, from mortal eyes, because their nature was so sublime that it was impossible

---

[2] I do not want to make too much of this, but the system described by Herbert's priestly spokesman has very definite gnostic overtones. The system proposed by the Christian gnostic Valentinus (fl. 150 A.D.), for example, contains a hierachy of deities headed by Bythos, the Supreme Father, known as the "unbegotten Monad and perfect Aeon." Successive pairs of "aeons" proceed from the union of Bythos with Sige (his "ennoia," or Thought) until there are thirty aeons altogether, forming the Pleroma. Only one of them, Nous (Monogenes) knows the Supreme Father. The lowest aeon, Sophia, because she wanted to know Bythos, produced yearning (Enthymesis), who, after a series of vicissitudes, was saved by Christ and given form. Out of this form came a Creator or Demiurge, who turns out to be the God of the Old Testament. For further details see J.N.D. Kelly, *Early Christian Doctrines* 23–24 (from which this account has been taken) and Elaine Pagels, *The Gnostic Gospels*, esp. 46–53, 113–18 [for Valentinus].

to see them, and instead God produced Celestials, which we can see and which benefit us, namely, Heaven, the Sun, the Moon, the Fixed Stars and the Planets. In these we are allowed by the Supreme God to see where we came from, because our noblest part could only have come from Heaven and the Stars, and our minds, being so complex, must have originated from a higher plane. Unless our crimes prevent it, we will return there again; those who have behaved themselves well will be housed there, everything will be as pleasant and convenient for them as it was on Earth, but magnified in pleasure and intensity.

It cannot be argued that because these [entities] are solid bodies, they are not divine, for they are operated by a divine mind, which makes their huge frames move at incredible speed. The fact that they are circular does not mean that they are not dignified enough to be gods; the more parts something has, the weaker and more inefficient it is, and is subject to all sorts of accidents and injuries, requiring assistance from outside. This is obvious from our own bodies, which have so many things wrong with them that they would hardly be fit for civilised life, or even for providing their own food and clothing, had God not provided them with hands and the organs of speech!

Moreover, it does not matter whether the motion of the Celestial Deities, or even of Heaven itself, is self-generated or necessary; if the former (as is logical to suppose of the planets), we ought at least to allow them to be inferior deities, and if the latter, then we should regard them as God's chief ministers. Nothing can be more certain, whether they are self-guided or governed by God's pleasure, than that they do preside over and manage our affairs, and should at least be paid external worship.

The Subcelestials are inferior to the Celestials, but as they are nearer to us they are more like us; they have airy or aetherial bodies, and are subject to almost the same limitations as we are. They are sometimes good, sometimes bad (to be simply evil is repellent to the nature of God; there is a maxim, that there can be no "highest degree" of evil), and as they are of this rather dubious nature, we ought to get them on our side. There is no-one who will not try to avoid impending evil as much as possible through propitiating a god. It is beyond dispute that these gods are more beneficial to man than men are to animals or animals to men, for they not only have intellects, but great strength, agility, and other god-like assets. Therefore if, like us, they use their free will to do bad things occasionally, they could do a great deal of damage to the human race, and anything made of elements, far beyond what we could ever do to animals. When it comes to punishing the wicked, they may punish mankind with as much reason as we punish an innocent animal. In fact, people are capable of behaving worse than any animals, for they often kill and destroy those animals that deserve their best treatment.

It would be very absurd for a wicked and impious person to think that he could ever be secure in his actions, or that he was not under the dire scrutiny of someone or other who will soon get revenge. Some of the above-mentioned gods or daemons were in their own natures either good or bad, but it is not known for certain whether they had freedom of will, and could incline either way, depending upon the occasion. If any of them were entirely evil, there would no point in trying to please them, but daily experience seems to indicate the contrary. It seems that the Supreme God has given the Supercelestials the power to manage everything happily throughout all time; the Celestials preside over human affairs and deliver the laws and covenants. The latter are visible only to us as the forms that govern the sublunary world, unless man's free will is brought into play, especially when right reason[3] is being employed. Lastly we have the Subcelestials, who are sometimes benign, sometimes malevolent, so that the authority of divine justice is apparent.

[All] this will be easier to understand if we consider the Celestial King-dom as either an aristocracy, an oligarchy, or a democracy. Where is there any form of government established by which everything in Heaven or on Earth is managed? Who can show us what the proper duties of each [form] are? Why should some [forms] be better than others? The most disparate and contradictory parts of Nature may be united, but if there were several deities of equal power, would there not be terrible disorder and revolutions

---

[3]For Herbert, "right reason" is synonymous with what he calls "Natural Instinct" in *De veritate*. Because it is not subject to the vicissitudes of chance, environment or possibility, it is the highest form of reasoning. He defines it as "an immediate emanation of the mind, co-extensive with the dictates of Nature, so that it directly supports the doctrine of self-preservation, and is so essential that even in death it cannot be destroyed" (*DV* 123). Its ultimate goal is grace, or the understanding of the divine. The Cambridge Platonist, Benjamin Whichcote, put it this way:

> For this is Fundamental to all Religion; that Man
> in the Use of his Reason, by Force of Mind and
> Understanding, may as well know, that there is a
> God, that governs the World, as he may know by
> the Use of his Eyes, that there is a Sun. For are
> we not made to know there is a God? If we were
> not made to know he is, we could never know.

("The Use of Reason in Matters of Religion," *Select Sermons* (1698); Patrides 47).

in Nature if every one of them attempted to advance his own interests? There would be nothing to unite or reconcile the opposing parts of the world.

We therefore conclude that there is one Supreme God who is blessed from all time, but he also adopted some others of the same happy nature to keep him company, and made them partake of his happiness. He can advance others into the supercelestial society and make them participate in all the good things; it is therefore rational to suppose that God [himself] is either sedentary, or that he wanders about alone, or that he is fixed to the celestial orb and continually turns it for his own enjoyment. [It is rational to suppose] that he made the world and had delivered some laws by which it might be governed from its beginning. No-one builds a city without establishing laws, and no-one can be governed without them; God has no reason to change his laws as the times require, because he knows the beginning and the end of every event and of all things. It would be ridiculous to think that God has to think up anything new or fresh, or that his establishment of things from the beginning was simply arbitrary and that he will never go back on it for any reason whatsoever. When God had formed the world out of Chaos, he made some laws by which it was to be governed, and did so because he did not want his serenity interrupted and disturbed every day by unimportant matters, which could waste ages. It would be very troublesome for him to try and reconcile the different prayers and requests of human beings, particularly those from people who, good and pious though they were, might ask something of God that would injure or hurt others as good as themselves. It would be better to suppose that those things which were lawfully requested were decreed anyway from time immemorial. When the regular means, such as fervent prayers, faith, supplication and so forth, were used and things did not turn out the way people wanted them to, they would have to conclude that it had been decreed that way from all eternity. What more could we ask of the Supreme God than after leading a good life here, we might be made happy forever, and does it matter whether this is achieved by eternal decree or by prayers? God will be adored and praised whether he made the connexion between means and end from the beginning of time, or whether he does it now; in short, if this or some other order were not established, we could not possibly understand how the Supreme God is free from all cares and burdens. The ancients truly said that only the eternally-blessed had no business to do, nor required anyone to do it for him.

I now come to discuss the kind of worship that is to be paid to these particular [secondary] gods, for I have already indicated that the Supreme God was to be worshipped with a pure mind free from vice, with faith, hope, and love, and with praises and thanksgiving. The Celestial Gods are to be worshipped only in honour of the Supreme God, but so that their worship would not seem meaningless, it was thought proper to add some rites and ceremonies, such as bowing, kissing the fingers or hands, turning from east to west (or the other way) to demonstrate God's universality, so that we could declare openly the worship and adoration [of these gods] next to the Supreme God. Then some incense, or their symbolic animals, such as a horse for the Sun and a cow for the Moon, could be offered to them. It is also useful to propitiate the Subcelestial Gods, because, for reasons about which we know nothing, they are uncertain in their nature and may incline either way. The best thing to do is offer them something which they might like; what this might be is best ascertained from their bodily forms, which, being made of either air or aether, might suggest that something should be made for them out of the gross elements, but reduced to a more suitable substance, for they require food and their elemental nature may be refreshed by cognate elements. That is why they like the smell of fat, and so animals appropriate to their taste and smell should be sacrificed to them. Some fine spirits are made in the liver, heart, and brain; these ascend, and are therefore the objects of worship. It is beyond a doubt that everything loves its like, so they would always be ready to tell people which sacrifices they found agreeable."

There are some very noble truths here, albeit mixed up with some probability, improbability and falsehood (about which more later). The priests passed them on to the masses, who are always more likely to believe than to question such things, and the latter were easily swayed. Now as there were people who tried to confirm what they had been told about the Supercelestial deities through magical practices, so there were educated people who doubted what they said, although they did not confront the priests, who were continually near the gods and oracles. They knew that there was nothing necessary [in these ideas] but that falsity should be denied, and doubts raised about half-truths and conjectures. At last the people, disatisfied with what the priests told them, asked them about the elements and about things composed of elemental matter, and especially whether some worship should be paid to famous men. And the priests answered them this way.

"We confirm that some worship should be paid to the elements, even though they are the lowest and most obscure parts of the world, because without them the universe would be incomplete, and the image of the Supreme God, manifest in all his works, would be imperfect. Those who worship the superior world yet neglect the inferior world are as stupid as those who should respect a person's head and neck, but despise and condemn his other parts, however impressive, however beautifully-proportioned and symmetrical they were. Let us consult Orpheus, who describes the Supreme God (whom he calls Zeus)[4] like this: "the heaven, adorned with glittering stars, is his head and hair; out of this come two golden horns, one the east, the other the west. The sun and moon are his eyes, the air his breath, the wind his wings, the earth his stomach, girded with the ocean."[5] Orpheus does not mean that these were individual parts of the Supreme God, but that his showing God by His external form would create a good idea of Him. But to get back to the point, we say that the elements are, in themselves, worthy of some form of worship. All animals have an elemental nature, and there is nothing invisible making them up other than what is derived from the elements, and ultimately dissolved into them again. We should not ignore them, for they are the material principle and ultimate end of all things. Nor can it be objected that the soul, which is of celestial origin, takes precedence; for if the human body, which is so near and precious to it, excites a sort of reverence within us for its majesty, how much more reverence is due to the elements, which influence everything that has size and matter with, as some say, the vegetative and sensitive soul.[6] If this is true, and if vegetation and motion, which is a species of vegetation and sense, and sensation itself depend on the temperature of the elements, why do we make exhaustive enquiry into the causes of some things that we have in common with the

---

[4]Orphic theology posits an "egg," which is described as "the primal *prima materia* . . . this theology praises him as the First-begotten [*Protogonus*] and calls him Zeus, the ruler of all things and of the whole cosmos" (Damascius, *De principiis* 123 [Grant 107]).

[5]This quotation from "Orpheus" Herbert attributes, in a marginal note, to "Porphyry and other Platonists." Similar sentiments may be found, for example, in Hermetic theology, as for example the *Poimandres* (V, 6): "if, however, thou wishest to see him, consider the Sun, consider the course of the Moon, consider the order of the Stars . . . the most honourable parts for being evident, but having concealed the base" (Chambers 39–40).

[6]Herbert's priest refers to the tripartite division of the soul by ancient philosophers, including Aristotle. The vegetative (or nutritive) soul is at the bottom, and is possessed by everything that lives (i.e. plants, animals, humans). The sensitive soul is possessed by animals and humans, and governs the operation of the five senses, perception, the feeling of pleasure or pain and, most importantly, desire. It also governs memory and movement, which Aristotle recognises is present to a degree in all animals. The third part is, of course, the rational soul, which only man possesses. The relation of the soul to the body, as described by the priest, is also rather Aristotelian, for Aristotle sees the soul and body not as separate substances, but elements of a single substance. And, further, the matter which links up with a soul to form a living thing existed from all time and will continue after the union of soul with body has ceased to be. The union is complete, then, only while it lasts.

animals, and not pay attention to the elements, from whom we receive so many blessings?[7]

The air, which we continually draw in and breathe out in reciprocal motion and which supports and renews life, ought to be worshipped; if it ever becomes too thin, or infectious, or too thick, our lungs cannot take it in and we die. Water also should be worshipped, because it gives us moisture, without which our bodies would soon crumble into dry and shapeless dust. But if it is too cold, like the waters of the Styx, or too hot, like some baths are, or poisonous because it runs through metallic pores in the earth, death will follow immediately. The Earth is worthy of veneration, too, because it supports us and gives dimension to our bodies, because without it the whole fabric would dissolve; it carries us, as it were, upon its shoulders, preserving us from the great abyss between our feet and its centre. Like a common mother and nurse, the Earth gives us all food and clothing. But if by some supernatural means it sends forth pestilential vapours, or emits water from its depths which can overwhelm entire cities, or does not allow crops to grow plentifully, the consequences will be plague, floods, famine and universal desolation. Fire, which originates from the sulphurous veins of the Earth, the collision of clouds, the striking of stones together, the rubbing of sticks and from some oily substance, appears bright and shining like some unexpected deity. By reason of its powerful and effective heat, present in all natural generation, it seems to be the form and soul of the other elements. Too much of it burns everything and it threatens the whole world with destruction; therefore it ought to be venerated before all other sublunary things.[8]

It might be objected that the elements are not spontaneous, but necessary agents, but it is probable that they are both. We might allow that fire, either by fate or through its own inflammable nature, always ascends; but it will turn obliquely towards appropriate fuel and exercise the same kind of freedom as animals do when they feed. The air, also, blows where it likes; the water, especially that of the seas, ebbs and flows in reciprocal motion, swelling and rising up to avoid a vacuum. If the Earth spins by its own internal power, as some people say it does, it still has many other motions,

---

[7] For many ancient philosophers, the elements were the material cause of generation. Aristotle discusses this in *De generatione et corruptione* II, i. And see below.

[8] The priest has now turned, in part, to Heraclitus. For the latter, fire was the symbol of the cosmic process because it was the one element that was in perpetual motion. "This world-order, the same for all, no god made or any man," he says, "but it always was and is and will be an ever-living fire, kindling by measure and going out by measure" (Fr. 5.12; Robinson 90).

or else many phenomena could not be explained. Although natural necessity may make one motion proceed from another, it does not follow that there are no spontaneous motions. The motion of the heart in us is necessary, because when it stops we cease to live at the same instant; but the motion of the eyes is voluntary, dictated by the free soul, and can move any way it wants, to which I might add the internal actions of the soul. As both these motions are present in animals, why should they be denied to the elements whose motion may in some respects be necessary or compulsive but is in others free and voluntary. Even if we grant that the elements move only by mere natural necessity, they are still the Supreme God's ministers, and the parts of which the world is made up. They are also the authors of all bodily nature and therefore are due some respect.

The whole world is so made that no-one who ventures outdoors can notice anything remarkable without reverent awe, so we now ought to enquire about those things which are made up of elements, and in particular about humanity, and see whether some animals, or some famous people, should have some worship paid to them. As there are hierarchies of things, so there should be hierarchies of worship suitable to each rank or degree. There is nothing in this wide world which does not deserve some sort of veneration, or which does not have something to do with the worship of the gods, such as bread, corn, wine, milk, or some herbs and animals pertaining to the gods.

Let us begin with man, who, after the elements, is of a middle nature, between the eternal and the perishable.[9] The world could not exist without the elements, but it could without man; in fact the earth would probably be a pleasanter and more fruitful place if the wickedness of mankind did not bring down divine retribution on all sublunary things. But just as an evil man is the worst of all animals, so a good, pious man is by far the best. The Supercelestial Deities are good in themselves, but man is so by reason of his free will, and while he has a propensity for evil, he may still advance, by means of virtue and piety, to immortality and great reward. If man could always conform to the rules of piety and honesty (which he never could), he would be the happiest of all the blessed, and next to the Supreme God. What others got by chance would be the just reward for his merit. Now, as we doom the wicked to an eternally miserable state, it is just that the good should be rewarded with eternal happiness, and therefore worshipped and adored. When [the good] are advanced into heaven by God, he makes them the judges and disposers of human actions; the latter are in part governed by eternal laws, [in part] by what is written in the heart,

---

[9]Or, as Donne puts it, "I am a little world made cunningly/ Of elements, and an angelic sprite" ("Divine Meditations," 5, l. 1–2; Smith 310).

and [in part] from the goodness or evil inclinations of the will, man's very thoughts.

It would be ridiculous to imagine that people who go to heaven lose or are deprived of any of the faculties that their souls exercised while they lived on earth, or that they are lazy and careless about our affairs, or so useless that they cannot manage them. Indeed, it is very just to make one man the judge of another, for he can bring common reason and conscience to the contemplation of our actions. If God had given this task to the Celestial Deities, they would have decided everything by the eternal laws of Heaven and the rigidity of Fate, caring not at all for the influence of man's will on his actions. And if God himself should get involved in human affairs, he would not be able to lead his blessed and serene life. So, then, this jurisdiction was given from the beginning to men who had been admitted to Heaven, for they can best deliberate and judge the right or wrong of human actions, and allot rewards and punishments after life, by those laws which are written in the eternal statutes of Heaven and the stars, and the universal consent of all mankind. There is no doubt that God will confirm the justice of their judgments; but if He should reserve some for his own judgment (as he is not strictly obliged to obey his own laws, and can exempt himself if he wishes), [those raised to Heaven] will be mediators between Him and humanity, and because of this they should be made propitious. The honesty and piety of their lives, their heroic deeds, or something that they have invented which gives great benefits determines who they are; such are our judges, if mortals have any representation in heaven, which it is reasonable that they should, because they are citizens of the world. In any well-established commonwealth, ordinary people have some authority, just as the aristocracy does; the laws of the former are known as plebiscites. In this way mankind becomes the plebeians in this World-City, when they raise their heroes to Heaven.

Now the common people only, and not the patricians, were under obligation to the plebiscite, and therefore it might happen that if someone should make an unreasonable request, the gods may well reject it as unfit, because they are more competent to judge. Therefore all the petitions of the plebeians will not advance someone to immortality unless he has been exemplary in piety and virtue. What will people not attempt to do to partake of eternal life, riches, and all that they could possibly desire? Indeed, this doctrine affords the strongest reasons for the practice of virtue and the avoidance of wickedness. These deities, once they are established in Heaven, should be offered prayers and sacrifices, but no more than those generally offered to Heaven.

As these deities, by God's permission, manage human affairs, I will now show the order and degree that is present in the heavenly kingdom, for they do not all have equal authority, and who is chief amongst them. I should remind you that they are bound by the eternal law, from which it is impossible for them to depart. We should prostrate ourselves before them as we make our solemn vows, for not only do they know our actions, both good and bad, but they are acquainted with the secret thoughts we have in our hearts. If they did not know these, no check could be made on the inner recesses of the conscience, and no exact rule would exist for justly judging mankind's actions. Mortals can judge only the externals, but those deities judge the innermost things, for which reason they should be venerated. We will let you know, from Nature's intimate secrets and from their own oracles, about the hierarchy of the gods and about their rites, but only if you will seriously consider what has already been said, and help us carry out this pious and necessary work; in fact, it is your duty to do so."

After they had made such empty speeches, which had very little solid truth in them, the priests then started to put together their theological systems. From first principles they established it so that nothing seemed more obviously true or orthodox, and nobody dared have any doubts or hesitation about anything that they were told about those things which came, so they were told, from the secret counsels of the gods themselves. By degrees, the priests came to manage everything just as they pleased; by pretending to keep a divine oracle for communication between themselves and the Supreme God, they unanimously agreed to manipulate the people, and they received answers from [the god] that firmly bound the people to them in blind obedience. Matters went so far that although the testaments were questionable and the oracles eventually proved false, it was nevertheless thought the height of impiety even to seem to doubt their truth or to interpret them in any other way than in that given [by the priests]. But the priests did not stop there: having gotten rid of the most reasonable parts of their religion, they corrupted peoples' minds with the most horrendous rites and ceremonies, offering up human sacrifices to the gods, the custom being abolished by the Romans and in other nations who were under their rule.

Nevertheless, the pure worship of God came to consist of only those sacrifices which the priests ate, only the prayers which they invented, the sacred mysteries which they alone performed, the oracles of their own designing, their own interpretations of auguries, their own rites and ceremonies, feasts and games which they thought up, and finally those dreams which occurred in temples and which none but they could interpret. Thus those most certain and basic articles of religion, such as faith in God, a firm and solid hope in

him, and that love which unites man with God, were totally neglected, or, at
the least, postponed until another era.

   I am now going to show what the pagans once thought of the noble faculties of the soul, which are so closely united with it, what they understood
by virtue, and how the erring soul was purified. The priests always tried
very hard to eradicate or stifle these principles in men's minds, although
they themselves knew them well, and were convinced of their truth. It will
therefore be quite in keeping with my present purpose to prove that these
principles were not unknown to the ancient pagans, and that whether one
looks into their religion or their law, one will find the most extraordinary
means used to encourage people in virtue, and to deter them from wickedness. The Church Fathers, uncompromising enemies of the pagans that
they were, completely misrepresented the matter; they pass over the more
orthodox part of pagan religion in silence, but use the old superstitions and
rites as an excuse for uttering the most severe invective against it. They
ingeniously exposed the madness of the sacred rites, pictured them as most
ridiculous and reproached the priests for the insane practices which they
had invented when they were stirred up by a divine spirit and were raving
violently. The Fathers subsumed all those things which had some obvious
merit; matters concerning the mind, virtue, piety, faith, hope and harmony
were thought of by them as healthy; indeed these goddesses (as the pagans
had called them) were held in great estimation and honour, and were most
enthusiastically pulled into the Christian religion. Because of this, I have
judged them not as bad parts, but as good parts of [pagan] religion, and they
will be examined as such. And these sane parts are the most ancient and
universal that can be found in the huge pile of superstition and error, a few
mature ears of wheat in a field otherwise full of darnel, thorns, thistles and
burrs (those plants which Pliny calls the sick and diseased produce of the
earth). Of the former one might be able to collect several handfuls, and I
know that to this extent there are a few sound things in pagan religion which
anyone might lay hold of. Of all the things that are relevant to this argument
I would like to note one in particular: if the old religious cults of gods and
goddesses could be divided into piles, scarcely an impression could have
been made on them in this volume. This work will be completed by people
who are more learned than me and who have more spare time; no-one, as
far as I know, has written particularly about all the ancient religions. Not
even that noble Frenchman, du Choul, has managed to do so.[10] Many people

---

[10]Guillaume du Choul (fl. 1550) was a French antiquarian, about whom very
little is known outside his book *Discours de la réligion des anciens Romains* (Lyons,
1556). He apparently planned a larger work on all ancient religions, which he

have incidentally illustrated the genealogy and history of the pagan heroes through their books but no-one, I think, has sorted through the disorderly pile and presented it all together in a viable form. I myself have given it a general shape, but I am in my sixties, entangled in business and other duties; may I not be forgiven if I leave the field to others?[11] It will be enough if I show the scope and fashion of the ridiculous priestly doctrines, [and indicate] that they did not dazzle everyone and deflect them from the pure worship of the Supreme God.

When the priests had invented new rites and established oracles, they always pretended that they had done so by the authority and command of Jupiter or some other god; the poor wretched masses had neither the courage nor the will to suspect these things as questionable or to reject them. However, those amongst them who were intelligent and judicious enough did consider these things human inventions. Sometimes they asked to be admitted to the most holy and secret parts of the temples so that they could hear for themselves what came out of their gods' mouths; the fact that the priests were present was only one kind of evidence, and it might well need corroboration by another person. They promised that they would devote themselves entirely to the priests and their doctrines if the latter would allow them this privilege. The whole exercise was designed to discredit [the priests]; they did not in the least believe that God spoke in an articulate voice or that he delivered his commands and revelations *sotto voce*.

---

mentions in his introduction, but it never appeared in print; it was entitled *Traité sur les images des dieux*. Herbert is probably alluding to this latter work. Seznec quotes the Italian scholar Jacopo Strada (1515–88) as praising du Choul for his learning, and he was highly-regarded by Montaigne (Seznec 247 n. 100).

[11] Herbert was about sixty-two in 1644–45, when he completed this work, and in bad health. It should also be remembered that he was writing in the midst of the Civil War, and was trying to resolve his doubts about which side he should take in the conflict. His mental state at the time was not good either; his family, like so many others at the time, was divided in its loyalties and his debts were still quite large. All his brothers and sisters except Sir Henry Herbert were dead, and so were most of his close friends. He was not on close terms with any of his family except his daughter Beatrix (with whom he lived in Montgomery Castle) and his grandson Edward. Indeed, it might not be too far-fetched to imagine that the writing of this work was undertaken partly for what we would now call "occupational therapy," and that Herbert took solace in this accomplishment at such a difficult time in his life. It was at this time, of course, that his castle came under siege by Parliamentary forces and that he eventually surrendered it to them, bringing down on his head the opprobrium of those who had assumed that he would join the Royalist side.

On the other hand, some of the most penetrating and intelligent minds did submit in a sense to the religious worship that was performed in their times, [but they did so] in order that the lewd and debauched, who could not distinguish truth from falsehood, should not completely reject or condemn all [genuine] religious worship. The wise and good of those times were content if they could extract good juice from the dry parts of religion; what they aspired to was nobility of spirit, the worship of the Supreme God, and the tacit rejection of what the priests imposed, which left them in doubt or indifferent. If at any time the priests went as far as requiring them to declare their assent and consent to [priestly] doctrines and precepts, and this was done with the authority of the whole priesthood, they then obeyed the Pontifex Maximus and the entire College of Priests.

Now, to make it clearer still what the ancients thought about religious worship, I will follow Vossius and divide all worship into Proper, Symbolic and Mixed categories. The first is the worship of the Supreme God, the Sun, Moon, Heaven and the whole world in themselves. Symbolic worship is worshipping God in the Sun, Heaven or World, as in the active principle of generation, as with the Sun or Heaven, or in the passive, as with the Moon and the Elements. Mixed worship, the lowest form, is when God is worshipped in the Sun, the Sun in Fire or Hercules, Fire in Flame or coals, and Hercules in his statue or image.

In ancient times it was believed that proper worship was due only to God. Wise people did not think that the Sun itself, which can burn the world up and reduce it to ashes, was the Supreme God, or anything but a part of the world itself. [They did not think] that any worship terminated in the Sun, or did not refer to anything beyond it. Whoever contemplates the Universe, composed as it is of so many contradictory and opposing parts, must conclude that it was first made, and is now governed, by ONE. We should not, therefore, pay proper worship to it, but should understand that there is something superior to it and more blessed, which acts only by the internal power of its own mind. I doubt whether [the Sun, the Moon etc.] were ever made the principal objects of adoration, for while they did exist, they were not "gods" because they needed each other.

The poor were always panting for a better and happier state than anything they could attain [here] either by Fate or hard work, and they thought that perfect and complete happiness could only be found in the Eternal and Blessed God and by being allowed to join his society. They tried very hard to make themselves like God through their piety and virtue so that they would be fit for eternal happiness. Thus if we judge mankind by ourselves, or through the common interpretations of others, we will conclude that although the pagans paid symbolic or mixed adoration to many gods, they paid proper worship to God alone. Although it may be true that the priests invented many strange rites and ceremonies to establish the worship of God, their main objective was to awaken the human mind so that as it became accustomed to religious duties it would become animated with something divine. Some of their sacrifices were indeed horribly barbaric and cruel, and because of that aroused either terror or disgust in the spectators, but at the same time they did indicate to the wicked how dreadful divine vengeance could be when an enraged God was presented to them by their own priests as being unappeasable without bloody sacrifices and human victims.

I now intend, if God will give me life and strength, to discuss at length an ancient doctrine which has been in the minds of mankind far longer than any of these rites and customs, many of which are either abolished now, or out-of-date. I shall now examine the more orthodox doctrines of the pagans, although these also were defiled and contaminated by rites and ceremonies.

XV

The More Reasonable Aspects
of Pagan Religion

In our present age, there are many very learned theologians who will claim that the pagans worshipped the same God as we do. The difference is, [they say], that the worship they gave him was erroneous and idolatrous, and they assert that it is equally sinful to worship the true God in a mistaken way as to worship a false god in an honest manner. This is not to say that they thought the pagans rejected the mind, virtue, faith, piety or any other aspects of real religion, but that they mixed superstitious, profane and cruel rites with them. It has never been denied that virtue, faith, hope and love were in themselves the way to worship God. I will therefore show here what aspects of real religion were adhered to amongst the pagans, so that a proper balance may be obtained.

Cicero, in Book II of *De legibus*, gives us an outline of ancient religion which is worth examining here, because it contains the opinion of the pagans on religious matters. He says, "Men have no other way to get to heaven other than through the mind, virtue, piety, and faith." Now, although Cicero believed that people whose merit had given them immortality, such as Hercules, Bacchus and Aesculapius were deserving of worship, he never thought that could have obtained blessedness by any sort of worship at all, but only by having a pure mind, all the virtues, that piety upon which all virtue is sometimes founded (that is, just and agreeble knowledge of God), and the holy faith which produces those virtues. Anyone who would like to have a correct idea about pagan religion ought to note this statement carefully; the pagans did not depend at all upon the external worship of their gods or upon the prayers and vows they made to them; they depended upon virtue itself as the admission to Heaven.[1] Cicero tells us in *The Nature of the Gods* how goddesses came to be so-called:

> [Balbus is speaking] Or a quality which manifests some great power is itself named as a god, such as Faith or Reason, both of which we have actually seen consecrated in the Capitol by Marcus Aemilius Scaurus. There was also a previous consecration of Hope by Aulus Atilius Colatinus. You can see

---

[1] Compare this with the views of Pomponazzi in *De immortalitate animae*. Pom-

from here the temple of Virtue, restored by Marcus Marcellus, and originally consecrated many years ago during the Ligurian War by Quintus Maximus. Wealth, Salvation, Liberty, Concord, Victory — all of these, because they had great power which seemed to demand a divine origin, have been named as gods.

In *De legibus*,[2] he says further:

> It was a good thing that the Mind, Piety, Faith and Virtue had some consecration paid them and that there are public temples dedicated to them in Rome, because those people who possess these virtues (that is, all good people) may be thought to have the gods themselves living within their souls.

Pliny[3] mentions these also, and adds Chastity, Concord and Clemency; and Dionysius of Halicarnassus adds Justice, Clemency, Themis and Nemesis, which his ancestors worshipped. He says:

> Numa was the first to dedicate a temple to public Faith, and to assign money out of the treasury for sacrifices to her, as well as to certain other gods.[4]

Peace, Quiet, Hope and Happiness also had public temples.

From all of the above it is quite obvious that according to pagan doctrine everything could be reduced to rules of virtue and piety, which are necessary for living well and happily here and for all eternity afterwards. They still thought that many more things, such as sacrifices, rites, ceremonies and a great deal of other such things were necessary for the demonstration of their piety, but unless their souls were governed by [piety and virtue] they would not get to Heaven. Thus far, then, the ancients agree with us; we cannot obtain salvation without the Mind, Virtue, Piety and Faith; it would appear, then, that the pagans agreed with us not only in the worship of the Supreme God, but also in the essentials of that worship. Anyone who consults the writings of those few pagan theologians and philosophers who remained living amongst the Christians will readily admit that they, like us, espoused piety and virtue. That is why Celsus[5] dared challenge Origen to show why

---

ponazzi, like Herbert, is concerned primarily with man, whom he says is "not of simple but of multiple, not of fixed, but of an ambiguous nature, and is placed in the middle between mortal and immortal things" (Kristeller *Renaissance Thought* I, 135). This is the standard place of man on the Great Chain of Being, but the point is, for both Pomponazzi and Herbert, that moral virtue, as Cicero also says, can be attained on earth, so that every human being can thus contribute to universal good.

[2] Cicero, *NG* II.60 (148).

[3] [Herbert's marginal note]: Cicero, *De legibus* II.

[4] Pliny, *Natural History* II.7 [Herbert's note].

[5] Celsus (fl. 160–85 A.D.) was a Platonist philosopher, whose book *Alethes logos* (The True Word) was a great anti-Christian polemic, is known also to have written

the Christian religion was better at inculcating virtue now than pagan religion had been in the past. Indeed, some people go further and assert that [pagan] precepts are stricter than those of Christianity, and therefore are better at promoting virtue, and I shall say something about each of these views.

The Mind

By Mind the ancients understood nothing less than right reason. Beyond everything they respected a sound mind, for without one nobody could make a proper choice of religion, lead a holy life according to its precepts, and reject false or doubtful doctrines.

First, there are principles of religion which derive from the Mind or from right reason, such as; 1. There is a Supreme God; 2. He ought to be worshipped; 3. Virtue is the most important aspect of his worship; 4. We ought to repent from our sins; 5. There are rewards and punishments both in this life and in the hereafter.[6] Others derive only from the authority of the priests. To the former, the pagans gave their firm and entire assent, but the others they thought at best probable and doubtful. They did not condemn or reject in their entirety the revelations, traditions and dreams of their priests, but they were somewhat cautious, and did not allow themselves to be dazzled by them or risk basing their entire religious system on them. They did not think that any doctrine should be held by faith alone, however plausible it was, because they easily discovered how they could be manipulated this way. The ancients deified the mind because, as Varro, Augustine, Lactantius and others say, they wanted to be endowed with good minds. Livy tells us that the praetor T. Octacilius promised to build a temple to the Mind, and when he became duumvir he dedicated it and had it built in the Capitol.

---

a handbook for Christians who wanted to become pagans. In his book, which is quoted almost in its entirety by Origen in *Contra Celsum*, Celsus uses a Platonistic point of view, but his speakers are Jews from Egypt. He argued, amongst other things, that Christianity had no ancestral traditions (unlike Judaism), but at the same time advocated the abandonment of the old, established polytheistic religion which held the very fabric of society together. Celsus placed a great emphasis on ancient tradition, and saw Christianity as a menace to society. Interestingly enough, he wrote under Marcus Aurelius, whose philosophical views led him to consider the Christians dangerous and subversive for much the same reasons as Celsus.

[6] Again, Herbert repeats the Five Religious Common Notions from *De veritate* (see Chapter I). Here he emphasises the rationality of these principles as they correspond with right reason (*ratio recta*).

Virtue

Virtue is next, as it is the genuine offspring of a good mind, or, as Cicero calls it, "the perfection of Nature." I believe that virtue is as much the perfection of the soul as the soul is of the body, and those who have examined the writings of the ancients will find them full of panegyrics to virtue. People esteemed it so much that they thought they could get to Heaven through it alone, and they had no less doubt that a virtuous person could get there, even if he did not know where it was, than a traveller, walking on the right path leading to a magnificent city, knows he will get to where he is going.

I need only mention a few examples here. Plato says that we can try to be like God through prudence, justice, and holiness. Ficino says that happiness may be acquired through these as well as fortitude and temperance, but that souls are united to God by love alone. Cicero says that all virtue consists of three things: the first is understanding what is true and consistent in everything, what was most agreeable to everyone, and what causes everything. The second is subduing the impulsiveness of the mind. The third is exercising temperance and fortitude as much as fairness and humanity allow. Cicero also affirms that virtue unites us with God, and Seneca says that it enlarges the soul and prepares it for the knowledge of higher things, thus making it worthy to be admitted to God's society. Poets, as well as philosophers and orators, have written extensively on this subject.

The Romans worshipped Virtus and paid divine honours to her, as Augustine, citing Varro, says in his *City of God*. The first temple to Virtus was built by Scipio Numantinus, and Marcellus then built one to Virtus and Honos, using the spoils of his Sicilian victory. In his "Life of Marcellus" Plutarch says that when Marcellus wanted to dedicate this temple, the priests prevented him from doing so because they said that it was not right to put two gods in the same building. Marcellus then began to add on to the former building, but he was very displeased, and saw the obstruction as a bad omen. In his speech against Verres, Cicero mentions the temples of Honour and Virtue being so built that no-one could go into that of Honour without [passing through] that of Virtue.[7] Marius built another temple to Honour and Virtue after he had defeated the Cimbri, but he built it low, so that it would not get in the way of the public auguries and so that the augurs would not have it demolished! As Marius was a very astute and intelligent man, he knew that the priests and augurs would not be too happy about a temple to Virtue; they would not, for his sake, have permitted their beloved profits, which they reaped from the common people by flying their birds and such

---

[7]Cicero, *NG* II 62 [147].

like nonsense, to be diminished in any way, nor the credit of their prophecies to be impaired.

Piety

This is the natural result of the two former concepts, for without a sound mind and virtue, piety is worthless; when the Mind or right reason is not operating, our natures are apt to invent and worship imaginary deities. And without adding virtue, all this religious worship has no value whatsoever.

In ancient times, Piety was divided first into that which is exercised towards God, second into that which concerns our country and parents, and third into that which we exercised towards neighbours and people that deserved well of us. Cicero notes that "piety and sanctity appease the gods," and further, "there can be no other piety towards the gods other than an honourable opinion about them and a true understanding; we should believe that we can expect from them only what is just and fair." Valerius Maximus, Pliny, Dionysius of Halicarnassus and many others offer examples of piety towards parents and others. Seneca says of Scipio Africanus,

> I am absolutely sure that his soul went back where it came from, namely to Heaven, not because he was the valiant and skilful commander of great armies (for mad Cambyses[8] was, too, and very successful) but because of his eminent moderation and piety.

There is no point in listing other examples, which, as Pliny tells us, are infinite. M. Acilius Glabrio dedicated a temple to Pietas in the Herb-Market because of a famous instance of piety shown by A. Quintius and M. Acilius to their mother who was imprisoned while about to give birth; the temple was erected in the very place where the prison stood.[9]

Concord

When the Mind is combined with Virtue and Piety, the certain and necessary result is harmony. Some people distinguish harmony from peace by stating that the latter refers only to a disagreement between two parties, whilst the former concerns many parties. Both were worshipped by the ancients,

---

[8]Cambyses [Kambuya] was king of Persia 529–21 B.C. He conquered Egypt in 525 B.C. (Herodotus III, 1–15) but suffered a series of reverses and, apparently, went insane.

[9]Herbert gives no reference for this story. Manius Acilius Glabrio dedicated a temple to Pietas in 181 B.C., which had been "vowed at Thermopylae" (*OCD* 387), where his father, Marcus Acilius Glabrio (Praetor, 196 B.C.) had defeated King Antiochus of Syria. I can find no account such as the one printed above, but it may be in Pliny.

because they wanted to lead quiet and sedate lives free from all troubles. Concordia is pictured holding a cup in her right hand and a cornucopia in her left; sometimes she has a sceptre, out of which fruit came, and sometimes she has two right hands joined together. Aristides,[10] in his *Oration on the Goddess Concord* to the Rhodians, depicts her as decorous, firm and agreeable, and, by the goodwill of the gods, allowed to descend from Heaven. Jupiter gives her the power to fix the hours; only she can confirm all things and make flowers grow in the fields and trees give fruit. She presides over possessions, city affairs, the bestowal of people in marriage and the nursing and education of children.[11]

There were many temples to Concord in Rome; the first was built by the fifth dictator, M. Furius Camillus,[12] in the Capitol. Plutarch and Ovid tell us that there was a room full of images which was used for entertainment and where the Senate used to meet. Pliny mentions it many times, and says that when P. Sempronius Longus and L. Sulpicius were consuls,[13] one Flavius vowed a temple to Concord if he could reconcile the patricians and the plebs. When no money was forthcoming from the treasury, he built a temple of brass with the fines of moneylenders. Livy also mentions this temple, and Pliny speaks of a temple to Concord in which the censor Quintius Martius set up an image of Concord which he had made; C. Cassius,[14] when he was censor, placed it in the Curia and dedicated an altar to the same goddess. There were three other temples in Rome, the last of which was either built or repaired by the Empress Livia. Augustine also mentions a temple of Concord in Book III of his *City of God*. From Livy we may understand who had the power to dedicate temples:

---

[10]Aelius Aristides (c. 117–89) was an Athenian sophist who travelled throughout a great part of the ancient world lecturing and teaching. He was renowned for his ceremonial speeches on various topics, all of which he wrote in the Attic style. They are full of "glowing periods, rhetorical devices, and refined feeling" (*OCD* 90).

[11]Concordia is the personification of agreements, both those between states themselves or amongst the various bodies within those states. She later became the personification of agreements made between members of Rome's imperial family or between the emperor and someone else. The turbulent 3rd century abounds in coins bearing the image of the goddess and the inscription CONCORDIA AVGG. It was wishful thinking for the most part, given the number of usurpers!

[12]This is said by modern scholars to be a conjecture (see *OCD* 224); Camillus is supposed to have dedicated the temple in 367 B.C.

[13]Publius Sempronius Longus and Lucius Sulpicius were consuls in 216 B.C.

[14]Gaius Cassius Longinus, the murderer of Caesar, is probably the subject of Herbert's example. The date is between 44 and 42 B.C.

Licinius Macer[15] dedicated a temple to Concord in Vulcan's Field, at which the patricians became very angry; according to the custom of their ancestors no-one but a consul or an emperor had that privilege.

Peace and Quiet

Near the Forum there was a very impressive temple of Pax, begun by Claudius and completed by Vespasian. Some people, following Jerome, say that [the emperor] Titus deposited the spoils from the Temple of Jerusalem there. Galen tells us that learned people used to go there to dispute, so that they could clear their doubts in peace. If only our modern divines would observe this custom in the temple of their souls! There was an altar to Pax in Rome; she was depicted as a woman, holding an ear of corn or, sometimes, a caduceus,[16] and crowned with laurels, olive-leaves or roses. Aristophanes makes Aphrodite and the Graces her companions.[17]

Quies, as well as Concordia and Pax, had a temple in Rome, which was built outside the Hill Gate. Because the epithet "quies" is given to the word "orcus," or hell, Vives thinks that the worship of Quies was concerned only with the dead.

Chastity

After Concordia and Pax we have Pudicitia,[18] because chastity may be much endangered by an easy but ill thought-out Concord. She was worshipped by the Romans, but referred only to conjugal chastity; Juno, Venus and Hymen were known as conjugal deities, although Juno was the preserver of the marriage-bed. As Seneca says in his Medea, "You conjugal deities and you, O Lucina!/ Preserver of the happy bed." Pudicitia had two names, *Patricia* and *Plebeia*; the patricians dedicated a temple to the first near the Cattle Market which no-one who had been married more than once could enter. Plebeia had a small chapel erected by Verginia, who, although herself

---

[15]This is probably the Licinius Macer who, as praetor in 68 B.C., advocated the rights of the common people, and killed himself when condemned for extortion (66).

[16]The caduceus is the herald's staff, similar to that carried by Mercury in his images.

[17]The Greek equivalent of Pax is Eirene, about whom there are no myths and who had few cults, although she was worshipped at Athens. She is the personification of peace, but the Roman Pax seems to be more related to political peace, and appears to have been introduced by Augustus.

[18]It might be noted, after reading the excessively melodramatic story of Verginia in Livy (or the speech following), that the cult of Pudicitia degenerated long before Imperial times.

patrician, had married a pleb. Her sister had her expelled from the patrician rites, and she resented this so much that, gathering together all the plebeian ladies, she complained of what had been done, and built an altar in a small chapel. Then she made a speech in which she told them that as the men emulated each other in bravery, the women might do so in chastity. She said that this altar was as chaste and holy as that of the patricians, and that no-one except a woman who had been married to only one man might sacrifice at it.[19] And Valerius Maximus says, "those who were content with marrying once were honoured with the crown of Chastity."

Faith

Faith was always worshipped, although not, as I respectfully point out, in the way that some churchmen take it today. The pagans never believed that anyone could get to heaven simply by displaying faith; virtue and piety had to be joined with it to prepare the way. There are some so-called theologians who assert that eternal happiness can be acquired by faith alone, so the word needs some explanation. Henri Estienne says that the pagans meant the same by faith as we do by conscience, but I disagree, because if we look at a comparison of various ancient authors we will find that they usually took faith to mean what we mean by fidelity. The word *fiducia* then meant what faith does now; this can be seen from Livy, where he tells us what *fiducia* or faith may be given to the virtues of a man called Theodorus.

I am aware that faith sometimes, though very rarely, meant being persuaded of something, or having a strong opinion. I think that is how Cicero is using it in Book II of *De legibus*, when he says that faith, together with right reason, virtue and piety give us admission into Heaven. This faith [*fiducia*], which is concerned with a future life, is entirely different from that which depends on the authority of its relator. Now, as there was no written word of God, how could the ancients have had such a strong faith in the past? They never took the word to mean conscience, or gave it any theological value at all; it had a human or civic meaning, concerned with bargains, contracts, societies, leagues, and trading.[20] Amongst the ancients the virtues were the same as ours, but faith was quite different; I do not

---

[19]This is the same Verginia who was killed by her father to save her from the advances of Appius Claudius. She was actually not married to a pleb, but betrothed to one, Lucius Icilius, whom Livy describes as "a keen and proven champion of the popular cause" (231). For more details see Livy III, 42–51 [231–40].

[20]Herbert is perfectly correct here. Fides is the personification of Good Faith. Fiducia, on the other hand, means specifically "confidence," "reliance," "trust" and so forth. It also has a specific legal meaning as in a legal "trust."

doubt, however, that when their minds were full of virtue and piety, they shared with us the hope of a more glorious state. That they had great respect for faith may be seen from Cicero's oration for Marcellus; here he says that "there can be no good faith [*fides*] where there is no piety."

Cicero tells us that there was a temple of Faith in the Capitol, next to that of Jupiter, and he says that Collatinus[21] dedicated it. Festus, citing Agathocles, says that it was dedicated on the Palatine by Aeneas before the time of Romulus. Dionysius and Plutarch say that Numa Pompilius was the first to dedicate a public temple to Faith, and that he assigned money from the treasury to it as he did for other gods. I would be inclined to believe this rather than Festus or Agathocles[22] because it may be found in Livy as well. There is no doubt that the temple of Jupiter was near that of Faith, and it is more probable because the most sacred oath sworn amongst the Romans was sworn by Faith. Jupiter himself is called Fidius; Silius Italicus says that Faith came before Jupiter, and describes it as "a silent god in the breast." The flamens who sacrificed to Faith were dressed in white, as Numa had laid down. Cartari notes that the right hand was dedicated to Faith because it should defend it, but he does not give his reference. This might be the reason, that on ancient images of Faith, the right hands of two images are joined together.

The notion of faith, as we have noted in the Introduction, was somewhat different for pagan religion than it was for Christians. Jaeger notes, for example, that Galen criticized Christians for relying on faith, believing it to be "mere subjective evidence [which] indicates the lack of a sufficient epistemological foundation for their system" (32). This led, in turn, to positions like that of Tertullian, who maintained that as Christianity was not a "philosophy" it did not have to follow the same rules. For Cicero, the question was different again; as Jaeger points out (33), the speaker in Book III of *Nature of the Gods* (Cotta) is the Pontifex Maximus of Rome as well as a sceptic philosopher; he rejects the arguments of his friends on philosophical grounds, but instead of positing philosophical alternatives he argues that religion must be maintained because of its tradition and its links with the state. Cotta does not even try to answer philosophically, because, having logically refuted their arguments, he knows that they could also refute his; therefore, he sees the whole question as a matter of "faith."

[21] See Chapter XI.

[22] Agathocles (2nd century B.C.) was a Greek historian and philosopher, author of the *History of Cyzicus*, a work containing a great deal of mythological information. It survives only in fragments, but is cited by Cicero, Pliny, and Athenaeus.

Hope

"Hope," says Cicero, "is the expectation of good," and the Romans wor-shipped Spes as a goddess. He also tells us that Hope leads heroes to sacrifice themselves for immortality, and he mentions the hope of ascending into Heaven in other contexts as well, so that amongst the pagans it may be said that a firm hope meant the same to them as faith [*fiducia*] does to us, and it was thought of by all as a divine virtue. There is a famous passage in Plato's Republic where it is shown what great men and eminent philosophers do about attaining a more blessed state:

> [Cephalus speaks] For let me tell you, Socrates, that when a man begins to realize that he is going to die, he is filled with apprehensions and concern about matters that did not before occur to him. The tales that are told about the world below, and how the men who have done wrong here must pay the penalty there, though he may have laughed them down hitherto, then begin to torture his soul with the doubt that there may be some truth in them. And apart from that the man himself, either from the weakness of old age or possibly as being now nearer to the things beyond has a somewhat clearer view of them. Now he to whom the ledger of his life shows an account of many evil deeds starts up even from his dreams like a child again and again in affright and his days are haunted by anticipations of worse to come. But on him who is conscious of no wrong that he has done a sweet hope ever attends and a goodly, to be nurse of his old age, as Pindar too says. (I, 330d–31a)[23]

From this it will be evident that a better state was the object of hope amongst the pagans; it was so deeply engraved upon their minds that even the fear of death cannot eliminate it until, as long as other faculties are not deficient, it has brought humanity to its ultimate happiness. As Ovid notes, "There is nothing owing to us for our merits, / But there is great hope in God's goodness."

It would seem, then, that as the pagans worshipped the same God as we do, and had the same idea of virtue, then we must all have the same common hope of immortality. As Cicero says, "Men's souls are immortal, but the virtuous enjoy celestial things." And in *De senectute* he says, "We should not complain about the fact that we are going to die, because the consequence is immortality." Cicero mentions a temple of Spes and Livy says that it was in the Herb-Market; he also states that P. Victor built a temple to Spes in the 7th quarter of the city. Another was built by the Tiber when M. Fulvius[24]

---

[23]Translated by Paul Shorrey (Hamilton and Cairns 579–80).

[24]Marcus Fulvius Nobilior (d. after 170 B.C.), soldier and politician, was consul in 189 and censor in 172. He was a great patron of culture and a builder of many temples.

was censor, and Dio mentions another. She was depicted in several ways on ancient coins, but for that you can consult Rozsfeld.[25]

Liberty

After Hope comes Liberty, then Safety and Happiness. The last hope terminates in eternal Liberty. Cicero says that liberty actually means living as one pleases, and who would not live happily if it were possible? The pagans believed, therefore, that when pious people died, they were able to partake of the enjoyments of Liberty, so that this noblest faculty of the soul might not be a needless creation. The Romans worshipped Liberty as a goddess who presided over that liberty which is a most desirable quality in a well-constituted commonwealth; yet the pagans did not think that the after-life was devoid of it, indeed they imagined that those heroes who had ascended into Heaven were in a state of perfect liberty, enjoying not only heavenly bliss but as much bodily pleasure as they wanted, with no restrictions. This is plain from reading the poets (not to mention the philosophers), who allowed them to do anything that was not directly contradictory to Nature.

Cicero, in *The Nature of the Gods*, mentions a temple to Liberty (Book II), and Vettori mentions one on the Aventine Hill. There was also a Palace of Liberty, which is frequently mentioned by [ancient] authors, but I am not sure what went on there; perhaps there were auctions there, as there were in some other temples? Livy mentions a temple to Liberty with beautiful brass statues and columns which was built by Tiberius Gracchus, whose porch was repaired and enlarged by Aelius Paetus[26] and Cornelius Cethegus,[27] and Suetonius tells us that it was restored yet again by Pollio.[28] When Cicero was

---

[25]Johann Rozsfeld [Rosinus] (1551–1626) was a German antiquarian and sub-rector of the Ratisbon Gymnasium. His *Antiquitatum Romanorum corpus absolutissimum* (1583) was a valuable source for both mythology and the history of ancient buildings in Rome.

[26]Sextus Aelius Paetus Catus, a distinguished Roman jurist, was consul in 198 B.C. His works include the *Tripertita*, an interpretation of the Law of the Twelve Tables.

[27]Gaius Cornelius Cethegus (d. 63 B.C.) was a Roman senator who conspired against the state and joined Catiline. He was put to death by Cicero, who was then consul.

[28]Gaius Asinius Pollio (76 B.C.–5 A.D.) was a Roman scholar, soldier, statesman and literary critic. He built the first public library in Italy, and wrote a history of the Civil Wars.

exiled, the tribune P. Claudius[29] dedicated [the former's] house to Liberty. Dio states that the Romans, in gratitude to Julius Caesar, built by public decree a temple to Liberty. This is enough said about liberty, which is the most important possession that an honest man can have both now and in the life to come.

Safety

The goddess Salus was worshipped by the ancients so that she would give them security, not only individual bodily security, but that more general kind which pertained to the State. They venerated her so much that they only mentioned her name on festival-days, as Macrobius tells us. Cicero mentions the temple of Salus and Livy writes of one built by the censor Junius Bubulcus,[30] which gave its name to the gate next to it, the Porta Salutaris. The Romans, as the ancients often note, frequently consulted the auguries of Salus, and Dio informs us how this was carried out:

> After the Romans had been free from war for a year, they consulted the auguries of Salus once again. It is a kind of divination by which they are told whether they can request the permission of the gods for the people's safety, as if it were impious to ask without permission. A particular day is set aside every year for this, on which no army must be in the field, and no enemy in sight. Therefore these rites are not performed when the danger is immediate, or when there is civil strife. Otherwise, it would be impossible for the Romans to observe the day exactly, and in any case it would have been absurd to implore safety from God when they were killing each other, or whether they conquered or were being conquered.

This indicates how arrogant the priests were, [decreeing] that public petitions for safety could not be made without their permission. They thus contrived in every way to bring the peoples' neck under their yoke, but this was very unjust; who, either in peace or war, should not be allowed to ask the gods for safety, and without the priests' permission?

---

[29]Publius Clodius [not Claudius] Pulcher (d. 52 B.C.) was a notoriously loose-living Roman politician. He was the deadly enemy of Cicero, and a friend of Caesar, with whose wife he conducted an affair. He was praetor (61), tribune (58) and aedile (56). His most famous act is his driving Cicero into exile. He was murdered by Milo, whom the returned Cicero defended.

[30]Caius Junius Bubulcus was consul three times (317, 313, 311 B.C.). He actually built the temple to Salus when he was dictator, not censor (302 B.C.) and after a celebrated victory over the Aequi. Smith (151) mentions that the temple was famous for its paintings by Q. Fabius Pictor.

Happiness

Felicitas has long been worshipped as a deity, in the hope that she will bestow happiness on humanity; some people think there is little difference between Happiness and Blessedness, and they are often synonymous in ancient writers. But they are not the same; the ancients believed that Happiness came from external causes, whilst Blessedness pertained to the inward action of the soul. Thus philosophers thought that only Virtue could make one happy; Fortitude would overcome fear and terror, and Temperance would repress the fire of lust. Herodotus, quoting Solon, makes this distinction very clear. When answering Croesus's question, [Solon] said that no man can truly be called blessed "before he has ended his life in virtue," which means that people may be called "fortunate" in this life, but "blessed" only after death. And Ovid also says that "I call no-one happy/ Before his death and funeral rites." No-one can properly be said to be *beatus* (blessed) in this life, and the pagans applied the term only to people who had gone to enjoy eternity in the Elysian Fields.

St. Augustine writes that "Felicitas was a Roman goddess who had a temple and an altar, and proper rites were performed for her" (*City of God*, IV).

[Some Others]

There was a temple to Ops, the goddess of help, and Victoria, so that enemies might be defeated, and other temples erected to aspects of rulers, such as Caesar's Clemency, the Justice of Augustus, and even Poppaea's Fecundity. But I have already been rather long-winded about these pagan deities, insofar as some of them were not even good people, let alone gods, and because of them religion became degraded, especially when the power of government was vested in one person. By flattery, almost all the worship which should have been paid to the Supreme God, and even to the heroes, went to living emperors, so that flattery undermined superstition itself as it had subverted religion before it. What is most objectionable about this is that while superstition may gain ascendancy over the stupid and fearful masses, flattery is only effective with the lowest and vilest.

Expiations and Lustrations[31]

Before I discuss the above rites, some of which I may look upon favourably, I should register my disapproval of them, but not of the ends for which they

---

[31]I have retained Herbert's original sub-heading for the following reasons. The word *expiatio* may be translated as "atonement," "appeasement," or "expiation." *Lus-*

were carried out, for they were very useful in guiding the ignorant masses. Furthermore, I would ask any modern priest who condemns them to tell me whether he could have invented anything better.

I will start with expiations and lustrations, together with those other solemn rites supposed to be useful for the purging of the soul. Having examined those virtues through which the ancients thought Heaven could be reached, it is now necessary to add those things which helped those who had deviated from the true path back to the right way and cure them from errors; this, they believed, could be done through expiations and lustrations, and without them no-one could be freed from either his crime or its punishment. The pagans had the same ideas about sin and vice as we do; they believed that all sin or vice originated either from anger, which, when stirred, could grow into malice or fury, from covetousness and depravity exerting themselves in various ways, from bad company, or from imprudence and ignorance about what was evil. The pagans, especially philosophers, prescribed the following remedies: 1. Restrain evil desires; 2. Atone for those sins which are in the conscience, and with the assistance of a priest perform an expiation to purify the soul; 3. Stay away from wicked and debauched people or conversation; 4. Understand plainly what is meant by good, and how to avoid evil; 5. Correct and curb the human passions; 6. Make frequent and properly devout atonements, according to the directions of the priests, so that the gods may be made favourable.

Plato[32] advises people who had evil or troubled thoughts in their minds to pray to the *Dii averrunci*, amongst whom the Greeks counted Zeus, according to Lucian, and Apollo, according to Aristophanes. Afterwards [Plato] recommends that people keep good company, and further, apply themselves to philosophy as the best way to purify their souls. Nothing was advised by either the theologians or philosophers of Greece and Rome except that which encouraged people to live well and happily, and to preserve them from evil. All wicked people, [however], should expect to suffer eternal punishment after this life, especially if their vices had become natural or

---

tratio is rather more complex. The latter referred to a specific ceremony performed every five years by the Roman censors as a purification rite. It was also applied to such rites as the Ambarvalia or Amburbia (see below), and the general ceremony seems to have involved a procession around something, sacrificial activities, and shouting, chanting or singing. A lustration, then, is a public or state ceremony, and was often, but not always, connected with expiation.

[32]"When thoughts of such things assail you, hasten to the rites that baffle chance, hasten in supplication to the altars of the gods . . . hasten to the company of men of virtuous repute" (Plato, *Laws* IX, 854b–c; Hamilton and Cairns 1415).

habitual. Cicero, in a letter to Atticus, says that "our remorse for having sinned is great and long-lasting; the gods will be satisfied, however, if our souls are purged and cleansed either here or elsewhere." It was believed that man, in his own nature, was neither good nor evil, but could incline either way according to his upbringing. Vice and sin were not so completely rooted in man's nature that they could never be weeded out and destroyed, so that unless the soul was stubbornly bent on sinning, internal purification or external admonition might restore it again to a good state. As Seneca says, "he who repents of his sins is always innocent."

The ancients, then, did not believe that so many people were condemned to eternal punishment, because they considered that divine wrath had a limit, and that God would not completely destroy his handiwork when he could repair it or reinforce it instead. Not even mortals ever build houses so that they can burn them down. Both priests and philosophers believed that reparation could be made through repentance, and they continually encouraged people to practice it, although it could not be done without their assistance. They were right to do this, because although our souls are naturally inclined to repent, merely by the internal dictates of conscience, we also find that it is necessary to do so without any motivation. Indeed, it is no more than turning back to the right path from which we have strayed. Thus Periander[33] says, "when you have done something wrong, atone for it," and so it seems that repentance was a remedy against all evil for the pagans, a plank after a shipwreck onto which they could climb at the least offence. Cicero says, "those things which seem small offences, and which many people ignore, should be carefully avoided," and he means in case they become habits and that we should not atone for them. Thus a subconscious or hidden disease often proves as fatal as an obvious one; indeed, the less it is perceived, the more dangerous, even incurable, it might become, and repentance is the only sure medicine against the illnesses of the soul. This is probably what Menander[34] meant when he said that "repentance is one of man's crises," for when the fever of man's mind is over, he is restored to his

---

[33]Periander (d. 585 B.C.) reigned as tyrant of Corinth 625–585. He was a great patron of philosophy and poetry; Plutarch set his *Symposium of the Seven Wise Men* at Periander's court. Another great admirer was Herodotus (see 1.23–24, 3.48–53, 5.92–95).

[34]Menander (c. 342–290 B.C.) was the greatest writer of the "New Comedy" in Athens, and author of over 100 plays. Only the *Dyskolos* has been preserved intact. Plautus and Terence were greatly influenced by him. There is a modern translation by Carroll Moulton (New York: Mentor Books, 1977).

pristine state. The ancients were not ignorant of the power that sin holds over the mind; as Lucretius confesses,

> Thus the conscious-ridden mind,
> In terrified anticipation, torments itself with
> Its own goads and whips. It cannot not see the end
> Of suffering, nor the end of punishment,
> And is afraid that death will just intensify pain.[35]

He was afraid that death might be the beginning of misery rather than the end, and that men would suffer even more severe punishments afterwards.[36] It is therefore quite evident, from here and from many other places, that the pagans considered repentance as the universal atonement or sacrament of Nature.

But now the priests began to involve [atonement] in a great number of mysterious rites and ceremonies which obscured it, and thus they made people believe that only they had the power and authority from the divine. They told the masses that if they would only devote themselves entirely to their priests they might rest secure; [the priests] appointed themselves mediators between God and Man, and [claimed] that God had delegated the power to them of procuring pardon for sinners. However, the wiser and bolder amongst the pagans thought this to be impious and arrogant; as Cicero says, "there can be had no expiation for sin and impiety from other mortals," and Ovid says, "It can never be easy to fall into crime/ And think that it can be washed away with river-water." Cicero, however, thinks that some lesser sins many indeed be expiated, but "any sacred rite that is performed, yet does not expiate sin, is impious; let the public priests expiate what they may." It was to the great detriment of virtue that they set themselves up for God's vengeance, and nothing was ever so destructive to virtue and injurious to the true adoration of God than the religious fraud of priests. Is there anything that a wicked person will not do when he knows that he can make an easy atonement for his sins?

---

[35] Lucretius, *On the Nature of the Universe* III, 1018–23. Adapted from the prose translation of R.E. Latham (Harmondsworth: Penguin Books, 1951).

[36] In all fairness to Lucretius, this is not what he is saying at all. What he is doing in this passage is painting a picture of the fears that beset people who have not been reading their Epicurus properly. Lucretius has explained (in the passage directly before these lines) that people feel like this because they are "wedded to the self" (128). Death, for Lucretius, is simply an eternity of "not-being," and those torments which we think are coming after death simply take place here and now, in our own lives.

I must acknowledge, however, that if the precepts of true repentance had accompanied those sacred rites, they might have anticipated God's secret counsels and judgments. If the words "penitence" or "repentance" seem rather modern for some people, I will not argue, because I can prove that the pagans had a sense of the divine anger, and that they repented for their sins.[37] It is beyond a doubt that what we term "repentance" was, indeed, amongst them a feeling of sorrow that they had sinned, and that they might have provoked God's anger. If they had not been so afflicted, surely they would not have invented so many sacred rites to pacify the gods, built and dedicated so many temples, and made so many prayers and vows. It would be tedious for me to rehearse all the public testimonies that they gave of their sorrow and remorse for offending the gods, and it is obvious from the authority of their writers that the pagans were always ready to blame themselves for God's wrath and for their sins, and that they contemplated the divine vengeance humbly and penitently in their minds. I am equally sure that the pagans repented of those things that caused them evil, and although the word "penitence" is rarely found used in the modern sense in their writings, we have adopted it from them, and have rediscovered it. As Seneca so aptly says, "The knowledge of sin is the beginning of salvation," for once a sinner comes to feel horror for his sins, he will soon repent, and will return to the practice of that virtue from which he had strayed.

The pagans believed that repentance, or sorrow for their sins, was effective and sufficient when the offence was committed against the Supreme God, but not when crimes were perpetrated against other human beings; this required that justice and compensation be made here and now. However, if the priests attempted to argue that repentance was not a sufficient atonement for divine justice, then these points might be advanced: 1. The Supreme God is the father of all, and would thus not reject a penitent child; 2. Human beings are naturally prone to sin; 3. People generally sin because they want

---

[37] It might be of use here to clarify the two terms "penitence" and "repentance." Repentance, to a Protestant (or at least to a non-Catholic like Herbert) was something inward, perhaps akin to the modern word "contrition." A Catholic, on the other hand, performs an act of "penance" to obtain forgiveness for sins; this act is outward, even public. Herbert makes a show of objectivity, or at least neutrality on the difference between the two, although it is hard to imagine him having much sympathy for Catholicism, and many of his readers would have none whatsoever. On the other hand, if either act is imposed by a priestly hierarchy, Herbert is not in favour of it, so while he may be anti-Catholic in his anti-clericalism, what he attacks might also be applied to the more extreme varieties of Protestantism, and even to Lutheranism in some cases, as Kortholt, Musaeus and the other Lutheran critics of Herbert clearly recognised.

something for themselves, not in defiance of God, which means that they did not sin with evil or malice in mind, or to insult God; 4. Sufficient punishment for this type of crime may be dealt out in this life; 5. If any further punishment was needed, God could inflict it after this life, for a short or long period, according to the gravity of the sin.[38]

Now, if God can inflict fitting punishment, there would be no reason to have recourse to bloody sacrifices (which were invented by the priests) to appease Him, as if God took pleasure in the shedding of blood, either of oxen or, which is horrible beyond words, of humans. Could an ox, moreover, really make amends for a human, or one person for another, and

---

[38]This passage caused great problems for some of Herbert's readers, who were convinced that he did not take sin as seriously as he should. And indeed, what Herbert proposes here is hardly a Christian and nowhere near a Calvinist point of view, although he does note that one effective argument is the claim that humans are naturally prone to sin. But Herbert does not suggest even here that they are naturally doomed to damnation; in fact, as he states at the beginning of this work, the fact that man is prone to sin means that God should be all the more willing to forgive. In *De veritate*, Herbert had said that sin was "an almost necessary compulsion" (180), and he believed even in this early work that God would always be lenient to those who were suitably repentant. Richard Baxter, for one, did not agree; he thought that Herbert was thereby saying that all men were good, which was as ridiculous as Calvin saying that they were all depraved. "None perisheth," Baxter wrote, "for the mere sin of Adam, nor merely for want of innocency required of the first law" (*More Reasons for the Christian Religion* [1672], 569). Baxter saw that if God himself dealt directly with sin, as Herbert suggests here and in the present work, then the role of Christ is at best superfluous. The problem is that Herbert was not worried about this: he sees no need for a redeemer and he likely did not believe in original sin either. But compare Pascal, "We know God only through Jesus Christ. Without this mediator all communication with God is broken off. Through Jesus we know God" (*Pensées* 85–86).

On the subject of "further punishment," it might be noted that as the Protestants discarded Purgatory, those sinners who were not quite as bad as the ones who went to Hell, but who were nevertheless unworthy of Heaven, posed a theological problem. It was traditional Church doctrine that Hell was eternal punishment, and to deny this would have been heretical. On the other hand, punishment could be shortened for venial sins or sins that a soul in Purgatory had not yet expiated. People were initially concerned about the consequences of the abolition of Purgatory, which looked as if people would now have to burn in Hell even for minor sins. That this point was indeed important to Herbert is obvious from the beginning of the present work; he does not want to contemplate the possibility of all sinners from all times being perhaps condemned to burn forever in Hell. To him this was cruelty, pure and simple, and any religion that condoned it was unworthy of the God it purported to worship.

was the substitution just and fair? No; these sacrifices were instituted to strike fear into the people and so that the priests and their friends might feast themselves with what was left over.

I am now coming to those rites which the pagans used for the purification of their souls. There were many kinds and methods of expiation and they had many names, such as *expiationes, expiamenta, piamenta, piamina, Februae, lustrationes, purgationum animae* and *purificationes*. The words differ very little in their meanings, because they all had to do with purgation or purification amongst the pagans. Not everything could be so expiated, and I have shown from Cicero and others that crimes against human beings could not be atoned for, and they did not think that all sins could be washed away by piacular or lustral rites which only had the power to absolve the conscience from some sorts of sins. And when a public lustration was performed for any crime, the magistrate did not have the authority to add punishments to it. Lustration and expiation were also performed for the welfare and prosperity of the city or for the armed forces, and the greater the crowd that attended, the more effective the lustration would be. Dionysius tells us how the public expiation of a city was carried out:

> When the conspiracy had been defeated, the Senate ordered that a lustration be performed for the whole city. The person responsible for the civil war had made it necessary that this be done. It was impious to perform any rites or sacrifices before expiation was made for the crime and that the stigma be removed by the customary lustrations. When the Chief Priest had performed all the religious ceremonies according to custom, the Senate then ordered public thanksgiving returned to God, and instituted games.

It is worth noting here what great respect they had for these public expiations; no-one dared perform any religious rites or offer sacrifices until they were over. Dionysius also mentions another public lustration in Rome; the Roman army was paraded, and their weapons were lustrated before they set out on their march. A bull, ram and he-goat (or, as Livy reports, a sow, sheep and bull) were led three times around the camp and then sacrificed. Livy also mentions some strange rites performed by the Macedonians in their military lustrations, where they cut up a dog. Dionysius speaks of lustrations for the army after a war; there were also public and private expiations in times of strife. Manslaughter could be expiated by piacular sacrifices, and when they were being performed, the accused was placed under a yoke. Dionysius tells us about M. Horatius Tergiminus, who killed his own sister, and Livy mentions him as well; he was expiated at the public's expense. Herodotus reports that amongst the Greeks and Lydians there was expiation for manslaughter, and Diodorus Siculus has information on Ethiopian expiations. Pliny gives an account of the Februae, which are similar to other expiations:

> It was popular opinion that the Februae were any rites performed to cleanse a guilty conscience, to procure pardon for sins and rest for the souls of the dead.

Festus says that the Februae were so-called because February, being the last month of the year, was when people performed the Februae, lustrations and purgations for 12 days at a time, and that everyone was occupied during that period in procuring peace and quiet for the souls of the departed. There were piacular sacrifices, lighted torches and wax candles placed around their graves. Ovid tells us that the Februae "were those expiations which our ancestors used," and, according to Columella and Tibullus, even the fields and fruit were lustrated. Tibullus writes, "That you may favour us, we lustrate fruit and fields, /And perform the ancient rites in them." See also Vergil in his *Eclogues* and *Georgics*. Sextus Pompeius notes that "the Ambarvalia is that sacrifice which is led around ploughed land, when divine rites are performed for the harvest." Amburbiae were rites performed for the lustration of city districts, for which see Lucan, *Pharsalia* I. The Romans also performed expiations for their houses and the spirits of the dead.

Dreams could also be expiated through washing the body and offering sacrifices, as we understand from Persius, *Satire* I, Juvenal, *Satire* I, and Tibullus, *Elegies* I, v and III, iv. The *lustrici dies* of girls was the eighth day, and of boys the ninth, because that was when they were purified and given names. Macrobius tells us, "These days were formerly those on which children were purified and had names given to them." The people who performed them were known as *lustratores* (men) or *lustratices* (women). Suetonius mentions these days in his "Life of Claudius," and Persius, in *Satire* II writes:

> See an old woman, bringing a cradle to the gods,
> Taking up the baby boy; with wet lips his head
> She anoints, with her finger moistened with lustral spit,
> Making her expiation . . .

(Satire II, ll. 30–34)

I could say more, but I would like to be brief. These were most of the rites used by the pagans in purgation and purification of the soul.

Purgation was important in the ceremonies of Bacchus, to which Vergil alludes in the line concerning "Bacchus's mystic fan" in Book I of the *Georgics*. This fan is made of willow and is broad like a sieve used by farmers to gather harvests; they use it to fan the corn. Columella[39] says, "The ears [of corn] are best threshed with clubs, but cleared with fans." Servius, commenting on the line I have just quoted from Vergil, notes:

> They were called Bacchic Mysteries because the sacred rites of Liber Pater concerned the purification of the soul, and people were purged by the mysteries as the corn was by the fan. So it was said that when Set tore Osiris to pieces, Isis put them in a sieve. Liber Pater is the one whose mysteries employ a fan, because, as I have said, he purged souls and makes them free.

A little later on [Servius says]: "Some call Liber Pater Licnetes, and the fan licnos. It is the custom to lay a child on it as soon as it is born." This name for Bacchus is also mentioned by Plutarch. Harpocration says that the fan is "convenient for all beginnings and sacrifices." Concerning the fan, you may refer to Grotius and Heinsius; it is also mentioned in Matthew 3:12 and Luke 3:17, and Vergil mentions a threefold rite observed in Heaven for the purgation of souls: "Others naked are exposed/ Suspended on the winds, still others under huge whirlpools / Pay for their crimes, or are purged with fire." From this Vossius deduces that the pagans had a threefold purgation, by air, water, and fire, and Servius, commenting on Book VI of the *Aeneid*, notes that "three purgations are used in all sacred rites; people are either purged with fire and brimstone, washed with water, or fanned by the air." And Vergil, in Book I of the *Georgics*, says ". . . and for you/ Dolls hang on the lofty pine-tree." The small dolls (*oscillae*) were images with which sacrifices were offered to Saturn for people and their children. Macrobius says that the *oscilla* hung on the tree and was purged by air, and thus stood for the external purification of the soul, rather like those images which, as I have mentioned earlier, were thrown into rivers to take the place of human beings. I note here that the purgations were performed only by those parts which composed man's body, so that when his elemental part was purified, everything else would be as well. The pagans thought that they were the seat of vice, and from there the latter insinuated itself into the soul.

I know that these rites are rather ridiculous, but do we not have now what is equivalent to them? Without some sort of rites and ceremonies the people would have too much freedom, and the priests too little time to exercise power and authority, so it was sufficient that these things were invented for the purification of the soul. Indeed, if the priests had been able to make people feel penitence and horror for their crimes, mankind would have been

---

[39]Lucius Junius Moderatus Columella (fl. 65 A.D.), writer on agriculture and the keeping of livestock and bees. His famous work is *De re rustica*, but there is a lost work, *De lustrationibus*. I can find no record of a translation before 1745.

better for it, and it is to be regretted that they were so very cautious, in case their impure flocks should actually get rid of their sins without assistance from them! They set themselves up as the only people who could be in charge of the Public Scrubbing-Brush, if I may call it such.

I hope that I have now sufficiently shown that as the pagans worshipped the same God and Father, and that they believed in the same virtues and penitence, as we do, which we acknowledge as the surest sign of God's divine grace. It was either generated from within them, as an internal sense of sin, or engraved by God himself upon their hearts. The bloody sacrifices and other cruel aspects of their religion were introduced only so that they might appease the wrath of God for their sins and wickedness, repent, and be able to stand purified and expiated before God.

Rewards and Punishments

Now that we have examined the kind of virtue which enables us to approach the divine, and penitence which puts us on the path of virtue, it now remains to investigate what the pagans thought about rewards and punishments. This is the last and most noble part of the old religious cults. They believed that there were rewards for good, and punishments for evil, in both this life and the life to come, depending on the goodness and justice of the Supreme God; all their writings abound with evidence that they acknowledged these as the most important attributes of the Supreme God. God was to be worshipped for himself, they asserted, because his highly-exalted nature was worthy of the highest praises, but at the same time they looked forward to a happier state than this present life as the outcome of his goodness. It was planted in their souls that God could and would grant them a better life if they behaved suitably. They did not think that God or Destiny had placed them in the world for no purpose and that they would at last return to oblivion. Neither [did they believe] that their life here was so perfect that there could be nothing nobler or more excellent; some secret promptings of nature hinted otherwise. God did not hate human virtue; he would distinguish between the just or pious and the wicked in their externally happy state. The ancient sages, theologians and philosophers freely taught that God would reward the good and punish the wicked.

On the other hand, they saw that good people here were oppressed and unlucky, and that certain bad people flourished and enjoyed all the pleasures and riches of the world. Yet divine justice was a sufficient argument that the good would be rewarded and the wicked punished in the next life. If this were not true, there would be no proof; there is a great deal of evidence from the past that good people suffered very much in those times, and Seneca observed, "Believe me, God does not give good men the good life, but tests them and proves them." This [testing] gives people ample time to exercise virtue, and when good people are prosperous, they are rarely examples of virtue; when things go wrong, however, they have the opportunity to show their resilience. But when the ancients saw that tyrants and other immoral people seemed to enjoy all the good things in life, they concluded that divine justice must punish them afterwards. So far, then, the notions of the philosophers, and even the priests, are sensible. It was when they decided in what places the good received their rewards and the wicked their punishments, such as the Elysian Fields, the Isles of the Blessed, the Stars and Heaven for the virtuous, and for the wicked Tartarus, Erebus, and the four infernal rivers, that they fall into error. It would have been easier to convince people that Divine Justice had allotted punishments after this life according to everyone's deserts, even if they did not know the place, manner, or duration of them. Instead, they stupidly determined the place to be in some dark subterranean caverns near the centre of the earth, or in spaces somewhere in the middle regions of the air, together with other circumstances equally absurd or uncertain. Their making Heaven and the Stars the dwelling-place of the blessed was not so strange, because mankind has usually held that the state of eternal happiness is only to be found in God or Heaven.

At this point some people may object that the pagans did not have such clear ideas about good or evil in their consciences, that they did not have just and virtuous rules to guide and govern their conduct as Christians have, and that they therefore could not have such a strong belief in either a better life or a dread of future punishments. To this I can answer as follows. As to our conscience, Cicero says that "its power is very great on either side," and so from a good conscience arises a great comfort of the mind, and, on the contrary, those who consciously lead vicious lives always have dismal forebodings of punishment before their eyes, which many of the ancients confessed. Lucretius the Epicurean, for example, says that "a conscious mind bites back." They also attest to the signs of a good conscience, which are fortitude, faith, constancy and joy, whilst those of an evil one are fear, terror, sorrow and despair.

Suetonius mentions the latter in his "Life of Nero" as not being able to endure the remorse of their own consciences, and Cicero says that "the Furies themselves haunt criminals." There are also external signs of a good conscience in the face or in speech: the body is held straight, the eyes and mouth look cheerful and fearless, and there are many other signs as well. A guilty conscience is accompanied by blushing, pallor, hesitation or abruptness in the speech, or trembling. There were many other indications of the conscience. And therefore, insofar as divine goodness gave the same intellect, freedom of will and other faculties to the pagans, as we can see from any of their writings and actions, there is no reason to object that the same goodness was also given to them, and the same consciences endowed with the same common principles which direct and activate us now. Nobody who knows a reasonable amount about them would be able, in any case, to deny it. I conclude, then, that [pagans] practiced the same virtues leading to eternal happiness, and had the same conscience and the same divine grace that we have. Does St. Paul [sic. Luke] not say in Acts 10 that the prayers and supplications of Cornelius, a mere pagan, would reach heaven? The pagans could have gathered undeniable arguments for divine justice and goodness from conscience alone, and from that they could have concluded that a future state existed. There is a pertinent passage in Cicero, where he says that "the weight of the conscience would be heavy if there were no divine reason for virtue and vice." That excellent man believed that divine justice would hardly be enough if virtue had no other reward besides popular praise, or that vice had no other punishment besides external blame or infamy here. Who would not be completely self-indulgent if all that was stopping him was a lack of public approval? Cicero thought that nothing could be more pleasing to the Greatest and Best God than that those people who had made themselves stand out like gods with their virtue should be admitted into divine society. And this was not just his opinion, but that of all the pagans; they deified heroes and called them by the names of stars, or called the stars by heroes' names, as I have already shown.

There were two Greek words for conscience, *synteresis* and *syneidesis*. The first referred to judgment, the second to will. Not only are some common notions, derived from universal wisdom (by which the world is governed), engraved on the conscience, but also those general axioms of theological or moral virtue, those rules and disciplines which correct the will and which determine what is good or just. Some examples are "do as you would be done by," or "when in doubt, choose the safest route." [The conscience], therefore, when freed from errors and imperfections, gives virtuous people the greatest comfort and support, but torments the wicked with unspeakable horror and anguish. So Cicero says that "everyone is tormented by his own wickedness and oppressed by his own folly; evil thoughts and a bad conscience terrify the mind." And Seneca advises that we should "have a greater care of conscience than of fame;" fame may deceive us, but conscience never will. Polybius writes, "there is no witness as formidable, no judge so impartial as conscience, which is in the mind of us all." Plutarch writes that "an evil conscience is like a festering sore which eats away at the body by degrees."

And a verse of Ovid also relates to this, "It is less to suffer than it is to deserve our fate."

But, as Cicero says, "how pleasant it is to be conscious of a good life, and the memory of good actions." Everyone will find out experimentally how true this is as he grows older, and nothing else beside it will relieve distress in the hour of death. It is a commonplace that when you travel, or when alone, you should be especially careful, so that evil thoughts do not creep in and get a foothold on your mind. When you are farthest away from an enemy, that is the time to beware. The Supreme God inspects our consciences rather than external actions, and judges from them what good or evil we have done. Seneca's advice to "commit nothing to your conscience that you cannot trust to a friend" is very apt, for whatever can be safely thought may be safely communicated. God searches our hearts and consciences, and he sees our most private secrets. Cicero says, "conscience is the greatest theatre for virtue," and although we may not have external opportunities for displaying our virtue, there is never a lack of evidence for it in the theatre of conscience. When our sins have been purged through repentance, God sees only that which is pure and clean; when the virtues are in their proper place (virtue does not operate at random, but adapts to particular occasions) they are ready to receive the praise for doing well and the blame for doing ill. The Common Notions sit as judges, and the Supreme God is the arbitrator. Menander says, "God is the conscience of all mortals," but this must be meant poetically, because the conscience is not a deity, but a faculty which has been built into the soul by God to judge between good and evil, and this produces the hope of a better life to come. Others say that conscience is not a deity but a daemon, genius or angel, assisting and informing the soul. Plato, Proclus and some later Platonists believed that when it was pleased it was called a Grace, and when angry, a Fury, for which see Ficino in his commentary on Plato's *Republic*. A good conscience, then, is the beginning of eternal salvation, and an evil one of future punishments, so that not only in the afterlife, but in this life, there are rewards and punishments in the theatre of conscience by way of a foretaste. But the pagans believed that the rewards were more glorious after this life and the punishments more unbearable.

Places of Reward and Punishment

Now we shall examine in detail some places of reward and punishment, according to ancient doctrines. Plato taught in the *Phaedo* that the pure soul passed on to pure and eternal things, to which the impure soul, infected with earthly matters, was attracted. It carried with it affectations and habits from both the understanding and the will which would either immediately prejudice it or work to its advantage. He adds that the souls are led by a genius, daemon, or angel to public judgment, and that when this is over they are sent through a place with three openings. Some, the purest, ascend to Heaven, others are cast down into Hell, and still others wander aimlessly about in the middle regions of the air, without a guide. The daemon or angel supports and improves the understanding of the good, but disturbs the imagination and emotions of the bad, thus making the rewards and punishments belong to the life after death.

Plato, describing the places designed for punishment, mentions four allegorical infernal rivers. *Acheron*, a purging river, runs under the earth and signifies care or sorrow. It has a correspondence with Air and with the southern climates of the world. *Periphlegethon* is the river of Fire and of the east, and, because of its heat, has the power to punish, and chastises souls for anger or lustful desires. *Styx* and *Cocytus* correspond with the Earth and with the west, and there hatred is punished through weeping and mourning. Ficino says that these two differ only in that Styx rises out of Hell while Cocytus flows, but he does not understand this correctly. After these comes Tartarus, or Hell itself, the lowest place in the infernal region, in which the very impious or wicked were punished, not to rehabilitate them, but to make an example of them, as Plato says in his *Gorgias*[40] and in Book I of the *Republic*.

The Platonists claimed that there were two kinds of sin, curable and incurable. Curable sins are sins that have not yet become habits, and have been committed with some misgivings; they are always coupled with serious

---

[40]The relevant passage in the *Gorgias* is 523–27 (Cairns and Hamilton 304–07). Socrates says, amongst other things, that "those who are benefited by suffering punishment by gods and men are those whose deeds are curable . . . those who have been guilty of the most heinous crimes and whose misdeeds are past cure, of these warnings are made, and they are no longer capable themselves of receiving any benefit, because they are incurable; but others are benefited who behold them suffering throughout eternity the greatest and most terrifying tortures because of their misdeeds" (305).

Herbert has a problem with the number of Cerberus's heads, and in deference to animal rights the record should be set straight. Hesiod, in his *Theogony* (l. 311) describes "the unspeakable,/ unmanageable/ Kerberos, the savage,/ the bronze-barking dog of Hades,/ fifty-headed" (141). The three-headed version seems to have appeared "in late archaic classical literature and art" (*OCD* 181), and the appellations Herbert quotes are Roman rather than Greek. In all fairness to Herbert, if not to Cerberus, H.J. Rose points out that "the number [of heads] is variously given, according to the individual writer's fancy" (55).

repentance. Incurable sins are habitual, committed without reluctance or intention of repenting; as they are beyond redemption they are termed incurable, and in the *Phaedo*, those wicked wretches that commit them are consigned to Tartarus, from whence they do not return.

It appears, therefore, that the pagans believed misgivings could alleviate sin, and that repentance could cure it completely; if any still remained, it could be washed away by a punishment specially ordained after life. Plato says that souls in this life are best purified through philosophy; thus philosophers, made complete and perfect through contemplation, are raised to Heaven and to celestial things. They mount up to a supercelestial place and live there for ever and ever. Porphyry and Iamblichus share much the same opinion, and assert that those souls perfectly restored to God can never again fall.

In the *Gorgias*, Plato describes Hell as a sort of dungeon where severe punishments take place, and he tells an interesting story about the last judgment of mankind. But Plato is not the only famous author to mention the four rivers of Hell, and there is no point in inserting other descriptions here. I cannot omit, however, mentioning that according to the ancient poets, the gods used to swear by the Stygian Lake, which encompasses the infernal regions. If they broke the oath, they had to divest themselves of their divinity for a year, and were not allowed to have nectar or ambrosia. The reason for this is explained in a further myth, but I am not sure of its significance; in any case, I have already mentioned it in the chapter about the worship of water.

There was another river, *Lethe*, which made mortals forget their pasts; the etymology of this name may be derived from Greek sources, as may that of the others by people who like to do these things. My purpose is to show that the ancients believed that some people suffered great grief and upheavals in their minds when they died and that others seemed merely to be sleeping, although their sleep was eternal death.

In Hell were Pluto's assistants, the Furies and Harpies, together with *Cerberus*, known by some as *Triceps* (three-headed), and by Hesiod as *Centiceps* (one hundred-headed). His duty was to lie at the Gates of Hell and welcome all who entered, but tear to pieces anyone who tried to get out.

The State of Souls

I am getting rather tired of these insipid and crazy poetic fictions, although it must be admitted that they do contain some spiritual sense. I now come to the philosophers, who held various opinions about the state of souls. They are in agreement about the diversity of the kind and degree of the rewards, whether they are to be found in Heaven, in the Stars, in some aetherial region where they eat airy fruit, on the Isles of the Blessed, or in the Elysian Fields. The pagans do not agree, however, about punishments. Plato, following the Pythagoreans, the Magi, and the Egyptian priests in Book IX of his *Laws*,[41] says that human souls return again in human bodies in which they suffer punishments suitable to the crimes they committed in life.

This seems also to have been the opinion of the Egyptian priests and the Magi. They believed that there could be no better purgatory for a sinner than suffering in a human body; Plotinus thought this idea so reasonable that he openly declares in his book *De providentia* that whatever Divine Providence does not punish in this life it will in the next. And it will not do so according to human reason and justice alone, but in a harsh manner: those that were formerly human souls will become the souls of animals. He was the only Platonist who held this opinion, for although Plato himself sometimes mentions the transmigration of souls, he does it so absurdly

---

[41]I am not sure of the passage in Book IX of Plato's *Laws* to which Herbert is referring. Book IX (Cairns and Hamilton 1414–40) discusses murder, its punishment, and the state of the deceased person's soul (871b–e). There is also a section on suicide and its implications (873c–d). There is no mention of either Pythagoras or Epicurus. There is a reference in Book X, however (903d), when the Athenian says that "a soul, in its successive conjunction first with one body and then with another, runs the whole gamut of change through its own action or that of some other soul" (*CH* 1459). It is to this passage that Herbert seems to be drawing attention.

Stories about Pythagoras are recorded by Philolaus of Croton, a contemporary of Socrates and Plato. If Herodotus thought that the Egyptians believed in the transmigration of souls he was wrong. Robinson thinks that "the belief could have reached Europe from the East, and the story . . . that Pythagoras travelled eastward as far as Babylonia before returning to settle at Croton, may actually be true" (61).

"Egyptians . . . grandfather." Herbert refers to the Hindu (not Buddhist) doctrine of *samsara*, or rebirth. Radhakrishnan writes that "the Hindu holds that the goal of spiritual perfection is the crown of a long, patient effort. Man grows by lives into his divine self-existence. Every life, every act, is a step which we may take either backwards or forwards. By one's thought, will, and action one determines what one is yet to be" (634). Herbert is well-informed on this subject, and realises that the Brahmins are the priestly caste. He would also have been aware of the reincarnation theories of both Pythagoras and the Orphics, but his sources, unfortunately, cannot be determined with any certainty. A relative, Sir Thomas Herbert, had resided at the court of the Moghul Emperor Jahangir, and had written a book on his travels. The catalogue of Herbert's books in the Jesus College Library lists no books of Herbert's which specifically deal with oriental religion, although Jan de Laet's *De imperio Magni Mongolis sive India Vera commentarius* (1631) might have contained some information.

that he either meant it allegorically or was joking, for which you may consult Ficino.

Amongst the Egyptians this opinion was very ancient. The Pythagoreans believed it, and modern people in India, whose priests are known as Brahmins (perhaps from Brahman) hold that there is *metempsychosis*, or the transmigration of souls into animals. This paradox has gained so much authority that people will not kill or eat animals, fearing that they might swallow their father's or grandfather's soul.

Plato's ideas about the state of souls after this life seem more plausible. He says that the primal nature of the sensation, the substantial origin of the other senses, which contains the whole power of the sensitive faculty after life, becomes closed up in itself. It then assumes an airy form, with which it may enter one body or go out from another. The human soul lives in this earthly body for only a short time, but in its airy form it lasts for many years — in its celestial or aetherial form it lasts for ever. Then he adds that when the souls assume their airy forms they take revenge for injuries done to them in this life, or to the bodies which then belonged to them.

I leave readers to judge all this as they may think fit, although there is nothing amongst the previous that carries more probability, except the common principles that God is good and just, and will therefore reward and punish both in this life and in the next according to our actions or thoughts. Yet great thinkers amongst the pagans began to stray beyond these boundaries, and they started to introduce many things that had no foundation in reason and had no faculty to support them. Thus a philosopher will add something, a priest another, and a poet many more, which will quite overturn the structure of truth, reducing it to a pile of rubbish. Whatever could be safely established about life after death besides these common principles unless we could consult the Inspector of the Human Conscience or partake in Divine Councils?

Some ancient writers have wisely said that good remains good, and wicked wicked, for all time, but no-one amongst them has shown us where those places are for rewards and punishments. Nor have they made any probable guess about the nature of punishment or its duration. The common dictates of reason cannot tell us whether a light punishment should be longer, or a more intense one shorter, and here the pagans heaped probabilities, possibilities and falsities on top of the glorious truth, almost stifling and smothering it, like people who make the roof of a house so heavy that the solid walls collapse. Nevertheless, the four articles I have mentioned before remained whole, and the fifth, too, *that there are rewards and punishments in life and after it*, will stand for ever and ever. If thousands of errors were piled on their bases, these five columns are so joined together that nothing, whatever its height, could endanger them or damage the building they support. They are, therefore, the foundation of Universal Divine Providence and of pure Religion, which never was and never will be concealed from any age or country. Whatever was promoted by priests in unintelligble language, mysterious myths, fictitious revelations and ambiguous rites and ceremonies imposed on the credulous masses had but a foundation of sand. The greatest philosophers in the whole world could not add anything to these five articles which could better promote true virtue, by which humans become god-like and fit for divine society, or piety, purity and a saintly life.

It might be worthwhile examining whether the additions which have been made to religion have diluted it and made it less strict by pretending that Divine Grace may be sooner obtained by auxiliary or external assistance. I know very well that tradition or great credulity has made people in all countries and in all ages believe that many things have dropped directly from heaven. These are either inconsistent in themselves or are of no value unless they are derived from the Five Religious Common Notions. People wore masks, daubed themselves with paint or had multicoloured clothes made, all of which was unseemly and dishonoured pure religion, whose reverend aspect and seamless coat was that of a noble and chaste lady. What is even more unfortunate is that, because of all this, parts of true religion were ignored or rejected, and people became atheists or condemners of Divine Justice and Providence. Even if they did embrace the whole religion, together with its attendant superstitions, they found themselves deserting right reason, the best rule of life. Those who did neither, adhered strictly to the Five Articles, while at the same time admitting to some things which were enjoined upon them by the supreme authority of the priesthood, even though they did not think that there was anything in them by which they could obtain God's plenty or bring them to Heaven.

If you look into the history of those times you will find that there was a bold attempt throughout them to reject the interpolations of the priests. People were not inclined, nor did they think it was safe, to oppose those things which God might be pleased to enact. In short, it was the duty of the person affirming the doctrine to prove it, and to allow people the freedom to judge it, and it was better for them to doubt than to deny it outright. The above articles, which are written in the heart, were favourably received by the ancient pagans, but they were not so taken by other doctrines. No-one could entirely credit the revelation of any priest, or a dream he had while lying all night in a temple, even if it were supposedly dictated by a daemon, genius or God himself. They did not have any faith in it when it was doubtful, or appeared to be a lie, or that there was only one witness, the priest himself. But you could argue that the priests were able to make some good come of these things. If something were good, it would naturally be received, but if it were evil nobody would believe, even if it were spoken by the actual voice of a so-called god. If it were said that something was spoken in the temple or from the tripod, I would ask who was nearby, or who was with the priest and could corroborate his testimony that it was God's voice? Was there anyone in former times so familiar with God that he knew his voice, or who heard God imitating a voice which made an evil or unjust pronouncement?

It is my opinion, then, that the pagans took the Five Articles as common principles, selected and isolated them from the rest, and recorded them inwardly as incontrovertible truths. Whatever else the priests might have added from oracles, revelations or dreams were received only as probabilities, or were totally rejected as reeking of fraud and imposture. But as every proposition that is made excites some new degree of knowledge, so there must be different degrees of assent or dissent in the audience. We may justifiably conclude that in that amazing hotch-potch of religion which the priests made and patched up, the pagans still held these propositions as undeniable, whilst others were more or less probable, and still others absurd, contradictory, impossible, or false.

It might be further objected that the truth could never be found whole or perfect, but was always shrouded in lies and fictions. I would answer that light or trivial truths, like things which are supported by air, or float on water, will eventually fall down or sink when a heavy weight is placed on them, and will not rise again until the weight is removed. But the Five Articles mentioned above were always, and will always be, of a divine nature, that, like sunbeams, which no weight can press down, or any wind blow away, have darted their glorious rays into the minds of people all over the world, wherever the natural use of reason is exercised. Now, since the priests imposed their frauds upon the people, the blame must be laid at their door, because the common people always submitted to whatever the priests commanded. Those who have a favourable outlook on the pagans may tax me with being too severe on them, because did they not truly practice virtue, have faith, give alms, and hold public prayers just as we do? Their priestly hierarchy was eminent and set a good example, and why should they not embrace their ancestors' religion as we have done? Surely they cannot be blamed entirely for supporting those things which have been handed down to them through the ages?

It is obvious that the pagans attempted to prepare themselves for the worship of God by abstaining from eating meat, and their philosophers, Porphyry being especially notable, and great rulers too, such as Numa Pompilius or the Emperor Julian, often fasted. Volaterranus says that

Amphiaraus[42] the High Priest commanded that priests who were intending to receive and deliver oracles should not eat meat for a day, or drink wine for three days. Alessandri says that the same applied to those who took care of sacred matters amongst the Trezenii. Apuleius tells us that people who wanted to be initiated into the sacred rites of Isis had to fast for ten days, and it is probable that fasting was also practised by the initiates of Cybele as well. This is referred to by Tertullian, who speaks of the *Castos* of Isis and Cybele as "a fast for ten days." This did not mean total abstinence from all forms of refreshment — doctors say that this would kill a healthy person within four days. Every fifth year, Livy says, a fast was decreed in honour of Ceres, as commanded by the Sybilline Books, and Dionysius also speaks of holy fasts sacred to Ceres, and adds that the Albanians[43] do not eat meat during times of public mourning. From Acts 10 it is evident that alms-giving and charity were practised by the pagans, and that they were acceptable to God. It was said of the Emperor Caracalla[44] that "he was neither sparing in his generosity nor backward in alms-giving." Stobaeus and Diogenes Laertius report that amongst the philosophers, Democritus[45] and Aristotle were very generous to the poor and needy, as was the orator Demosthenes.[46] Homer says "the gods will punish those who deny alms to beggars at their own door." This is borne out

---

[42] Amphiaraus was the son of either Oecles or Apollo, the latter being a "not unexampled genealogy for diviners" (*OCD* 44). During the expedition of the Seven against Thebes he attacked the city and was engulfed in a hole placed there by Zeus. The spot became a shrine and a cult developed.

[43] Albania was a country separated from Armenia by the Cyrus river, with the Caucasus on one side and the Caspian Sea on the other. Pompey was there in 65 B.C. "Their chief worship," the *OCD* notes, "was an orgiastic cult of the moon-goddess" (28). Things seem to have changed somewhat over the ages.

[44] Herbert does not give a source for this charitable view of the vicious and tyrannical Caracalla (211–17), but it would be interesting to know where he found it.

[45] Democritus of Abdera (c. 470–360 B.C.) was the Greek atomist philosopher, much-admired and quoted by Aristotle. Atoms, which are invisible realities, make up the world; they are infinitely various in shape and innumerable, and they exist in the void, which is infinite space. His fragments are printed in Freeman 91–120, and number in the hundreds. Democritus also developed an ethics, but from the surviving fragments it is difficult to piece it together.

[46] Demosthenes (384–322 B.C.) is known as the greatest of all Greek orators. His famous speech was the *Third Philippic* against Philip II of Macedon, and he is renowned for his rhetorical and political rivalry with the orator Aeschines. He committed suicide by sucking a poisoned pen after the Macedonians took Athens and he had been condemned to death.

by the fact that in ancient times great generosity was shown to the poor, so
that there were very few beggars.

We cannot deny, either, that public prayers were staged when anything
important was about to be undertaken. Caesar states in Book 41 that "the
Senate decreed twenty days of prayer." Cicero, speaking against Catiline,[47]
mentions supplications made to the gods by Senate decree, and that they
were performed at the shrines of all the gods. Making vows to the gods
was a very common occurrence amongst the ancients, and when they found
themselves in trouble they often prayed so hard that their knees became
sore. I do not know how anyone could doubt that the Supreme God ever
listened to them when he remembers the story of Cornelius, a pagan, in the
New Testament.

Although there was a hierarchy amongst the pagan priests, it was not
the same everywhere. The *Luperci*,[48] priests of Pan, were introduced by
King Evander of Arcadia before Rome was built, and they settled on the
Palatine Hill. Their sacred rites, for purifying the citizens, were performed
in February, and Dionysius tells us in Book I about the bizarre things they
did. Cicero, in his *Pro Caelio*, calls them "a savage group." The *Potitii*
and *Pinarii*, the priests of Hercules, were a very ancient order, taking their
names from two noble families who had undertaken to perform the rites of
Hercules in the Greek fashion for several centuries.[49] Long before this there
were priests not only in Greece but in the East, too, as well as amongst the
Aborigines. There are many instances amongst the ancients of their kings
themselves being priests; Livy and Dionysius tell us of the many orders of
priests founded by Numa Pompilius, and of others which he abolished and
whose offices were taken over by the *Flamines Diales*. He transferred the
ancient worship of Jupiter Juvans to them. According to Festus, there are
two sorts of flamines, the *patricii* and the *plebei*, so that du Choul, who
mentions the arch-flamines as superior, must be wrong. Festus says that
there were fifteen *Flamines Diales*, and they served Jupiter; some were

---

[47]Lucius Sergius Catilina (d. 62 B.C.) was the leader of a revolt against the
consulship of Cicero. He fell in battle against Cicero's colleague Gaius Antonius.

[48]The Luperci certainly did have rather bizarre rites. At the Lupercalia (February 15), goats and dogs were slaughtered, and young men, attired only in parts of the
skins round their waists, rushed around hitting people, usually women, with strips
of the goat-skins. This suggests that fertility was a good part of the ceremony, and
goats are, of course, associated with concupiscence.

[49]The Potitii and the Pinarii (Herbert, or his printer, has *Politii*) were indeed two
gentes who performed rituals for Hercules at the Ara Maxima in Rome, "his most
ancient place of worship" (*OCD* 416).

known as *Curiales* or *Curiones* or as *Quirinales* and *Martiales*, the priests of Quirinus and Mars.[50] Romulus appointed twelve *Arval Brothers*,[51] who performed the *Ambarvalia* sacrifices; they were so-called because before they sacrificed they walked round a ploughed field. Numa also appointed twelve *Salii*[52] to Mars Gradivus, who leaped around carrying shields and singing songs called *Saliaria*, after which they held Saliarian Feasts.

There were many orders of priests. Numa alone, for example, instituted sixty priests or ministers of the god in addition to those who were ordinary tribal priests, or the hundreds who performed sacrificial rites; all these numbers were increased in succeeding times. But Numa would neither allow a priestly office to be sold, or disposed of at random; he passed a law which said that two priests should be chosen out of each district who were over fifty years old and were distinguished for their family background and virtue as well as for their good health and prosperity. They were to hold office for life, free by virtue of age from military service, and from civic duties because of their positions. Numa ordered that some rites were to be performed by women, and some by boys who had both a father and mother living; also the wives of the priests were expected to assist them in the performance of their duties.

Dionysius tells us that the Romans borrowed many rites and customs from the Greeks; Roman virgins performed the same rituals as the Canephori did amongst the Greeks, and the Camilli[53] the same as the Kadoloi of the Greeks. Just as the Romans adopted Greek rites and customs, so did the latter adapt theirs from the Eastern peoples, for they were the ones who first spread myths in the world, and the most ancient superstitions derive from them.

---

[50]There were fifteen priests forming this group. The *Flamines Dialis* were the priests of Jupiter, and together with those of Mars and Quirinus they made up the *Flamines Maiores*. The others served less important deities such as Pales and Furinna, to mention just two of them. For further details, see *OCD* 364.

[51]The Arval Brothers (*Fratres Arvales*) are a unique order of ancient priests in that their records are still extant and have been edited by W. Henzen as *Acta Fratrum Arvalium* (1874). The *OCD* mentions also the *Carmen Arvale*, a ritual hymn with 5th century B.C. origins. Herbert may have known, possibly through his reading in du Choul, that discoveries concerning the Arval Brothers had been made in 1570 on the site of their sacred grove.

[52]The Salii (literal translation: jumpers or leapers) were twelve in number, and the adjective *Saliaris* came to be used to denote "splendid" or "magnificent," because of the feasting which was accurately described by Herbert. Mars Gradivus is the war-god who "walks in battle."

[53]Camilli, Canephori, Cadoli. Simpson (88) gives the plural of *Canephoros* as *Canephoroe*; their name (lifted directly from Greek) means "basket-bearers."

Numa Pompilius wished to have a *Vates* or prophet, whom the Greeks called *hieroscopos* and the Romans *haruspex*, from every tribe present at the sacred rites. He also made a law concerning priests and ministers of the god so they would be appointed by their districts and their election confirmed when approved by the augurs, who, together with the High Priests and two Sacrificers, sanctioned the laws. At the same time, the office of High Priest was responsible for the saying of solemn prayers, the performance of vows and any debate in the Senate about religious matters. Cicero, in one of his letters to Atticus, says that the High Priests were senators. They also settled disputes about sacred matters, or, acting as magistrates, disagreements between private persons. They were not obliged to give either the Senate or the people reasons for anything they did. Those who belonged to the highest order of the priesthood were known as Teachers of the Priests, Administrators, Keepers and the Interpreters of Holy Matters. When one of them died, the people did not elect another one, but the College chose someone they judged appropriate from the citizens, and he began his duties when their choice was approved by a happy augury.

The *Augurs* were believed to be expert in all sorts of prophecies; they made their predictions not only from the flight of birds, but from signs in the air, in heaven, or on earth. They also made conjectures from curses (which included offensive or threatening events, a voice coming from nowhere, or those meetings of humans with animals which were considered unlucky), winds, prodigies, oracles and portents. The Augurs were present at the sanctioning of laws and the appointment of magistrates, and were distinguishable from the priestly orders in that only they could preside over auguries and predictions, while the priests presided over sacred rites; success of transactions was reflected in the auguries, as Cicero, himself a public augur, tells us in *The Nature of the Gods*. Their College is frequently mentioned by writers. Romulus established four augurs, and their number was later increased to twelve, the same number as the High Priests, and the eldest was the Master. In the end, the High Priests and augurs appointed a senior person amongst them, known as the *rex sacrorum*, to preside over divine worship; although he was known as "king," his authority was purely religious, as Dionysius tells us. The *haruspices* inspected the sacrifices on the altars, from which some say they derived their name, but others take it from *haruga*, the place where the sacrifice was. I think the first is correct, because they were also known as *extispices*, those who looked at the entrails, and they were diviners as well as the augurs. The females were known as *haruspicae*. However, a complete discussion of this would require a whole volume to itself.

The pagans also had books which they considered sacred, such as the *libri Lintei*, containing the fate of the Roman Empire, which were kept in the temple of *Juno Moneta* at Rome. The Egyptians had a book written in red letters which they said came from a hawk and which was dedicated to the Sun, the grandfather of Osiris. Amongst the Greeks there were the celebrated volumes containing the Eleusinian mysteries, and there were others such as the Books of Apollo, the Etruscan Books and the Sybilline Books, which were all full of prophecies which no-one but the priests of the Sybil were able to open or read. There were still others which contained those mysteries, auguries and predictions which could be made from animal entrails. There were some known as the *Fulgurales* because they contained observations about lightning. The most famous of the remaining ritual books about the principal sacred rites were the eight books attributed to Numa Pompilius, where all the information on religion and sacred matters could be found.

Conclusions

In spite of the many arguments concerning the virtue, piety and antiquity of their priestly hierarchy, although it was very notable and respected, and although the pagans may produce sacred books full of prophecies coming from divinely-inspired prophetic spirits, and even though they seem to use the same methods (especially those directed by right reason) as we do for obtaining everlasting life, I say it is still impossible to acquit them from suspicion of and even the practice of idolatry. [The priests] provided the people with many occasions to fall into very serious errors because they did not understand the idea of symbolic worship, mythical history or strange rites, so that not all virtue and piety was restored and adorned by the Christian Church.

It will need further enquiry to discover what was good and bad in pagan religion. Everyone will agree that the five articles are sound and universal, although some people will not admit that they are sufficient to procure eternal happiness. Those who think this way seem to me to be pronouncing a bold, rash and severe sentence that divine judgments are not to be penetrated by mere reason. But I shall not presume to assert that they are completely sufficient; the opinion of those who judge more objectively and reverently about the decisions of God seems the most probable to me. Man can do all that is in his power; but it is not in him to rest his entire faith and assurance in the truth of traditions, and no person, using common sense or right reason, could add another article to our five which might make human beings more sincere and more pious, or better promote public peace and tranquillity. I know very well that there are many doctrines all over the world whereby sinners are offered the hope of redemption, which gives them great comfort and consolation, but I fear that unless [these doctrines] are carefully and properly explained, they could prove very harmful. If pardon from sin were to be so easily obtained, people would soon relapse, then fall into greater evils, for as they could depend on outside help to get into heaven, they could themselves neglect to perform their duties. But the priests will say that virtue and repentance were implied and encouraged; this might be granted, but common experience tells us that people have been more likely to try and procure eternal happiness by external means than from virtue or internal repentance.

If more is needed to complete religious worship of God than the five articles we have already discussed, the priests of both former and present ages will strongly assert that it may be found in some divinely-inspired oracle, or commanded by the word of God. But, with all respect to such great men, a lay person amongst the pagans might answer that the following things are needed to prove the truth of an oracle or what is the word of God:

1. That it be proved beyond all doubt that the supreme God did actually speak with an articulate voice and deliver oracles.

2. That the priest who heard the oracle was absolutely sure that it came from the supreme God, and not from a good or evil angel, and that he was not in a trance, or hallucinating, or in the stage between sleeping and waking.

3. That the oracle or word was accurately recited and delivered to the people, or, whenever possible, it was written down and recorded or transmitted to posterity through the handwriting of their priests, so that if anything was added to it or taken away, it could be corrected.

4. That everyone should understand that the doctrine which derived from the oracle or word of God should have such importance for posterity that it was necessary for it to become an article of faith, especially as most things of this nature relied on single pieces of evidence. When the priests have done all this, then the pagan laic will happily submit to their injunctions.

XVI

An Examination of Pagan Religion

I now consider that any religion at all, in any age or country, was only established to oblige people formally to do that which they did voluntarily before, so that universal peace and concord might be maintained this way. I began then, reluctantly, to admire the priests and how they had, by professing the same religion, stirred up and encouraged the common people to bitter dissent and animosity, making them act completely against what they knew to be their express duty. This made me wonder whether there were not some destructive and wicked, as well as merely vain and frivolous, opinions mixed with religious matters. I examined the most ancient and generally-known aspects of pagan religion, and I began to collect those which were absolutely necessary (as they were grounded on common reasons), and those which could be separated from the dirt and rubbish in which they lay. It was thus that I found those five religious common notions which I have so often mentioned, and thought myself far happier than Archimedes.[1] Nothing could have been more congenial to me than the pagans' universally and unquestioningly acknowledging the truth that there was one Greatest and Best God, in spite of the fact that they worshipped many other deities, and that he was to be venerated before all others with virtue and reverence. There could have been no better or surer sign of the divine grace operating in their hearts or a safer reason found (in spite of all the solemn [ceremonies of] purification and lustration) for the remission of their sins than sincere repentance. Nothing, moreover, was so in line with divine justice than that God would reward or punish everyone, here or in the life to come, according to his thoughts, words, and deeds.

Now when I had collected these great truths together, I made a further examination into what the priests had or could have added to them, by which we might get a clearer rule of faith, eternal happiness, honesty, and respect for life, and by which these would be promoted and a more peaceful way of life established. I found that there were indeed many things, but they

---

[1] Archimedes (287–212 B.C.), the pre-eminent mathematician of ancient Greece who was killed at the capture of Syracuse by the soldiers of Marcellus (see Chapter X). His cry of "Eureka!" is echoed by Herbert, who thinks that he, like Archimedes, has made a great discovery, namely that his religious common notions are adhered to throughout recorded history.

diluted and weakened the truth rather than strengthened or corroborated it, and therefore I decided to make further enquiry into what they were. So, as I began with the origins of pagan religion, so I intend to finish this book with a critique of it; I am completely indifferent to what the reader might think about me, as I am sufficiently prepared to deal with the most stringent contradiction.

Where will you find, for example, any of the great philosophers asserting that the Supreme God, always happy and living free from cares and troubles, left the government and administration of all sublunary things to inferior deities, particularly Heaven and the Fixed Stars, in which he had written the laws and eternal fate of the world? It would be very puzzling and highly improbable that the Supreme God in his wisdom should leave the "city of the world" completely destitute, from its beginning, of those laws by which it should be governed. No human being founds a republic or a city without making laws, and for this reason the pagans believed that there was a universal divine law established in the Heavens and Fixed stars especially, but also, to some degree, in the elements themselves and indeed in all universal Nature. From this, God's eternally unchanging decrees had never been altered, nor would they ever be. Amongst these laws were the beginning and end of things, and they also gave us the means to live pleasantly on earth and to attain a better life afterwards, for there were rewards for the good and punishments for the wicked, as well as many other things which could be acquired by constant observation of the laws. In short, things that were analogous or in agreement together would be constantly reduced to those laws. When God had settled and established them, he made the world, but he also made a good number of supercelestial deities before the ages of the world began.

Anything on earth that was subject to change and irregularity, and not easily understood, was managed by the Sun, Moon, and other Planets. The pagans, therefore, believed that people should pay them adoration before other Stars. Philosophers said that all compound beings were partly immutable, partly subject to change, and were governed by the conjunction of various Fixed Stars or Planets. They also speculated about the operations of the Elements, so that these, too, were venerated, and at last the whole world came to be worshipped. Then the Supreme God appointed some heroes whose deeds had deified them, as judges and mediators of all human affairs, to whom humans, with God's permission, should address prayers and who were sufficiently able to take care of particulars, and also some men who had led exemplary lives administered some of the particulars. Therefore the priests said that they should be propitiated by sacrifices as well. The subcelestial deities, such as daemons, lares, lemures and others I have mentioned before, being of a doubtful nature, were worshipped with sacrifices and other rites so that they would do no harm, because it was in people's interest to avert evil as well as to bring good fortune on themselves. The pagans thought that it was insulting to the Greatest and Best God to think that he was the cause of any evil which happened, unless when by his justice it was inflicted on sinners.

I shall only say something briefly about these matters, because I have spoken more about them already. I could wish that a more judicious pen could be employed on this subject, because neither age[2] nor such leisure as I have will allow me to examine all the small particulars of pagan religion. It is not that I am asking for an apologist for what I have said here, but simply that when the errors [the pagans made] have been exposed, the good parts might be allowed to appear in their true light, because any religion which flourished for so long and grew so widely must have had a true and solid foundation. Myths and stories about pagan gods are known to and exploded by schoolchildren, but I think that even the wisest men do not thoroughly understand the principles and causes which made up the basis of pagan religion. Allow me, then, to say something about this difficult subject.

First, when [the pagans] say that in the beginning the Supreme God established a certain divine law, fate, or order of being, I think we can easily understand what they meant in things acting necessarily, or by natural impulse. There is no reason at all why any of these actions should depend simply on the Fixed Stars, or the Elements, because God can implant something in the form of every natural being which is very different from the celestial or elemental nature, something which is proper only to this or that individual or species. I am inclined to this opinion because there are some principles and understandings implanted in the human conscience which no other animals possess. If these are ultimately derived from the Supreme God rather than by mediation on the part of the Heavens or the Fixed Stars, and if Man is the most advanced part of creation, then there is no reason to have recourse to the Heavens or the Fixed Stars as the causes of things that are regular or constant.

I can agree with this much, that the primary, if not the next, cause of all such things comes from the Heavens or Fixed Stars. But it is a mystery to me whether the divine laws about the beginning and end of things are written in the Heavens and Stars, or whether they influence how we provide

---

[2]Herbert was by now 63 years old and not in good health. He was also involved, whether he liked it or not, in the vicissitudes of the Civil War and with family disagreements. Herbert's old age in general was not a happy time for him; his health had never been good, but mental depression had set in and was taking its toll.

ourselves with food and shelter, or what they have to do with the secret decrees about eternal rewards and punishments. Yet it will all be the same, and the truth will be proved, when the means are properly connected with the ends, whether rewards and punishments were decreed by the Supreme God before time or subsequently, or even daily as the particular emergencies of human behaviour arise. God does not regard necessary actions as voluntary actions, and it is from the latter that he makes his judgment of humanity. I therefore infer the causes of rewards and punishments from God's eternal decrees (not the ones written in the Heavens and the Stars); in regard to these, there is nothing more worthy of God than that he should establish everything from eternity, and that it might be done without violating man's free will, which is imprinted in man as a part of divinity. Also, which is one and the same, that God should allot rewards and punishments as if they, too, were decreed from all eternity. But then why should people pray devoutly if the laws for reward and punishment were fixed and confirmed from the beginning? If prayers are part of the means for obtaining eternal happiness, virtue will be rewarded only through prayer, so that virtuous people will not grow proud and arrogant or overrate themselves. For the same reason God, by eternal decree, requires repentance or internal atonement for sins to make men humble, as well as everything else which keeps us within the bounds of duty. It is, then, the same thing when a man uses the right means, whether eternal happiness was decreed for him from the beginning for his virtue, piety or faith, or whether he obtained them every day through prayer. Man will equally possess his desires as if he daily inclined God to make new and sudden determinations of his actions.

The idea that God had established his laws from the beginning of the world was only believed by learned people, because they could not otherwise understand how God could remain free from trouble in his own blessed state. All they needed was the knowledge that God had given them the proper means for living well and happily, and that they ought to accept it and make use of it. They never debated whether what they had from the gods was decreed from the beginning, or was the effect of fresh deliberations [by God]. It could not be positively proved or denied that the Supreme God had associated with himself, from the beginning of time, some supercelestial deities who shared his happiness, but it seemed more probable to [the pagans] that he did, rather than later on advance mere mortals to that blessed state. Tranquillity was a quality which only individuals themselves could enjoy; no-one could be thought happy or blessed except in reference to many [others].

It might have seemed more probable that the extrinsic motions of things should depend upon the different aspects and motions of the planets, if it could have been demonstrated that the causes of those things which move constantly or regularly derived from the Fixed Stars, especially if the various configurations of Fixed Stars and Planets influenced those things which were subject to change. It is very difficult to draw any conclusions in so esoteric a matter, but I must confess frankly that this opinion seems so probable to me that I cannot see how any other cause could be assigned to these matters by the use of common reason alone. However, I must stress here that to pay proper divine worship to the Fixed Stars or Planets is a serious error, so that unless the worship of the Supreme God was symbolised in the Stars, the Stars in the Heroes, and the Heroes in their statues, I must entirely reject it. It is no good claiming that most people today in the East and West Indies worship the Sun, Moon, Stars and Elements, because any baby is impressed by them. God is visible in all single parts of the world, but the Supreme God is most particularly visible when all the parts are taken together; therefore the parts should not be worshipped, for adoration can only be safely paid to the Supreme God. It seems very strange to me that the pagans should have paid such religious worship to the Planets, rather than to Heaven or the Fixed Stars, when they believed that inexorable Fate was written in them, but perhaps they thought that was the only way to reach them.

Next, because the pagans thought that many things [on earth] necessarily came not just from the Heavens, Fixed Stars, Planets or Elements, but from lower principles as well, they concluded that the whole world [itself] should be worshipped. Here I must determine, as I did above, that unless this veneration was symbolic, it was wrong. I have already mentioned many reasons for proving that it was symbolic, and I leave readers to determine whatever they please from their own judgments.

It is not only perfectly compatible with right reason, but can be proven from internal sense, that not everything [on earth] depends on Heaven, the Fixed Stars, the Planets or the Elements, but to an extent on Free Will, which God in his goodness has given to human beings. It is from Free Will, inclined either to good or evil, that God judges mankind; although the evil of punishment comes from the former principles (the intervention of divine justice), man's Free Will is the originator of the evil of crime.

It is a mere conjecture, founded neither on reason nor on experience, that the heroes of the pagans who ascended into heaven were, in the next life, made the judges, patrons or mediators of those actions which sprang from man's Free Will exercised during his life. This is not unlike an opinion generally held nowadays: people attribute the same power and position to the souls of the blessed in heaven as the pagans did to their heroes. And what writer tells us that any of these people ever returned an immediate answer to the pagans' prayers or petitions? Now, if devout supplicants asked something which was just and fair according to the prescripts of eternal law, they succeeded, but if it was not, their prayers were fruitless. It was useless for them to pierce Heaven with their cries, or expect that the most eloquent speech would work to force God to grant anything that He considered unjustly requested or unsuitable. If we arranged for prayers to be said for an eternity, they would not alter God's eternal counsels or change his judgments.

The pagans might answer here that God is always happy and free from caring about particulars (except of each genus or species), and that he allotted this task from the beginning of time to those heroes who deserved it, and that they will not ignore the prayers of mankind but will rather procure a favourable answer for them from a superior deity. In a matter as ambiguous as this, there could be worked out no better expedient but that God should make some men the overseers and judges of others. Heroes, drawing on the eternal law for the certainty of their opinions, would not themselves be deceived, or deceive others. Yet this is a rather weak argument for the pagan doctrines, for mankind can have no intimate knowledge of God's nature, and our narrow reason is completely incapable of judging what is agreeable to the divine nature or Providence. At the same time, if the pagans' ideas about the blessedness of God, that he was free from cares, and their notions about Heaven, the stars and elements had been valid, some natural consequences might have followed, although I can say nothing about them here. All I can do is note that they considered these premises good grounds for the opinions that they held.

Now it would be absurd to imagine that all the heroes of antiquity were worthy of this employment, for it is well-known that they did many reprehensible things. Yet the pagans believed that God remitted their sins and placed them in power of judgment to interpret the eternal laws in the same way as the Heavens or Stars.

It may be answered here that while the heroes attained Heaven through remission of their sins, that did not make them the best people. Who does not laugh at many of the things done by Jupiter, Mercury, Venus and the rest, or condemn other things? Here again it might be said that amongst the many Jupiters, Mercuries and Venuses which were worshipped in antiquity, the priests attempted to expose or ridicule all those which did not belong to their own countries, and that they reproached them with either poetic or sacerdotal license with all the things that they had done on earth when they were human beings, in spite of their being revered as gods. The priests on the other side fired back at them with their scurrilous wit, so that there was no genuine or clear history of the pagan gods available any more. Now if this were true, why did they not censor, either by law or by public proclamation, the more ridiculous stories, so that people would not be encouraged by their bad examples? Why were these stories not obliterated from the world if they disgraced gods and men? The pagans say that there was allegorical meaning in the ancient stories, which the priests could explain, but here I shall not bother to contradict them, for they could hardly have been so stupid, besotted or absurd as to suppose that there was a kernel of truth in them under those fantastic shells. But still, what was worth knowing should have been publicly taught, even if the priests opposed it.

The pagans might also say that there are many good things about their religion and many glorious tales about their gods which ought to be believed, that there are some things also that are rather doubtful, and whose authority should be decided upon by the priests. The priests might then say, "We should believe whatever is told us by reliable people about the things of the past, even if they appear miraculous. Man's judgment is ignorant and rash if it rejects all probabilities as false, because they might be conducive to increasing the glory of God. Some credit is indeed due to secular accounts, but we should stick more firmly to the divine."

These Achillean arguments made me search carefully for common events and miracles in as many authors as I could obtain, so as to advance God's glory. But I could not find anything substantial; their sacred histories were like fables, their traditions very obscure and doubtful, their revelation nothing but imagination or the pointless inventions of priests lying in temples between sleep and wakefulness. Their oracles were fictions, deriving authority only from what some priest had said, and there was no foundation of their faith on either common or right reason. I must admit that the doctrine of heroes is not strange or crude, but does contain some noble and useful things; for example, they did not expect [the heroes] to be indolent, or simply indulgent in self-contemplation, or negligent of the affairs of mankind, the group to which they had formerly belonged. They were constantly busy doing those things which best suited them and were useful to gods and men. Indeed, I believe I could not have found them to have a better use, if the old women, poets, and priests had kept themselves within the bounds of reason when they related the stories [of the heroes]. Through this belief the pagans established a doctrine of immortality of the soul and of rewards for virtue.

If all that the pagans had said about their heroes were true, they still believed that they ought to pray first and foremost to the Supreme God. They did not think that God had delegated authority to others at the expense of his own honour and glory, or that he would permit the invocation of any gods before Him. And it must not be laid to the priests' charge that they called dead heroes by the names of stars; this was due rather to the grief or the flattery of the masses, or to the ambitions of their rulers. It did, however, prove a great incitement to virtue, for what good deed is there that a person will not attempt to carry out, however difficult it may be, if he believes that not only his head, but his name as well, will be placed amongst the stars?[3] The homonymity of the names of stars and heroes has caused grave errors to be made by people who do not know very much about pagan religion, but I cannot go into great details here. Being rather ignorant about the fact that stars were worshipped under men's names, and men by the name of stars, they imagined the worship of them was not symbolic, but proper; thus the commentators perpetrated many mistakes amongst themselves. And there was an immense amount of flattery, common in ancient times, which was the effect of overweening ambition, and very inappropriate; I cannot, however, much object to the ancients paying people heroic honours because it served to make people want to be virtuous.

The idea that the pagans had about making some deities, particularly the subcelestial, favourable to them through sacrifices and other rites, imagining that they had bodily needs and so forth, was promoted cautiously, because it would have been very insulting to the majesty of God [had it appeared] that he could not or would not protect and defend his own [creation]. Would it not be cowardly and treacherous for someone who fights under the standard of the Supreme God to desert him for another deity? And what could possibly hurt us that did not come from us directly? The person who has no evil or depraved thoughts drives the demons away; nothing is done, or can be done by them except by divine permission, and the fault for that is entirely ours.

Now this is a very ridiculous idea. Who can demonstrate that there was ever any collusion between these various deities, demons, and mankind? And even if we grant that some of them can assume airy forms, whoever saw one of them? Or when did one of them visibly attack anybody? I am not denying completely that air, aether and the heavenly bodies may have inhabitants, but I must freely plead ignorance about their natures or how we may propitiate them; I am very sure, however, that a person who leads a pious and religious life need not fear any demons.

Amongst the clever inventions of the priests we may count sacrifices, which they either used for themselves, or for loading the people down with religious forms and ceremonies. The priests made them into feasts for themselves, and, according to the number of sacrifices ordered by the High Priest, they ordered a group of notable eaters to take care of them, as we can see from Livy and Cicero, and in an ancient inscription mentioned by du Choul.

---

[3]Cf. Sir William Davenant, "Lovers, whose priests all poets are,/ Think every mistress, when she dies,/ Is chang'd at least into a star;/ And who dare doubt the poets wise?" ("The Lover and the Philosopher: To A Mistress, Dying," Gardner 275).

So much for the divinity of worship amongst the ancients, and the causes of it, as far as I can gather them from their writings. I would like to conclude with a passage from Varro (quoted from Augustine) to clarify some of what was said before:

> The name "mythical" applies to the theology used chiefly by the poets, "physical" to that of the philosophers, "civil" to that of the general public. The first type contains a great deal of fiction which is in conflict with the dignity and nature of the immortals. It is in this category that we find one group born from the head, another from the thigh, a third from drops of blood; we find stories about thefts and adulteries committed by gods, and gods enslaved to human beings. In fact, we find attributed to gods not only those accidents that happen to humanity, but even those which can befall the most contemptible of mankind.

He continues,[4]

> The second type . . . is one on which the philosophers have left a number of works, in which they discuss who the gods are, of what kind, and of what character they are; whether they came into being at a certain time, or have always existed: whether they derive their being from fire (as Heraclitus held) or from numbers (as Pythagoras believed) or from atoms (as Epicurus teaches us). And there are many other like questions, all of which can be better heard within the lecture-room than outside in the market-place.

And finally,

> The third variety is that which the citizens in the towns, especially priests, ought to know and practice. It contains information about which gods ought to be worshipped officially, and the rites and sacrifices which should be paid to each of them. The first type of theology is particularly suited to the theatre, the second to the world, and the special relevance of the third is to the city.

From these words of Varro, and from the opinion of Plato and the Platonists whom I have cited earlier, it appears that pagan religion was partly constructed from solid reason, partly from mysterious poetic fictions, and partly from priestly inventions. As I have dealt with the two former, I would like to say something of the last, although it would require an entire volume to deal with them properly, and although the main parts of their rites have already been discussed. I shall not take long about it, but my opinion is that these things are of no greater value than pagan faith or fables, but they

---

[4]Herbert (and Lewis) have combined the two citations from Augustine's *City of God*. They come from Book IV of Varro's *De lingua Latina*, which, outside citations by others, is only extant from Book V onwards. The quotations from Varro are adapted from Henry Bettenson's translation of Augustine, 234–36.

do at least appear to promote a greatly reverential fear of divine justice and gratitude for divine mercy.

However, the rites themselves were more like external pageantry than [a celebration of] God's honour, and as such they led people away from the worship of God to the magnificent pomp of mere empty ceremony, to the detriment of true and sound religion. The feasting, sports, and shows that were put on by the High Priest or his colleagues made the people withdraw from the direct worship of God, although this may be more due to state policy than to the intentions of the priests, for, as Cicero says in a letter to Atticus, "what the people feel is indicated by the theatre, or public spectacles."

I shall now discuss those reasons why the pagans have been accused of idolatry and superstition, and to clarify what I have to say I would like to note that there are two errors about religious worship, namely: 1. The true God may be worshipped in a false manner; 2. True worship may be paid to a false god. The first we may class as superstition, the second as idolatry. Aquinas tells us that "superstition is a vice completely opposite to religion." Whatever dilutes, destroys, obscures or subverts the pure worship of God is, indeed, superstition, but are not many people in modern times just as guilty of it as were the pagans of old? Women, as well as priests, were instrumental in the introduction of superstition; Strabo, quoting Menander, says "a single man is hardly ever superstitious," but I do not blame the women as much as I do the pagan priests, whom Bullinger describes as "wicked, vain, covetous wretches, indeed, genuine villains." Had the priests not promoted these effeminate superstitions, they would never have been so universal, and they spread so much that not only the pagans, but the Jews, as some tell us, were infected by them, for their ceremonial laws forbade and commanded so many things which did not make very much sense. Not only Quintilian, but many other ancient authors, mention Jewish superstition, as their writings testify. Cicero says that superstition "is present in all countries and oppresses the minds of most people." Again, Aquinas notes that "idolatry is the divine worship [*latreia*] of a creature, especially of an idol or of something resembling another thing." According to this notion, then, had pagan worship been proper rather than symbolic, or divine rather than hero-directed, they would not simply have been guilty of idolatry, but this is the kind of thing for schoolmen to argue about.

It seems clear, and Tertullian is one ancient author who confesses it, that idolatry was neither very ancient nor universal amongst the pagans. Varro says that the Romans worshipped the gods without images for over 170 years; if this had continued, he says, the worship of the gods would have been purer. He adds that "those who put up the first images of the gods taught the people to be fearless, and encouraged them to sin." The oldest Egyptian temples were without statues or images, as I have already mentioned. Herodotus and Strabo both note that the Persians had neither temples nor images, and Eusebius reports that the Assyrians published an order against idol-worship. It was in later ages, therefore, that the worship of idols and images crept into the world, and even then not everywhere. I cannot discuss here whether it derived from the cleverness of those who made the images, thereby gaining awe and reverence for them, or from the public honour and veneration that the masses accorded to people who had deserved well of their countries or mankind, or whether it grew out of the private respect that people had for their ancestors, or that some parents had for their children, or anything else.

There are many aspects of pagan religion which modern times consider as superstitious or idolatrous, but I have spoken of most of them already, and if any readers do not think that I have given these sufficient attention, they may use their own judgments in the matter. I would like to emphasise that anything which we call superstition was understood by the pagans only to mean the mystical or hidden adoration of some unknown deity, and that anything which we call idolatrous was a symbolic method of worshipping the Supreme God.

It is well-known that the pagans did fall into many errors, especially when they decreed divine honours to emperors, some of whom were horrible people. The also instituted priestly orders called by imperial names, such as those of Augustus, Helvius [Pertinax], Antoninus [Pius], [Marcus] Aurelius and Faustina. Yet it is not strange that they should have such priests, for an ancient law existed which stated that all deities should have a particular order of priests appointed to serve them. Thus superstition overcame the true, pure, ancient religion, for the masses were so credulous that they were far more inclined to embrace whatever was handed to them by either the state or the priests, engraving it upon their minds rather than speaking out against it. They thought that it was safer to make the mistakes of their betters than to adhere to the profounder doctrines of the philosophers, who were always the professed enemies of superstition. And so, as the purest and most chaste parts of divine worship were neglected, all religion degenerated by slow degrees into superstition. Nothing sound or solid remained, besides laws, unless there were some people, amongst the most perceptive, who could still distinguish our five articles amidst the vast heaps of rubbish in which they had been all but buried. At that point there was little hope for the pagans, who were by now so prone to sin and error that all the law could do was restrain them from committing the most heinous crimes.

Now, insofar as universal religion may be constructed from our five articles, there was no religion to be found in that nasty sewer of errors which could correct people's mistakes or get them back on the true path. The High Priest Mucius Scaevola,[5] and Varro, attempted to rectify some of the wrongs done to religion, particularly to explode fictions in it. And the Emperor Julian tried to purge pagan religion from its dross, and weed out its worst errors, but all to no avail, because they had become too deep-rooted.[6] Almost all Platonists and Stoics attempted to simplify religious practice to virtue and piety towards God and humanity, as we can see from all the remedies for the defects of the times that they supply in their works.

The Christians of those times either confirmed some of the better or more sacred doctrines than those of the philosophers, or made them their own, with the result that the rest of pagan religion was reduced to a dry and useless skeleton, and so it died out. The Christians joined the practicing of virtue and a pure life to their own religion, and any other part of the old beliefs was simply ridiculed by the Fathers of the Church. By their doing, other laws were substituted, which slowly gained momentum over the ages, and are now almost universal; the [priestly] hierarchy remained the authority in sacred matters, but I shall handle this matter in more detail later, if God gives me life and health to do it.[7] By what I have said, then, I hope it seems

---

[5]Quintus Mucius Scaevola (d. 82 B.C.) was a Roman statesman, lawyer and teacher. He does not appear to have actually held the title of Pontifex Maximus, but was known as "Pontifex" because of his great knowledge of religious laws. He was consul in 95, and the author of *Liber singularis definitionum*, an important legal treatise excerpted by Justinian in his *Digest of Roman Law*. Scaevola was murdered by order of Marius.

[6]See particularly in his *Orations*, addressed to the Sun-god. Julian tried specifically, and unsuccessfully, to improve the organisation and morale of the pagan priests, who had been declining in influence since the reign of Constantine I and his successors, particularly Constantius II. One of his measures against Christianity was to forbid children of Christians to be educated in the "Greek" manner, which would not seem a very good way of encouraging old pagan virtues.

[7]This is sometimes taken as Herbert's promise to write *A Dialogue between a Tutor and his Pupil*, which, if it is his, certainly fulfils the promise he made about a concentrated attack on the priesthood. It might be useful to say something about this work here, because of its great similarity to the present one in its arguments, and the forcible English prose in which it was written. At the outset, it is this author's opinion that the work is, indeed, Herbert's. Evidence presented by Gawlick in his [German] introduction to his edition of the work seems to point to its being by Herbert. R.D. Bedford terms it "at any rate, an unquestionably Herbertian production" (189). On the other side, Mario Rossi argues that the *Dialogue* is not Herbert's, and he gives these reasons: 1. A serious philosophical treatise should have been in Latin; 2. Herbert's handwriting does not appear on extant MSS; 3. There are no mentions of

clear that the philosophical opinions of the pagans about some of the eternal laws of the stars, planets, elements, and Heaven did carry some semblance of truth in them, and that common reason could not find a more sensible doctrine, in spite of the fact that it was next to impossible to determine what those eternal laws were. In spite of this, it was impious for them to have directly worshipped Heaven, the stars, or the elements. Even if what we have said about the heroes who had been admitted into Heaven seems plausible, it cannot be inferred that they should be worshipped instead of God, or that heroes had authority delegated to them from time immemorial.

As for the worship of subcelestials, this is a great affront to God's divine majesty because [it suggests that] he has neither the will nor the power to defend and protect humanity and that people would not have security unless they propitiated these deities. These sorts of superstitions should have been abolished, rather than made reasonable by a favourable explanation.

---

the work in Herbert's own MSS or letters; 4. Herbert did not have time after 1645 to write a book; 5. The views of the Tutor are even more extreme than the view expressed in DRG. Some of these objections can be easily refuted: Herbert had written a Latin treatise (the present work), and like his predecessor Bacon, who also used the vernacular (in *The Advancement of Learning*), Herbert may have wanted to reach a larger audience, so he wrote in English, using an accessible form (the dialogue). Furthermore, we have *Religio laici* in an English version, and no scholars deny Herbert's authorship. The passage in *DRG* that I have noted does say that he will write further about the subject. In *De veritate* he did the same, and produced *De causis errorum*. Herbert did have a record for delivering what he had promised. Then, as much of the material in the *Dialogue* is similar to that of *DRG* (as its first [1768] editor noted), Herbert did not require as great an amount of time to do original research as he had for other works. He had both *DV* and DRG to draw on by 1645. Further, the fact that a MS in Herbert's holograph does not exist now does not mean that it never did, and it is certainly possible that his hand does not appear on the MSS because he died before he had corrected it, but not before he had had a good copy made.

Gawlick, I believe, provides more evidence. Every secondary source that Herbert used in the *Dialogue* is listed in the Fordyce and Knox catalogue of works donated by Herbert to Jesus College, Oxford. Secondly, the author directly quotes both *De veritate* and *DRG* without credit, but carefully credits all other sources by name. Thirdly, the English style of the *Dialogue*, compared closely with that of Herbert's other English works (*Religio laici, The Life and Raigne of King Henry the Eighth, The Expedition to the Isle of Rhe*), points to the book being his. Lastly, we may add that other philosophers and serious writers used the dialogue form in English; they include Bunyan, Berkeley, Hume, and Joseph Butler.

The definitive edition, which contains an excellent German introduction, of the *Dialogue* is that of Gunter Gawlick (Stuttgart: Friedrich Frommann Verlag, 1972). It is Volume III of Herbert's *Works* in that series.

The Five Articles which I have extracted from pagan religion and laws ought to provide the best means for attaining a better life. The mistakes of the pagans, which sowed dissension and which consisted of myths and fictions invented by the priests, must be rejected. And as I come at last to the end of this volume, I condemn all those who oppose the implementation of Universal Peace and Divine Providence, and I submit myself to the censure or judgment of the Catholic and Orthodox Church.

FINIS

Bibliography

This list refers to those works consulted for the purposes of the introduction, notes, short biographies and quotations, as well as to works consulted by Herbert and checked by the translator. Any abbreviations cited in the text appear in brackets after the bibliographical citation. My general rule has been to refer to the original Greek or Latin if there is a doubtful text in Herbert, and to supply a translation based on a modern edition. I have also, of course, referred to and quoted from translations of some of Herbert's more frequently-used authorities.

Acosta, José de. *Historia natural y moral de las Indias* [1590]. Edmundo O'Gorman, ed. Mexico City: Fondo de Cultura Economica (1940), 1962.

Allan, D.C. *Doubt's Roundless Sea*. Baltimore: Johns Hopkins University Press, 1962.

Apuleius, L. *The Golden Ass*. R. Craven, tr. Harmondsworth: Penguin Books, 1979.

Aratus. See Germanicus.

Aristotle. *The Basic Works*. Richard McKeon, ed. New York: Random House, 1980.

Attwater, Donald. *The Penguin Dictionary of Saints*. 2nd edition [Catherine Rachel John, rev.]. Harmondsworth: Penguin Books, 1986.

Augustine [Aurelius Augustinus], Saint. *City of God*. Henry Bettenson, tr. Harmondsworth: Penguin Books, 1972.

Barkan, Leonard. *The Gods Made Flesh: Metamorphosis and the Pursuit of Paganism*. New Haven: Yale University Press, 1986.

Batman, Stephen. *The Golden Booke of the Leaden Gods* [London 1577]/ Fraunce, Abraham. *The Third Part of Yvychurche* [London 1592]/ Lynche, Robert. *The Fountaine of Ancient Fiction* [London 1599]. New York: Garland Press, 1976.

Baxter, Richard. *More Reasons for the Christian Religion*. London, 1672.

Baumer, Franklin L. *Modern European Thought: Continuity and Change in Ideas, 1600–1950*. New York: Macmillan, 1977.

Bedford, R.D. *The Defence of Truth: Lord Herbert of Cherbury and the Seventeenth Century*. Manchester: University of Manchester Press, 1979.

Beecher, Don A. and Massimo Ciavolella, eds. *Eros and Anteros: The Medical Traditions of Love in the Renaissance*. Ottawa: Dovehouse Editions, 1992.

Bell, R.E. *Dictionary of Classical Mythology, Symbols, Attributes, and Associations*. Oxford: Oxford University Press, 1982.

Bellarmine, Robert. *Spritual Writings*. J.P. Donnelly and Roland Teske, ed. and tr. New York: Paulist Press, 1989.

Bible, The Holy. King James Version (1611). Camden: Thomas Nelson and Sons, 1972.

Birley, A., tr. and ed. *Lives of the Later Caesars: The First Part of the Augustan History*. Harmondsworth: Penguin Books, 1976.

Blount, Charles. *Great is Diana of the Ephesians*. London, 1682.

——. *Religio laici*. London, 1682.

Boethius, Anicius Manlius. *The Consolation of Philosophy*. V.E. Watts, tr. Harmondsworth: Penguin Books, 1969.

Bottrall, Margaret. *Every Man a Phoenix: Studies in Seventeenth Century Biography*. London: John Murray, 1958.

Bowker, John. *The Targums and Rabbinical Literature*. Cambridge: Cambridge University Press, 1969.

Budge, Sir E.A. Wallis. *The Gods of the Egyptians*. 2 volumes. New York: Dover Books, 1969.

Burkert, Walter. *Greek Religion*. John Raffan, tr. Cambridge, Mass.: Harvard University Press, 1985.

Burtt, E.A. *The Metaphysical Foundations of Modern Science*. New York: Anchor Books, 1954.

Bush, Douglas. *English Literature in the Earlier Seventeenth Century*. New York: Oxford University Press, 1952.

Butler, John. *Lord Herbert of Chirbury 1582–1648: An Intellectual Biography*. Lewiston: Edwin Mellen Press, 1990.

Calcagnini, Celio. *Anteros sive de mutuo amore*. In *Opera aliquot*. Basileae: Froben, 1544.

Callimachus. *Hymns, Epigrams, Select Fragments*. Stanley Lombardo and Diane Raynor, tr. Baltimore: John Hopkins University Press, 1988.

Campbell, Joseph. *The Hero with a Thousand Faces*. Princeton: Bollingen Library Series, 1968.

Capella, Martianus. [*Works*]. Adolf Dick, ed. Stuttgartt: B.G. Teubner, 1978.

Carpenter, Nathaniel. *Geographica delineata*. London, 1635.

Cary, M., A.D. Nock, et al., eds. *The Oxford Classical Dictionary*. Oxford: Clarendon Press, 1968.

Cartari, Vincenzo. *Le imagini de i dei degli antichi, nelle quali si contengono gl'idoli, riti, ceremonie & altre cose apparenenti alla Religione degli Antichi* [Venice 1571]. New York: Garland Press, 1976.

Carter, Jesse B. *The Religion of Numa and Other Essays on the Religion of Ancient Rome*. London: Macmillan, 1906.

Carus, Paul. *The History of the Devil and the Idea of Evil*. La Salle: Open Court Publishing Company [1900], 1991.

Cassirer, Ernst. *The Platonic Renaissance in England*. James Pettegrove, tr. London: Nelson, 1953.

——. *The Individual and the Cosmos in Renaissance Philosophy*. Morris Domadi, tr. Philadelphia: University of Pennsylvania Press, 1963.

Catullus, P. Valerius. *Gedichte*. Viktor Pöschl, ed. Heidleberg: F.H. Kerle, 1960.

Ciavolella, Massimo and Iannucci, Amilcare, eds. *Saturn from Antiquity to the Renaissance*. Ottawa: Dovehouse Editions, 1992.

Cicero, M. Tullius. *The Nature of the Gods*. H.C.P. MacGregor, tr. Harmondsworth: Penguin Books, 1972.

——. *Tusculan Disputations, Book* I. A.E. Douglas, ed. and tr. Warminster: Aris and Phillips, 1985.

——. *Letters to his Friends*. 2 volumes. D.R. Shackleton Bailey, tr. Harmondsworth: Penguin Books, 1968.

Claudian. *De raptu Proserpinae*. J.B. Hall, ed. Cambridge: Cambridge University Press, 1969.

Clement of Alexandria. *Le Protréptique*. Claude Mondésert, ed. and tr. Paris: Éditions du Cerf, 1949.

Colie, Rosalie. *Light and Enlightenment: A Study of the Cambridge Platonists and Dutch Arminians*. Cambridge: Cambridge University Press, 1957.

Collistus, Nicehorus. *L'histoire ecclesiastique*. Paris: Antoine le Blanc, 1587.

Connell, J.C., See *Illustrated Bible Dictionary*.

Copleston, Frederick. *A History of Philosophy*. Volumes 1–5. New York: Image Books, 1962.

Cornford, Francis. *From Religion to Philosophy: A Study in the Origins of Western Speculations*. New York: Harper Torchbooks, 1957.

Costa, CDN., ed. *Seneca*. London: Routledge and Kegan Paul, 1974.

Craig, W.L. *The Historical Argument for the Resurrection of Jesus during the Deist Controversy*. Lewiston: Edwin Mellen, 1985.

Culverwell, N. *An Elegant and Learned Discourse of the Light of Nature*. Toronto: University of Toronto Press, 1981.

Cumont, Franz. *After-life in Roman Paganism*. New Haven: Yale University Press, 1923.

Dawson, Christopher. *The Historic Reality of Christian Culture*. New York: Harper Torchbooks, 1960.

Day, Terence P. *The Conception of Punishment in Early Indian Literature*. Waterloo: Wilfred Laurier University Press, 1982.

Des Places, Edouard, ed. *Oracles chaldaïques, avec un choix de commentaires anciens*. Paris: Société d'édition "Les belles lettres," 1971.

Dictionary of National Biography [Compact Edition]. 2 volumes. Oxford: Oxford University Press, 1975. [*DNB*]

Dionysius of Halicarnassus. *Roman Antiquitties*. 7 volumes. Earnest Cary, tr. Cambridge, Mass.: Harvard University Press, (1943), 1962.

Donne, John. *The Poems*. Harmondsworth: Penguin Books, 1982.

Dowden, Ken. *The Uses of Greek Mythology*. London: Routledge, 1992.

Dresser, Horatio. *A History of Ancient and Medieval Philosophy.* New York: Thomas Crowell, 1926.

Dryden, John. "Religio laici," in Keith Walker, ed. *John Dryden.* Oxford: Clarendon Press, 1987.

Du Choul, Guillaume. *Discours de la religion des anciens romains illustré* [Lyon 1556]. New York: Garland Press, 1976.

Duff, J. and A.M. Wight-Duff. *A Literary History of Rome from the Origins to the Close of the Golden Age.* New York: Barnes and Noble, 1963.

Du Mésnil du Buisson, [Count] Robert. *Études sur les dieux phéniciens hérités par l'empire romain.* Leiden: Brill, 1972.

Eisenbichler, K. and Olga Z. Pugliese, eds. *Ficino and Renaissance Neoplatonism.* University of Toronto Italian Studies 1. Ottawa: Dovehouse Editions, 1986.

Eliade, Mircea. *The Sacred and the Profane: The Nature of Religion.* Willard Trask, tr. New York: Harcourt Brace Jovanovich, 1969.

Emerson, R.L. "Heresy, the Social Order, and English Deism," *Church History* 37 (1968).

Ennius, Quintus. *The Annals.* Otto Skutsch, ed. Oxford: Clarendon Press, 1985.

Epicurus. *Letters, Principal Doctrines, and Vatican Sayings.* Russel M. Geer, tr. Indianapolis: Bobbs-Merrill, 1964.

Euripides. *The Bacchae.* Donald Sutherland, ed. and tr. Lincoln: University of Nebraska Press, 1971.

Eusebius. *The History of the Church.* G.A. Williamson, tr. Harmondsworth: Penguin Books, 1965.

——. *Ecclesiastical History.* 2 volumes. R.J. Deferrari, tr. Washington: Catholic University of America Press, (1955), 1965.

Fontenrose, Joseph. *Python: A Study of Delphic Myth and its Origins.* Berkeley: University of California Press, 1980.

Fordyce, C.J. and T.M. Knox. "The Library of Jesus College, Oxford, with an Appendix on the Books bequeathed thereto by Lord Herbert of Cherbury." *Proceedings of the Oxford Bibliographical Society.* Oxford: Oxford University Press, 1937. [*FK*]

Fox, Levi, ed. *English Historical Scholarship in the Sixteenth and Seventeenth Centuries.* Oxford: Oxford University Press, 1956.

Fox, Robin Lane. *Pagans and Christians in the Mediterranean World from the 2nd Century A.D. to the Conversion of Constantine.* Harmondsworth: Penguin Books, 1988.

Frazer, Sir J.G. *The Golden Bough: A Study in Magic and Religion* [Abridged Edition]. London: Macmillan, 1971.

Freeman, Kathleen, ed. and tr. *Ancilla to the Pre-Socratic Philosophers: A Complete Translation of the Fragments.* 2nd edition. Cambridge, Mass.: Harvard University Press, 1983.

[Fulgentius Planciades, Fabius]. *Fulgentius the Mythographer.* L.G. Whitbread, tr. Columbus: Ohio State University Press, 1971.

Galen, Cladius. *Three Treatises on the Nature of Science*. R. Waltzer and M. Frede, trs. Indianapolis: Hackett, 1985.

Gassendi, Pierre. *Selected Works*. C. Brush, tr. New York: Johnson Reprints, 1972.

Germanicus, Gaius [Caesar]. *Les phenomènes d'Aratos*. André leBoeuffle, tr. Paris: Société d'édition "Les belles lettres," 1975.

Gilson, Etienne. *Reason and Revelation in the Middle Ages*. New York: Scribner Libary [1938], n.d.

Giraldi, Lelio Gregorio. *De deis gentium libri sive syntagmata*. Ludguni: J. Junctae, 1565.

Grant, Frederick, ed. *Hellenistic Religions: The Age of Syncretism*. Indianapolis: Bobbs-Merrill, 1953.

Grant, Michael. *Greek and Latin Authors, 800 B.C.–1000 A.D.* New York: H.H. Wilson, 1980.

——. *Roman Myths*. New York: Scribners, 1971.

——. *The Founders of the Western World: A History of Greece and Rome*. New York: Scribners, 1991.

——. *The Rise of the Greeks*. London: Weidenfeld and Nicolson, 1987.

Halyburton, Thomas. *Natural Religion Insufficient, and Revealed Necessary to Man's Happiness*. Edinburgh, 1714.

Hammond, N.G.L. and H.H. Scullard [eds.]. *Oxford Classical Dictionary*. 2nd edition. Oxford: Oxford University Press, 1970. [*OCD*]

Harrison, Jane. *Themis: A Study of the Social Origins of Greek Religion*. Gloucester: Peter Smith, 1974.

——. *Prolegomena to the Study of Greek Religion*. Cambridge: Cambridge University Press [1903], 1922.

Harvey, Sir Paul. *The Oxford Companion to English Literature*. Oxford: Oxford University Press, 1969.

Harvey, Van A. *Handbook of Theological Terms*. New York: Dutton, 1978.

Heilbron, J.L. *Elements of Early Modern Physics*. Berkeley: University of California Press, 1982.

Helden, Albert van. *Measuring the Universe: Cosmic Dimensions from Aristarchus to Halley*. Chicago: University of Chicago Press, 1986.

Herbert of Chirbury, Edward, Lord. *De veritate*. Meyrick H. Carré, tr. Bristol: Arrowsmith, 1937.

——. *De religione gentilium*. Günter Gawlick, ed. Stuttgart: Friederich Frommann Verlag, 1967.

——. *The Antient Religion of the Gentiles, and Causes of their Errors Consider'd*. W. Lewis, tr. London, 1705.

——. *A Dialogue between a Tutor and his Pupil*. Günter Gawlick, ed. Stuttgart: Friederich Frommann Verlag, 1973.

——. *Poems on Several Occasions*. G.C. Moore Smith, ed. Oxford: Oxford University Press, 1923.

——. *Religio laici*. H.R. Hutcheson, tr. New Haven: Yale University Press, 1944.

——. *The Life of Edward, first Lord Herbert of Cherbury.* J.M. Shuttleworth, ed. London: Oxford University Press, 1976.

——. *The Life of Lord Herbert of Cherbury written by Himself.* Sir Sidney Lee, ed. and cont. Oxford: Oxford University Press, 1886.

Herodotus. *The History.* David Grene, tr. Chicago: Chicago University Press, 1987.

Hesiod. *The Works and Days/ Theogony/ The Shield of Herakles.* Richmond Lattimore, tr. Ann Arbor: University of Michigan Press, 1978.

Hill, Christopher. *Religion and Politics in Seventeenth-Century England* [Collected Essays Vol. 2]. Amherst: University of Massachusetts Press, 1986.

Hill, Eugene D. *Edward, Lord Herbert of Cherbury.* Boston: Twayne, 1987.

Hippocrates. *The Hippocratic Writings.* G.E.R. Lloyd, tr. Harmondsworth: Penguin Books, 1976.

——. *Oeuvres complètes.* Littré, ed. Amsterdam: A. Hakkart, 1978.

Homer. *The Illiad.* Richmond Lattimore, tr. New York: Harper and Row, 1964.

——. *The Odyssey.* Richmond Lattimore, tr. New York: Harper and Row, 1967.

Hopkins, E. Washburn. *Origin and Evolution of Religion.* New York: Cooper Square Reprints, 1989.

Horace [Q. Horatius Flaccus]. *The Complete Odes and Epodes.* W.G. Shepherd, tr. Harmondsworth: Penguin Books, 1983.

Hurtado, Larry W. *One God, One Lord: Early Christian Devotion and Ancient Jewish Monotheism.* Philadelphia: Fortress Press, 1988.

Illustrated Bible Dictionary. J.D. Douglas et al, eds. 3 volumes. Leicester: Intervarsity Press, 1980. [*IBD*]

James, William. *The Varieties of Religious Experience.* Harmondsworth: Penguin Books, 1982.

Jean, Georges. *Writing: The Story of Alphabets and Scripts.* Jenny Oates, tr. New York: Abrams, 1991.

Johnson, Paul. *A History of Christianity.* New York: Athenaeum Press, 1977.

——. *A History of the Jews.* London: Weidenfeld and Nicolson, 1987.

Jonas, Hans. *The Gnostic Religion.* Boston: The Beacon Press, 1958.

Jones, Richard Foster. *Ancients and Moderns: A Study of the Rise of the Scientific Movement in Seventeenth-Century England.* New York: Dover Books, 1961.

Josephus, Flavius. *The Complete Works.* William Whiston, tr. Grand Rapids: Kregel Publications, 1981.

Julian, Emperor [Flavius Claudius Julianus]. *The Works of the Emperor Julian.* 3 volumes. Wilmer Wright, ed. and tr. London: Heinemann, 1913.

Jung, C.G. and Carl Kerényi. *Essays on a Science of Mythology: The Myth of the Divine Child and the Mysteries of Eleusis.* R.F.C. Hull, tr. Princeton: Princeton University Press, 1969.

Kelley, J.N.D. *Early Christian Doctrines.* Revised edition. New York: Harper and Row, 1978.

Kirk, G.S. *The Nature of Greek Myths*. Harmondsworth: Penguin Books, 1974.

——. *Myth: Its Meaning and Functions in Ancient and Other Cultures*. Cambridge: Cambridge University Press, 1971.

Kitchen, K.A. See *Illustrated Bible Dictionary*.

Koestler, Arthur. *The Sleepwalkers*. Harmondsworth: Penguin Books, 1968.

Kortholt, Christian. *De tribus impostoribus magnis/ Qua Hieronymi Cardani et Edoradi [sic] Herberti de Animalitates Homini opiniones perspicue proponuntur, ac Philosophice examinantur*. Kiel, 1680.

Kramer, Samuel Noah. *Sumerian Mythology: A Study of Spiritual and Literary Achievement in the Third Millennium B.C.* New York: Harper Torchbooks, 1961.

Kristeller, P.O. *Renaissance Thought: The Classic, Scholastic and Humanist Strains*. New York: Harper and Row, 1961.

——. *Renaissance Thought II: Papers on Humanism and the Arts*. New York: Harper and Row, 1965.

——. *The Philosophy of Marsilio Ficino*. New York: Knopf, 1943.

Kuhn, Thomas S. *The Copernican Revolution: Planetary Astronomy in the Development of Western Thought*. Cambridge, Mass.: Harvard University Press, 1957.

Lactantius. *Minor Works*. Sr. Mary McDonald, tr. Washington: Catholic University of America Press, 1965.

Littleton, C.S. *The New Comparative Mythology*. Cambridge: Cambridge University Press, 1967.

Livy [T. Livius]. *The Early History of Rome*. A. de Selincourt, tr. Harmondsworth: Penguin Books, 1981.

Lucien of Samosata. *The Dialogues*. Paul Turner, tr. Harmondsworth: Penguin Books, 1966.

Lucretius [Carus], Titus. *On the Nature of the Universe*. R.E. Latham, tr. Harmondsworth: Penguin Books, 1951.

Lycophron. *Alexandra*. Lorenzo Mascialino, ed. Stuttgartt: B.G. Teubner, 1964.

Macrobius, Aurelius. *The Saturnalia*. P.V. Davies, tr. New York: Columbia University Press, 1969.

Malebranche, Nicolas. *The Search after Truth*. T.M. Lennon and P.J. Olcamp, trs. Columbus: Ohio State University Press, 1980.

Mandrou, Robert. *From Humanism to Science*. Brian Pearce, tr. Harmondsworth: Penguin Books, 1978.

Marcellinus, Ammianus. *History of the Later Roman Empire*. W. Hamilton, tr. Harmondsworth: Penguin Books, 1986.

Mattingly, Harold. See *Oxford Classical Dictionary*.

Mercatante, Anthony S. *Who's Who in Egyptian Mythology*. New York: Potter, 1988.

Milosz, Czeslaw. *The History of Polish Literature*. Berkeley: University of California Press, 1983.

Milton, John. *Paradise Lost*. Menston: Scolar Press Facsimilies, 1973.

———. *Paradise Regain'd and Samson Agonistes*. Menston: Scolar Press, 1968.

———. *Poems 1645*. Menston: Scolar Press, 1970.

Minucius, Felix. *Octavius*. R. Arbesmann, tr. Washington: Catholic University of America Press, (1950), 1962.

Morford, Mark and R.J. Lenardon. *Classical Mythology*. 3rd edition. New York: Longmans, 1985.

Musaeus, Johann. *Dissertationes duae contra Herbert de Cherbury Baro Anglorum*. Jena, 1675.

———. *Examen Cherburianismi*. Jena, 1705.

Needleman, Jacob, ed. *The Sword of Gnosis: Metaphysics, Cosmology, Tradition, Symbolism*. Baltimore: Penguin Books, 1974.

Nilsson, Martin. *A History of Greek Religion*. Oxford: Clarendon Press, 1925.

Noreña, Carlos G. *Juan Luis Vives*. The Hague: Martinus Nijhoff, 1970.

Orr, John. *English Deism: Its Roots and its Fruits*. Grand Rapids: W.B. Eerdmans, 1934.

Otto, Rudolf. *The Idea of the Holy*. J.W. Harvey, tr. Oxford: Clarendon Press, 1926.

Ovid [P. Ovidius Naso]. *Metamorphoses*. Mary Innes, tr. Harmondsworth: Penguin Books, 1955. [Ovid]

———. *Fasti*. Sir J.G. Frazer, tr. Cambridge, Mass.: Harvard University Press, 1989.

Pagels, Elaine. *The Gnostic Gospels*. New York: Vintage Books, 1981.

Parke, H.W. *The Oracles of Zeus*. Cambridge, Mass.: Harvard University Press, 1967.

Patrides, C.A., ed. *The Cambridge Platonists*. Cambridge: Cambridge University Press, 1969.

Pausanias. *Guide to Greece*. 2 volumes. Peter Levi, tr. Harmondsworth: Penguin Books, 1979.

Peck, H.T., ed. *Harper's Dictionary of Classical Literature and Antiquities*. New York: American Book Company, 1923.

Persius [Flaccus], Aulus/Juvenal[is], Decimus. *Saturae*. W.V. Clausen, ed. Oxford: Clarendon Press, 1968.

Philostratus, Flavius. *Imagines*. Arthur Fairbanks, tr. London: Heinemann [1931], 1960.

Pico della Mirandola, Giovanni. *Oration on the Dignity of Man*. R. Kirk, tr. Chicago: Gateway Press, 1956.

Plato. *The Collected Dialogues*. Edith Hamilton and Huntington Cairns, eds. Princeton: Bollingen Series, 1958.

Pliny the Elder [C. Plinius Secundus]. *Natural History: A Selection*. John Healey, tr. Harmondsworth: Penguin Books, 1991.

Plotinus. *The Enneads*. Stephen Mackenna, tr., John Dillon, abr. Harmondsworth: Penguin Books, 1991.

Plutarch. *De Iside et Osiride.* J.G. Griffiths, ed. and tr. Cardiff: University of Wales Press, 1970.

Popkin, Richard H. *The History of Scepticism from Erasmus to Spinoza.* New York: Harper and Row, 1968.

Praz, Mario. *Studies in Seventeenth-Century Imagery.* 2 volumes. London: Warburg Institute Studies (III), 1939.

Procopius. *The Secret Histories.* G.A. Williamson, tr. Harmondsworth: Penguin Books, 1966.

Prudentius, Aurelius Clemens. *The Poems.* H.J. Thompson, tr. Cambridge, Mass.: Harvard University Press, 1961.

Qu-ran, The Holy. Ustadh Abdullah Yusuf Ali, tr. Al-Madinah: King Fahd Holy Qur-an Printing Complex, 1987.

Reid, J.K.S. *Christian Apologetics.* London: Hodder and Stoughton, 1969.

Rémusat, [Baron] Charles de. *Lord Herbert de Cherbury, sa vie et ses oeuvres.* 2 volumes. Paris, 1824.

Rivers, Isabel. *Classical and Christian Ideas in English Renaissance Poetry.* London: Unwin, 1979.

Robinson, J.M., ed. and tr. *An Introduction to Early Greek Philosophy: The Chief Fragments and Ancient Testimony, with Connecting Commentary.* New York: Houghton Mifflin, 1968.

——— , ed. *The Nag Hammadi Library in English.* New York: Harper and Row, 1981.

Rose, R.J. *Gods and Heroes of the Ancient Greeks: An Introduction to Greek Mythology.* New York: Meridian Books, 1972 [Rose]

——— . *Religion in Greece and Rome.* New York: Harper Torchbooks, 1959.

Ross, Sir David. *Aristotle.* London: Methuen, 1964.

Rossi, Mario Manlio. *La vita, le opere, i tempi di Edoardo Herbert di Chirbury.* 3 volumes. Florence: G.C. Sansoni, 1947.

Sacks, Kenneth S. *Diodorus Siculus and the First Century.* Princeton: Princeton University Press, 1990.

Sandys, John E. *A History of Classical Scholarship.* 3 volumes. Cambridge: Cambridge University Press, 1903–08.

Scholem, Gershom. *On the Kabbalah and its Symbolism.* Ralph Manheim, tr. New York: Schocken Books [1960], 1977.

——— , ed. and tr. *Zohar: The Book of Splendor.* New York: Schocken Books [1963], 1974.

Scholtz, Heinrich. "Die Religionsphilosophie des Herbert von Cherbury." *Studien zur Geschichte des neueren Protestantismus,* V (1914).

Schuon, Frithjof. *The Transcendent Unity of Religions.* New York: Quest Books, 1984.

Seerup, Georg. *De legis Mosaici divine origine et auctoritate diatribe, adversus E. Herbertum baronem de Cherbury.* Copenhagen, 1678.

Seneca, Lucius Annaeus. *The Stoic Philosophy of Seneca: Essays and Letters.* Moses Hadas, tr. New York: Doubleday, 1954.

Seznec, Jean. *The Survival of the Pagan Gods: The Mythological Tradition and Its Place in Renaissance Humanism and Art.* Barbara F. Sessions, tr. Princeton: Princeton University Press, 1972.

Shapiro, Barbara J. *Probability and Certainty in Seventeenth-Century England.* Princeton: Princeton University Press, 1985.

Sherwin-White, A.N. *The Letters of Pliny: A Historical and Social Commentary.* Princeton: Princeton University Press, 1983.

Simpson, D.P. *Cassell's Latin-English/ English-Latin Dictionary.* London: Cassell, 1979.

Smith, G.C. Moore. See Edward Herbert, *Poems.*

Smith, W. and S. Cheetham. *Dictionary of Classical Antiquity.* 2 volumes. London: John Murray, 1975. [*SC*]

———. and S. Wace. *Dictionary of Christian Biography.* 4 volumes. London: John Murray, 1877. [*SW*]

Sorley, W.R. *A History of English Philosophy.* London: Putnam's, 1921.

Springern, Joel E. *A History of Literary Criticism in the Renaissance . . . .* New York [1899], 1924.

Staniforth, Maxwell, ed. *Early Christian Writings: The Apostolic Fathers.* Harmondsworth: Penguin Books, 1981.

Suetonius, Gaius. *The Twelve Caesars.* Robert Graves, tr. Rev. ed. Harmondsworth: Penguin Books, 1979.

Sykes, Egerton. *Everyman's Dictionary of Non-Classical Mytthology.* London: Dent, 1968.

Tacitus, P. Cornelius. *The Annals of Imperial Rome.* Michael Grant, tr. Harmondsworth: Penguin Books, 1989.

Teixidor, Javier. *The Pagan God: Popular Religion in the Greco-Roman Near East.* Princeton: Princeton University Press, 1977.

Tertullian. *Apologetical Works.* Sr. Emily Daly, tr. Washington: Catholic University of America Press [1950], 1962.

———. *De idololatria.* J.M. Waszink and J.C.M. van Winden, eds. and trs. Leiden: E.J. Brill, 1987.

Theocritus. *The Idylls.* Robert Wells, tr. Harmondsworth: Penguin Books, 1989.

Theodoret of Cyrrhus. *Eranistes.* Gerard H. Ettlinger, ed. Oxford: Clarendon Press, 1975.

Tibullus, Albius. *Poems.* Philip Dunlop, tr. Harmondsworth: Penguin Books, 1972.

Tillyard, E.M.W. *The Elizabethan World Picture: A Study of the Idea of Order in the Age of Shakespeare, Donne and Milton.* New York: Vintage Books, n.d.

Titius, Gerhard. *Disputationes theologica oppositione libro* De religione gentilium. Helmstedt, 1667.

Trinkaus, Charles. See Eisenbichler and Pugliese, eds., *Ficino.*

Trismegistus, Hermes. *The Divine Pymander and Other Writings.* John D. Chambers, tr. New York: Samuel Weiser, 1975.

Vallée, Gérard. *A Study in Anti-Gnostic Polemics: Irenaeus, Hippolytus, and Epiphanius.* Waterloo: Canadian Corporation for Studies in Religion, 1981.

Varro, M. Terentius. *De lingua Latina.* 2 volumes. R.G. Kent, ed. and tr. Cambridge, Mass.: Harvard University Press, 1951.

Vergil, P. *Vergili Maronis Opera.* R.A.B. Mynors, ed. Oxford: Clarendon Press, 1969.

———. *The Pastoral Poems.* [Latin text with tr. by E.V. Rieu]. Harmondsworth: Penguin Books, 1954.

———. *The Georgics.* L.P. Wilkinson, tr. Harmondsworth: Penguin Books, 1982.

———. *The Aeneid.* R.L. Fitzgerald, tr. New York: Viking Books, 1976.

Vincent of Lerins. *The Commonitories.* R.E. Morris, tr. Washington: Catholic University of America Press [1949], 1970.

von Leyden, W. *Seventeenth-Century Metaphysics: An Examination of Some Main Concepts and Theories.* London: Duckworth, 1968.

Vossius [Vos], Gerardus Joannes. *De theologia gentili.* 3 volumes. [Amsterdam 1641]. New York: Garland Press, 1976. [*DTG*]

Walker, D.P. *The Ancient Theology: Studies in Christian Platonism from the Fifteenth to the Eighteenth Century.* Ithaca: Cornell University Press, 1972.

Walpole, Horace, ed. *The Life of Lord Herbert of Chirbury by himself.* Strawberry Hill Press, 1764.

Warhaft, Sidney. "Stoicism, Ethics and Learning in Seventeenth-Century England." *Mosaic* 1:4 (July 1968).

Wiley, Margaret L. *The Subtle Knot: Creative Scepticism in Seventeenth-Century England.* London: Allen and Unwin, 1952.

Willey, Basil. *The Seventeenth-Century Background.* London: Chatto and Windus, 1949.

Wind, Edgar. *Pagan Mysteries in the Renaissance.* New York: W.W. Norton, 1968.

Wood, Derek, co-ordinator. *The Illustrated Bible Dictionary.* 3 volumes. Leicester: Inter-Varsity Press, 1980. [*IBD*]

Yates, Francis. *Giordano Bruno and the Hermetic Tradition.* London: Routledge, 1964.

Zeller, Eduard. *Outlines of the History of Greek Philosophy.* L.R. Palmer, tr. New York: Dover Press, 1980.

Index

This Index includes references to scholars (ancient and modern) quoted in the Introduction and in notes to chapters, as well as authorities used by Herbert. For deities, Herbert's major discussion is indicated by the first listing, e.g., Adonis, god 78–80.

– B –